Hands-on PostScript

Michael B. Spring

David S. Dubin

Department of Information Science
University of Pittsburgh

Hands-on PostScript

Library of Congress Catalog No.: 92-71207

ISBN: 0-672-30185-7

94 93 92   8 7 6 5 4 3 2 1

Interpretation of the printing code: the rightmost double-digit number is the year of the book's printing; the rightmost single-digit number, the number of the book's printing. For example, a printing code of 92-1 shows that the first printing of the book occurred in 1992.

Preface

This book is about the PostScript language. PostScript was initially developed as a page description language that could be used to communicate between application software and printers in a device-independent fashion. (The introduction contains a little more on the history of PostScript.) In the simplest of terms however, PostScript has become the *de facto* standard for page description and final form document interchange. It is also a serious contender as a display device language and a graphics interchange standard. Lastly, it is becoming an increasingly popular programming language in its own right. Researchers use PostScript to plot the results of their work, graphic artists develop simple and precise graphics with it, and computer and information scientists use it to demonstrate stack and object-oriented programming.

This book is a response to the growing demand for help in learning PostScript. It provides an introduction to both the PostScript language and the concept of drivers. We have made every effort to make the book comprehensible to the casual programmer who might know only BASIC. At the same time, we have worked very hard to make the book interesting to the professional programmer who needs to produce a limited amount of PostScript output.

Experienced programmers who come to us ask for examples that closely match what they need so they can modify the code for their situtation. After several PostScript projects, they invest in their own reference manuals. The examples in this book have been selected to offer a wide range of examples to copy and modify. We encourage applications programmers who needs to create some small output in PostScript to liberally modify these examples as they see fit.

At the other end of the continuum, many folks who are not programmers or are just learning a little programming have developed more than a passing curiosity about PostScript. Almost anyone can use the language with dramatic effects. Without belittling PostScript's tremendous power there is a sense of reward in using its simple commands to control a PostScript printer. This book is also written with casual programmers' needs in mind—the chapters are written in a direct and straightforward manner. Casual programmers may find some of the discussions about stack manipulations and early and late binding over their heads, but if a reader skips these sections, it should not seriously affect his or her ability to work with a specific example.

We have taught PostScript to graduate and undergraduate students, to executives and salespersons, to housewives and high school students. It is a rich and complex language that can absorb you with its intricasies for years. At the same time, anyone can write a simple PostScript program knowing only one or two rules which can be learned in under five minutes. Most importantly, we are convinced that anyone with an interest and a willingness to invest a little time can quickly begin to create some very exciting and rewarding output.

Dedication

To

Melinda, who kept the ship afloat through the tumult of writing,
Francese whose birthday party was missed,

and

Gail, with fond memories.

Document Design and Composition

This document was produced using the Scribe Document Production Software, copyright Unus, Inc. Scribe is exclusively licensed to Cygnet Publishing Technologies, Inc. A variety of micro-, mini-, and mainframe computer systems were used to enter and edit the manuscript's components. Final editing was done on a DECstation 5000/200 and a SUN Sparc. Graphics were composed and tested via PostScript previewers on these workstations before being sent to a variety of printers for final testing.

One of Scribe's advantages is the system's capability to work on documents that consist of multiple files. Scribe's capability to include an Encapsulated PostScript (EPS) file both as an EPS file and as a simple text file was of particular interest to us. This means that with one or two exceptions where we needed to make some special point, the PostScript listings in the book are the very listings that produced the related graphic; if there was an error in the listing, the graphic would not be produced.

The document was designed by Michael B. Spring. It employs principles of informational composition and printing as put forth by Jan V. White and Edward Tufte. Body text is set in a Times Roman font. Heading text is set in Helvetica Bold, and examples and program listings are set in Courier.

All graphics were designed and executed in PostScript by Michael B. Spring, David S. Dubin, Richard Baker, Jeffrey Deppen, Roberta Pavol, Bryan Sorrows, Molly Sorrows, Kathy Vrudney, and Janice Zappone. PostScript files were tested on a variety of printers including DEC LPS40s and Apple LaserWriters. They were also tested on DECstation 5000/200 and a SUN Sparc PostScript page previewer. BASIC, Pascal, and C programs were also tested on a variety of machines and compilers. While the files are generic, there may be minor adjustments that need to be made in some environments to account for PC biased I/O functions and procedures. All files on the Mac disk have been run in a Mac environment.

The basic cover design was developed by Michael Spring. This design was completed by Hayden Books.

Acknowledgements

Most books have many parents. This one was born during a phone call from Gregg Bushyeager. Gregg, who had just joined Prentice Hall Computer Publishing convinced me that although it had been only five months since my last book, which it had taken six years to write, I was ready to begin another book . . . and finish it in a little over three months!

Several other people at Hayden provided valuable assistance and support. Publisher Mike Britton and Associate Publisher Karen Bluestein were most supportive of our efforts to produce the book. The Editorial Production Coordinator, Karen Whitehouse, managed all of our requests, and kept us on an even keel as we managed the competing demands of a production publishing system. Julie Sturgeon provided many editorial suggestions. Howard Peirce proofread the document noting in the process many ways in which the document could be improved. Finally, despite our best efforts to index the document ourselves, we fell woefully short of a quality index. Joelynn Gifford showed us the value of professional indexing by providing us with a large number of additional suggestions. Where the index fails, it is due to the inadequacies of automated indexing systems. Where it succeeds, it is due to Joelynn's efforts.

Completing this book in the time frame set out required a lot of help. Most importantly, it took David Dubin, a Ph.D. candidate in the department who was just crazy enough to consider working on the project. The students in my document processing class were invited to help, and those that took the challenge were in for a real-life electronic publishing experience! All of the students in the document processing class contributed by commenting on the early chapters and making clear which concepts were hard or easy to understand. They all contributed to the book in one way or another. I thank them all: Richard Baker, Jeffrey Deppen, Toni Hebda, Kristin Hopkins, John Krupka, Philip Manion, Roberta Pavol, Bryan Sorrows, Molly Sorrows, Kathy Vrudney, Sang Yoon, and Janice Zappone.

Several graduate students' work is represented in the various chapters and is noted there. Some personal comments about these contributions are also in order. Janice Zappone, a physics teacher who has just completed her Master of Information Science, brought a sense of joy and enthusiasm to the project that helped greatly. It has been a long time since I programmed in BASIC, and then it was only as a passing fancy. Janice was willing to go back and brush up her BASIC. In addition, she produced text and explanations that required little modification. After the last class, after grades were submitted and graduation assured, Janice offered to write another section of the book because it was fun! It is hard to describe how much such a student affects a teacher—it is a wonderful feeling. Janice was by no means alone when it came to hard work. Jeff Deppen, like Janice, also took on more than his share. I thank Jeff for that and for the insight he brought to thinking about PostScript in new ways. Jeff was working on some graphics projects at the same time he was working on the PostScript. His co-mingling of concepts led to some very useful insights.

Richard Baker, Toni Hebda, Roberta Pavol, and Kathy Vrudney had full-time jobs and family responsibilities. Yet they worked on, at night and on weekends, to complete their projects. I thank each of them for the special knowledge they brought to the project. I also thank their families and coworkers for allowing this project to intrude. Finally, Molly and Bryan Sorrows were working on a major research project at the same time the book was being written. They specifically asked before the course began if it would have the very heavy workload my courses seem to be known for. I told them it would not, that I was working to make the course load more reasonable, but that was before Gregg called. In any case, they suffered through the workload while they were working on their project. They inevitably showed up bleary-eyed at the last minute, on their way to gather data somewhere in the country, to hand in the work they had stayed up all night finishing. I thank them for sticking with the project.

When the time came to bring it all together and ensure appropriate consistency, the enormity of the task came home. Terry McArdle worked on description of the PostScript operators, developing a consistent approach to defining the operators. Terry worked long and hard over the holidays. Patricia Thomas, who has worked with me on a number of projects, waded through the manuscript and provided a important initial review. Marty Lindner also provided early feedback on the manuscript. Elaine Newborn from Cygnet Publishing Technologies was most helpful. The document design we wanted to employ needed some major and minor modifications to the standard Scribe approach. Elaine was helpful and courteous in answering both difficult and stupid questions. Jeff Cepull of the University Instructional Resource Center provided gracious assistance in refining the PostScript basis for the cover. Mary Kerr made the revisions and editorial corrections. She worked long into the night and coordinated the task of switching between the hundreds of individual files that make up the source manuscript.

Along with David, I would like to acknowledge and thank our loved ones who wondered during the holiday season of 1991 what had happened to us!

Michael B. Spring
spring+@pitt.edu
Pittsburgh, PA
January 1, 1992

About the Authors

Michael B. Spring is an assistant professor of Information Science at the University of Pittsburgh. His research involves the application of technology to the workplace with particular attention to interface design and large scale electronic document processing. He received his bachelor's in psychology from the College of the Holy Cross, Worcester, MA, and his Ph.D. from the School of Education, University of Pittsburgh. For more than a decade prior to joining the Department of Information Science, Dr. Spring served as associate director and then director of the University External Studies Program at the University of Pittsburgh. Dr. Spring has authored numerous articles and book chapters in the areas of office automation, text and document processing, information technology standardization, and educational technology. He is the author of *Electronic Printing and Publishing: The Document Processing Revolution*. He has led research projects in custom-on-demand publishing, intelligent text conversion, and document database publishing. Current research efforts include intelligent interfaces, reference models for human-computer interaction, and virtual reality. He has consulted with major corporations and nonprofit institutions on related topics ranging from office automation to large document processing, to information technology standards and trends.

David Dubin is a doctoral student and teaching fellow at the University of Pittsburgh's Department of Information Science. He received a bachelor of science in Humanities and Communications and an M.S. in Library and Information Science from Drexel University. David's research is in the areas of document processing and retrieval.

Table of Contents

Part 1. Introduction to PostScript 1

1. Background and Overview 3
   1. PostScript Origins 4
   2. Overview of the Book 5
   3. How to Use This Book 6
      a. Listing of Disk Files 8
   4. PostScript Programming Conventions 10
   5. Driver Programs 11

2. Introduction to PostScript 13
   1. PostScript Syntax 15
   2. How a PostScript Printer Works 18
   3. PostScript Objects 18
   4. PostScript Stacks 19
   5. Operation of the Interpreter, Revisited 20
   6. Some Basic Operators 22

3. Structured and Encapsulated PostScript 25
   1. Introduction 25
   2. Why Structure PostScript Files? 26
   3. The Basic Organization of Programs 28
   4. Some Document Structuring Conventions 29
   5. Encapsulated PostScript: EPS 33

4. The PostScript Coordinate Space 35
   1. Measurements and User Space 36
   2. The Default Imaging Area 38
   3. Changing the Default Imaging Area 39
   4. The Imaging Process 47
   5. The Graphics State Stack 49
   6. Code for Coordinate System with Default Image Area 53

Part 2. PostScript Programming Examples 55

5. Letterhead 57

1. Objectives 57
2. Operator Explanations 58
   a. The Simplest Letterhead 58
   b. Centering the Letterhead 60
   c. Useable Letterhead. 62
3. A Note about PostScript Comments 64
4. Explanation of the Listings 65
   a. Version 1: Simple Letterhead 65
   b. Version 2: Centered Letterhead 66
   c. Version 3: White Text over a Gray Bar 69
5. Additional Refinements and Uses 73
6. What Went Wrong?. 73

6. Certificate 75

1. Objectives 75
2. Operator Explanations 76
3. Explanation of the Listings 85
   a. Version 1: Simple Certificate 85
   b. Version 2: Certificate with Scrollwork 88
   c. Version 3: A Final Touch 92
4. Suggested Improvements 96

7. Envelopes 97

1. Objectives 97
2. Operator Explanations 98
   a. Simplest Envelope 98
   b. Intermediate Envelope 98
   c. Complex Envelope 99
3. Explanation of the Listings 102
   a. Version 1: Simple Envelope Program 102
   b. Version 2: Intermediate Envelope Program 105
   c. Version 3: Complex envelope 107
4. A Word about Device Dependence 109
5. Enhancements 111
6. Why Didn't It Print? 111

8. Place Cards 113
1. Operator Explanations 113
    a. Version 1: The Simplest Place Card 114
    b. Version 2: Text Scaled to Available Space 116
    c. Version 3: Text with a Logo 119
2. Essential Features 120
3. Explanation of the Listings 121
    a. Version 1: Simplest Place Card 121
    b. Version 2: Text Scaled to Available Space 124
    c. Version 3: Text with a Logo 125
4. Problems and Modifications 128

9. Wrapping Paper 131
1. Objectives 131
2. Operator Explanations and Definitions 132
3. Typesetting Concepts 134
4. Coordinate Space 135
5. Program Listing Discussion 138
6. Wrapping Paper Wrapup 143

10. Greeting Card 145
1. Objectives 145
2. The Use of Procedures 146
3. Operator Explanations 147
4. Explanation of the Program Listing 148
    a. General Overview 151
    b. The Procedures ctr, rit, and shadow 151
    c. Border Procedure 153
    d. Clearit Procedure 153
    e. Front Procedure 153
    f. Inside Procedure 154
    g. The Main Program 154
5. Changing or Adding to the Design 154

11. Keyboard Templates 155
1. Objectives 155
2. Command Explanations 156
3. Explanation of the Keyboard Template Listing 157
    a. Initial definitions 160
    b. Definition of procedures 162
    c. Main Program 167
4. Suggestions for Modification 168

12. Christmas Ornament 169
1. Objectives 169
2. Operator Explanations 169
a. A Bulb 170
b. Two Christmas Tree Bulbs 170
c. Complete Christmas Tree Bulb 171
3. Explanation of the Listings 172
a. Version 1: A Christmas Tree Bulb 172
b. Version 2: Two Christmas Tree Bulbs 174
c. Version 3: A Personalized Christmas Tree Bulb 177
4. Possible Modifications 183
5. Possible Errors 183

13. Poster 185
1. Introduction 185
a. Objectives. 185
2. Command Explanations 186
a. The Simple Poster Operators 186
b. One-Page Poster Commands 188
c. Multi-Page Poster Commands 188
3. Modular Design and Programming Style 189
4. Simple Poster 190
a. Explanation of the listing 193
5. One-Page Poster. 197
6. Multi-Page Poster 204
7. Further Modifications 210

Part 3. Simple PostScript Drivers 211

14. Drivers 213
1. Introduction 213
2. Drivers 213
3. How to Program a Driver. 215
4. Building a PostScript Driver 216
a. A Very Simple Driver 216
b. Adding Variability. 218
c. Expanding the Prologue 219
d. Calculation by the Driver 220
5. Font Metric Files: Providing More Information to the Driver. 222
6. Further Improvements 226

15. Fonts 227
1. Definitions 227
2. Character Manipulations 229
3. Font Metric Files 233
4. Encoding Vectors 238

16. Drivers for a Greeting Card 241
1. Greeting Card Driver: BASIC 241
a. Building the Driver 242
b. Putting It All Together 246
c. Suggested Enhancements 249
2. Greeting Card Driver: Pascal 249
a. Files Used and Created 250
b. Version 1 of the Greeting Card Driver 251
c. Version 2 of the Greeting Card Driver 257
d. Suggested Enhancements 266
3. Greeting Card Driver: C 268
a. Program Specifications 268
b. Explanation of the Listings 269
c. Possible Modification 293
d. Possible Errors 293

17. Drivers for a Certificate 295
1. Certificate Driver: BASIC 295
a. Introduction 295
b. Creating the Driver 296
c. Putting It All Together 300
d. Suggested Enhancements 303
2. Certificate Driver: Pascal 304
a. Explanation of the Listing 306
b. Suggested Enhancements 312
3. Certificate Driver: C 312
a. Program Specification 312
b. Explanation of the Listing 312
c. Possible Modifications 318
d. Complete Listing 318

18. Drivers for a Poster 325
1. Poster Driver: Pascal 325
a. Review of Multi-page Printing 326
b. Explanation of the Listing 329
c. Complete Listing of the Pascal Driver 332
2. Poster Driver: C 339

a. Explanation of the Listing. 345
3. Further Enhancements 346

19. Name Tag Driver in C. 347
1. Introduction 347
a. Explanation. 347
b. Objectives 348
2. Building a Simple Name Tag Driver. 348
a. Setup Functions 352
b. User Interface Functions 353
c. Final PostScript Creation Functions 354
d. Output Results. 355
3. Version 2: Adding an Interactive Procedure 357
4. Version 3: Printing Background Text and Using Font Metrics Files . . . 358
a. Background Printing 359
b. Font Metrics Files 360
c. Results 364
5. Further Modifications 367

20. Label Driver in C 369
1. Introduction 369
2. Building the Label Driver 370
3. Setup Functions 373
4. User Interface 376
5. PostScript Output. 377
6. Summary. 377
7. Program Enhancements 378
8. Possible Errors 378
9. Complete Listing of the Driver. 378

Part 4. Command Reference 387

21. Operator Reference 389
1. Path Operators 391
2. Font and String Operators 396
3. Painting Operators 400
4. Stack Operators. 400
5. Mathematical Operators 403
6. Logical Operators. 407
7. Dictionary Operators 411
8. Array Operators. 414
9. Control Operators. 416

10. Coordinate Operators 419
11. Graphics Operators 421
12. Conversion Operators 424
13. Device Operators. 425

Index 427

List of Figures

Figure 4.1	Grid of Default Page Coordinates	40
Figure 4.2	PostScript Coordinate System with Default Image Area	42
Figure 4.3	Impact of Scaling on Coordinates and Image Area	43
Figure 4.4	Impact of Rotation on Coordinates and Image Area	45
Figure 4.5	Impact of Rotation on Line Placement Relative to Image Area	46
Figure 4.6	Rotation and Translation for a Landscape Page	48
Figure 4.7	Opacity of PostScript Objects	49
Figure 4.8	Exploding PostScript Logo	50
Figure 4.9	Impact of Gsave and Grestore on Output	52
Figure 5.1	Simple Letterhead	67
Figure 5.2	Centered Letterhead	70
Figure 5.3	Improved Letterhead	72
Figure 6.1	Simple Certificate	87
Figure 6.2	Certificate with Scrollwork	91
Figure 6.3	A Final Touch	94
Figure 7.1	Output from Simple and Intermediate Envelope Program	104
Figure 7.2	Output from Complex Envelope Program	110
Figure 8.1	Simplest Place Card	123
Figure 8.2	Text Scaled to Available Space	126
Figure 8.3	Text with a Logo	129
Figure 9.1	Personalized Wrapping Paper	133
Figure 9.2	Page Coordinate System. Gray Box is Printable Page Area.	136
Figure 9.3	Effect on Coordinate User Space With Rotation	136
Figure 9.4	Effect on Coordinate User Space with Rotation and Translate	137
Figure 9.5	Wrapping Paper Coordinate Space/Printable Page Area	138
Figure 10.1	Output of Greeting Card Listing	150
Figure 11.1	A Laptop Keyboard Template	161
Figure 12.1	A Christmas tree Bulb	175
Figure 12.2	Two Christmas tree bulbs	178
Figure 12.3	Personalized Christmas Tree Bulb	182
Figure 13.1	A Simple Poster	194
Figure 13.2	One-Page Poster Program	201
Figure 13.3	Poster with Center Slogan Scaled to Fit	203
Figure 13.4	Enlarged Poster With Translation of Origin	208
Figure 14.1	Output from a Simple Driver	218
Figure 14.2	Multiple Strings and Horizontal Centering	223
Figure 15.1	Character Widths for Helvetica 18 Point Font	230
Figure 15.2	Outlined Characters	231

Figure 15.3	Characters as Clip Path for Special Effects	232
Figure 15.4	Character Set with Standard Encoding	237
Figure 15.5	Character Set with ISO Latin Encoding	239
Figure 16.1	Example of Driver Output	248
Figure 16.2	Output of Initial Version	258
Figure 16.3	Output created by the Enhanced Driver	267
Figure 16.4	Output of Simple Greeting Card PostScript Program	277
Figure 16.5	Output of Greeting Card with Formatting PostScript Program	282
Figure 16.6	Output of One Page	286
Figure 17.1	PostScript File Output	302
Figure 17.2	Output of Certificate PostScript Program	315
Figure 18.1	Sample Output of the Pascal Driver	330
Figure 19.1	Printed Output of Version 1	356
Figure 19.2	Printed Output of Version 3	366
Figure 20.1	Sample Diskette Labels	374

Program Listings

Listing 3.1	Basic Structure of a DSC Compliant File	29
Listing 3.2	Selected DSC Comments	31
Listing 4.1	Grid of Default Page Coordinates	38
Listing 4.2	Example of Layering	47
Listing 4.3	Exploding Logo	49
Listing 4.4	Listing for Exploding Logo with Gsave and Grestore	51
Listing 4.5	PostScript Coordinate System with Default Image Area	53
Listing 5.1	Simple Letterhead	65
Listing 5.2	Centered Letterhead	66
Listing 5.3	Improved Letterhead	69
Listing 6.1	Simple Certificate	85
Listing 6.2	Certificate with Scrollwork	89
Listing 6.3	A Final Touch	92
Listing 7.1	Simple Envelope Listing	102
Listing 7.2	Intermediate Envelope Listing	106
Listing 7.3	Complex Envelope Listing	107
Listing 8.1	Simplest Place Card	121
Listing 8.2	Text Scaled to Available Space	124
Listing 8.3	Text With a Logo	125
Listing 9.1	Listing to Produce Wrapping Paper	139
Listing 10.1	Greeting Card Program Listing	148
Listing 11.1	A Laptop Keyboard Template	157
Listing 12.1	A Christmas Tree Bulb	172
Listing 12.2	Two Christmas tree bulbs	176
Listing 12.3	Personalized Christmas Tree Bulb	179
Listing 13.1	A Simple Poster	191
Listing 13.2	One-Page Poster Program	198
Listing 13.3	Multi-Page Poster Program	204
Listing 14.1	A Simple Driver	217
Listing 14.2	PostScript Output from a Simple Driver	217
Listing 14.3	Driver Outputting Multiple Strings	218
Listing 14.4	Driver Outputting Multiple Strings with Horizontal Centering	219
Listing 14.5	Driver for Vertical and horizontal centering	221
Listing 14.6	Outputting with Multiple Strings and Horizontal Centering	221
Listing 14.7	Horizontal centering via string width calculation	222
Listing 14.8	Function to calculate width of a string	225
Listing 14.9	Excerpt from a simplified font metric file	225
Listing 15.1	Program to List Fonts Available on a Printer	228
Listing 15.2	Outlined Characters	231

Listing 15.3	Characters as Clip Path for Special Effects	231
Listing 15.4	Excerpts from an Adobe Font Metric File	233
Listing 15.5	Character Information Excerpts from an AFM File	234
Listing 15.6	Kern Pair Excerpts from an AFM File	235
Listing 15.7	Composite Character Excerpts from an AFM File	236
Listing 15.8	Changing the Standard Encoding Vector	238
Listing 16.1	PostScript Prologue	242
Listing 16.2	BASIC Prologue Code	243
Listing 16.3	Occasion Input Code	243
Listing 16.4	Occasion Output Code	244
Listing 16.5	PostScript Segment 1 Generated	244
Listing 16.6	Message Input Code	245
Listing 16.7	Input Verification Code	245
Listing 16.8	Message Output Code	246
Listing 16.9	PostScript Segment 2 Generated	246
Listing 16.10	Subroutine Control	246
Listing 16.11	Example of Driver Output File	247
Listing 16.12	Introduction to the Driver	249
Listing 16.13	Prologue File	250
Listing 16.14	PostScript Program Produced by the Pascal Driver	250
Listing 16.15	Version 1: Pascal Driver for Greeting Card Program	252
Listing 16.16	Enhanced Pascal Driver for Greeting Card Program	257
Listing 16.17	Output produced by Version 2 of the program	265
Listing 16.18	Simple Greeting Card Generator	269
Listing 16.19	Output of Simple Greeting Card Generator	276
Listing 16.20	Additional Code for Formatting	278
Listing 16.21	Prologue for the Card file	279
Listing 16.22	Output of Greeting Card with Formatting Generator	280
Listing 16.23	New Functions for the Final Greeting Card Generator	281
Listing 16.24	Changes for the Final Version	284
Listing 16.25	Output of Complete Greeting Card Generator	284
Listing 16.26	Complete Greeting Card Generator	287
Listing 17.1	PostScript Prologue File	296
Listing 17.2	File Name Selection	297
Listing 17.3	File Creation	297
Listing 17.4	Awardee Name Input	298
Listing 17.5	Date Input	298
Listing 17.6	Reason for Certificate	298
Listing 17.7	Verification Routine	299
Listing 17.8	Printing Variable Data	299
Listing 17.9	Personalized Output	299
Listing 17.10	Subroutine Control Module	300
Listing 17.11	Driver Output	300
Listing 17.12	Enhancements	303
Listing 17.13	String Input Routine	303
Listing 17.14	Using the String Input Routine	304
Listing 17.15	Prologue for the Pascal Driver	305

Listing 17.16	The Pascal Certificate Driver	306
Listing 17.17	Output of Certificate Generator	313
Listing 17.18	Certificate Prologue	316
Listing 17.19	Certificate Generator.	319
Listing 18.1	Output from a Sample Run of the Pascal Driver	326
Listing 18.2	The Prologue File for the Pascal Driver	328
Listing 18.3	The Pascal Poster Driver.	332
Listing 18.4	The C Poster Driver	339
Listing 19.1	Version 1: Simple Name Tag Driver	348
Listing 19.2	Version 1 Output Listing	355
Listing 19.3	Listing of New Code in Version 2.	357
Listing 19.4	Listing of Code for Printing Background Text	359
Listing 19.5	Listing of Code for Using Font Information.	360
Listing 19.6	Version 3 Output Listing	364
Listing 20.1	Sample PostScript Output	370
Listing 20.2	Prologue File.	373
Listing 20.3	Label Driver in C	379

Part 1
Introduction to PostScript

This part of the book contains several chapters that introduce the PostScript programming language. The first chapter provides some background on PostScript and an overview of the book. The second chapter provides a brief introduction to PostScript, the syntax of the language, and a few of the more basic commands. The third chapter explains how PostScript uses some commenting conventions to provide an additional level of structure to PostScript files. This chapter also includes a brief discussion of the Encapsulated PostScript (EPS) file format. The fourth chapter explains how PostScript deals with coordinates and manipulations of the coordinate system.

Chapter 1
Background and Overview

This book is an introduction to programming in PostScript. Over the last several years, a growing number of users have become interested in achieving special effects on PostScript printers by writing little programs in PostScript. This book is intended for these users.

In some ways, PostScript is a simple, intuitive language like BASIC or Logo. In other ways, PostScript is a rich, highly capable, demanding, and sometimes esoteric language. Programmers who write PostScript drivers to serve as a back end to commercially distributed software need to know and program PostScript in this second form. The average user, however, can quickly learn enough PostScript to achieve interesting results on a printer in just a few minutes, and this book is designed to make that possible.

To give you an example of how easy PostScript can be, consider the following "program":

```
% -- % begins a comment that ends with end of line
72 72 moveto
% this command moves 1 inch up and 1 inch over on
% an  8.5-by-11-inch page -- there are 72 units/inch.
144 144 lineto
%draws a line from that point to a point two inches
% up and two inches over.
showpage
%ejects a page from the laser printer.
```

On the other hand, if you look at the listing of the program on page 38 you will probably not understand much of it at this point in time. This book is intended to help you start with programs such as the preceding example and quickly move to more powerful and useful programs.

Readers who find this book useful and work more than a few hours a week to learn PostScript will want to expand their collection of PostScript reference works to include the *PostScript Reference Manual*. *Hands-on PostScript* makes PostScript easy to understand by not introducing some of the language's complexities. Where appropriate we explain some of the nuances of PostScript in footnotes. On the other hand, nothing in this book is done by slight of hand. When we provide a listing, it is that precise listing that produces the associated graphic. Every listing in the book has been run on several different PostScript interpreters and has produced the correct results. Indeed, the listings used in this book are the original electronic files used to run the programs.

1. PostScript Origins

Some of the concepts that underlie the development of PostScript and other page description languages may be traced back as far as 1976 to the Evans and Sutherland firm which developed "Design System," a system to build complex three-dimensional graphics databases. Based on this early research, the Xerox Palo Alto Research Center (PARC) began in 1978 to develop a language called JaM. JaM, which is named for *J*ohn Warnock *a*nd *M*artin Newell, is a forerunner to the Interpress page description language. It is also a predecessor of the PostScript language developed by Warnock, Geschke, Brotz, Paxton, Taft, and others at Adobe Systems, a company Warnock and Chuck Geschke formed in 1982. All these efforts owe some intellectual heritage to the FORTH programming language, especially in their use of stacks, object-orientation, and postfix, or reverse polish, notation. Why this concern with developing new languages to describe pages? The original impetus for JaM and then Interpress was the development of laser printers. Laser printers differed dramatically from other computer printing devices in that they were raster-oriented rather than character oriented. And although dot-matrix devices were also raster devices, laser printers reflected a significant improvement in resolution. It was possible to think about printing in new ways. Basically, a laser printer could represent a low-end phototypesetter. Everyone would be able to produce quality output historically reserved to those who could afford to have their material published.

It was clear the timing was appropriate for a rich graphical language that would provide a standard means for communication between composition software and display, originally printing, devices. The developers of PostScript also had the foresight to realize the language should be independent of any given device; it needed to be a device-independent language for describing what was to be printed. PostScript is a computer programming language for communicating high-level graphic information to digital (laser) printers.[1]

[1] In reality, there are many different kinds of digital printers—inkjet, ionographic, as well as thermal, magnetographic, and electrostatic. However, the consumer market at the current time is dominated by the laser printer.

PostScript was introduced in the LaserWriter in January, 1985. Some have suggested that PostScript will ultimately dominate not only hard copy display but screen displays as well. Indeed, the NeWS on the SUN uses display PostScript as its imaging model, as does the NeXT workstation. An additional set of commands have been added to the base PostScript language to accommodate screen displays' specialized needs. Finally, in 1990, Adobe released PostScript Level 2. This version is the first major improvement of the base language and reflects both new and revised commands.

Hewlett Packard's Graphics Language (HPGL) and its PCL5 Printer Language probably still drive more laser printers than any other language. Xerox's Interpress is likely responsible for more printed pages than any other language due to the high speed of the printers that use it and the large number of these machines in specialized commercial applications. However, PostScript has become the *de facto* page description and final form interchange format. It is known by more people, incorporated in more applications, and running on more different types of printers than any other language. It has also had more influence on the international standard for page descriptions than the other languages. With the definition of the structuring conventions for PostScript, we will surely see a whole new family of software products based on PostScript as the universal language for document interchange emerging over the next few years.

2. Overview of the Book

Hands-on PostScript is divided into four parts:

1. Introduction to the PostScript Language
2. PostScript Programs
3. PostScript Drivers
4. PostScript Reference

The first part, provides a simple introduction to the PostScript language, including the general syntax rules and the underlying philosophy. This section also discusses the commenting conventions PostScript programmers use that allow for PostScript preprocessors and for Encapsulated PostScript—PostScript programs that may be included by other programs in PostScript output. The final chapter in this part discusses the PostScript coordinate space. Understanding PostScript coordinate space proves essential in the long run for those interested in using PostScript's full capabilities.

In the second part of the book, we introduce a number of different, useful programs. We have tried to pick applications that cannot be done as well or as easily with standard word processing or database packages. Obviously, utility is in the eye of the user, and whether the same result can be achieved in another way depends of the user's expertise. We hope that even if you do not like our specific implementation, we still provide the necessary information to enable you to modify the PostScript program to your needs. In the early chapters, the code is as simple as possible, and we try to slowly introduce new operators. For this reason, it is important for someone who is trying to learn PostScript to go through these chapters in sequence. If you already know PostScript, simply go to the example of your choice. Some of the programs introduced toward the end of this section require some resources that may have to be purchased. For example, you can use PostScript to produce a design for a T-shirt, but you have to pay to have it put on actual cotton clothing. Similarly, you can use PostScript to produce business cards, but you will probably want to have the actual cards printed in color and cut by a printer.

The concept of a device driver is introduced in the third part of the book. A general overview of the functionality of a device driver is presented, along with examples of actual code. There are different sample programs, with each one presented in one or more languages. The simplest versions are presented in BASIC, the next level in Pascal, and the most sophisticated in C. While this book is not intended to help people learn new languages, the translations are simple enough that most of the programs can be cross-translated without too much work.

Finally, the fourth part provides a quick reference manual to PostScript. It presents the full set of PostScript operators by type. When you are reading a PostScript program, you need to find commands based on their spelling. For that reason, we have provided a list of the commands in alphabetical order which can be xeroxed to provide a quick index to where the command may be found. However, readers will more often want to discover if there is a PostScript command that does x, y, or z. For that reason, we have grouped the commands by what they do, hoping this enables you to find the ones that are relevant to your plans. As mentioned earlier, a full reference manual is beyond the scope of this book and is unnecessary, as one already exists. We urge readers who find they are working a lot with PostScript code to purchase the *PostScript Reference Manual.*

3. How to Use This Book

It would be nice if everyone who wanted to use PostScript were willing to spend the time to sit down and learn the language in all its intricacy. However, this is not how we learned PostScript, and in the five years we have been giving PostScript assignments in our courses, almost every student has been drawn to examples they could modify and elaborate. This book is written so you may choose to ignore the opening chapters and go right to the sections that provide examples.

There is nothing wrong with this—feel free! We have made every effort to include all the information you need to know about the example in the chapter that introduces it. You should be aware that the explanations in the earlier chapters are more detailed than those in the later chapters.[2]

Each of the example chapters has an introduction that includes a description of the project and the chapter's objectives. Next, commands that might be new to you in the chapter are explained. Then, a simple PostScript program is presented. Depending on the example, more sophisticated versions of the program are presented. Finally, the chapter offers suggestions for how you can further enhance the program.

PostScript makes extensive use of structures called "stacks" (See Chapter 2). When the program makes extensive use of stacks, we use a picture like the following to give you a sense of what the stack contains:

this is on the top of the stack
This is in the middle
this is the bottom of the stack

Hopefully, this makes it easier to visualize the kinds of things that make the PostScript language very exciting to work with.

For every listing shown in the book, be aware of two things. First, there is a copy of almost every listing on the accompanying disk, so you can begin by copying the file rather than rekeying it. Second, and most important, the figures in the book are derived directly from the listings. The listings are not rekeyed versions of the programs that produced the figures, they are the actual programs that produced the figures. We used this technique as a final check on debugging our programs. If the program listing was not correct, the figure you see would not have been produced.

Note: If you rekey one of the listings in the book and it does not produce what is in the figure, it is an error in the rekeying. Check the spelling carefully; assume nothing! The listings do produce the figures you see in this book.

---

[2]You should also be aware that while we try to explain the full details about what is going on, it has been necessary in places to simplify the descriptions for the purpose of clarity.

a. Listing of Disk Files

The disk contains the PostScript programs shown below. They are listed in the order in which they occur in the book. The titles give a brief indication of what the program does.

1. spac_ps1.ps: Printer Workspace Grid
2. spac_ps2.ps: Coordinate System Transformation Test
3. spac_ps3.ps: Impact of Scaling on Coordinates
4. spac_ps4.ps: Impact of Rotation on Coordinates
5. spac_ps5.ps: Impact of Scaling on Coordinates(2)
6. spac_ps6.ps: Impact of Rotation and Translation on Coordinates
7. spac_ps7.ps: Layering of Graphics in Postscript
8. spac_ps8.ps: Using Scale and Translate for Special Effects
9. spac_ps9.ps: Use of Gsave, Grestore, Scale, and Translate
10. lttr_ps1.ps: Basic letterhead
11. lttr_ps2.ps: Centered letterhead
12. lttr_ps3.ps: Final letterhead
13. cert_ps1.ps: Basic Certificate
14. cert_ps2.ps: Certificate with Scrollwork
15. cert_ps3.ps: Final Certificate
16. envl_ps1.ps: Simple Envelope
17. envl_ps2.ps: Intermediate Envelope
18. envl_ps3.ps: Advanced Envelope
19. plac_ps1.ps: Basic Place Card
20. plac_ps2.ps: Place Card with Scaled Text
21. plac_ps3.ps: Place Card with Scaled Text and Logo
22. wrap_ps1.ps: Wrapping Paper
23. card_ps1.ps: Greeting Card
24. temp_ps1.ps: Keyboard Template
25. orn_ps1.ps: Basic Christmas Ornament
26. orn_ps2.ps: Two Sided Christmas Ornament
27. orn_ps3.ps: Final Christmas Ornament
28. post_ps1.ps: One Page Poster
29. post_ps2.ps: Advanced One Page Poster
30. post_ps3.ps: Multi Page Poster
31. font_ps1.ps: Font Directory List
32. font_ps2.ps: Partial Font Character List
33. font_ps3.ps: Stroking using Charpath
34. font_ps4.ps: Clipping using Charpath
35. font_ps5.ps: Font Character Set
36. font_ps6.ps: Font Character Set (ISO Latin Encoding)

The following font files are also contained on the disk. The file use is explained in Part 3, of the book on drivers. The files contain information on the width of each character in the indicated fonts.

1. helv_b_r.fxw: Helvetica-Bold font x widths
2. pala_b_i.fxw: Palatino-BoldItalic font x widths
3. pala_b_r.fxw: Palatino-Bold font x widths
4. tiro_b_i.fxw: Times-BoldItalic font x widths
5. tiro_l_r.fxw: Times-Roman font x widths
6. zcha_l_r.fxw: ZapfChancery-MediumItalic font x widths

Finally, the disk also contains a series of files in various languages which may be used to write PostScript programs. The various files' uses are explained in the chapters, but the files generally follow the following form. The first four letters indicate the focus of the program: CERTificate, CARD, NAMEtag, etc. The letter after the underscore indicates the language in which the program is written: B is for BASIC, P is for Pascal, and C is for C. After the language indicator a number indicates the program version; there are one to three versions of each. Where there is more than one version, the higher number(s) represents enhancements to the basic program. Finally, there are the file extensions. The file extensions .c, .bas, and .pas. indicate the language. The extension .psp stands for PostScript prologue, a file that is read by a driver program and written to the beginning of the output file. The extension .txs stands for text-setup and indicates a file that provides basic text information to the driver. Files with the extension .txi are text input files and provide a mechanism for automating interactive input. One final note: When a .txs or .txi file exists for one version but not for earlier versions, it is probably because the earlier versions did not use the file. If a later version is not listed, it is because it has not changed from an earlier version.

The files below are grouped by chapter and presented in the order they are found in the book.

1. Files for the card drivers:
    - card_b1.bas
    - card_b1.psp
    - card_p1.pas
    - card_p1.psp
    - card_p2.pas
    - card_c1.c
    - card_c1.txi
    - card_c2.c
    - card_c2.psp
    - card_c2.txi
    - card_c3.c
2. Files for the certificate drivers:
    - cert_b1.bas
    - cert_p1.pas
    - cert_p1.psp
    - cert_c1.c

- cert_c1.psp

3. Files for the poster drivers:
   - post_p1.pas
   - post_p1.ps
   - post_p1.psp
   - post_p2.ps
   - post_c1.c
4. Files for the nametag driver:
   - name_c1.c
   - name_c1.txi
   - name_c2.c
   - name_c3.c
5. Files for the label driver:
   - labl_c1.c
   - labl_c1.psp

4. PostScript Programming Conventions

There is a set of conventions that PostScript programmers are increasingly using. All of the listings in the book reflect the general intent of these conventions and implement several of them. A more careful explanation is provided in Chapter 3.

What is commonly referred to as "Structured PostScript" is a PostScript program that has some special comments in it. The comments, which are simply lines that begin with the characters *%%* or *%!*, separate the program into the following sections:

1. header
2. prologue
3. script or body
4. trailer

The script, or body, can be further broken down by comments into the commands that generate each page. These conventions allow programmers to write software to manipulate the PostScript code.

What is commonly referred to as Encapsulated PostScript or EPS is simply a PostScript program which follows a small subset of the structured PostScript commenting conventions.[3] Encapsulated PostScript simply requires that the first line be a comment identifying the file type and PostScript version, followed by a bounding box comment. The last line of the file should be an end-of-file comment. The following is a legitimate Encapsulated PostScript program:[4]

```
%!PS-Adobe-3.0 EPSF-30.
%%BoundingBox: 0 0 612 792
showpage
%%EOF
```

To keep track of our programs and ensure they work, we used a few of the structuring comments that make it possible to draw the figures in this book. All these comments may be deleted without affecting the way the program operates. Readers interested in structuring conventions will want to see Chapter 3 on page 25.

5. Driver Programs

After learning PostScript, the next step is to write programs that write PostScript programs. These programs are called device drivers, driver programs, or drivers. This book contains a number of of driver examples. A bit of driver program theory is provided in commonsense form. Some of the driver programs are written in three languages; we provide examples in BASIC, Pascal, and C. When the same driver is written in multiple languages, the simplest example is in BASIC and the most sophisticated example is in C. In all cases, even novice programmers will note that the user-interface component of the programs is too simplistic. This oversight is intentional. We do not wish to distract the user by unnecessarily complicating the code. It will require additional work to bulletproof the user interface in these examples before they can seriously be used, especially by non-programmers.

[3]As Chapter 3 explains, there is actually more to creating Encapsulated PostScript than is described here.

[4]This program actually does nothing more than eject a page.

Chapter 2
Introduction to PostScript

PostScript has been described many different ways. As you begin to write programs in PostScript, it is useful to consider the following characteristics:

- PostScript is a graphical language. Despite the fact that it is mostly used to describe characters and words, it is a graphical language at heart. This opens up wonderful possibilities. If a letter is indeed nothing more than a sophisticated set of filled-in curves, there will be ways to use these graphic objects to create exciting effects.
- PostScript is designed to describe pages. The available commands are optimized to help describe document pages and all their contents: text, images, and primitive graphics. Thus, it is a page description language (PDL).
- PostScript is designed to be device independent; you are free to describe what you want to do in a purely mathematical way. It is each device manufacturer's responsibility to map that description onto particular device.
- PostScript is designed to be understood by both people and machines and to be easily transported over almost any kind of electronic circuit.

Keeping these points in mind makes it a easier to understand why things work as they do. Beyond these design considerations, also keep in mind these facts about how the PostScript language works:[5]

- PostScript is a stack-based language. There are four stacks that are used, but we focus only on the main stack here—the operand stack. Consider what happens if you give PostScript a command to add two

[5]PostScript, like any computer language, is an artificial language. Humans constructed it to allow them to accomplish some goal through instructions to a computer. PostScript, or any other computer language, can seem idiosyncratic or even erratic at times. This is most often caused by the fact that we do not understand the underlying language rules and operations.

numbers. PostScript puts the two numbers on the stack and then tells the processor to add them. What happens if there are not two numbers on the stack to add? The "program" dies. It is hard to imagine you would forget to give the computer two numbers before asking it to add, but in fact this is one of the main error sources in writing PostScript. To help relieve some of the problems that new programmers encounter in this respect, we show you the contents of the stack when it begins to get complicated and hard to remember. A stack with five numbers looks like this:

34
23
45
123
19

In this case, 19 is the first number given to the computer and 34 is the last. The top of the stack contains the number 34 and the bottom contains the number 19.

- PostScript uses a form of notation known as postfix. This simply means you provide the objects of interest first, followed by the operation or action you want to perform. This is closely related to the fact that PostScript is a stack-oriented language. Generally, there are three ways of stating operations. Infix notation is closest to natural language: take 2 from 3, or 3 – 2. Prefix notation puts the operation first and then provides the operands: add 3 4. Finally, postfix provides the operands first, followed by the operation: 2 3 add. Keep in mind that 2 is "pushed" onto the stack first, followed by 3. This is not very important for addition, but it becomes crucial for operations such as subtraction where the order of the operands is important.
- PostScript is an object based language. The operands are really objects as far as PostScript is concerned. The objects are pushed on and popped off the operand stack. It is important to keep this in mind because having the wrong kind of object on the stack is another possible error source. For example, if the stack contained the following:

34
Hello
23

and the PostScript interpreter encountered the instruction "add," it would try to add 34 to Hello and result in an error.

- PostScript is an interpreted computer language. This has important implications. The most important thing to remember, particularly if you do not program regularly, is that at any given point,[6] the interpreter knows only what it has been told to that point. In many languages, you may define procedures or variables at any point in the program and allow the compiler to organize them for you. This is not the case in PostScript.

- PostScript is primarily an application-to-device interchange language. Normally, professional programmers write programs that write PostScript and send it directly to the printer. For this reason, most PostScript interpreters do not provide very extensive or helpful feedback. This situation is improving, but generally it is up to the programmer to take care and go slowly in developing programs.

1. PostScript Syntax

In PostScript, a scanner, or parser, examines the incoming character sequence and groups the characters as appropriate-to-form objects. The PostScript syntax is the set of rules which governs this process of tokenizing the incoming character stream to create objects.

The most basic rule to remember is that tokens are isolated by "white space." We did not say "a space," because to the PostScript scanner, "a space" is only one form of "white space." Other forms include the tab, the carriage return, the linefeed, the formfeed character, and the null character. Any combination and any number of these in a row constitute "white space"—one space is the same as 100 tabs or formfeeds. Therefore, the following two PostScript programs are identical:

- Example 1

```
12
13
moveto
```

- Example 2

```
12


                         13           moveto
```

In a PostScript program, there is only one place where the scanner ignores white space: when it occurs on a line following a percent sign (%) and before a carriage return or a linefeed character. Characters between a percent character and a car-

[6] As always, there are exceptions in terms of early and late binding for those who are familiar with such concepts. A brief explanation is provided on page 21 of this chapter. For a full explanation, refer to the *PostScript Language Reference Manual*.

riage return or linefeed character— also known as a newline—are considered to be comments. Thus, in the following example the scanner will create the number objects 12, 13, 14, 15 and 19:

```
12
13
14 15 %comment here % 16 17 18
19
```

The numbers 16, 17, and 18 are part of the comment that begins with the first percent symbol (%) and which includes a percent symbol (%), ending with the newline symbol that exists in the computer file between the 18 and the 19.

The characters

```
( )
< >
[ ]
{ }
/
%
```

are reserved. The ( ) characters are used to delimit a string.The [] characters define an array. The <> characters delimit strings encoded in hexadecimal notation. The {} characters delimit a packed array or procedure. For all practical purposes, it is easiest to think of the {} characters definitions for a procedure or sequence of PostScript commands. Finally, the / character introduces a name literal.

In PostScript, a number is identified as a sequence beginning with a digit, +, or – and followed by any number of digits, a decimal point, or, under certain conditions, letters which represent numbers.[7] Numbers may take integer or real (radix) form. The following are legitimate numbers:

```
123

-123

0.0

+.006

-3.4
```

Generally, a string is delimited by parentheses. Within a string, the \ character is an escape character allowing the following characters to be represented:

---

[7]Introducing non-decimal number representations at this point would unnecessarily complicate matters. For the purist, however, note that PostScript recognizes numbers of the form *n#sssss*, where *n* is a number between 2 and 36 and *s* is any element in the appropriate symbol set for a radix *n* number. The symbol set consists of the digits followed by the letters of the alphabet. Thus, 20#1ja3 is a legitimate number.

- \n is a newline
- \r is a return
- \t is a tab
- \b is a backspace
- \f is a formfeed
- \\ is a \
- \(is a (
- \) is a)
- \ddd is octal character ddd
- *newline* is an indication of line continuation

\ddd is used to represent characters using their octal representation of their character code. In a string, it returns the character that is represented by the 3-digit octal code **nnn**. 101 is the octal representation of the character code for the letter A. 102 is the octal representation of the character code for the letter B:

```
(\101\102C) show
```

```
is equivalent to
```

```
(ABC) show
```

Angle brackets (<>) are used to delimit a string that is represented by pairs of hexadecimal digits. The following two strings would be equivalent

```
(HELLO)

<48454C4C4F>
```

In PostScript, it is sometimes desirable to place a name literal on the operand stack. For example, you might wish to inform PostScript to look for a given font. This is done by prefacing the name with a / to inform PostScript that the letters and/or numbers that follow are a name literal and not a command or number:

```
/Helvetica findfont
```

instructs PostScript to find the font named Helvetica.

An array is a list of objects delimited by [] characters:

```
[123 /abc (xyz)]
```

defines an array consisting of the number object 123, the name literal abc, and the string "xyz."

A procedure is an executable array and it is indicated by {} characters. For example:

```
{2 3 add}
```

is an object that is an executable array.

2. How a PostScript Printer Works

The PostScript printer does three different things. The first is scanning. PostScript code written by a programmer or by software is sent to the printer. From the printer's point of view, it arrives as a stream of characters. The printer scans and tokenizes this incoming character stream into objects. In this scanning phase, the engine identifies the different types of objects based the syntax rules described earlier and converts the characters to the appropriate object type. "Object" is a special term, but for now, simply realize that a number is one kind of object and the command "showpage" is a different kind of object.

This leads to the second printer activity, the interpretation phase where the appropriate action is taken for each object. This is the interpretation phase. One important product of the interpretation phase is the construction of a virtual image in PostScript's coordinate space. This interpretation phase takes place concurrently with the scanning phase.

The last printer activity is imaging. Based on a command such as showpage, the virtual image constructed in the PostScript coordinate space is converted to a bitmap that can be transferred to a page, screen, or other physical medium.

This book is most concerned with the interpreter phase where the virtual image is constructed. How the character stream is tokenized and how the image is converted to a particular output device are topics beyond the scope of this book.

The interpreter sequence of operation is straightforward. Objects identified as operands are moved onto the operand stack. Objects identified as names are executed, removing operands as appropriate from the operand stack and pushing back results as appropriate. In reality, this action is actually more complicated, but for clarity, it is necessary to have a better understanding of the various types of objects PostScript recognizes, and the four stacks. After introducing these topics, we return to a description of the operation sequence.

3. PostScript Objects

Part of PostScript's power is that everything in PostScript is considered an object. Each object has a type, a value, and one or more attributes—for example, whether it is executable. PostScript objects are either simple or composite. Simple objects are integers, names, reals, booleans, and other unary objects. Composite objects have structure. For example, an array is a composite object in that it is a one-dimensional collection of objects. A dictionary is an associative table of pairs of objects. A string is a composite object, in this case an array whose elements are integers between 0–255.

The following objects are simple objects broken into three groups:

- Numeric
    - integer
    - real
    - boolean
- Nominal
    - name—literal
    - operator—executable
    - file
- Special
    - Null
    - Save
    - Mark
    - FontID

The following composite objects are defined:

- Strings
- Arrays, including packed arrays and procedures
- Dictionaries

In Level 2 and Display PostScript, an additional series of composite objects are added, including condition and lock (Display PostScript) and gstate and packedarray (Level 2).

4. PostScript Stacks

Earlier, it was mentioned that the operand stack is where operands are stored until an operator consumes them. PostScript actually uses four stacks. They are all "LIFO" or last-in, first-out stacks. That simply means if the numerals 1, 2, 3, and 4 are "pushed" onto a stack, the result is as follows:

4
3
2
1

If you take an element off the stack, it is the top element, 4. The last object onto the stack is the first object off the stack.

Each object occupies one place on the stack. Thus, a stack might contain the following:[8]

[8]We have used syntax conventions to identify various types of objects.

`4`
`[1 2 3 4 5]`
`(Hello, my name is John)`
`/Helvetica-Bold`
`/inch`
`{72 mul}`

In addition to the operand stack, the stack most directly under your control, there are the dictionary stack, the execution stack, and the graphics state stack.

The dictionary stack contains some number of dictionaries. It always contains at least two dictionaries: userdict and systemdict. The system dictionary, or systemdict, contains the names and associated procedures for all the standard PostScript operators. The operators "add" and "sub," along with all the other commands in PostScript, are defined here. When an object is tokenized as name, it is looked up here and if found, the appropriate action is taken. The user dictionary, userdict, is where user-defined commands are stored. The command:

```
/inch {72 mul} def
```

associates the name "inch" with the procedure 72 mul. If you write:

```
1 inch 2 inch moveto
```

you are really writing:

```
1 72 mul 2 72 mul moveto
```

which is the same as writing a moveto with the default PostScript units.

The execution stack stores procedures that are suspended by the interpreter while it completes execution of an embedded object. This provides a mechanism by which PostScript can handle procedures embedded in procedures.

Finally, PostScript has the capability to save the current graphics state and restore it at a later point. There are a variety of conditions under which it is desirable to save the graphics state. One of the most common is when an operation would change the current point, which is one of the parameters of the graphics state that is saved (see Chapter 4 for more details).

5. Operation of the Interpreter, Revisited

The interpreter simply executes the various object types in one of two ways:

- Numeric objects, special objects, dictionary objects, strings, literals, executable arrays, and packed arrays are pushed onto the stack.
- Executable name objects are looked up in the current dictionary stack and executed.

The interpreter executes names by passing control to the operator, which pops the necessary number of objects (operands) off the stack and pushs the result(s) onto the stack.

While this process is straightforward, there are complexities you need to consider. Given the way the process works, it is easy to write a program that contains errors. The more common types of errors are:

- The interpreter is instructed to do something—add—but the objects available on the stack are not the correct type (e.g. in the case of add, the top two objects on the stack had better be numbers).
- The interpreter is instructed to do something for which it expects objects to be on the stack and there are none.
- The interpreter receives a command to do something but cannot proceed because one or more prerequisite actions have not been taken. For example, before the command "show" can be used to place text on a page, three conditions must be met:
    1. A font must be selected and set.
    2. A point for the text to be shown must selected.
    3. The text to be shown must be provided.

  If one or more of these things are not done, issuing the show command results in an error condition.
- Finally, while it is not very common, it is also possible to "overflow" the operand stack—to put too many things on the stack. The typical size of the operand stack in a Level 1 implementation is 500. Putting 501 objects on the stack before removing any results in an error condition.[9]

One important aspect of interpreter operation that you should be aware of is the process of definition and definition binding. Soon you will see it is possible to define operations in PostScript. For example:

```
/i {72 mul} def
```

This causes the name **i** to be defined as the procedure {72 mul}. This means that whenever the interpreter encounters **i**, it pushes 72 onto the stack and multiplies the top two objects on the stack. This makes it possible for people who think in inches to write a PostScript moveto command as follows:

```
1 i 1 i moveto
```

The importance of early and late binding is related to the definition of the operator

[9]The authors first encountered this error when designing a logo that was built from lineto commands derived from points obtained from a scanner.

"mul." In this example, we intend for **i** to multiply the number preceding it by 72. That is fine as long as the definition of mul does not change.[10] However, if the program redefines mul as add—which can be done, although it is not advised—it redefines **i** as 72 add rather than 72 mul. You can avoid this by using the bind command:

```
/i {72 mul} bind def
```

This associates the actual operation that is performed when a multiply command is encountered with **i** rather than the name of the operation. Giving mul a new definition does not change the definition of what is associated with **i**.

6. Some Basic Operators

Chapter 21 on page 389 provides a description of the basic classes of operators along with a defintion of the more basic operators. These definitions include examples where appropriate. As you get started with PostScript, it does not hurt to have a sense of the basic operators.

- Path Operators
    - arc
    - arcto
    - clip
    - closepath
    - lineto
    - moveto
    - newpath
    - rlineto
    - rmoveto
- Font Operators
    - findfont
    - scalefont
    - setfont
    - setlinewidth
    - show
- Painting Operators
    - fill
    - stroke

[10]Examples are used here to make the concept clear. It should be noted the problems that can occur with early and late binding are generally with more complex situations. Further, be aware the standard PostScript commands should only be changed with the greatest of care.

- Stack Operators
    - dup
    - exch
    - pop
    - roll
- Mathematical Operators
    - add
    - sub
    - mul
    - div
    - mod
- Logical Operators
    - eq
    - gt
    - ge
    - lt
    - le
    - and
    - or
    - not
- Array Operators
    - array
    - put
    - get
    - length
- Control Operators
    - if
    - ifelse
    - for
    - forall
    - loop
    - exit
    - repeat
- Coordinate Operators
    - rotate
    - scale
    - translate
- Graphics Operators
    - currentpoint
    - setlinewidth
    - gsave
    - grestore

Chapter 3 Structured and Encapsulated PostScript

1. Introduction

Chapter 2 mentions the use of the % character to indicate a comment. In PostScript, a % character indicates that all characters to the next linefeed or carriage return are part of a comment. The PostScript interpreter ignores comments. Most of the PostScript programs in this book include comments at the beginning and the end which conform to Adobe's Document Structuring Conventions (DSC). In general, DSC comments make the logical structure of the program more comprehensible.[11] This chapter introduces some of the conventions for structuring PostScript files and explains why they are recommended. It also introduces the basic conventions for Encapsulated PostScript (EPS). PostScript files conforming to the EPS conventions are becoming a graphical interchange standard. Many document processing applications allow users to import graphics that are in EPS format. Almost any single-page PostScript program can be specified in EPS format.

The goal of this chapter is to provide an understanding of Adobe's Document Structuring Conventions. This understanding may be applied in two ways. First, it enables you to create small programs that conform to the EPS conventions so they can be imported into other computer applications. Second, it is possible to write

[11]The comments used in the PostScript programs in this book do conform to the Document Structuring Conventions, but more importantly, they conform to the additional requirements set out for Encapsulated PostScript (EPS). The purpose of the comments used, in reality, is to allow us to include the listings as PostScript graphics, which our processor defines as those conforming to the the EPS standard.

programs in a language such as C, Pascal, or BASIC that performs some useful operation on a DSC PostScript file. For example, it is possible to take pages 23–37 out of a 400-page document and send them to a laser printer. Assuming you only want 14 pages, you could write a program to save both printing time and money. Interested readers will want to continue their study of EPS and DSC in the latest edition of *PostScript Language Reference Manual.*

2. Why Structure PostScript Files?

There are many reasons why PostScript files are structured. Imagine you have two copies of a PostScript file, both versions of price lists. Which one is the most current? There are a number of ways you could find the answer. However, imagine the PostScript files conformed to DSC. You can now assume one of the first several lines in the file is:

```
%%CreationDate:  <some date>
```

By checking the dates the two files were created, you can make some reasonable assumptions about which is more current. Information in the file can also be used by other programs to manage the manipulation of PostScript files—e.g. the information can be used so only selected information is printed or transmitted. In organizations where documents can be thousands of pages, the ability to print only needed material can be significant. The PostScript listings and figures in this book are examples of why you want to use Document Structuring Convention (specifically EPS) comments in a PostScript program. This book was laid out electronically using a publishing program that permits the importation of graphics in a variety of formats; EPS is one of them. By structuring the program listings consistent with EPS requirements, figures are drawn by referencing the same file that contains the listing. Consistency between the two is guaranteed, even in the face of changes to the code.

Although you can read DSC and EPS comments, they are not meant for humans as much as they are for other computer programs. Later in this book, programs to write PostScript programs are discussed. Programs that write other programs, in the sense used here, are called drivers. The programs that use the comments placed in PostScript programs may be collected into groups called *document managers*. Document manager refers to any program which intervenes between the source of the PostScript code and the interpreter which executes the code. A document manager may be built into the laser printer, run on the computer on which the PostScript is generated, or be part of some specialized device separate from the printer and the generating computer—e.g. a print server that serves as an intermediary to the generating device and the printer.

Ultimately, the goal of document structuring comments is to provide information to a document manager that enables the program to perform some service for the user. There is no specified mapping between specific services and comments. It is up to software developers to make use of the standard in any creative way they imagine.

When a PostScript program adheres to the DSC form, you can assume it also aheres to the *Prologue and Script Model* described in Section 3, The Basic Organization of Programs. The most important feature of this adherence is the characteristic of page independence, which means that any page can be printed without relying on definitions or graphics state changes made in previous pages.

The most common document manager service a beginning programmer is likely to use is selective printing; page independence is the prerequisite. PostScript programs can be very long, but often you want to print or view only a single page or a small range of pages. By taking advantage of page independence and the cues provided by DSC comments, a computer program (or human) can selectively execute only those portions of the PostScript program that produce the desired pages. Similarly, with the growing popularity of page previewers—software that allows you to preview a PostScript program on the screen—the use of DSC comments becomes critical. For example, a previewer that we use has the option of using comments in the process of looking at a file. When we previewed this book, it took the system one second to look at page 100 of the PostScript output using comments. Getting to the same page without comments took the system more than 100 times longer (115 seconds).[12]

Document management services currently available include:

- *Print format manipulation:* For example, it may be useful to put more than one logical page on a physical page—as could be the case with slides or overhead transparencies. N-Up printing uses reduced versions of pages printed n to a single physical page so they can be proofed without using as much paper. Similarly, pages could be printed duplex—front and back—or shifted to allow for binding, etc.
- *Print services:* This includes selective or range printing, which is particularly important for previewers. Banner/trailer pages are another service: these are pages which precede and follow a print job with information about who it belongs to, the date and time it was printed, and so forth.
- *Accounting services:* Information in the document could be based to feed an accounting system. Although this is not recommended given

[12]In reality, reaching pages as high as 300 without comments proved to be such a complex task, it not only took much longer but occasionally crashed the workstation!

the open nature of the documents, there might be situations in which you could exercise such controls.

- *Resource management:* Certain resource allocation services allow document managers (print spoolers in particular) to manage laser printers as a resource. They are primarily useful in environments with large printing volumes and where multiple printers are linked into a network. Some DSC comments include information which can allow printers to more efficiently manage virtual memory and font caches; such management strategies can make a difference in the long run when printers are in use during most of the working day. Other examples of this kind of service include printer rerouting, where a print job is automatically routed from a busy printer to a free one, and parallel printing, where a large print job is broken up over several printers, each simultaneously printing a range of pages.

- *Document interchange:* Other programs can use comments to define the nature and scope of a graphic or page of text. As mentioned, numerous PC applications have the capability to import PostScript. The last section of this document explains how to make a PostScript program conform to EPS (Encapsulated PostScript format).

3. The Basic Organization of Programs

As mentioned in Chapter 2, there are certain structuring conventions that help to maintain the robustness and modularity of PostScript programs. Although PostScript interpreters do not enforce these conventions, it is necessary to respect them to conform to DSC. The basic model for DSC is a prologue followed by a script. This is the heart of the program structuring conventions. A PostScript program which conforms to the Document Structuring Conventions is divided into two main sections. The first, the prologue, contains procedure definitions and document information. The second, the script, uses the procedures defined in the prologue along with the standard operators to place marks on pages. The *PostScript Language Reference Manual* includes extensive discussion on programming within this model, including guidelines on which specific PostScript commands should and should not be used in each section. However, the principles you should follow can be summarized in a few rules:

- Any definition referred to on more than one page belongs in the prologue. The goal is to make each page independent, so you should be able to remove the code for any particular page without affecting other pages.

- The prologue is for definitions only. No marks should be placed on the page while the prologue is executing.

- Changes in variables and the graphics state should not carry over from one page to another. It should be possible to bracket the code for each page within a **gsave/grestore** pair. In fact, if pages include changes to the current coordinate space, it is probably a good idea to include **gsave** and **grestore** .

Much is unsaid here, but remember, the goal of this section is not to make you an expert at producing DSC compliant PostScript but to help you to see how programs might be written to make use of this additional structure.

4. Some Document Structuring Conventions

Comments that contribute to document structuring, with the exception of the First one, are preceded by a double % character in columns one and two. Of course, like any other comments, the PostScript interpreter ignores these comments, beginning with the double %%. Using a double rather than a single % character is simply a convention which document management software can be programmed to recognize as an indication of a DSC comment. Each DSC comment appears on its own line, and the double %% characters are always in the leftmost two columns.

Following each double %% character (with no space in between) is a DSC keyword. The keyword identifies the specific comment, and its spelling is case-sensitive. Some keywords are followed by a colon followed by one or more arguments. There is always a single space between the colon and the first argument.

The basic DSC comments that would appear in a program are illustrated in Listing 3.1. As you can see, they reflect the prologue/script model.

Listing 3.1: Basic Structure of a DSC Compliant File

```
%!PS-Adobe-3.0
%%Title: <textline>
%%Creator: <textline>
%%CreationDate: <textline>
%%Pages: <integer>
%%Version: <real> <integer>
%%EndComments
%%BeginProlog
  .
  . <Procedure definitions here>
  .
%%EndProlog
%%BeginSetup
  .
  .
  .
%%EndSetup
%%Page: <label> <integer>
```

```
%%BeginPageSetup
  .
  .
  .
%%EndPageSetup
  .
  . <PostScript Commands for the page here>
  .
%%PageTrailer
  .
  .
  .
%%Trailer
  .
  .
  .
%%EOF
```

The comments make major divisions of the program explicit. Although the prologue goes from the beginning to the comment %%EndProlog and the script goes from the next line to the end of the file, a little more detailed breakdown is possible:

header	Contains creation information and overall information about the document. This section contains only comments and ends with "%%EndComments".
prologue	Procedures are defined here preferably via a dictionary, along with any named variables and constants.
script	Page output information is contained here. The most significant comments are those that identify the separation of the pages"%%Page: pagelabel pagenumber,"but further information may be provided by structuring the program in terms of page setup, actual commands, and trailer information.
trailer	The trailer section contains document information that could not be easily put in the header at the time the file was created. In this case, the comment in the header would include the argument"atend,"which is an indication to the document management software to look for a parallel comment in the trialer comments for the information. A common example might be the total number of pages in the document.

The script or body is broken down into pages. Further structuring at the page level is achieved by three types of comments:

- structure comments
- resource requirements

- query comments

While the focus of this book does not permit full treatment of the comments, you may want to know the comments include such details as Listing 3.2.

Listing 3.2: Selected DSC Comments

```
%RGBCustomColor: red green blue string
%%HSBCustomColor: hue saturation brightness string
%%CMYKCustomColor: cyan magenta yellow black string
%%DocumentPaperSizes: sizename sizename...
%%DocumentPaperForms: formname formname...
%%DocumentPaperColors: colorname colorname...
%%DocumentPaperWeights: integer integer
```

Most readers have little trouble understanding how a document manager might use comments such as those above about paper color or size.

As you can see, there are a number of DSC comments not described in this chapter; however, the ones described in the following chart are appropriate for nearly all PostScript programs. With the exception of the first comment (%!PS-Adobe-3.0), and the last (%%EOF) no one comment is required in absolutely every program. The DSC compliance rule is as follows: If whatever a comment refers to or makes explicit (such as a section of the program) is present, that presence *must* be signaled by the appropriate comment. Obviously, in the case of general information (such as creator or version), unless that information is present, a document manager cannot use it to provide a service. As indicated, certain information, such as the number of pages in the document, can be deferred from the header to the trailer section (see chart). Under these circumstances, the header comment takes the string **atend** instead of its normal arguments, and the comment is repeated with the appropriate arguments in the trailer section. Here are the explanations for the DSC comments presented in Listing 3.1:

%!PS-Adobe-3.0	This comment must be the first line of a PostScript program. It signals a document manager that the program conforms to Version 3.0 of DSC.
%%Title:	This comment is followed by a text string which is the name of the document. It might be extracted by a document manager for entry in a log or display on a banner page.
%%Creator:	This comment is followed by a text string which is the name of the program's creator. The creator might be a person or a PostScript driver program (see Chapter 14).
%%CreationDate:	This comment is followed by a text string indicating the date and time the document was created. The information does not have to be in any particular format.

%%Pages:	This comment is followed by an integer equaling the number of pages in the document.
%%Version:	This comment is followed by a real number equaling the document's version number, followed by an integer equaling the revision number.
%%EndComments	This comment indicates the end of the header comments (i.e. those DSC comments just described).
%%BeginProlog	This comment signals the start of the program prologue, which includes global level definitions such as procedures.
%%EndProlog	This comment signals the end of the program prologue.
%%BeginSetup	This comment signals the start of part of the script where changes to the graphics state are made for the entire document. Examples of commands that occur in the setup section include setting the current font or rotating the coordinate space to print in landscape mode.
%%EndSetup	This comment signals the end of the setup section.
%%Page:	This comment is followed by a text label, which is followed by an integer. Both the label and the integer indicate the start of a particular page and refer to the page number. The label, however, need not be ordinal; for example, labels such as "first," "second," "third," could be extracted by a document manager which provides a pagination service.
%%BeginPageSetup	This comment signals the start of the page setup section, which is like the program setup except that changes to the graphics state are specific to the particular page.
%%EndPageSetup	This comment signals the end of the page setup section.
%%PageTrailer	This comment should immediately precede any page comments that were deferred using the atend convention.
%%Trailer	This comment should precede any document comments that were deferred using the **atend** convention.
%%EOF	This should be the last line in the PostScript program.

5. Encapsulated PostScript: EPS

One of the questions often asked about PostScript is how to create EPS files. By definition, an EPS file is a PostScript file that can be used as an image or graphic in another PostScript file. This interest is often a need to create a small file that is to be incorporated in another document, such as data from an experiment or a photo on a resume. EPS is becoming an increasingly popular format for importing graphics into other applications. To import the graphical representations of the listings in this book into the formatting program, the formatting program needed to see them as EPS compliant PostScript programs. At the base level, a PostScript program must contain two comments to be EPS compliant:

%!PS-Adobe-3.0 EPSF-3.0	The version comment informs the application the file conforms to the EPS file format.
%%BoundingBox:	This comment is followed by four integers indicating the X and Y coordinates for the lower left and upper right corners, respectively. Applications which scale the imported image to fit within a portion of the page (such as the one used to layout this book) need this information.

Experience suggests that some processors look for an additional command at the end of the EPS program. We know of one previewer that gives a warning if there is not a %%Trailer comment. One formatting system complains if the last line is not %%EOF. While these are legitimate comments, their requirement is beyond the scope of the convention.

A further word is in order on the BoundingBox comment. The integers that follow the keyword specify the extent of the image in the default coordinate space. So,

```
%%BoundingBox: 100 100 200 200
```

specifies the application program should anticipate there is no imaging outside this space. Imagine this image is to be put into a space that is 3 inches by 6 inches. This means the original image, which was 100 × 100 units or about 1.4 inches square, easily fits in the larger space. It could be doubled in size with a scale command and still fit. It could also be anamorphically scaled—doubled in the X direction and quadrupled in the Y direction—and still fit. Many application programs use the information in the BoundingBox comment, along with information about the space to be filled, to offer you many scaling and clipping choices. One last note: It has been indicated on several occasions that the relationship between the DSC comments and the actual PostScript code is one of honor. If the actual image in our example went from (50,50) to (300,300), there could well be unanticipated side effects in bringing an EPS file into another document. Some applications allow the host program to clip any part of the image that is outside the bounding box, but this might not have the desired effect.

Beyond the commenting conventions, there are a number of programming guidelines associated with Encapsulated PostScript. The guidelines are all designed to protect the graphics state and stack contents of which PostScript program into which you import the EPS file. For example, programmers are encouraged to keep all procedure definitions in their own dictionary to avoid overwriting one of the same name associated with the host program. Certain PostScript commands are illegal in EPS because they empty the entire contents of one or more stacks. In general, these guidelines are intended to protect the host PostScript program that houses the encapsulated program. Programmers are responsible for encapsulating their programs so they do not damage the environment within which it is placed.

You are encouraged to pursue a thorough treatment of EPS guidelines in the current edition of the *PostScript Language Reference Manual*.

Chapter 4
The PostScript Coordinate Space

Some people are excited about PostScript because of the possibility of defining graphic objects and images in PostScript in a way that is not constrained by the particular device you are using. For example, it is possible to give the following commands:

```
100 100 moveto
.00001 setlinewidth
.5478 setgray
10000 10000 lineto
showpage
```

We are not aware of any display device that could fully implement these commands. The specified line is less than one-millionth of an inch thick and spans a distance of more than 100 inches. Nevertheless, we can specify the line and the output device will try to render it as accurately as it can.[13]

PostScript provides the capability to specify text and graphics unconstrained by any particular output device's capability, either in terms of the resolution of the rendering or the extent of the space that may be rendered.

This means it is possible to write a single program that produces output on both low- and high-resolution devices. For example, the code that produced the page you are currently reading was initially sent to a page previewer (low-resolution device) where images of the pages were displayed on a computer screen for proofing. Over a number of iterations, stylistic and content corrections as well as format and design improvements, were made to the manuscript. Once we achieved a reasonable level of clarity, we used the same formatting system to produce the same kind of PostScript code. This time, instead of previewing it on the screen, the code was sent to a laser printer (medium-resolution device), where pages were

[13]This particular line is so fine, all the devices we know of would render it as one device-pixel wide.

produced for review and proofing. When all corrections had been made, PostScript code was sent to a phototypesetter (high-resolution device) to make the masters for printing.

PostScript can also create images that are not bound by a predefined space such as a page. You can put text and graphics in a space that is infinitely large.[14] While the general applications of this are somewhat limited, there are significant. For example, it is possible to create a large poster that is many feet high by many feet wide. Any standard PostScript laser printer can print the poster by printing the various pieces, creating tiles that can be put together to form the whole image.

This chapter takes a brief look at how the author of a PostScript program can manipulate the coordinate space to achieve selected effects. It only scratches the surface of the complex and sophisticated coordinate system transformations available in PostScript through graphics state matrix manipulations. Generally, this discussion is limited to the more simple transformations performed individually. The chapter begins with an explanation of the measurements used in PostScript and defines "the user space." The next section, introduces the basic transformations. Finally, the purpose and use of the graphics state stack is introduced.

1. Measurements and User Space

Measurements and the user coordinate system, or space, present a minor problem for many first-time PostScript users. While the numbers used for positioning in most PostScript programs may seem strange at first glance, they look very familiar to printers and others who use the unit of measurement known as a "point." For all practical purposes, a point is 1/72 of an inch. The point is PostScripts default unit of measurement. If there are 72 points to an inch, an 8.5-by-11-inch page is 612 × 792 points wide. The center of that page is also 306 across by 396 up. These numbers, when they are first encountered in programs, are confusing to many users. There are ways to avoid using these numbers,[15] but we suggest you familiarize yourself with them for three reasons:

1. One of the ways to learn more about PostScript is to read code that others have written. Most of this code uses the default measurement

[14] In reality, the imaging space is bound by the printer's memory.

[15] The two most common ways are to define an inch as the procedure 72 mul, i.e. "/inch {72 mul} def." Having done this, all movements can be specified in inches, e.g. "2 inch 2 inch moveto." Another way to accomplish the same goal is to make the first command in the file 72 72 scale. This changes all units to inches. Now the command 1 1 moveto is interpreted as a movement to a point one inch over and one inch up on a sheet of paper.

or a multiple of it.[16] So it is good to get a sense of how default page coordinates are translated in points. A 1-inch margin is 72 points. The center of a page is at 306, 396, etc.

2. While it is easy to think in inches, many of us do not think well in fractions of inches. For example, there are "ruling lines" around figures and program listings in this book. How wide are these lines in inches? In points they are 1 point thick, which is 1/72nd of an inch or .013888 inches wide. Many of the measurements you make on a page of text are awkward fractions of an inch, but they are nice round, whole, points.

3. Fonts are most often described in terms of their point size. The discussion gets very complicated here because the letters of a 36-point font are not a half-inch high.[17] Nonetheless, fonts are most often discussed or thought about in terms of their point size. Normal reading fonts are in the 9 – 11 point range, for example. For children or elderly readers, you might choose 12 or even 13 points. These sizes do not easily translate to inches or centimeters.

We urge readers who are serious about PostScript to commit some time to learning the default coordinate system.

The space where you work, the PostScript coordinate space, is often referred to as the user space. For those who remember coordinate geometry from high school, the user space is nothing more than the Cartesian Coordinate System. For those that have not had a lot of math, the concept is still relatively simple. Consider taking a few pieces of graph paper. Put one down and mark the lower left corner 0,0. This means this point is 0 units in the X, or horizontal, direction and 0 units in the vertical, or Y, direction. If you imagine that every line on the graph paper is 10 units from the previous line, you can count from 0,0 in the horizontal or vertical direction. Put an "X" on your sheet so you remember it. Now, put another sheet to the right of it, and you could count more lines going to the right. If you put pages at the top, you could count further up in the Y direction. What we have done so far is define one quadrant or one quarter, of the Cartesian Coordinate System. You could add pages to the right and above indefinitely.

---

[16]Some systems use a coordinate system with 720 or 7200 units to the inch to allow for more precise placement, particularly if the output might be sent to typesettters.

[17]In reality, the "point size" of a font is a measure of the size of a box within which all the letters of the alphabet fit. A few minutes of drawing letters on a ruled page—the kind of paper you used to practice penmanship in elementary school—will convince you that no letter goes from the highest point of the highest letter—any capital—to the lowest point of the lowest letter—e.g. y or g. Thus, any particular 36-point character is in reality slightly less than 36 points.

You could also add pages to the left of the first page you put down. The horizontal lines would be continuations of the horizontal lines on the page with the "X." The vertical lines, however, would be on the other side of zero. Indeed, you have entered into the region of negative X coordinates. Points on this sheet would be represented in the form –20,30. Similarly, you could put a sheet below the original sheet. In this case, the vertical lines would continue from that original sheet, but the horizontal lines would be on the other side of zero. On this sheet, the coordinates would represented in the form 30, –50.

You now have a number of sheets to the right and above the original, one sheet to the immediate left of original, and one sheet immediately below the original. There is one space still empty: the space to the left and below the original sheet. The upper right corner of a sheet here would touch the 0,0 spot on the "X" sheet. In this area, both the horizontal and vertical coordinates are negative. If you imagine these sheets going out in all directions, you have defined the space in which one can put text or draw objects. Unfortunately, as many novice programmers have discovered, drawing something does not mean it is printed. You need to know which area of the user space is being imaged or printed. You can control this, but you start by looking at the default area.

2. The Default Imaging Area

Initially, the page printed by a standard laser printer using 8.5-by-11-inch paper is the space defined by the rectangle that has one corner at 0,0 and the other corner at 612, 792. Listing 4.1 shows a program listing. You are not expected to understand the program at this point; rather, compare the output depicted in Figure 4.1 with the program listing and see if you can recognize what some of the numbers mean or what a command might do. This program, which is included on your disk, a grid on a piece of paper, as shown in Figure 4.1. If you send this file, called SPACE_PS1.PS, to your laser printer, it provides a reference sheet you can use to identify the point coordinates of a particular place on the page.

Listing 4.1: Grid of Default Page Coordinates

```
%!PS-Adobe-3.0 EPSF-30.
%%BoundingBox: 0 0 612 792
%%Title: (Workspace Grid)
%%Creationdate: (9/04/91:13:13)
%%EndComments
/Helvetica-Bold findfont
10 scalefont
setfont
.5 setlinewidth
.8 setgray
/nstr 10 string def
0 10 792
```

```
{0 exch moveto 612 0 rlineto stroke}
for
0 10 612
{0 moveto  0 792 rlineto stroke}
for
1 setlinewidth

0 72 792
        {dup dup
        0 exch moveto
        600 0 rlineto .2 setgray stroke
        4 sub 312 exch moveto 0 setgray  nstr cvs show
        }
for
0 72 612
        {dup dup
         0 moveto
        0 792 rlineto stroke
        dup nstr cvs stringwidth pop 2 div sub
        396 moveto nstr cvs show
        }
for
showpage
%%EOF
```

Printing this page is also useful because it shows you the actual printing limits of your particular laser printer. The laser printer we tested it on clipped the first 15 points and the last 20 points in both directions. So, if a printing goes from 1,1 to 10,10, even though it is correctly stated, it would not appear on the output page.[18]

3. Changing the Default Imaging Area

To change the default imaging area, it is necessary to "transform" the coordinate system. From a graphics point of view, there are three basic transformations that can be made. PostScript has a rich set of commands for performing these transformations individually and together. This section briefly describes these transformations in their most basic form. Although it is beyond the scope of this introduction to provide a full description of all the transform commands, we will introduce the basic ones and provide a sense of their impact. The three transformations are:

[18]Device space is independent of the user space, and mapping between user space and device space is normally transparent to the user. The process of converting the user image to device pixels is called scan conversion. The process of accommodating the image given the undesirable effects that can occur in rasterization is called tuning. Tuning is a particular concern when device resolution is a significant fraction of the size of the images or text characters that are being drawn.

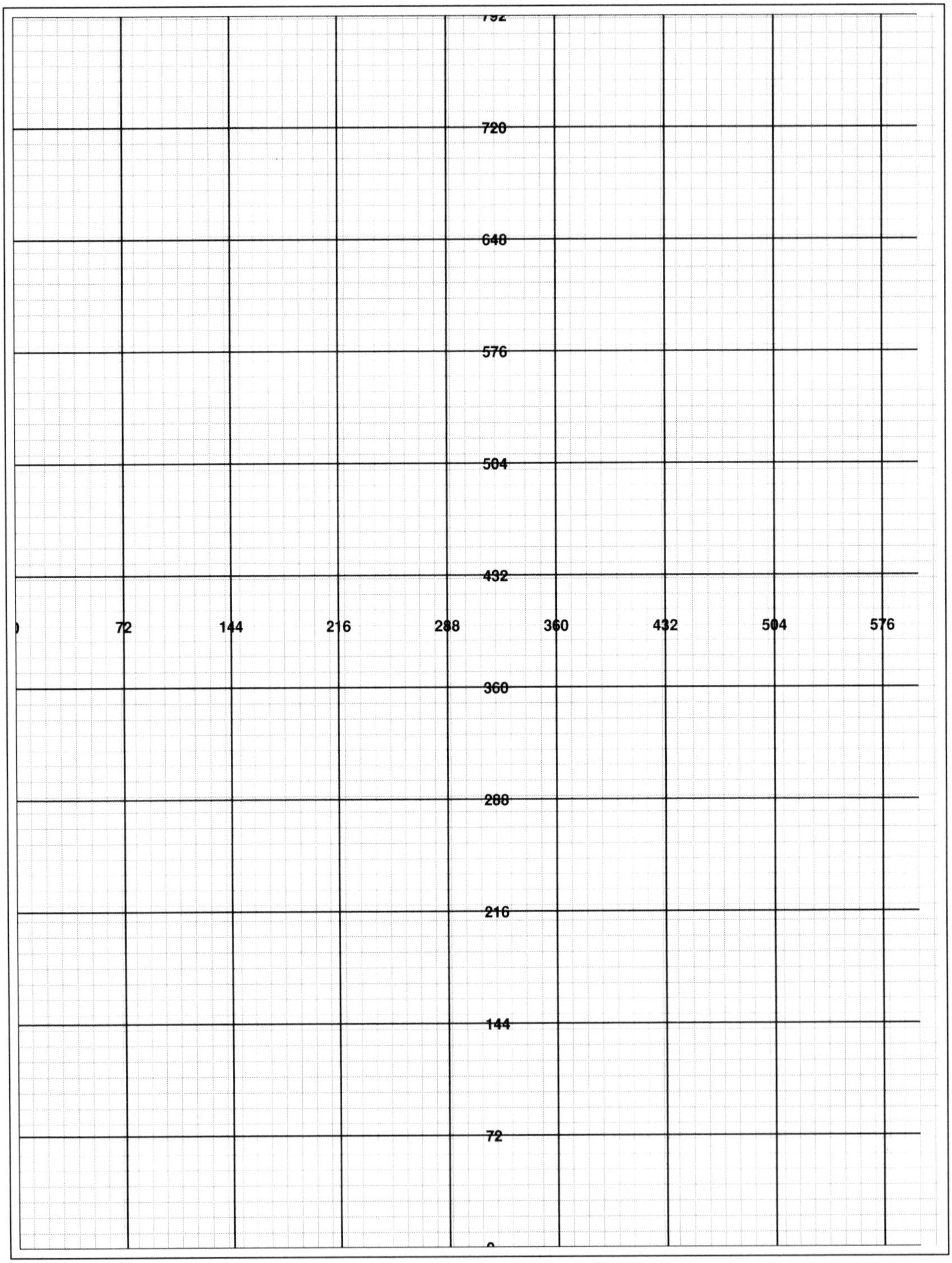

Figure 4.1: Grid of Default Page Coordinates

- scaling
- translating
- rotating

Figure 4.2 shows a picture of the PostScript coordinate system with a shaded square representing the part of the system that is imaged if the showpage command is given. The program[19] that is used to make these images has five sections:

- A section to depict the page that will be printed, which never changes;
- A section where commands can be added before a transform;
- A section where transform commands can be added;
- A section where commands can be added after the transform;
- A section which draws the coordinate grid, showing the impact of the changes made on the coordinate space.

The section of the program that we change is between the comments shown below:

```
% place pre transformation commands here


%rotations, translations, and scaling commands
%may be placed here
%The gray box always shows the area to be printed



%place post transformation commands here
```

Consider, as a simple example, the PostScript command:

```
10 10 scale
```

This causes the default unit of measurement to increase by a factor of 10 in both the X and Y directions. Another way to imagine this is to change the default unit of measure from approximately 1/70th of an inch to approximately 1/7 of an inch. Before the scale command, a line from 100,100 to 200,200 is on the printed page. After the scale command, it is still in the user space, which continues indefinitely in all directions, but it is no longer found on the printed page. Figure 4.3 shows the effect of the "10 10 scale" command.

[19]The code that produced this and many of the other figures in this chapter is included at the end of this chapter in Listing 4.5. You may wish to copy and experiment with the code to get a sense of the various transform commands.

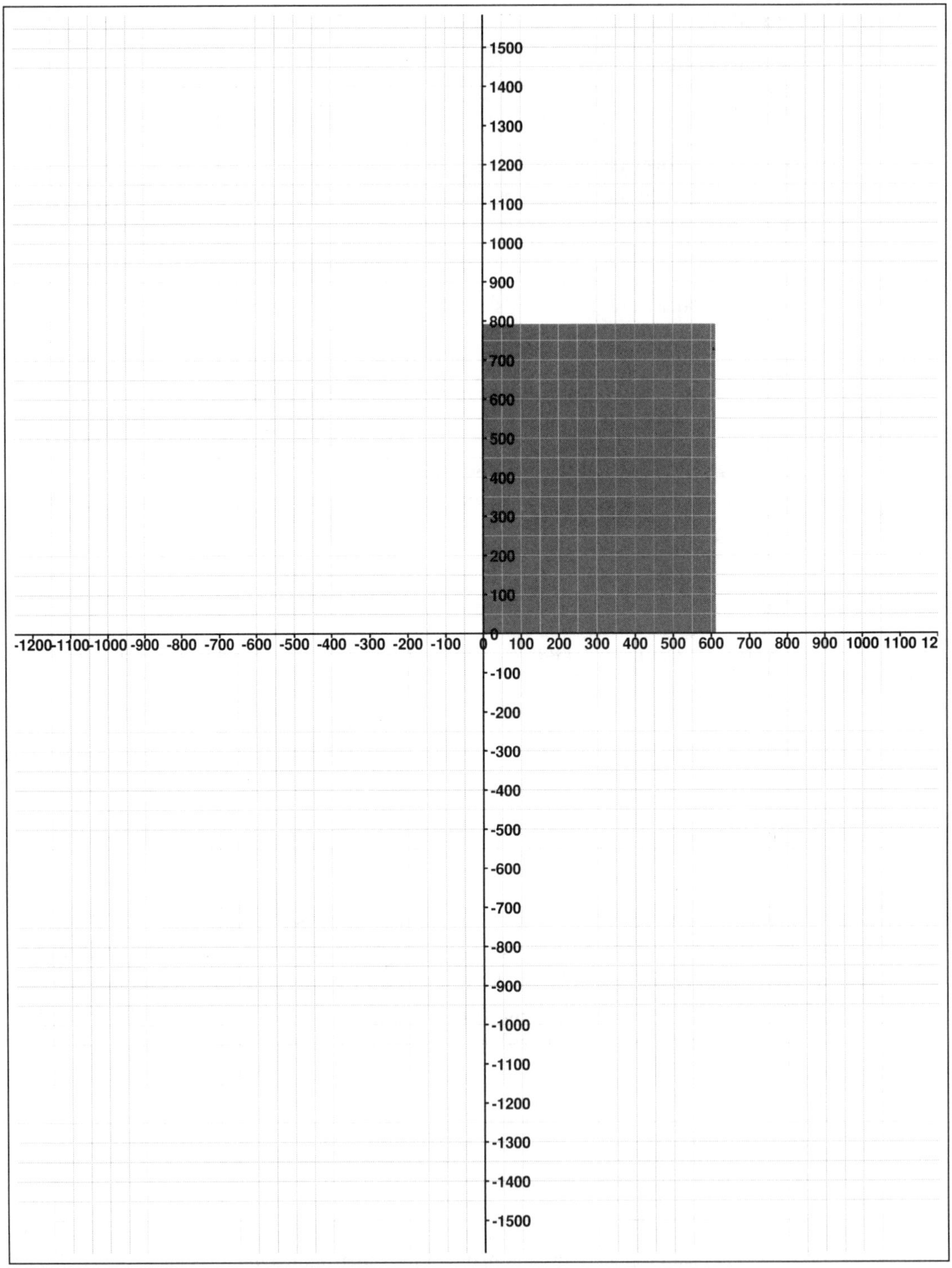

Figure 4.2: PostScript Coordinate System with Default Image Area

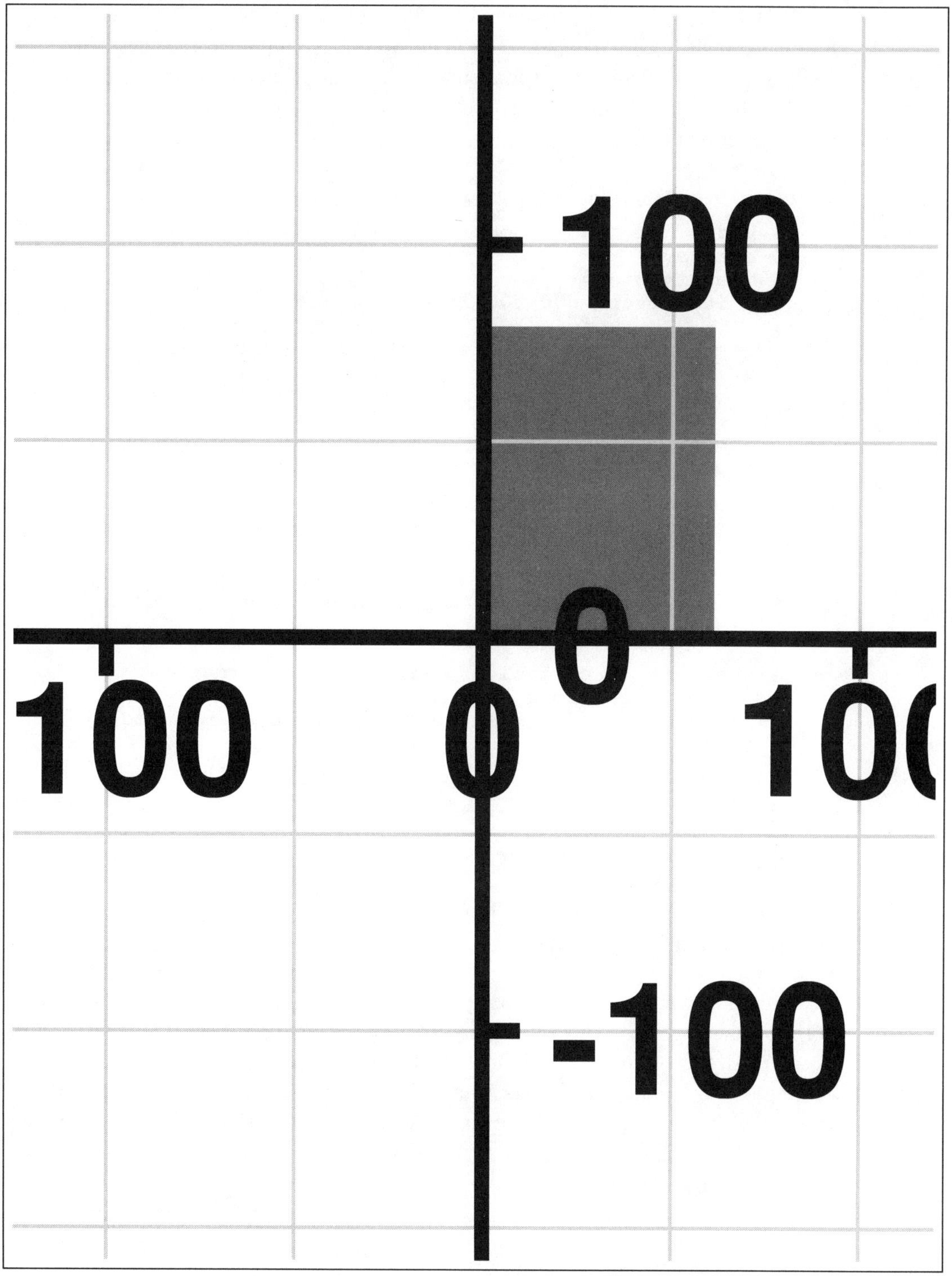

Figure 4.3: Impact of Scaling on Coordinates and Image Area

By the way, if the first command in a PostScript program is "72 72 scale," the user has transformed the default coordinate system from points to inches! The command "1 1 moveto" moves to a point on the page 1 inch up from the bottom and 1 inch over from the left. Any moveto beyond 8.5 in the X direction or 11 in the Y direction is off the page.

Figure 4.4 change the center portion as follows:

```
% place pre transformation commands here
0 setgray
10 setlinewidth
100 100 moveto 600 600 lineto stroke

%rotations, translations, and scaling commands
%may be placed here
%The gray box always shows the area to be printed
-90 rotate

%place post transformation commands here
```

Note the line drawn from 100,100 to 600,600 is now going from –100,100 to –600,600. If you do the rotation first and then draw a line from 100,100 to 600,600 as shown below:

```
% place pre transformation commands here


%rotations, translations, and scaling commands
%may be placed here
%The gray box always shows the area to be printed
-90 rotate


%place post transformation commands here
%
0 setgray
10 setlinewidth
100 100 moveto 600 600 lineto stroke
```

the result would be Figure 4.5.

This is a good example because you often want to print on a page in landscape format—the page is 11 inches wide by 8.5 inches high. In PostScript, you can accomplish this by rotating and then translating the coordinate axis. If you are willing to specify the coordinates as mixed positive and negative numbers, the translation is not necessary. However, most people feel most comfortable expressing page coordinates as positive integers. To accomplish this, use the following rotation and translation:

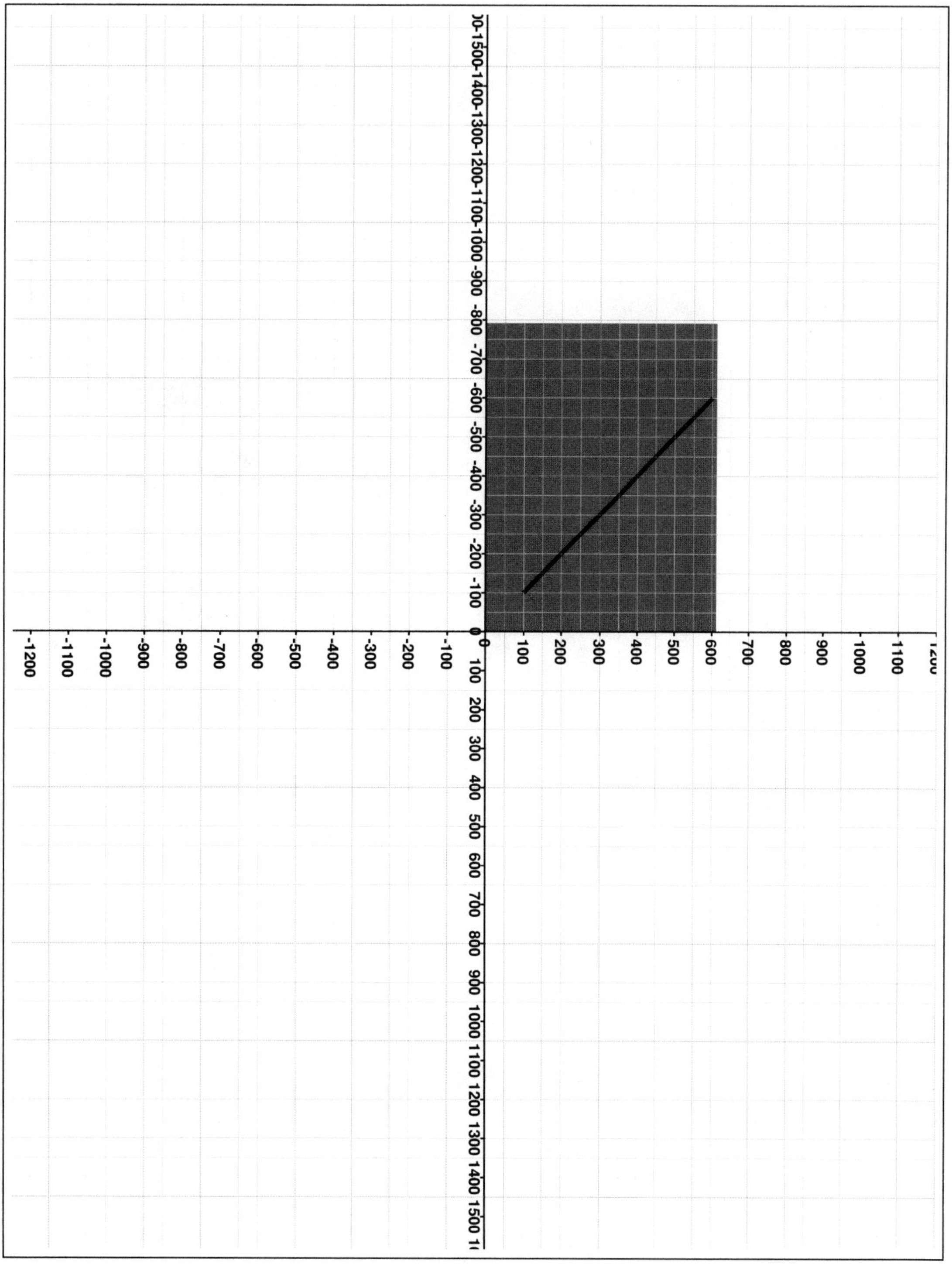

Figure 4.4: Impact of Rotation on Coordinates and Image Area

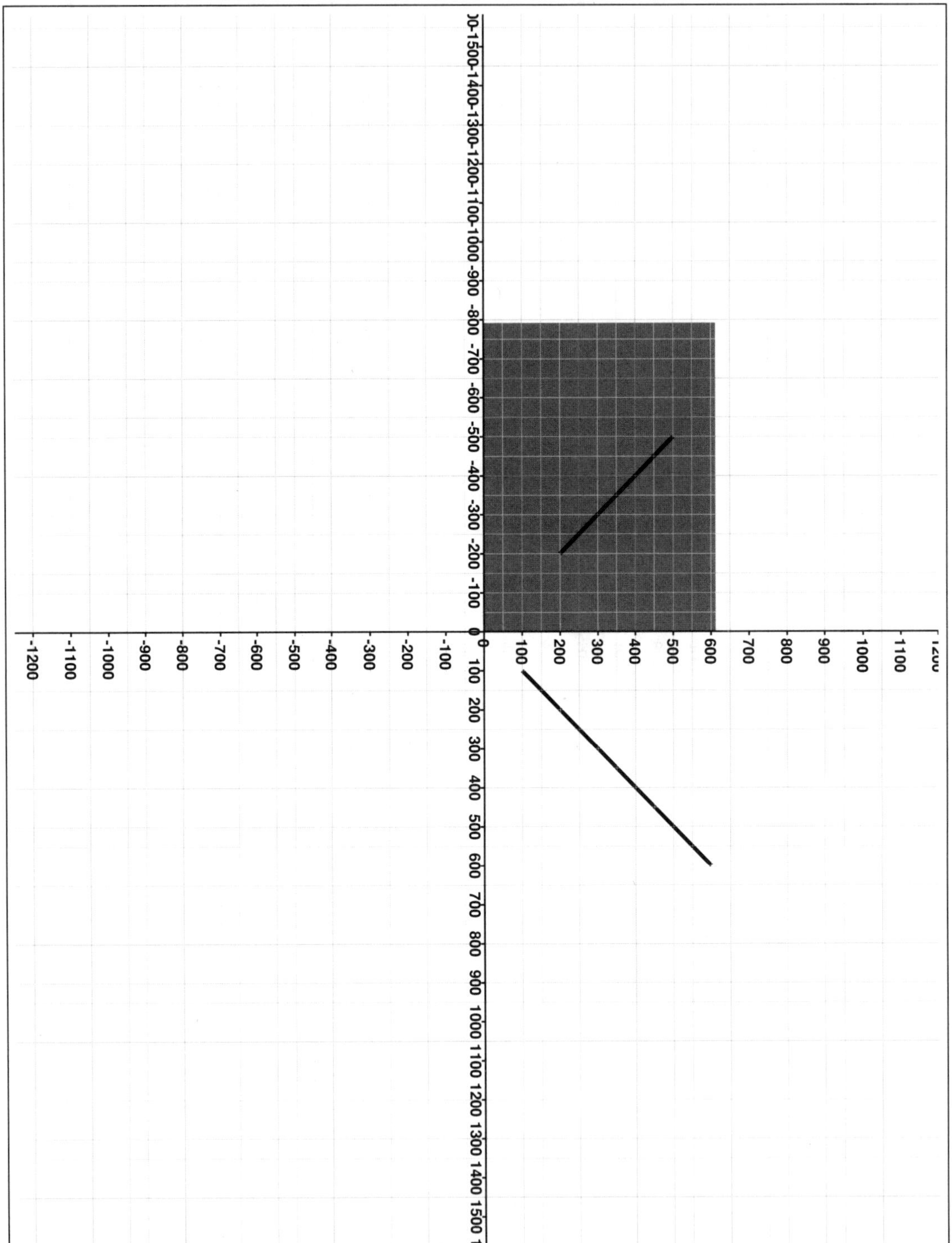

Figure 4.5: Impact of Rotation on Line Placement Relative to Image Area

```
% place pre transformation commands here

%rotations, translations, and scaling commands
%may be placed here
%The gray box always shows the area to be printed
-90 rotate
-792 0 translate

%place post transformation commands here
%
0 setgray
10 setlinewidth
100 100 moveto 600 600 lineto stroke
```

As a result, the image print area is moved, as shown in Figure 4.6.

4. The Imaging Process

One of the most frustrating situations when working with PostScript is a program you know is syntactically correct but yields no output.[20] You have already learned one of the reasons why an image might not appear on a page—incorrect placement in the coordinate space. Now, let's address another less common reason for unanticipated results.

Imagine that you give the commands in Listing 4.2:

Listing 4.2: Example of Layering

```
%!PS-Adobe-3.0 EPSF-30.
%%BoundingBox: 0 0 612 792
%%Title: (Coordinate System and Transformations)
%%Creationdate: (9/07/91:08:00)
%%EndComments
100 100 moveto
0 setgray
10 setlinewidth
200 200 lineto
stroke
.5 setgray
150 150 50 0  360 arc
fill
showpage
%%EOF
```

[20]For example, consider that you wrote a program where the last command was a show page. When you run the program, the page comes out, but what you expected to see is not there. You know the program has no syntax errors; otherwise, it would not have gotten to the showpage command.

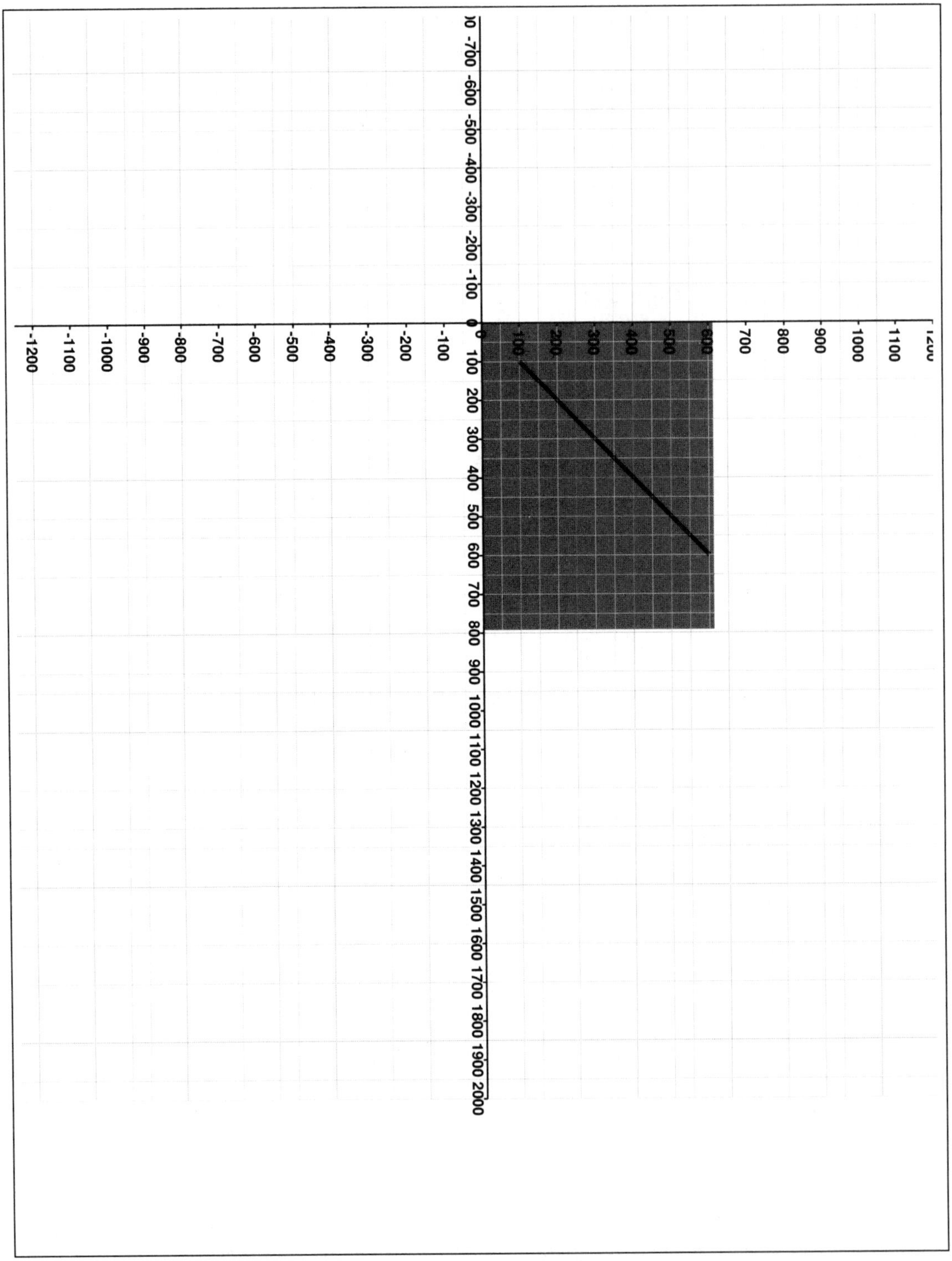

Figure 4.6: Rotation and Translation for a Landscape Page

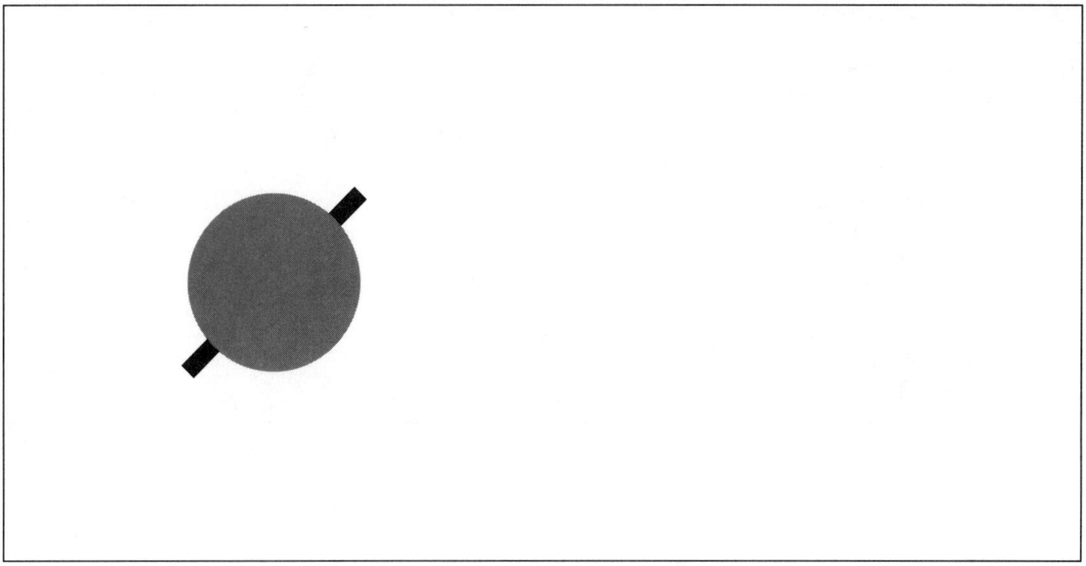

Figure 4.7: Opacity of PostScript Objects

Based on these commands you might expect to see a gray circle with a solid black line through it. In reality, you only see the ends of the lines, as shown in Figure 4.7. The gray circle is opaque: it is a solid laid on top of the line. The line does not show through.

If you remember text is really a complex graphic outline that is filled in, it should be apparent that although it is impossible to layer a shaded circle over text, it is possible to layer text over a shaded circle or other graphic with very positive results.

5. The Graphics State Stack

As you begin to manipulate the coordinate space to achieve special effects, the problem of returning to the original graphics state can become a problem. Consider for example, that you find it useful to create a logo that explodes and moves. This might easily be done by a loop that repeatedly prints a name after translating, scaling, and changing the gray scale. Take Listing 4.3 for an example.

Listing 4.3: Exploding Logo

```
%!PS-Adobe-3.0 EPSF-30.
%%BoundingBox: 0 0 612 792
%%Title: (Coordinate System and Transformations)
%%Creationdate: (9/07/91:08:00)
%%EndComments
/Helvetica-Bold findfont
```

```
10 scalefont
setfont
1 setlinewidth
10 100 translate
0 .03 1 {setgray
.5 .75 translate
1.045 1.075  scale
0 0 moveto
(Hands-on Postscript) show
} for
0 setgray
0 0 moveto
(Hands-on Postscript) show
showpage
%%EOF
```

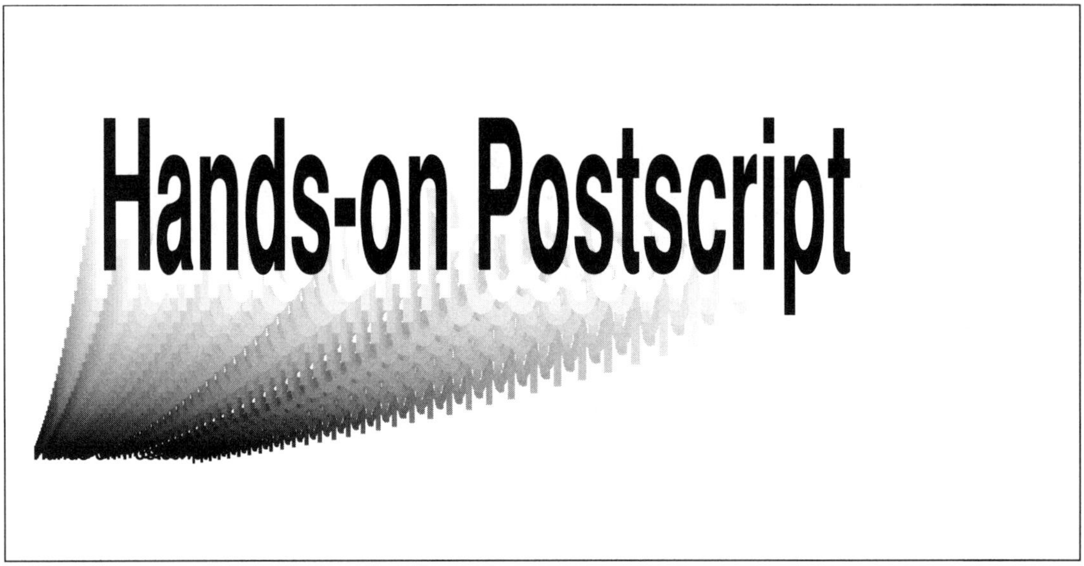

Figure 4.8: Exploding PostScript Logo

It would be very difficult, if not impossible, to calculate the impact of all the scale and translate directives that created the logo, as some of the following examples show. PostScript provides a facility called the graphics state stack that makes this chore unnecessary. By issuing the command gsave, you can save a number of characteristics of the current graphics state, including the current transform matrix. To return to the state that existed at the time the gsave command was issued, we simply issue a grestore. So, you can save the graphics state, make changes to it, and restore the original version by making the following modification to our program (The results of Listing 4.4 are shown in Figure 4.9):

Listing 4.4: Listing for Exploding Logo with Gsave and Grestore

```
%!PS-Adobe-3.0 EPSF-30.
%%BoundingBox: 0 0 612 792
%%Title: (Coordinate System and Transformations)
%%Creationdate: (9/07/91:08:00)
%%EndComments
/Helvetica-Bold findfont
10 scalefont
setfont
1 setlinewidth
gsave
10 100 translate
0 .03 1 {setgray
.5 .75 translate
1.045 1.075  scale
0 0 moveto
(Hands-on Postscript) show
} for
0 setgray
0 0 moveto
(Hands-on Postscript) show
10 20 moveto (10 20 before grestore) show
grestore
10 20 moveto (10 20 after grestore) show
showpage
%%EOF
```

Other parameters—beyond the transform matrix—the appropriate graphics state commands save and restore include

- color
- position
- path
- clipping path
- font
- linewidth
- linecap
- line join
- miter limit
- dash pattern

A few other devices independent and a number of device-dependent parameters are also a part of the graphics state, but these are beyond our current discussion. As always, see the *PostScript Language Reference Manual* for further details.

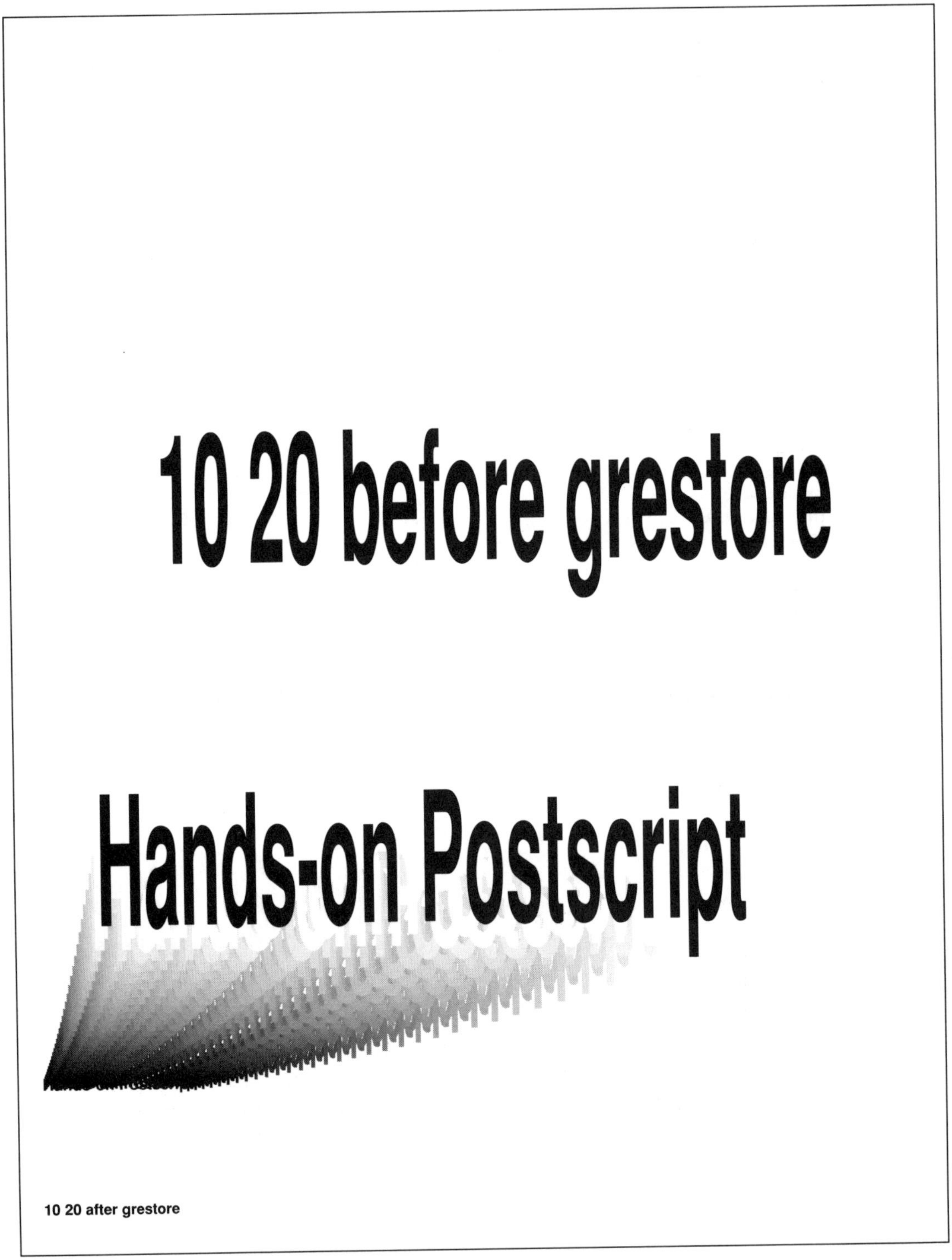

Figure 4.9: Impact of Gsave and Grestore on Output

6. Code for Coordinate System with Default Image Area

Listing 4.5 provides a program that allows you to insert various matrix manipulation commands as indicated, and to see the effect they have on the coordinate system.

Listing 4.5: PostScript Coordinate System with Default Image Area

```
%!PS-Adobe-3.0 EPSF-30.
%%BoundingBox: 0 0 612 792
%%Title: (Coordinate System and Transformations)
%%Creationdate: (9/07/91:08:00)
%%EndComments
/Helvetica-Bold findfont 40 scalefont setfont
1 setlinewidth .5 setgray
/nstr 10 string def
312 396 translate
.25 .25 scale
0 0 moveto  612 0 rlineto 0 792 rlineto -612 0 rlineto
closepath fill

% place pre transformation commands here

%rotations, translations, and scaling commands
% may be placed here
%The gray box always shows the area to be printed

%place post transformation commands here


1 setlinewidth .8 setgray
-2000 50 2000 {-2000 exch moveto 4000 0 rlineto stroke} for
-2000 50 2000 {-2000 moveto  0 4000 rlineto stroke} for
4 setlinewidth 0 setgray
-2000 0 moveto 2000 0 lineto stroke
0 -2000 moveto 0 2000 lineto stroke
-2000 100 2000{
        dup 0 exch moveto 10 0 rlineto
        gsave stroke grestore
        8 -16 rmoveto nstr cvs show} for
-2000 100 2000 {
        dup 0 moveto 0 -10 rlineto
        gsave stroke grestore
        dup nstr cvs stringwidth pop 2 div neg  -30 rmoveto
        nstr cvs show} for
showpage
%%EOF
```

Part 2
PostScript Programming Examples

This section of the book contains a series of PostScript programs. Every effort has been made to make each chapter self-contained—everything that you need to know to do the project is in the chapter. The earlier chapters are simpler and are explained more completely than the latter chapters; you decide where to begin. The chapters in this section describe programs that can be run and completed with any laser printer and computer.

Chapter 5
Letterhead

This chapter introduces the first programming project—producing letterhead or stationery. The program is presented in three stages; each demonstrates a few features of the language and illustrates how they are used. In PostScript programming, particularly if you do not have access to on-screen preview and error detection, it it best to start simple and be sure the program works at a basic level before adding bells and whistles. There has more than one occasion where a simple typo prevented a program from running. Without diagnostics, you could spend hours looking for an error that, in the last analysis, is very obvious. This chapter begins with the simplest program that performs something relatively useful and then expands and enhances it. A few additional ways to enhance this program after you learn a little more about PostScript are suggested at the end of the chapter.

1. Objectives

The objectives of this chapter are:

- To show that PostScript programs can be simple and direct, making them both easy to write and easy to understand;
- To provide a letterhead program that can easily be adapted for personal use;
- To demonstrate how this book introduces operators in the context of examples that do something useful; these operators enable you to
    - move around a "page"
    - draw simple lines
    - put text on a page
    - do simple arithmetic
    - "manipulate the stack"
    - control the printer
- To introduce the notion of structuring and encapsulating PostScript programs.

2. Operator Explanations

These programs essentially consist of moving the current point to various places on the page and then laying down strings of text. Before proceeding with a line-by-line analysis of the listings, here is a summary of the operators introduced in these first programs:

a. The Simplest Letterhead

The first program is one of the simplest and most useful PostScript programs. It uses six operators to put text on a page to form a simple letterhead. Three of the operators—**findfont**, **scalefont**, and **setfont**—may almost be considered a single command as they are most often used together.[21] The letterhead is not elegant by any means, but the program can be keyed and run without creating major problems. The operators used in the first program include:

findfont

Description: The **findfont** operator consumes a literal key from the top of the stack and returns the font dictionary `font` associated with `key` in the `FontDirectory`. If the font is not found, the action is implementation-dependent. The system may substitute a default font, attempt to search any disk files for the specified font, or it may generate an "invalidfont" error and refuse to continue. You may redefine **findfont** operator to implement different font-finding strategies.

Arguments: `key`

`key` is an object defining a font dictionary and can be obtained via a call to **definefont** operator. Fonts built into the output device are usually automatically enrolled into the `FontDictionary` and do not need to be registered via **definefont** operator.

Results: `font`

The **findfont** operator function returns a font dictionary `font` that is associated with the argument `key` in the `FontDirectory`.

In these programs, **findfont** locates the Helvetica font, the typestyle chosen for this project.

[21] In Level 2 PostScript, these three operators have been combined into a single operator, selectfont, which accomplishes the same goal of finding, scaling, and setting a font.

moveto

Description: This operator starts a new subpath of the current path. **Moveto** operator sets the current point in the graphics state to the user space coordinate (X,Y) without altering the current path. The (X,Y) coordinate is acquired by popping two number objects from the stack.

Arguments: **`num`**$_1$**`,  num`**$_2$

`num`$_1$ and **`num`**$_2$ may be either integers or real number objects, where **`num`**$_1$ represents the X coordinate and **`num`**$_2$ represents the Y coordinate. If the previous path operation was also a **moveto** operator or an **rmoveto** operator, then the previous point is deleted from the path and the point **`num`**$_1$**`,  num`**$_2$ replaces it.

Results: **`none`**

The **moveto** operator moves the current point to where you want to place text strings on the page.

scalefont

Description: This operator expects a number and a font on the stack. They are popped and the **`font`** is scaled according to **`num`**.

Arguments: **`font, num`**

The **`font`** is scaled from the original 1-unit character coordinate space by the amount **`num`** specifies in both the X and Y dimensions.

Results: **`font`**

The **scalefont** function returns a font properly scaled in the X and Y dimensions according to the **`num`** argument.

The **scalefont** operator scales the Helvetica font to a 14-point size.

setfont

Description: This operator expects a font on the stack. It pops **`font`** off the stack and sets the font dictionary parameter in the graphics state to **`font`**.

Arguments: **`font`**

The **`font`** is used to inform the graphics state of the font to use.

Results: **`none`**

The **setfont** operator makes the current font 14-point Helvetica.

show

Description: This operator pops a string off the stack and displays it at the current point using the current typeface, font size, and orientation as set in the current graphics world.

Arguments: **`string`**

Character spacing is determined by the character's width, which is part of the font definition. The current point is adjusted by the sum all the imaged characters widths. The current point must be defined, otherwise a "nocurrentpoint" error is generated.

Results: `none`

All three programs use the **show** operator to print text strings at various points on the page.

showpage Description: **showpage** transmits the current page to the raster output device, causing any marks painted on the current page to appear. Quite simply, **showpage** converts the information in the user space into the device space, making whatever transformations and modifications are necessary.

Arguments: `none`

Although **showpage** operator does not take any arguments on the stack, certain entries in the device dictionary affect operation, such as the **#copies** userdict variable that defines the numbers of copies that will be produced of each page.

Results: `none`

b. Centering the Letterhead

The second program uses an algorithm to center lines of text on the page. This is accomplished with math, string, and most importantly, "stack" operators. The additional operators introduced in the second program include:

div Description: This operator expects two numbers onto the stack. They are removed and the result of dividing the bottom number, num_1, by the top number, num_2, is pushed onto the stack.

Arguments: num_1 num_2

num_1 and num_2 may be either integers or real number objects. Argument num_2 must not be zero.

Results: `real`

The **div** operator function returns a number of type real that represents the mathematical division of the two arguments. See the **idiv** function if you desire an integer result.

dup Description: This operator duplicates the top element on the operand stack. Only the object is copied, so duplicated composite objects share their values with the original object.

Arguments: `any`

The object to be copied may be of any type. The original is popped off the stack.

Results: **any_1 any_2**

Two objects of the same type and value of the argument **any** are pushed onto the stack. Again, for composite objects, the operator **dup** operator only duplicates the reference object. The values of the composite object are shared by both references.

These programs use **dup** to duplicate text strings so the **stringwidth** operator has a copy of the text string to measure.

exch Description: This operator expects two objects on the stack. They are removed and their sum is pushed onto the stack.

Arguments: **any_1 any_2**

num_1 and **num_2** may be any object.

Results: **any_1 any_2**

The **exch** function exchanges the top two elements on the stack.

These programs use **exch** to swap operands before subtraction so that the correct number is subtracted.

pop Description: This operator pops the top object from the stack and discards it.

Arguments: **any**

Results: **none**

These programs use **pop** to dispose of unwanted values the **stringwidth** operator leaves on the stack.

stringwidth Description: The **stringwidth** operator removes a string from the top of the operand stack and replaces it with the X and Y values of the current point that would occur if the string were given as the operand to the **show** operator under the current font settings. See **show** for more information on how the return values are calculated.

Arguments: **string**

string is the string of text that **show** uses to calculate the proper width of the string if it were to be displayed on output with the current graphics state. Note the width of the string is strictly defined as the movement of the current point and, as such, the method that **show** uses to calculate the entire string width is irrelevant.

Results: **num_1, num_2**
num_1 represents the X coordinate and **num_2** represents the Y coordinate of the calculated current point.

These programs use **stringwidth** calculate the horizontal width of the string; the vertical dimension is discarded.

sub

Description: This operator expects two numbers on the stack. They are removed and their difference is pushed onto the stack.

Arguments: $\mathbf{num_1}$ $\mathbf{num_2}$

$\mathbf{num_1}$ and $\mathbf{num_2}$ may be either integers or real number objects.

Results: **num**

The **sub** operator function returns a number of type real or integer that represents the mathematical difference of $\mathbf{num_2}$ substracted from $\mathbf{num_1}$ arguments. The type is determined to be integer only if both arguments are of type integer and the result is within the range of representable integers for the PostScript interpreter. Type real is assigned to the result if both conditions are not met and some loss in the result's precision may occur.

c. Useable Letterhead

Finally, a few additional graphics operators are added, along with a change in a system definition to make a number of copies of letterhead. By the time you finish this book, you should consider this program excruciatingly simple. At that point, we hope you improve on the design, but for now, this should be acceptable. The operators introduced in the third program include:

lineto

Description: This operator appends a straight line segment to the current path from the current point to the point indicated by the two numbers popped off the stack.

Arguments: $\mathbf{num_1}$, $\mathbf{num_2}$

$\mathbf{num_1}$ and $\mathbf{num_2}$ may be either integers or real number objects, where $\mathbf{num_1}$ represents the X coordinate and $\mathbf{num_2}$ represents the Y coordinate. Lack of a current point generates "nocurrentpoint" error.

Results: **none**

These programs use **lineto** to draw a gray bar underneath the white.

rmoveto

Description: This operator starts a new subpath of the current path. **rmoveto** sets the current point in the graphics state to the user space coordinate (X,Y) without altering the current path. The (X,Y) coordinate is acquired by popping two number objects from the stack. Unlike **moveto**, however, the two coordinates are interpreted in a relative manner from the (X,Y) of the current point as opposed to the absolute coordinates, with respect to the origin.

Therefore, the new subpath is constructed at a point relative to the current point by the amount specified in the arguments ($X + \mathbf{num_1}$, $Y + \mathbf{num_2}$). The new current point is ($X + \mathbf{num_1}$, $Y + \mathbf{num_2}$). The original current point must be defined or a "nocurrentpoint" error results.

Arguments: **num_1, num_2**

num_1 and **num_2** may be either integers or real number objects, where **num_1** represents the X coordinate and **num_2** represents the Y coordinate. If the previous path operation was also a **moveto** or an **rmoveto**, then the previous point is deleted from the path and the point **num_1, num_2** replaces it.
Results: **none**

The last programs use **rmoveto** to move the current point to the left a distance equaling one half the width of a string. This is a more elegant way to center a string around a point.

setgray Description: This operator expects a number on the stack. It pops **num** off the stack, sets color space to DeviceGray, and finally sets the gray shade parameter in the graphics state to a value corresponding to **num**. **num** may be in the range from 0 to 1, with 0 corresponding to black and 1 representing white.

Arguments: **num**

The **num** is used to inform the graphics state which gray level to use—if it is above 1 or below 0, the nearest legal value is substituted.

Results: **none**

The **setgray** operator is used in the last program to set the gray value for the line, to change back to black ink when black text should be drawn, and to change to white text which overlays the gray bar.

setlinewidth Description: This operator expects an integer on the stack. It pops **int** off the stack and sets the line width parameter in the graphics state to the argument value. That number is stored in the active graphics state as the width (in points) for any lines drawn until either the value is changed or another graphics state becomes active.

Arguments: **int**

Specifically, **int** controls the thickness of lines rendered by subsequent execution of the **stroke** operator: **stroke** paints all points whose perpendicular distance from the current path in user space is less than or equal to half the absolute value of **int**. This means stroked lines can vary by as much as 2 device pixels, depending on their positions. Also, an argument of 0 for the **int** causes **stroke** to image the lines at the device's finest resolution.

Results: **none**

The gray bar drawn in the third version is actually a thick line.

setlinecap Description: This operator expects an integer on the stack. It pops **int** off the stack and evaluates it to determine the shape to put at the ends of open subpaths painted by the **stroke** operator.

Arguments: **int**

int must be in the set {0, 1, 2}. If it is not, an error occurs. If **int** is 0, the line has a butt cap: the stroke is squared off at the path's end point. There is no projection beyond the end of the path. If **int** is 1, the line has a round cap: a semicircular arc with diameter equal to the line width is drawn around the end point and filled in. If **int** is 2, the line has a projecting square cap: the stroke continues beyond the path's end point for a distance equal to half the line width and is squared off.

Results: **none**

The third version of the program draws a thick line with rounded edges.

stroke Description: This operator paints a line centered on the path, with sides parallel to the path segments, and in compliance with the settings of the current graphics state. **stroke** operator implicitly performs a **newpath** after it finishes painting the current path. If this concerns, bracket your call to **stroke** operator with **gsave** and **grestore** calls.

Arguments: **none**

Results: **none**

3. A Note about PostScript Comments

All of the program listings here have been commented. A comment in PostScript is anything between a % character and the next newline character. PostScript comments that begin with double % characters provide information about the document's structure. When typing, feel free to take any and all comments out: they have no impact on the program. Chapter 3 contains more information about the use of comments to structure files for various preprocessors as well as Encapsulated PostScript.

4. Explanation of the Listings

Listings 5.1, 5.2, and 5.3 for the programs Listing 5.1, Listing 5.2, and Listing 5.3. correspond to the output displayed in Figure 5.1, Figure 5.2, and Figure 5.3, respectively. The first version prints a three line name and address in the upper left corner of the page. The second version centers the name and address around a point in the middle of the top of the page. The third version adds a centered phone number line, which is overlaid in white lettering on a dark gray background.

a. Version 1: Simple Letterhead

The first listing, 5.1, consists of 10 lines of code and comments.

Listing 5.1: Simple Letterhead

```
%!PS-Adobe-3.0 EPSF-30.
%%BoundingBox: 0 0 612 792
%%Title: (letterhead example 1)
%%Creationdate: (8/21/91:16:21)
%%EndComments
/Helvetica findfont
14 scalefont
setfont
36 730 moveto
(David S. Dubin) show
36 714 moveto
(Dept. Information Science) show
36 698 moveto
(University of Pittsburgh) show
showpage
%%EOF
```

Keep in mind the line-breaks do not contribute to the language's syntax. (except to mark the end of comments). The points to break lines were chosen to enhance readability, but the entire program (minus the comments) could have been written as one long character stream. Nevertheless, the explanation shall proceed line by line.

The first line pushes the name of the Helvetica dictionary on to the operand stack and then executes the **findfont** operator. The slash preceding the dictionary name indicates it is a literal. Literals are simply pushed on the operand stack. The **findfont** operator removes the dictionary name from the top of the stack, looks up the Helvetica dictionary in the font directory, and pushes that dictionary (scaled for one-point characters) on to the stack. The second line pushes the number 14 over top of the dictionary and then calls the **scalefont** operator, which removes both from the stack and scales the dictionary for 14-point type. The scaled dictionary is left on the top of the stack. The third line invokes the **setfont** operator which removes the scaled dictionary from the top of the stack and makes fourteen point Helvetica the current font.

The fourth line moves the current point to the coordinates 36, 730. The ordering of the operands for the operator **moveto** are deliberately intended to suggest Cartesian coordinates, but in the long run, it is more helpful to imagine first the X then the Y coordinates being pushed on the stack and the **moveto** operator removing them in reverse order. Since none of the programs in this chapter ever have more than three items on the stack at once, it should be relatively easy to keep track of them. The coordinates 36, 730 are chosen because 36 points from the left is a half inch (72 points to the inch) and 730 points from the bottom is almost an inch from the top (11 inches = 792 points).

The fifth line begins by pushing the first text string on to the operand stack (strings are delimited by parentheses); the **show** operator removes the string and lays it down on the page. In the following lines, each **moveto** moves the current point back to 36 points in on the horizontal axis and down 16 points on the vertical axis. This last choice respects the rule of thumb: when laying down parallel lines of text of a uniform size, the vertical distance to move each time should be about 1.1 times the typesize. The last line invokes the **showpage** operator, which prints and ejects the current page.

b. Version 2: Centered Letterhead

Listing 5.2: Centered Letterhead

```
%!PS-Adobe-3.0 EPSF-30.
%%BoundingBox: 0 0 612 792
%%Title: (letterhead example 2)
%%Creationdate: (8/21/91:16:21)
%%EndComments
/Helvetica findfont
14 scalefont
setfont

(David S. Dubin) dup stringwidth pop
2 div 306 exch sub
730 moveto show

(Dept. Information Science) dup stringwidth pop
2 div 306 exch sub
714 moveto show

(University of Pittsburgh) dup stringwidth pop
```

David S. Dubin
Dept. Information Science
University of Pittsburgh

Figure 5.1: Simple Letterhead

```
2 div 306 exch sub
698 moveto show

showpage

%%EOF
```

The second version of the letterhead program is similar to the first, but with some changes. Instead of moving to a point and then displaying a string, the string is pushed on to the operand stack and a number of operations are performed before the **show** operator displays the string. Obviously, one of those operations is a **moveto**, which moves the current point to the appropriate place to display the string. There are nine operators and operands between each string and the **show** operator; each function is explained in the following list. Overall, the nine commands subtract half the width of the string from 306 (which represents a point in the center of the horizontal axis of our page). The result of that subtraction is the X coordinate for the point at which the string should be displayed. The Y coordinates for each string are identical to those used in the last program; they are pushed over top of the X coordinate, the **moveto** operator removes both operands, and the **show** operator displays the string.

1. The **dup** operator makes a second copy of the string and pushes it on top of the first. this is necessary because the **stringwidth** operator needs a copy to measure, and that copy is not preserved. After the **dup** operator, the stack holds two copies of the string, one on top of the other.

2. The **stringwidth** operator removes the top copy of the string from the stack and replaces it with the X and Y coordinates of the point where the current point would be if the string were shown. At this point, the stack consists of a Y coordinate with an X coordinate below and the string below that.

3. The **pop** operator disposes of the Y coordinate from the top of the stack. The **stringwidth** operator placed two numbers on the stack. Because the Y value is not needed, **pop** is used to discard (pop) it from the stack.

4. The value **2** is pushed onto the stack on top of the X coordinate. You want to divide the X coordinate by two to have a value which is half the length of the string.

5. The **div** operator removes the 2 and the X value and divides the former by the latter. The quotient is pushed on top of the stack (i.e. on top of the string).

6. At this point, the number 306 is pushed on top of the halved string width. Subtracting the latter from the former results in the X coordinate for the point at where the string should be displayed. However, the two operands on the stack are not in the proper order for subtraction.

7. The **exch** operator swaps the positions of the 306 and the halved width value. If the subtraction were carried out without this exchange, the resulting value would be negative.
8. The **sub** operator removes the top two numbers and subtracts the top one from the one underneath. In this case, a value equaling half string width is subtracted from 306. The stack now consists of this value, and the string is below that value.
9. The Y coordinate used in the last program version is now pushed on top of the X coordinate that was just calculated. You want to use the same vertical coordinates as in the last version.
10. The **moveto** operator removes the X and Y coordinates and changes the current point to one whose X coordinate differs from 306 by half the string width. By a happy coincidence the original string is back at the top of the stack, and so is ready for the **show** operator.

The final version of the letterhead program uses a more elegant method for centering a string around a point. The string width is calculated and halved as we just described, but the resulting value is made negative to move the current point to the left of the point chosen for the string center.

c. Version 3: White Text over a Gray Bar

Listing 5.3: Improved Letterhead

```
%!PS-Adobe-3.0 EPSF-30.
%%BoundingBox: 0 0 612 792
%%Title: (letterhead example 3)
%%Creationdate: (8/21/91:16:21)
%%EndComments
36 686 moveto
576 686 lineto
16 setlinewidth
1 setlinecap
.25 setgray
stroke

0 setgray
/Helvetica findfont
14 scalefont
setfont

306 730 moveto
(David S. Dubin) dup
stringwidth pop
2 div 0 exch sub 0 rmoveto
show
306 714 moveto
```

David S. Dubin
Dept. Information Science
University of Pittsburgh

Figure 5.2: Centered Letterhead

```
(Dept. Information Science) dup stringwidth pop
2 div 0 exch sub 0 rmoveto show
306 698 moveto
(University of Pittsburgh) dup stringwidth pop
2 div 0 exch sub 0 rmoveto show

306 682 moveto
1 setgray
(Phone (412) 555-3413) dup stringwidth pop
2 div 0 exch sub 0 rmoveto show

showpage
%%EOF
```

A few additional changes have been made from the second version of the program to the third version. The first six lines of the code in Listing 5.3 describe drawing the horizontal gray bar. Lay this down first because all figures, text, and lines in PostScript are opaque, so the material underneath must be placed first. The **moveto** operator moves the current point to where want to place the lower left corner of the bar. The bar is in fact a line, whose length is defined with **lineto**, its thickness with **setlinewidth**, and its color with **setgray**. The **stroke** operator makes the line visible on the page. Use the **setlinecap** operator to round off the ends of the bar. You can experiment with different **linecaps** by changing the parameter from a one to zero or two.

The method for centering the strings is slightly different because it uses the **rmoveto** operator. As previously explained, **rmoveto** takes the relative offsets from the current point as arguments. Imagine these values being added to the X and Y coordinates of the current point to define a new current point. The strategy for centering the string is first to move to the point you want to center the string (306, 730 for the first string). Then the stringwidth is calculated and halved as in the previous version. That halved, value is then subtracted from zero, and another zero is pushed over top of the negative value. **rmoveto** then consumes the top two values on the stack to change the current point to one which has the same Y value but whose X value is lowered by half the string width.

There are three calls to the **setgray** operator in this listing. The first (after the line cap is set) defines the pattern for the bar. The second occurs immediately after the **stroke**, where you want to switch back to black ink for the first three text strings (zero is pure black and one is pure white). The last **setgray** occurs immediately before the last string is pushed on the stack and switches from black to white ink.

Figure 5.3: Improved Letterhead

5. Additional Refinements and Uses

Once you successfully execute these three listings, try some of the following experiments:

- Change the name and address strings to your own name and address.
- Experiment with different line widths, caps, and gray levels. Remember to set the gray value back to zero before trying to display black text.

Here are other ways that this program might be improved:

- Expand the letterhead concept to make a buckslip by creating small rectangles in front of text strings. To create the small rectangle in front of text, type:

```
1 setlinewidth
100 100 moveto
110 100 lineto
110 110 lineto
100 110 lineto
100 100 lineto
stroke
115 100 moveto
(buck slip message) show
```

- A line at the bottom of the page that provides telephone or address information in a smaller font size. This requires another **moveto** and a restate the **findfont**, **scalefont**, and **setfont** sequence.

6. What Went Wrong?

It is possible that something went wrong with this first program. Problems for these first programs fall into two categories:

1. Errors that cause the program to halt with no output:

No output	Check all spellings—spacing does not matter as long as there is at least one space between each key word. Make sure your computer can send a file to the printer. The simplest way to check this is to put the word "showpage" in a file. If that file does not cause your laser printer to eject a page, you have a problem.

2. Errors that cause a blank page to be ejected:

White on white	Make sure you do not set gray levels to place white ink on a white background.
Tiny characters	Unless you scale fonts to a specific size, the default is 1 point high.
Undefined current point	Make sure that you have not moved the current point to some place that is not defined in the user space. The **rmoveto** operator is the likely culprit.
Lack of **show** or **stroke**	It is the **show** and **stroke** operators that actually lay the marks on the page. Lines drawn without a **stroke** remain invisible, and strings pushed on the stack without a **show** are buried.

Chapter 6
Certificate

This chapter presents a programming project to produce a certificate.[22] Three variations are provided. The first example is a simple certificate. The second example adds scrollwork to the certificate. The third example adds a medallion background to the certificate.

1. Objectives

The objectives of this chapter are:

- To provide a certificate program that is easy to create and personalize
- To demonstrate looping structures
- To demonstrate procedures
- To demonstrate operators that allow you to
    - to center lines of text
    - to draw simple arcs
    - to rotate and translate axes
    - to draw curves
    - to constrain the print output area with clipping

[22]The certificate presented here was developed by Janice Zappone, a Pitt MSIS graduate who teaches Physics and Computer Science at the Mt. Pleasant Area High School in Pennsylvania.

2. Operator Explanations

The simplest certificate example uses only font changes. Procedures are defined to facilitate the frequent font changes and to center the output lines. In the second example, loops repeat arcs to create scrollwork around the edge of the certificate. In the final example, a background medallion embellishes the certificate. You will use the following operators:

arc Description: This operator expects five arguments on the stack, consisting of two coordinate values, a distance specification, and two angle values. They are removed and the current point and current path are altered according to the following interpretation of the arguments to create a line segment and a circular arc in the user space. Note any scaling transformations alter the shape that is imaged in device space, possibly causing a non-circular shape. The first and second coordinate values are X and Y offsets, respectively, relative to the current origin of the user space that represents the center of the arc. The arc has a radius equal to the distance specification. The arc starts at an angle equal to the first angle value in degrees counterclockwise from the positive X axis and ends at an angle equal to the second angle value, also in degrees counterclockwise from the positive X axis. After the **arc** operator command, the current point is equal to the arc's endpoint. The current path is the aforementioned arc if the current point is undefined or is equal to the arc's starting point. If the current point is defined and is different from the arcs starting point, a straight line segment is appended to the current path before the aforementioned arc is appended to the current path. The line segment starts at the value of the current point at the start of the **arc** operator command and terminates at the start arc's point.

Arguments: $\mathtt{real}_1$ $\mathtt{real}_2$ $\mathtt{real}_3$ $\mathtt{real}_4$ $\mathtt{real}_5$

$\mathtt{real}_1$ and $\mathtt{real}_2$ are the X and Y coordinates relative to the origin of the user space that specify the center of the arc. $\mathtt{real}_3$ represents the distance in user space units from the X and Y coordinate values represented by $\mathtt{real}_1$ and $\mathtt{real}_2$. $\mathtt{real}_4$ and $\mathtt{real}_5$ are the angles relative to the positive X axis of the user space that specify the arc's start and end points.

Results: `none`

bind Description: The **bind** operator causes the interpreter to replace all executable operator names in a procedure with the actual operators themselves. This has two effects. First, the procedure executes faster, as operator names do not have to be searched for in the current dictionary stack. Second, if definitions of any of the operators are changed after the procedure has been bound, the procedure operation is not affected. For each procedure object in **proc**

whose access is unrestricted, **bind** applies itself recursively to **proc**, makes the process read-only, and returns **proc** on the stack.

Arguments: `proc`

The executable names that refer to operator object values which make up the array **proc** are replaced by the actual operators they refer to.

Results: `proc`

The **bind** function returns the same procedure it was given, except that all references to executable names are replaced by the actual operators they referred to.

clip

Description: This operator does not take any arguments or push any results onto the stack. However, it does alter the current path: **clip** operator takes the area of the user space considered to be inside the current path (as determined by the nonzero winding rule) and the area considered to be inside the current clipping path (as determined by the winding rule in use at the time of the clipping path's creation). It then returns a new path that, generally, is the intersection of both of these areas. It is not possible to enlarge the clipping path unless the **initclip** or **initgraphics** operators are called, both of which reset the clipping region to its initial value.

Arguments: `none`

Results: `none`

closepath

Description: This operator does not use any arguments or push any results onto the stack. It is intended to provide an easy way to append a straight line segment to the current path from the current point to the point that represents the start of the current subpath. (This is especially helpful when drawing Bézier curves and arcs, where the required line segment can be tedious to calculate.)

Arguments: `none`

Results: `none`

Note that **closepath** operator terminates the current subpath. Any operator that appends to the current path begins a new subpath. If the current subpath is already closed or the current path is empty, **closepath** operator does nothing.

curveto

Description: This operator expects six numbers on the stack and uses them to create a Bézier curve. The arguments are removed from the stack and no objects are pushed onto the stack. If **currentpoint** is undefined when this operator is executed, a "nocurrentpoint" error results.

Arguments: $\mathbf{num_1}$ $\mathbf{num_2}$ $\mathbf{num_3}$ $\mathbf{num_4}$ $\mathbf{num_5}$ $\mathbf{num_6}$

$\mathbf{num_1}$ through $\mathbf{num_6}$ may be either integer or real number objects and represent three pairs of (X,Y) points. **currentpoint** fulfills the requirement for the fourth pair of points. The entire curve is contained within the user space box defined by the four pairs of points. The start of the Bézier curve is the **currentpoint** and the end of the curve is the point indicated by the third pair of arguments, **(num_5, num_6)**. Points **(num_1, num_2)** and **(num_3, num_4)** provide input for geometric modifications to the curve, as defined by the following pair of parametric cubic equations: $x(t) = a_x t^3 + b_x t^2 + c_x t + x_0$ and $y(t) = a_y t^3 + b_y t^2 + c_y t + y_0$.

Results: **none**

def Description: This operator consumes two objects of the form **key** and **value** from the stack and adds them to the current dictionary.

Arguments: **key value**

key is associated with **value** in the current dictionary. If **key** exists, the new **value** replaces the associated **value**. If **key** does not exist already in the current dictionary, the dictionary must have room for one more entry. If it does not, a "dictfull" error is generated. **key** may consist of any object. If **key** is a name literal, it is converted to a name literal prior to storing the entry.

Results: **none**

The current dictionary is modified so it contains a **key** with an associated **value**.

div Description: This operator expects two numbers onto the stack. They are removed and the result of dividing the bottom number, **num_1**, by the top number, **num_2**, is pushed onto the stack.

Arguments: **num_1 num_2**

num_1 and **num_2** may be either integers or real number objects. Argument **num_2** must not be zero.

Results: **real**

The **div** operator function returns a number of type real that represents the mathematical division of the two arguments. See the **idiv** function if you desire an integer result.

dup Description: This operator duplicates the top element on the operand stack. Only the object is copied, so duplicated composite objects share their values with the original object.

Arguments: **any**

The object to be copied may be of any type. The original is popped off the stack.

Results: **any_1 any_2**

Two objects of the same type and value of the argument **any** are pushed onto the stack. Again, for composite objects, the operator **dup** operator only duplicates the reference object. The values of the composite object are shared by both references.

exch Description: This operator expects two objects on the stack. They are removed and their sum is pushed onto the stack.

Arguments: **`any`$_1$ `any`$_2$**

`num`$_1$ and **`num`$_2$** may be any object.

Results: **`any`$_1$ `any`$_2$**

The **exch** function exchanges the top two elements on the stack.

findfont Description: The **findfont** operator consumes a literal key from the top of the stack and returns the font dictionary **`font`** associated with **`key`** in the **`FontDirectory`**. If the font is not found, the action is implementation-dependent. The system may substitute a default font, attempt to search any disk files for the specified font, or it may generate an "invalidfont" error and refuse to continue. You may redefine **findfont** operator to implement different font-finding strategies.

Arguments: **`key`**

`key` is an object defining a font dictionary and can be obtained via a call to **definefont** operator. Fonts built into the output device are usually automatically enrolled into the **`FontDictionary`** and do not need to be registered via **definefont** operator.

Results: **`font`**

The **findfont** operator function returns a font dictionary **`font`** that is associated with the argument **`key`** in the **`FontDirectory`**.

for Description: This operator expects a start value, an increment value, a final value, and a procedure on the operand stack. The procedure is executed a number of times, and each execution increments a counter variable by the value of the increment operand. The counter begins at the start value, and when it reaches the final value, the loop ends.

Arguments: **`num`$_1$ `num`$_2$ `num`$_3$ `{operator(s)}`**

The first **`num`$_1$** is the loop counter's starting value. The second **`num`$_2$** is the loop counter's increment value, and the third operator, **`num`$_3$**, is the loop counter's destination value. An operator or group of operators enclosed in the curly brackets indicates the number of times the loop executes.

Results: **`none`**

grestore

Description: This operator pops a graphics state from the top of the graphics state stack and makes it active. It undoes any changes that were made to the graphics state since the last **gsave**.

Arguments: **`none`**

Results: **`none`**

gsave

Description: The **gsave** operator pushes the current graphics state onto the graphics state stack. This operator is often used before changes that are difficult to recover from are made to the graphics state. It is also used to isolate changes to the graphics state made for a small subsection of the program so those changes do not have unintended effects on commands executed later.

Arguments: **`none`**

Results: **`none`**

moveto

Description: This operator starts a new subpath of the current path. **Moveto** operator sets the current point in the graphics state to the user space coordinate (X,Y) without altering the current path. The (X,Y) coordinate is acquired by popping two number objects from the stack.

Arguments: $\mathbf{num_1}$, $\mathbf{num_2}$

$\mathbf{num_1}$ and $\mathbf{num_2}$ may be either integers or real number objects, where $\mathbf{num_1}$ represents the X coordinate and $\mathbf{num_2}$ represents the Y coordinate. If the previous path operation was also a **moveto** operator or an **rmoveto** operator, then the previous point is deleted from the path and the point $\mathbf{num_1}$, $\mathbf{num_2}$ replaces it.

Results: **`none`**

neg

Description: This operator expects two numbers on the stack. They are removed and their sum is pushed onto the stack.

Arguments: **`num`**

`num` may be either an integer or a real number object.

Results: **`num`**

The **neg** operator function returns a number of the same type as the **`num`** argument.[23]

[23]If the number is the most negative number, the result is a real (otherwise the result is out of bounds of the maximum representable integer for that interpreter.)

newpath Description: This operator initializes the current path to be empty, causing the current point to be undefined.

Arguments: **`none`**

Results: **`none`**

After the command is executed there is no path and the current point is undefined.

pop Description: This operator pops the top object from the stack and discards it.

Arguments: **`any`**

Results: **`none`**

repeat Description: The **repeat** operator executes **`proc int`** times, where **`int`** is a non-negative number, or until the **exit** or **stop** operators are called. If the **exit** or **stop** operators are called, the **repeat** operator terminates prematurely.

Arguments: **`int proc`**

`proc` is a set of zero or more PostScript commands.

Results: **`none`**

Although **repeat** operator does not directly leave results on the stack, the procedure that is executed may alter the stack after the invocation of the **repeat** procedure has completed.

rlineto Description: This operator appends a straight line segment to the current path from the current point to the point indicated by the two numbers popped off the stack. Unlike **lineto**, however, the two coordinates are interpreted in a relative manner from the (X,Y) of the current point as opposed to the absolute coordinates, with respect to the origin. Therefore, the line is constructed from the current point (X,Y) to a point relative to the current point by the amount specified in the arguments (X + $\mathbf{num_1}$, Y + $\mathbf{num_2}$). The new currentpoint is (X + $\mathbf{num_1}$, Y + $\mathbf{num_2}$).

Arguments: $\mathbf{num_1}$, $\mathbf{num_2}$

$\mathbf{num_1}$ and $\mathbf{num_2}$ may be either integers or real number objects, where $\mathbf{num_1}$ represents the X coordinate, and $\mathbf{num_2}$ represents the Y coordinate, with the aforementioned special interpretation. Lack of a current point generates "nocurrentpoint" error.

Results: **`none`**

rmoveto Description: This operator starts a new subpath of the current path. **rmoveto** sets the current point in the graphics state to the user space coordinate (X,Y) without altering the current path. The (X,Y) coordinate is acquired by popping two number objects from the stack. Unlike **moveto**, however, the two coordinates are interpreted in a relative manner from the (X,Y) of the current point as opposed to the absolute coordinates, with respect to the origin. Therefore, the new subpath is constructed at a point relative to the current point by the amount specified in the arguments (X + num_1, Y + num_2). The new current point is (X + num_1, Y + num_2). The original current point must be defined or a "nocurrentpoint" error results.

Arguments: num_1, num_2

num_1 and num_2 may be either integers or real number objects, where num_1 represents the X coordinate and num_2 represents the Y coordinate. If the previous path operation was also a **moveto** or an **rmoveto**, then the previous point is deleted from the path and the point num_1, num_2 replaces it.
Results: `none`

rotate

Description: This operator expects one or two arguments on the stack. The first argument is always an angle value, either in integer or real form, and the second argument, if present, is a matrix. The horizontal and vertical axes for the current user space are rotated counterclockwise a number of degrees equal to the **num** argument.

Arguments (Form 1): `num`

Results: `none`

Arguments (Form 2): `num, matrix`

Results: `matrix`

The **rotate** function occurs in two varieties: in one, the user supplies a matrix; the other operates on the current transformation matrix (CTM). If a matrix is supplied, the CTM is not altered in any way.

scale

Description: This operator has two versions, one that operates the current transformation matrix (CTM) and affects the user space, and the other that operates a matrix that is provided.

Arguments (Form 1): num_1 num_2

num_1 and num_2 may be either integers or real number objects and represent the X axis and the Y axis scaling factors, respectively.

Results: `none`

Arguments (Form 2): num_1 num_2 `matrix`

num_1 and num_2 may be either integers or real number objects, and represent the X axis and the Y axis scaling factors, respectively. In the matrix case, scaling is also done along the X and Y axes. Scaling does not affect the graphics state or, more importantly, alter the CTM.

Results: `matrix`

scalefont Description: This operator expects a number and a font on the stack. They are popped and the **`font`** is scaled according to **`num`**.

Arguments: **`font, num`**

The **`font`** is scaled from the original 1-unit character coordinate space by the amount **`num`** specifies in both the X and Y dimensions.

Results: **`font`**

The **scalefont** function returns a font properly scaled in the X and Y dimensions according to the **`num`** argument.

setfont Description: This operator expects a font on the stack. It pops **`font`** off the stack and sets the font dictionary parameter in the graphics state to **`font`**.

Arguments: **`font`**

The **`font`** is used to inform the graphics state of the font to use.

Results: **`none`**

setgray Description: This operator expects a number on the stack. It pops **`num`** off the stack, sets color space to DeviceGray, and finally sets the gray shade parameter in the graphics state to a value corresponding to **`num`**. **`num`** may be in the range from 0 to 1, with 0 corresponding to black and 1 representing white.

Arguments: **`num`**

The **`num`** is used to inform the graphics state which gray level to use—if it is above 1 or below 0, the nearest legal value is substituted.

Results: **`none`**

setlinewidth Description: This operator expects an integer on the stack. It pops **`int`** off the stack and sets the line width parameter in the graphics state to the argument value. That number is stored in the active graphics state as the width (in points) for any lines drawn until either the value is changed or another graphics state becomes active.

Arguments: **`int`**

Specifically, **`int`** controls the thickness of lines rendered by subsequent execution of the **stroke** operator: **stroke** paints all points whose perpendicular distance from the current path in user space is less than or equal to half the absolute value of **`int`**. This means stroked lines can vary by as much as 2 device pixels, depending on their positions. Also, an argument of 0 for the **`int`** causes **stroke** to image the lines at the device's finest resolution.

Results: **`none`**

show

Description: This operator pops a string off the stack and displays it at the current point using the current typeface, font size, and orientation as set in the current graphics world.

Arguments: `string`

Character spacing is determined by the character's width, which is part of the font definition. The current point is adjusted by the sum all the imaged characters widths. The current point must be defined, otherwise a "nocurrentpoint" error is generated.

Results: `none`

showpage

Description: **showpage** transmits the current page to the raster output device, causing any marks painted on the current page to appear. Quite simply, **showpage** converts the information in the user space into the device space, making whatever transformations and modifications are necessary.

Arguments: `none`

Although **showpage** operator does not take any arguments on the stack, certain entries in the device dictionary affect operation, such as the **#copies** userdict variable that defines the numbers of copies that will be produced of each page.

Results: `none`

stringwidth

Description: The **stringwidth** operator removes a string from the top of the operand stack and replaces it with the X and Y values of the current point that would occur if the string were given as the operand to the **show** operator under the current font settings. See **show** for more information on how the return values are calculated.

Arguments: `string`

`string` is the string of text that **show** uses to calculate the proper width of the string if it were to be displayed on output with the current graphics state. Note the width of the string is strictly defined as the movement of the current point and, as such, the method that **show** uses to calculate the entire string width is irrelevant.

Results: $\mathtt{num}_1$, $\mathtt{num}_2$
$\mathtt{num}_1$ represents the X coordinate and $\mathtt{num}_2$ represents the Y coordinate of the calculated current point.

stroke

Description: This operator paints a line centered on the path, with sides parallel to the path segments, and in compliance with the settings of the current graphics state. **stroke** operator implicitly performs a **newpath** after it finishes painting the current path. If this concerns, bracket your call to **stroke** operator with **gsave** and **grestore** calls.

Arguments: `none`

Results: **none**

translate Description: This operator has two versions:

Arguments (Form 1): **num_1 num_2**

This version of **translate** operator shifts the user coordinate system **num_1** units in the X direction and **num_2** units in the Y direction. The current transformation matrix is updated and the operation relocates the origin point. **num_1** and **num_2** may be either integers or real number objects.

Results (Form 1): **none**

Arguments (Form 2): **num_1 num_2 matrix**

This version of **translate** operator alters **matrix** by providing the transforms for shifting a user coordinate system **num_1** units in the X direction and **num_2** units in the Y direction. The current transformation matrix (CTM) is not altered and the operation has no effect on the current graphics state. **num_1** and **num_2** may be either integers or real number objects.

Results (Form 2): **matrix**

3. Explanation of the Listings

Listing 6.1, Listing 6.2, and Listing 6.3 correspond to the output displayed in Figure 6.1, Figure 6.2, and Figure 6.3, respectively.

a. Version 1: Simple Certificate

The simple certificate program, Listing 6.1, creates the figure 6 certificate, Figure 6.1, which depends on attractive and dramatic fonts for its style. The ZapfChancery-MediumItalic[24] font is ornate and appealing. The stark Helvetica font used for the name contrasts sharply.

Listing 6.1: Simple Certificate

```
%!PS-Adobe-3.0  EPSF-30.
%%BoundingBox: 0 0 612 792
%%Title: (Certificate example #1  certex1.eps)
%% Creationdate:  (9/16/91:14:30)
%%Endcomments
```

[24]If ZapfChancery-MediumItalic is not available on your printer, try Times-Italic. While not as ornate, it is attractive.

```
/font {findfont exch scalefont setfont} bind def
/center {dup stringwidth pop 2 div neg 0 rmoveto} bind def

612 0 translate
90 rotate
72 72 moveto
7 setlinewidth
0 468 rlineto
648 0 rlineto
0 -468 rlineto
closepath
stroke

70/ZapfChancery-MediumItalic font
396 460  moveto
(CERTIFICATE) center show
26/ZapfChancery-MediumItalic font
396 415  moveto
(of) center show
70/ZapfChancery-MediumItalic font
396 360  moveto
(RECOGNITION) center show
24/Helvetica font
396 290  moveto
(Father Time) center show
24/ZapfChancery-MediumItalic font
396 245  moveto
(For 100 years of dedicated service to) center show
396 225  moveto
(Life, Liberty and the Pursuit of Happiness) center show
396 190  moveto
(______________ ______________ ______________) center show
396 160 moveto
(______________ ______________ ______________) center show
396 130  moveto
(______________ ______________ ______________) center show
12/ZapfChancery-MediumItalic font
396 110 moveto
(September 16, 1991) center show
showpage
%%EOF
```

Certificates are printed in Landscape style. The **translate** operator moves the 0,0 origin 612 points to the right. No vertical translation takes place. The Y axis is at the right edge of the print area. The **rotate** operator turns the axes counterclockwise 90 degrees: the X axis is located where the right edge of the print area was and the Y axis is where the bottom was. The next seven commands draw a 7-point rectangular border, where the text of the certificate is to be placed.

The program uses two procedures. The **font** procedure simplifies multiple font changes by allowing the name of the font and its size to be passed as a parameter. The **center** procedure centers each line of output. Each procedure is examined later in detail.

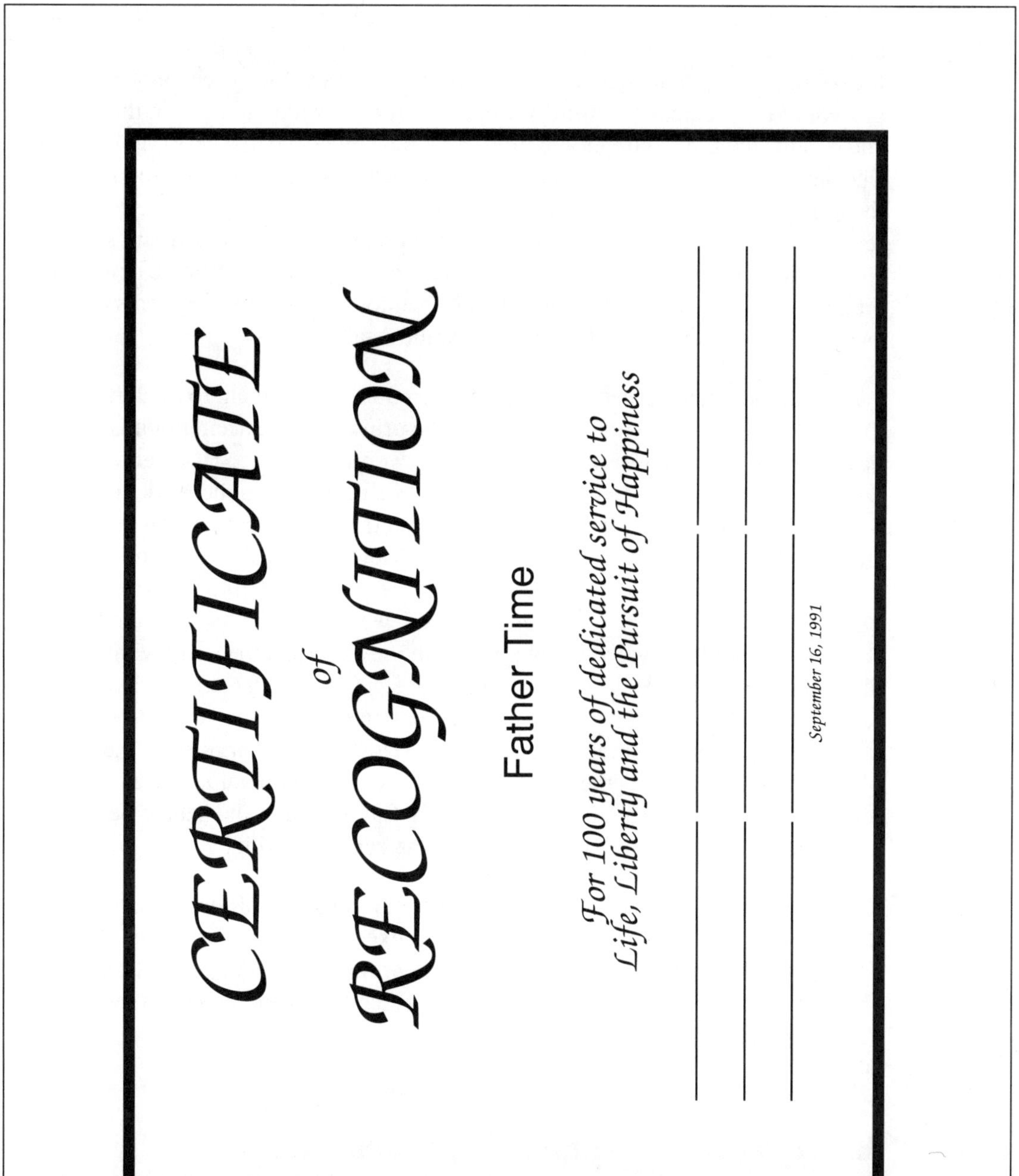

Figure 6.1: Simple Certificate

Five font changes are effected. The **font** procedure is provided with a point size and font name. The point size, 70, is pushed on the stack, followed by the literal font name, ZapfChancery-MediumItalic.[25] When **font** is encountered, the procedure is executed. The **findfont** operator removes the literal from the stack and obtains the font dictionary identified by the key (ZapfChancery-MediumItalic). The dictionary is pushed onto the stack. The **exch** operator takes the top two items, the font dictionary and the point size, from the operand stack. They are replaced in reverse order, point size on top. The **scalefont** opererator takes the point size and font dictionary from the stack, scales then accordingly and pushes the new font dictionary back on the stack. The **setfont** operator pops the font dictionary and establishes it as the current font in the graphics state.

All output lines are centered. Centering requires movement to the left of the line center by half the width of the data to be printed. The current point is positioned at the center of the line at a proper vertical distance. The **center** procedure is given a string. (see line 18). The string is pushed onto the stack. The **dup** operator makes a copy and places both back on the stack. **stringwidth** takes the string from the stack, calculates the X and Y widths and pushes them on the stack. The Y dimension is 0; it is not needed, so the next operator, **pop**, removes it. Next, 2 is pushed onto the stack, **div** is encountered, which requires two operands. The 2 and the stringwidth X value are popped from the stack and the stringwidth value is divided by two. The result is pushed onto the stack. The **neg** operator takes the result and makes it negative. A 0 is pushed onto the stack. The **rmoveto** operator takes two arguments from the operand stack. The 0 is the Y argument; the negative of half the string width is the X argument. The **rmoveto** operator causes the current point to move to the left by a value of half the width of the data to be printed. This is the correct position to start printing the centered string.

The **bind** operator associates the binary representation of the procedure directly with the key. This effectively speeds execution of the procedure by a measurable difference Experiment: Time the printing with and without **bind**. Without **bind**, each key in the instruction must be found and processed every time the procedure is executed.

b. Version 2: Certificate with Scrollwork

This version, Listing 6.2, of the Figure 6.2 certificate, has scrollwork around the edge of the box for a more ornate finish.

---

[25]Font names must be precise. Spelling, capitals, and dashes must be correct.

Listing 6.2: Certificate with Scrollwork

```
%!PS-Adobe-3.0  EPSF-30.
%%BoundingBox: 0 0 612 792
%%Title: (Certificate example #2  certex2.eps)
%% Creationdate:  (10/16/91:11:30)
%%Endcomments
/font {findfont exch scalefont setfont} bind def
/center {dup stringwidth pop 2 div neg 0 rmoveto } bind def
/landscape {612 0 translate 90 rotate} bind def
/portrait {796 0 translate 90 rotate} bind def
/corner {0 0 36 90 360 arc stroke}bind def
/scroll {newpath 0 36 translate 0 0 36 90 270 arc stroke} bind def

gsave
  landscape
70/ZapfChancery-MediumItalic font  396 460  moveto
(CERTIFICATE) center show
26/ZapfChancery-MediumItalic font  396 415  moveto
(of) center show
70/ZapfChancery-MediumItalic font  396 360  moveto
(RECOGNITION) center show
24/Helvetica font     396 290  moveto
(Father Time) center show
24/ZapfChancery-MediumItalic font  396 245  moveto
(For 100 years of dedicated service to) center show
396 225  moveto
(Life, Liberty and the Pursuit of Happiness) center show
396 190  moveto
(_______________ _______________ _______________) center show
396 160 moveto
(_______________ _______________ _______________) center show
396 130  moveto
(_______________ _______________ _______________) center show
12/ZapfChancery-MediumItalic font
396 110 moveto
(September 16, 1991) center show
grestore

gsave
  5 setlinewidth  .9 setgray
    2{gsave
        72 72 translate  corner  0 36 576 {scroll} for
      grestore
      landscape
      gsave
        72 72 translate  corner  0 36 396 {scroll} for
      grestore
      portrait
     } repeat
grestore
 72 72 moveto  7 setlinewidth
 0 648  rlineto  468 0 rlineto 0 -648 rlineto  closepath
 stroke
 showpage
 %%EOF
```

Once the interior of the certificate is complete, the scrollwork is added. The scrollwork and the black line do overlap. Because the scrollwork is gray and the box line is black, the line must be drawn after the scrolls are completed. Otherwise, the line appears dotted with gray.[26]

Several additional procedures are used that must be explained before continuing with a description of the program. Repeated operations use procedures. The orientation of the page is changed several times. You can easily switch page orientation by using the **landscape** and **portrait** procedures. The **corner** procedure draws the 3/4 circle at each corner. The **scroll** procedure draws the half circle used many times for the scrolls.

Each program segment is bracketed by **gsave** and **grestore** to preserve the graphics state. This enables you to develope the segments independently. Additionally, **gsave** and **grestore** are used to simplify the looping structure for the scrolls.

The **landscape** procedure executes the same sequence of operators as shown in Listing 6.1. The axes are translated, then rotated. The result is landscape orientation. The **portrait** procedure changes the orientation from landscape to portrait. The **translate** operator moves the 0,0 origin to the right 796 points. No vertical translation takes place. The Y axis is at the right edge of the print area. **Rotate** turns the axes counterclockwise 90 degrees. The X axis is located where the right edge of the print area was and the Y axis is where the bottom was. The result is portrait orientation.

Each corner of the finished certificate has a 3/4 circle on the outside of the box. The **corner** procedure creates this partial circle. The procedure expects the 0,0 position to be the starting point for the circle when the procedure is executed; the axes must be adjusted before executing the procedure. The radius of the circle is 36 points. The arc starts a half inch from the corner on the Y axis and continues counterclockwise 270 degrees to the X axis, a half inch from the corner.

The **scroll** procedure accomplishes its task by emptying the current path with **newpath**. The axes are translated from the current point up the Y axis a half inch. The half circles are started every half inch and have a radius of a half inch. They begin on the positive Y axis and continue counterclockwise to the negative Y axis. Each time this procedure is executed, the 0,0 position moves up the Y axis a half inch.

---

[26]All marks in PostScript are opaque, so even white or light gray can show up over black.

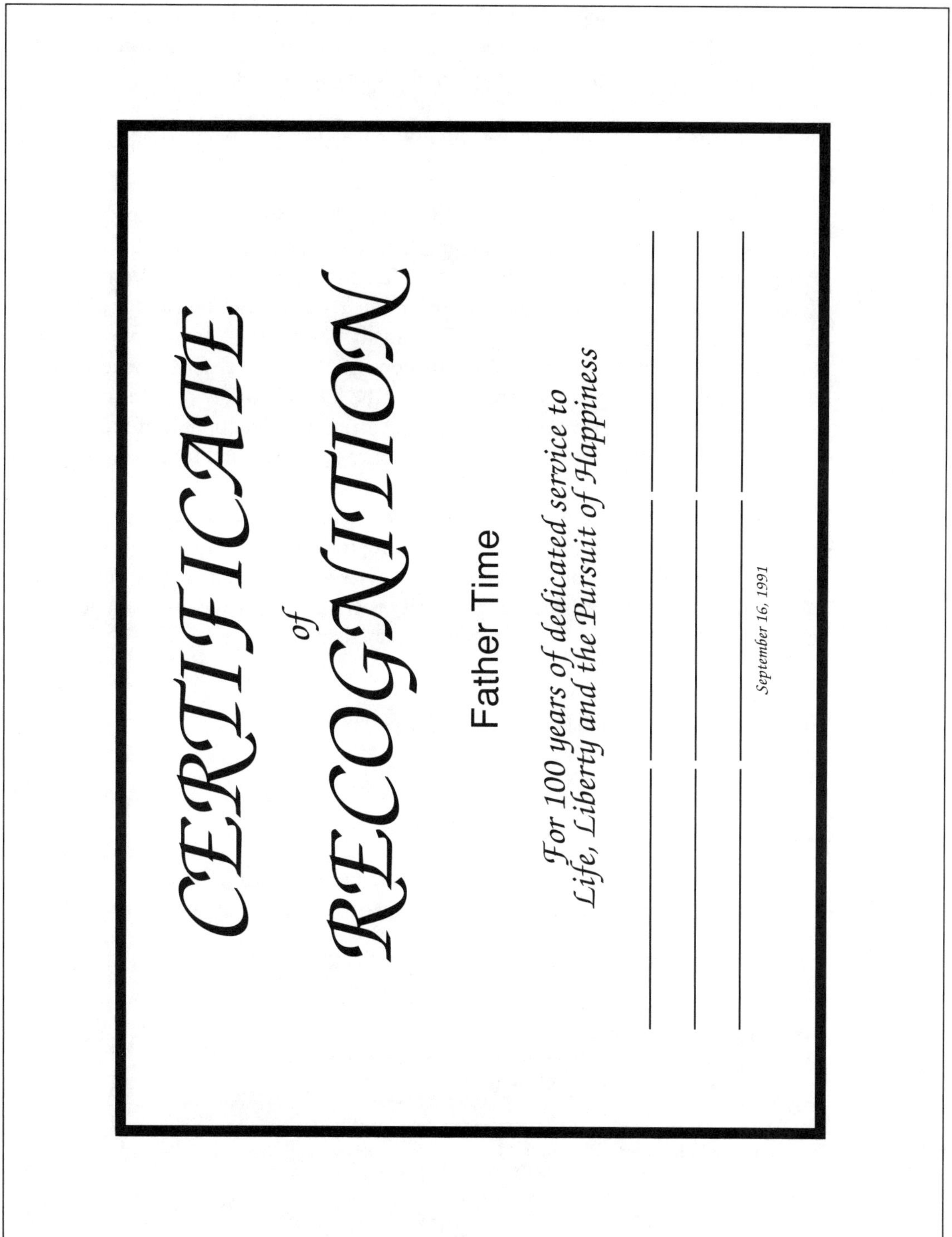

Figure 6.2: Certificate with Scrollwork

The first program segment begins with **gsave**, then changes the orientation to landscape. The certificate text is identical to the first version. The **grestore** operator restores the portrait orientation of the page.

The **gsave** operator protects this graphic state. The line width changes and the color changes to a light gray.

The repeat loop is executed twice. It applies the scrollwork to a long side and a short side of the page each time. The graphics state is saved because it is changed in the following process. The origin is translated to a position 1 inch from the left side in the X direction and 1 inch upward in the Y direction. The **corner** procedure is executed. The loop is completed as previously described. A **for** loop executes the **scroll** procedure beginning with 0, in steps of 36 until it reaches the terminal value of 576. At this point the scrollwork for the left side of the paper is completed. The **grestore** operator returns the axis from near the top left of the page to the bottom left corner. The **landscape** procedure translates and rotates the page so it is in position to apply the scrollwork to the short side. Next **gsave** is executed. The start point in moved in 1 inch from bottom and side. The short side is completed first by **translate** and **corner** procedure, followed by a **for** loop with the terminal value adjusted for the different size. The graphics state is restored so the page orientation is landscape. The **portrait** procedure is executed and the loop is repeated for the second time. The graphics state is restored.

The last task is to draw the box around the certificate text and inside the loop. This is the same set of instructions as the first version.

c. Version 3: A Final Touch

The final version, of the certificate Listing 6.3, places a light medallion on the certificate, Figure 6.3, as a background for an official-looking document.

Listing 6.3: A Final Touch

```
%!PS-Adobe-3.0  EPSF-30.
%%BoundingBox: 0 0 612 792
%%Title: (Certificate example #3  certex3.eps)
%% Creationdate:  (10/29/91:12:30)
%%Endcomments
/font {findfont exch scalefont setfont} bind def
/center {dup stringwidth pop  2 div neg 0 rmoveto} bind def
/landscape {612 0 translate 90 rotate} bind def
/portrait {796 0 translate 90 rotate} bind def
/corner {0 0 36 90 360 arc stroke}bind def
/scroll {newpath 0 36 translate 0 0 36 90 270 arc stroke} bind def
/box {newpath 72 72 moveto 0 648 rlineto 468 0 rlineto
      0 -648 rlineto   closepath} bind def
```

```
gsave
box clip  newpath
306 396 translate  .95 setgray  5 setlinewidth
  2 {30 {0 0 moveto  40 40 80 -40 432 0 curveto 360 30 div rotate
        }repeat
       -1 1 scale
    }repeat  stroke
1 setgray  0 0 8 0 360 arc fill
grestore
gsave
landscape
70/ZapfChancery-MediumItalic font  396 460  moveto
(CERTIFICATE) center show
26/ZapfChancery-MediumItalic font  396 415  moveto
(of) center show
70/ZapfChancery-MediumItalic font  396 360  moveto
(RECOGNITION) center show
24/Helvetica font     396 290  moveto
(Father Time) center show
24/ZapfChancery-MediumItalic font  396 245  moveto
(For 100 years of dedicated service to) center show
396 225  moveto
(Life, Liberty and the Pursuit of Happiness) center show
396 190  moveto
(______________ ______________ ______________) center show
396 160 moveto
(______________ ______________ ______________) center show
396 130  moveto
(______________ ______________ ______________) center show
12/ZapfChancery-MediumItalic font  396 110 moveto
(September 16, 1991) center show
grestore

gsave
  5 setlinewidth  .9 setgray
  2{gsave  72 72 translate  corner  0 36 576 {scroll} for
    grestore
    landscape
    gsave  72 72 translate corner 0 36 396 {scroll} for
    grestore
    portrait
   }repeat
grestore
7 setlinewidth box stroke
showpage
%%EOF
```

One additional procedure is included with this version. The **box** procedure is used because the same path is used for the box around the certificate and the clipping path used for the medallion. No new operators are used. They are placed in a procedure to reduce the length of the program.

The only modifications in this program are the medallion at the beginning and the **box** procedure at the end. The balance of the program is unchanged.

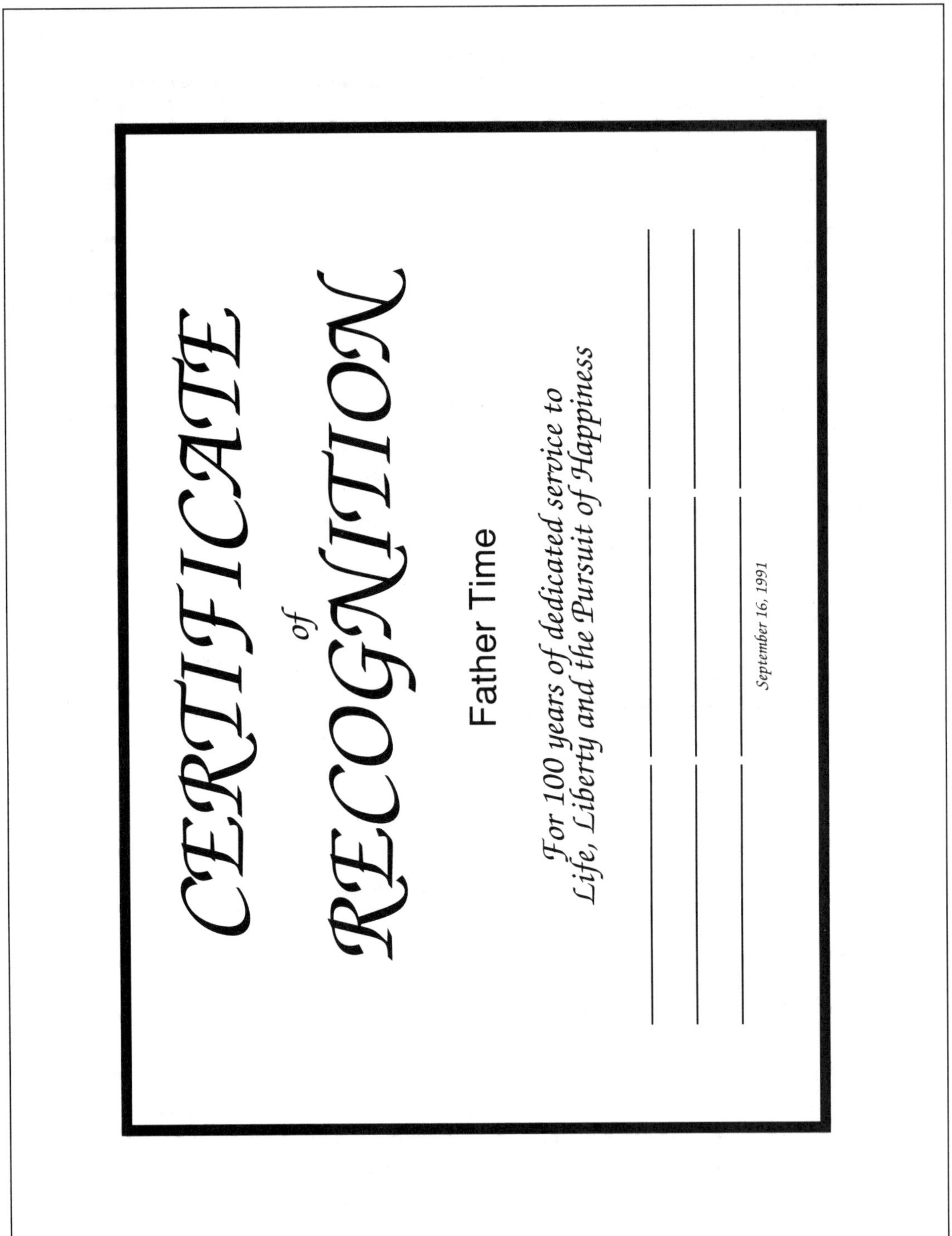

Figure 6.3: A Final Touch

The medallion is created by constructing a Bézier curved path from the center of the certificate to the outside. The axes are rotated 12 degrees and another curve is constructed. This is repeated until the axes have completed 360 degrees. The X coordinate is then negatively scaled. This causes the curve to bend in the opposite direction and creates a leaf effect in the medallion. This is repeated with rotation for 360 degrees. The leaves overflow the certificate into the border area. To prevent this, a clipping path is set at the 9-by-6.5-inch boundary of the certificate. When the medallion is completed only the portion inside the path is retained.

The **box** procedure constructs a path. The **clip** operator sets a limit on the work area. The **newpath** operator is invoked because **clip** does not empty the current path. The axes are translated to the center of the page. A gray color is selected and the line width set to 5 points. The drawing process is repeated twice with negative X scaling between the repetitions. The lines are created with the **30 {..} repeat**. If you desire more leaves are desired, increase the repetitions from 30 and change the **30 div** operand to the same number. This ensures complete rotation through 360 degrees with no repeats. The curve is drawn from the center to the outside. It is long enough to reach into the corners. After the medallion is stroked, the color is set to white and a small circle is cleared in the center of the medallion.

The text of the certificate is completed. The scrollwork is placed on the outside. Finally, the **box** procedure creates the current path for the outline.

4. Suggested Improvements

The name of the awardee should remain at the center of the certificate, but other changes are encouraged. These are easily accomplished:

- Replace RECOGNITION with MERIT.
- Substitute ACHIEVEMENT for CERTIFICATE, delete OF and replace RECOGNITION with CERTIFICATE. The certificate can be adapted to other occasions by changing the text.
- Change the number of signature lines.
- Create a small medallion similar to the large one to replace a column of signature lines. Make it darker than the large one.
- Create a small medallion by printing "recognition" in a circular pattern.

Chapter 7
Envelopes

This chapter provides a program for printing envelopes on a PostScript printer.[27] In this chapter, you are introduced to several new PostScript operators and presented with three successively more advanced programs for printing envelopes. In addition, this chapter addresses the issue of device dependence using PostScript.

1. Objectives

The objectives of this chapter are:

- To provide a program that prints envelopes on a PostScript printer.
- To provide examples of how to modify and enhance the PostScript programs provided.
- To discuss device dependence using PostScript.
- To introduce several new PostScript operators and provide increased familiarity of some operators which have been introduced in previous chapters. The operators introduced in this chapter include:
  - **bind**
  - **begin/end**
  - **definefont**
  - **dict**
  - **forall**
  - **gsave/grestore**
  - **ifelse**
  - **index**

[27]The envelope program and chapter were developed by Bryan Sorrows. Bryan's work in information science entails the capture and visualization of biomedical information.

- **length**
- **ne**
- **pop**

2. Operator Explanations

a. Simplest Envelope

The simplest envelope program prints a return address and a destination address on an envelope in the most straightforward way. The only new operator introduced is:

currentpoint Description: This operator pushes two numeric objects representing the current point's the X and Y values. The values are retrieved from the active graphics state.

Arguments: `none`

Results: $\texttt{num}_1$ $\texttt{num}_2$

The **currentpoint** operator function returns two numbers of type real which represent the X and Y coordinates of the current point in the graphics state. The current point is the trailing end point of the current path. A "nocurrentpoint" error is generated if **currentpoint** is undefined.

b. Intermediate Envelope

The intermediate envelope program proceduralizes the repetitive sections of code from the simple example and introduces several new operators.

The operators introduced are:

bind Description: The **bind** operator causes the interpreter to replace all executable operator names in a procedure with the actual operators themselves. This has two effects. First, the procedure executes faster, as operator names do not have to be searched for in the current dictionary stack. Second, if definitions of any of the operators are changed after the procedure has been bound, the procedure operation is not affected. For each procedure object in **proc** whose access is unrestricted, **bind** applies itself recursively to **proc**, makes the process read-only, and returns **proc** on the stack.

Arguments: `proc`

The executable names that refer to operator object values which make up the array **proc** are replaced by the actual operators they refer to.

Results: `proc`

The **bind** function returns the same procedure it was given, except that all references to executable names are replaced by the actual operators they referred to.

For example: if the definition of print in the program is bound when defined, and later the value of **ptsize** which is an operator used to define print operation is changed, the change in the definition does not affect the ptsize print.

grestore Description: This operator pops a graphics state from the top of the graphics state stack and makes it active. It undoes any changes that were made to the graphics state since the last **gsave**.

Arguments: `none`

Results: `none`

gsave Description: The **gsave** operator pushes the current graphics state onto the graphics state stack. This operator is often used before changes that are difficult to recover from are made to the graphics state. It is also used to isolate changes to the graphics state made for a small subsection of the program so those changes do not have unintended effects on commands executed later.

Arguments: `none`

Results: `none`

c. Complex Envelope

This version is enhanced to print in the opposite orientation and to print characters not found in the standard encoding of fonts.

The operators introduced are:

begin Description: The **begin** operator causes the named dictionary, **dict**, to be pushed onto the dictionary stack so it is the current dictionary (i.e. the first dictionary looked at by later commands).

Arguments: `dict`

Results: `none`

The **begin** operator function makes **dict** the current dictionary. It becomes the first dictionary consulted during implicit name lookups and by the **def, load, store,** and **where** operators.

definefont Description: This operator registers a font dictionary **`dict`** as the object **`key`**, usually a name literal. **definefont** operator first checks to see if the dictionary is syntactically correct and can be properly loaded. If so, **definefont** creates an entry with a key **`FID`** and value of object **`fontID`**. An error is generated if the dictionary does not have the capacity to hold this value. The **`key`** value is then associated with **`font`** in the global **`FontDirectory`** font dictionary. The **findfont** operator is used to retrieve the font for use.

Arguments: **`key font`**

The name literal **`key`** is associated with the dictionary object **`font`** as specified, allowing **findfont** access to the specified dictionary. The **`font`** parameter must not have an existing FID associated with it.

Results: **`font`**

The **`font`** dictionary object is pushed back onto the stack.

dict Description: The **dict** operator consumes the top value on the stack and creates an empty dictionary with room for that number of key-value pairs.

Arguments: **`int`**

`int` must be non-negative.

Results: **`dict`**

The **dict** operator returns a dictionary object with a maximum capacity of **`int`** key-value pair entries. If an attempt is made to add more than **`int`** key-value pairs to the **`dict`**, a "dictfull" error is generated.

end Description: The **end** operator takes the current dictionary off the dictionary stack. The dictionary immediately below the popped dictionary becomes the new, current dictionary. An error is generated if a user-defined dictionary is not on the stack, as the two system dictionaries cannot be popped. This operator does the opposite of the **begin** operator.

Arguments: **`None`**

Results: **`None`**

forall Description: The **forall** operator executes a procedure for each element of a string or array. A procedure object is expected on top of the stack (the procedure to be executed) with the string or array underneath it. The **forall** operator pushes each string or array element onto the stack and executes a procedure. The procedure may or may not act the stack element. With strings, the stack objects are codes, or numeric values, of the characters.

Arguments (Form 1): **`array proc`**

Arguments (Form 2): **packedarray proc**

Arguments (Form 3): **dict proc**

Arguments (Form 4): **proc proc**

Note if the first operand in any of the forms is empty (i.e. has length zero), **forall** operator does not execute at all.

Results: **None**

ifelse

Description: The **ifelse** command pops three objects from the stack, evaluates the first argument and, if it is true, executes the second argument, the **proc**$_1$ procedure. Otherwise, it executes the third argument, the **proc**$_2$ procedure.

Arguments: **boolean proc**$_1$ **proc**$_2$

proc is a set of zero or more PostScript commands.

Results: **none**

Although **ifelse** operator does not directly leave results on the stack, the procedure that is executed may alter stack after the invocation of the **ifelse** procedure has completed.

index

Description: The **index** operator command pops an integer object off the stack and uses that integer as an index to access the **int** entry from the top of the stack. A copy of the **int** entry is pushed onto the stack.

Arguments: **any**$_n$**...any**$_1$**, any**$_0$**, int**

int must be a non-negative integer, and **n** = **int** above. Element counting begins at zero, not one.

Results: **any**$_n$**...any**$_1$**, any**$_0$**, any**$_n$

n = **int** above. The very last instance of **any**$_n$ shown here is the copy of the element that gets pushed onto the stack.

length

Description: This operator behaves differently based the arguments it is given on the stack.

Arguments (Form 1): **array**
Arguments (Form 2): **packedarray**
Arguments (Form 3): **dict**
Arguments (Form 4): **string**
Arguments (Form 5): **name**

Results: **length**

If the argument type is an **array**, **packedarray**, or **string**, **length** returns the number of elements in its value. If the operand is a dictionary, only the current number of key-value pairs in the dictionary is returned. See **maxlength** for information about determining the maximum capacity of a dictionary. Finally, if the argument is a **name** object, the number of characters in the text string that defines it is returned.

ne

Description: This operator expects two objects on the stack. They are removed and a boolean is pushed onto the stack. The boolean object is true if the objects are not equal, and false otherwise. Certain objects are considered equal even though they have different types. Integers and reals may be considered equal if they represent the same mathematical value. Strings and names are equal if they have the same sequence of characters.

Arguments: $\mathbf{any_1}$ $\mathbf{any_2}$

$\mathbf{num_1}$ and $\mathbf{num_2}$ may be any type of object.

Results: **boolean**

The **ne** function returns a number of boolean as described.

3. Explanation of the Listings

There are three versions of the envelope program. Each one is progressively more complex and introduces new operators. Listings can be found in Listing 7.1, Listing 7.2, and Listing 7.3. The output from Listing 7.1 and Listing 7.2 are identical and can be found in Figure 7.1. The output from Listing 7.3 can be found in Figure 7.2.

a. Version 1: Simple Envelope Program

The first version of the envelope program, Listing 7.1, will print a return address and destination address on the top of a portrait page. There is no standard path for envelopes to travel through a PostScript printer. The envelope tray could feed from the right, left or middle, in landscape or portrait orientation. The output from the program shown is in Figure 7.1.

Listing 7.1: Simple Envelope Listing

```
%!PS-Adobe-3.0 EPSF-30.
%%BoundingBox: 0 0 612 792
%%Title: (Simple Envelope)
%%Creationdate: (11/3/91)
%%EndComments

/inch {72 mul} bind def

/eh 4 inch def          % Envelope Height
/ew 9.5 inch def        % Envelope Width
```

```
-90 rotate               % Landscape
-792 0 translate         % Reset coordinate axis for new orientation
0 612 eh sub translate   % Set coordinates for envelope


%% Print Return Address

/NewCenturySchlbk-Italic
findfont 12 scalefont setfont

.3 inch eh .3 inch sub moveto    % move in enough to right and down
                                 % that printing gets put on page

currentpoint
(Naive Novice) show
14 sub moveto
currentpoint
(Room 214) show
14 sub moveto
currentpoint
(School of Information Science) show
14 sub moveto
currentpoint
(University of Pittsburgh) show
14 sub moveto
(Pittsburgh, PA 15206) show

%% Print address

/Helvetica findfont 12 scalefont setfont
ew 2 div 1 inch sub         % Set X coordinate 1" left of middle
eh 2 div                    % Set Y coordinate in middle of envelope
moveto
currentpoint
(Professor PostScript) show
14 sub moveto
currentpoint
(Adobe Systems Incorporated) show
14 sub moveto
currentpoint
(Mountain View, CA 94039) show

showpage
%%EOF
```

This program begins by defining an operator called **inch**, which replaces the top item on the stack with that item's value multiplied by 72. This effectively converts between inches and points.

The next two definitions use the **inch** procedure to define the size of the envelope. Since the rest of the program uses these definitions of envelope width and height, you can easily modify the program to produce any size envelope.

This program prints envelopes in landscape orientation. The **rotate** operator is

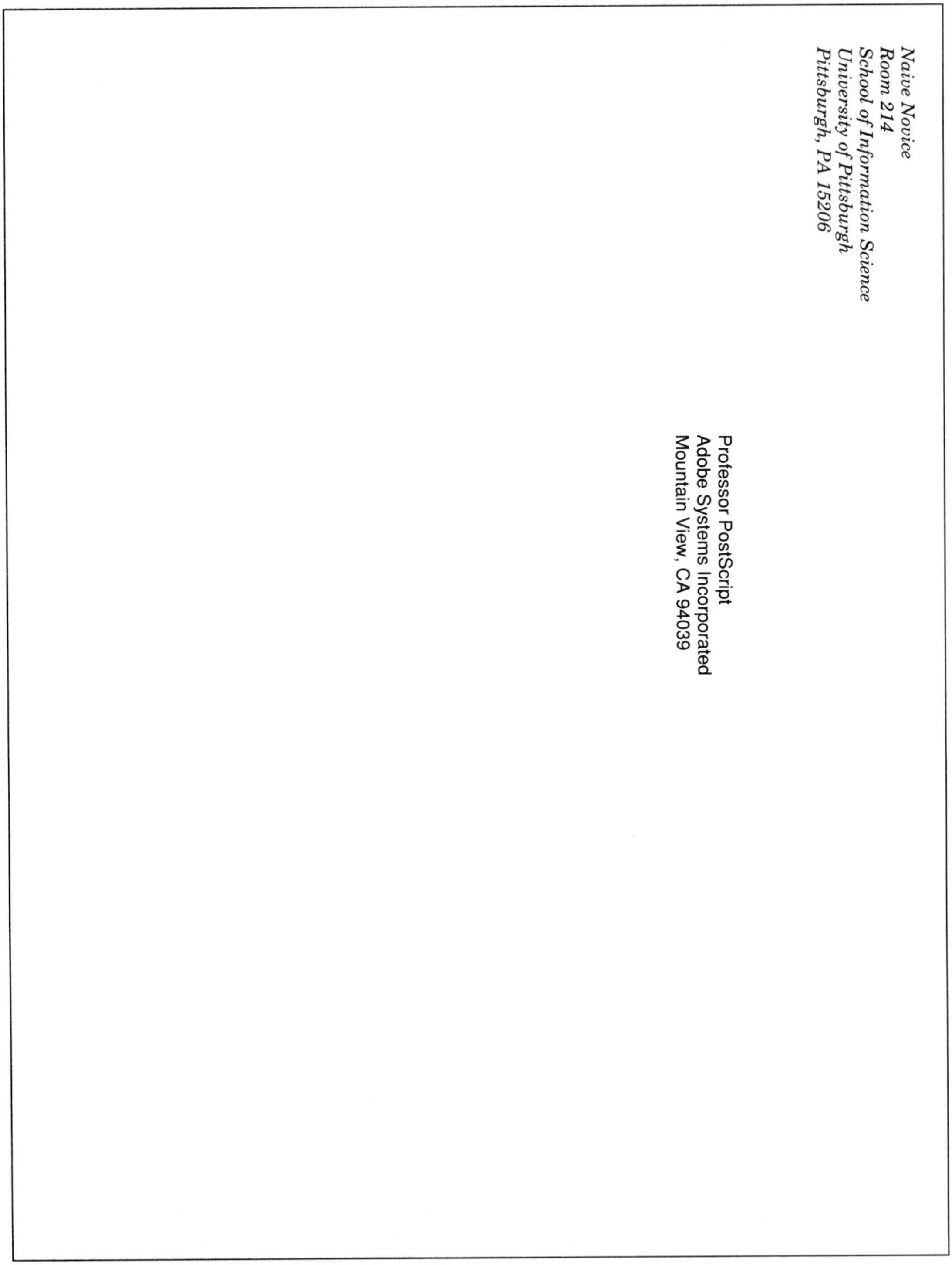

Figure 7.1: Output from Simple and Intermediate Envelope Program

used to rotate to landscape orientation and **translate** is used to transform the area that will be printed back into the positive coordinate space. The **rotate** operator moves the coordinate axis clockwise 90 degrees. The **translate** that follows moves the origin to the bottom left of an 8.5-by-11-inch sheet of paper. The second **translate** moves the origin to the bottom left corner of an envelope.

In preparation for printing the return address text, the **findfont**, **scalefont**, and **setfont** operators set the font to New Century Schoolbook-Italic and 12 points. The program also sets the current point to .3 inches in and down from the top left point of the envelope.

The next operators in the program print the return address. The **currentpoint** operator pushes the current X and Y values onto the stack. The string to be printed is then pushed onto the stack, where **show** pops it back off to display the line of text. After **show** is executed, the current point is the X and Y value for the point at the end of the string. The starting point for the next line of text must be calculated from the X and Y values that were used for the beginning point of the last string, not the current point after the string was printed. To allow for this, the **currentpoint** operator was used to push those values onto the stack before the string was printed. The values can now be accessed; 14 is subtracted from the Y value that is on the top of the stack and the current point is moved to lastX (.3 inch), lastY–14. This series of operators is repeated for each line of the return address.

After printing the return address, the font change to Helvetica, and the current point moves toward the middle of the envelope for printing the destination address. Each line is then placed on the page and the current point is moved down the page to print the next line.

The **showpage** operator causes the printer to put the description of the page onto an envelope.

b. Version 2: Intermediate Envelope Program

The second version of the envelope program can be found in Listing 7.2. This version prints an envelope identical to one produced by the first version, as shown in Figure 7.1. However, the second version exploits some of the PostScript interpreter strengths by proceduralizing the repetitive code found in the first listing.

Listing 7.2: Intermediate Envelope Listing

```
%!PS-Adobe-3.0 EPSF-30.
%%BoundingBox: 0 0 612 792
%%Title: (Intermediate Envelope)
%%Creationdate: (11/3/91)
%%EndComments

/inch {72 mul} bind def

/eh 4 inch def          % Envelope Height
/ew 9.5 inch def        % Envelope Width
/ptsize 12 def          % initial pointsize



/print
{dup stringwidth pop exch
show
neg ptsize 1.1 mul neg rmoveto
} def
% no bind so that we can change the ptsize at will


-90 rotate              % Landscape
-792 0 translate        % Reset coordinate axis for new orientation
0 612 eh sub translate  % Set coordinates for envelope


%% Print Return Address

/NewCenturySchlbk-Italic
findfont ptsize scalefont setfont
.3 inch eh .3 inch sub moveto % move in enough to right so first char prints
(Naive Novice) print
(Room 214) print
(School of Information Science) print
(University of Pittsburgh) print
(Pittsburgh, PA 15206) print

%% Print address

/Helvetica findfont ptsize scalefont setfont
ew 2 div 1 inch sub        % Set X coordinate 1" left of middle
eh 2 div                   % Set Y coordinate in middle of envelope
moveto
(Professor PostScript) print
(Adobe Systems Incorporated) print
(Mountain View, CA 94039) print
showpage


%%EOF
```

In this program, the **print** procedure is defined. To make this procedure self-contained, the current point is not pushed onto the stack before the string is pushed onto the stack, as it was in Listing 7.1. The **currentpoint** operator could be issued inside the procedure before the **show operator**, but then the stack would need to be rolled to bring the string back to the top of the stack for the **show** operator. Instead, the procedure issues a **stringwidth** operator. The Y offset is popped, and the X offset is exchanged with the second copy of the string. The string is then shown. The X offset is made negative.

Because the next line should always be 110 percent of the point size lower than the current line, the procedure uses an **rmoveto** operator to move relative to the last line rather than calculating the absolute coordinates needed for the **moveto** operator.

This procedure is not defined with the **bind** operator because if it were bound, **ptsize** definition changes made during the execution of the program, would not be reflected when the **print** procedure was executed. An example of this would be if the user wanted to change the point size between the return address and the destination address.

c. Version 3: Complex envelope

This envelope program contains several additional enhancements. The program is shown in Listing 7.3 and the output can be seen in Figure 7.2. This program produces an envelope that travels through the printer in the opposite orientation as the previous examples. The program enables you to print characters encoded with ISO Latin Encoding, such as foreign characters.

Listing 7.3: Complex Envelope Listing

```
%!PS-Adobe-3.0 EPSF-30.
%%BoundingBox: 0 0 612 792
%%Title: (Advanced Envelope)
%%Creationdate: (11/3/91)
%%EndComments

/inch {72 mul} bind def

/eh 4 inch def          % Envelope Height
/ew 9.5 inch def        % Envelope Width
/ptsize 12 def          % initial pointsize

/print
{dup stringwidth pop exch
show
neg ptsize 1.1 mul neg rmoveto
} def
```

```
% no bind so that we can change the ptsize at will

/center {
exch 2 div exch dup 3 1 roll
stringwidth pop 2 div sub
0 rmoveto show
} bind def

/box {
dup 0 rlineto
dup 0 exch rlineto
neg 0 rlineto
closepath
stroke
} bind def

/NewCenturySchlbk-Italic
findfont
dup length dict begin
{1 index /FID ne {def} {pop pop} ifelse} forall
/Encoding ISOLatin1Encoding def
currentdict
end
/NewCenturySchlbk-Italic-ISOLatin1 exch definefont pop

90 rotate                          % Landscape
11 inch ew sub      % x
eh neg              % y
translate           % Reset coordinate axis for R.H. envelopes


%% Print Return Address
/NewCenturySchlbk-Italic-ISOLatin1
findfont ptsize scalefont setfont
.3 inch eh .3 inch sub moveto % move in enough to right so first char prints
(Na\357ve Novice) print
(Room 214) print
(School of Information Science) print
(University of Pittsburgh) print
(Pittsburgh, PA 15206) print

%% Print address

/Helvetica findfont ptsize scalefont setfont
ew 2 div 1 inch sub          % Set X coordinate 1" left of middle
eh 2 div                     % Set Y coordinate in middle of envelope
moveto
(Professor PostScript) print
(Adobe Systems Incorporated) print
(Mountain View, CA 94039) print


gsave
ew 1 inch sub
eh 1 inch sub
translate
0 0 moveto
```

```
1 setlinewidth
.75 inch box
0 .5 inch translate
0 0 moveto
.75 inch (Place) center
0 ptsize 1.1 mul neg translate
0 0 moveto
.75 inch (Stamp) center
0 ptsize 1.1 mul neg translate
0 0 moveto
.75 inch (Here) center
grestore

showpage
%%EOF
```

Given the width of a space and a string, the **center** procedure centers the string in the middle of the space. This procedure centers text inside of a box.

Given the width of a square, the **box** procedure draws a square of that size with the bottom left point of the square on the current point.

In this version, the encoding for the New Century Schoolbook font is changed from Standard to ISOLatin.[28] This enables to specify foreign characters in the address. The same could be done for the Helvetica-Normal font used for the destination address.

This program rotates the page 90 degrees in the positive direction (the axis rotate 90 degrees counterclockwise). In this orientation, the envelope feeds stamp side first, so the axis must be moved in so the origin is still at the bottom left corner of the page.

After printing the return and destination address, code that prints a "place stamp here" box on the upper right corner of the envelope, with the text centered in the box, was added to this version this example shows your return address be centered in a similar manner.

4. A Word about Device Dependence

One of PostScript's major goals was to develop a device-independent page description language. Although this is possible for describing where and how to place objects in a coordinate space, some printer capabilities such as media han-

[28]See Chapter 15.

Place
Stamp
Here

Professor PostScript
Adobe Systems Incorporated
Mountain View, CA 94039

Naïve Novice
Room 214
School of Information Science
University of Pittsburgh
Pittsburgh, PA 15206

Figure 7.2: Output from Complex Envelope Program

dling are inherently device-dependent. As stated earlier, printers can feed envelopes from the right side of the tray, the left side, or the center, and in any orientation. There can be a separate envelope bin or the printer can require you to manually feed in envelopes. Although it may not be a problem for a PostScript file that goes directly to a printer to be device-specific for that printer, device-specific code causes problems for document storage and interchange, which is one of PostScript's important strengths.

There are several approaches to solving this problem. In Level 1 PostScript, the **statusdict** is used for device setup. The keys to the dictionary entries and the values associated with those keys are nonstandard, i.e. they are device-specific. In Level 2, Adobe has standardized the handling of device setup with the **setpagedevice** operator. Using this approach, each Level 2 printer is prepared for a standard set of requests. The printer is capable of responding to all requests, even if the response is to indicate that the printer can't handle a given capability. A third approach is to place device-specific operators in the comments section of the program. In this way, a pre-processor can scan these comments for device setup information without interfering with document storage and interchange.

5. Enhancements

There are several ways these programs could be improved. The most obvious is the to print a logo on the envelope. This can be easily accomplished by including an encapsulated PostScript description of the logo.[29] Some users may like their return address centered on the left of the envelope. Version 3 of the program shows one way this can be done.

6. Why Didn't It Print?

One area that can cause major possible problems when printing envelopes is determining the paper feed and orientation. Once this is determined, the **translate** and **rotate** operators can be used to set the origin to the bottom left point on the envelope. You should review the **translate** and **rotate** operators carefully so the addresses print in the current page region and onto the envelope. This should be the only needed change.

This rather basic program introduces no new problems beyond the nemesis of not having a current point before issuing an **rlineto**, **rmoveto** or **show** operator. If

[29]See Chapter 3.

you have a PostScript device that gives error messages, these problems can be caught easily, but often PostScript printers do not return an error message and you are left to find the problem on your own.

Chapter 8
Place Cards

Often at meetings or panel discussions, participants are assigned name cards to place in front of them on the table. Hand-printed cards do in a pinch, but they are less attractive and less legible than laser-printed ones. This chapter introduces the programming principles required to produce name cards for panels or meetings.[30] Three variant forms of a program are shown. Each variation of the program is discussed and the results are illustrated.

The objectives of this chapter are:

- To explain rotation, translation, scaling, and clipping in PostScript programming, and to demonstrate, via examples, their effect on printed text;
- To provide a place card program that can easily be adapted for personal use.

1. Operator Explanations

Several of the operators, including **findfont**, **scalefont**, **setfont**, **moveto**, **rmoveto**, **lineto**, **dup**, **pop**, **div**, **stroke**, **setgray**, **stringwidth**, **show**, **setlinewidth** and **showpage**, are fully described in earlier chapters. These operators are discussed later in a context specific to the listed programs.

[30]This chapter was originally developed by Dr. Toni Hebda to produce bumper stickers. Dr. Hebda is exploring the application of information science in the medical field with particular attention to wellness programs and health education, areas in which she provides consultation

a. Version 1: The Simplest Place Card

The first program produces a card comprised of text only. Three operators, **findfont**, **scalefont**, and **setfont**, permit you to select of 100-point Helvetica font for this project. **Moveto**, **show**, and **showpage** are used to select the initial coordinates and output selected text to the printed page. This program also uses the following operators:

def

Description: This operator consumes two objects of the form **`key`** and **`value`** from the stack and adds them to the current dictionary.

Arguments: **`key value`**

`key` is associated with **`value`** in the current dictionary. If **`key`** exists, the new **`value`** replaces the associated **`value`**. If **`key`** does not exist already in the current dictionary, the dictionary must have room for one more entry. If it does not, a "dictfull" error is generated. **`key`** may consist of any object. If **`key`** is a name literal, it is converted to a name literal prior to storing the entry.

Results: **`none`**

The current dictionary is modified so it contains a **`key`** with an associated **`value`**.

The operators **gsave** and **grestore** were introduced in other chapters. In this program, the graphics state is saved before scaling takes place, and is later restored to the pre-scaling status. A full description of these operators is found in the operator reference.

rlineto

Description: This operator appends a straight line segment to the current path from the current point to the point indicated by the two numbers popped off the stack. Unlike **lineto**, however, the two coordinates are interpreted in a relative manner from the (X,Y) of the current point as opposed to the absolute coordinates, with respect to the origin. Therefore, the line is constructed from the current point (X,Y) to a point relative to the current point by the amount specified in the arguments ($X + num_1$, $Y + num_2$). The new currentpoint is ($X + num_1$, $Y + num_2$).

Arguments: num_1, num_2

num_1 and num_2 may be either integers or real number objects, where num_1 represents the X coordinate, and num_2 represents the Y coordinate, with the aforementioned special interpretation. Lack of a current point generates "nocurrentpoint" error.

Results: **`none`**

rotate Description: This operator expects one or two arguments on the stack. The first argument is always an angle value, either in integer or real form, and the second argument, if present, is a matrix. The horizontal and vertical axes for the current user space are rotated counterclockwise a number of degrees equal to the **`num`** argument.

Arguments (Form 1): **`num`**

Results: **`none`**

Arguments (Form 2): **`num, matrix`**

Results: **`matrix`**

The **rotate** function occurs in two varieties: in one, the user supplies a matrix; the other operates on the current transformation matrix (CTM). If a matrix is supplied, the CTM is not altered in any way.

At one point in this program, the axes are rotated negative 90 degrees. This means text must be located at negative X and positive Y coordinates to be rendered on the printed page if no other adjustments are made to the program.

setdash Description: This operator expects an array and a number on the stack. They are removed and their sum is pushed onto the stack.

Arguments: **`array, offset`**

The top value on the stack is the offset into the dash pattern used for each line.[31] The second value is given as an array (placed between [ ]), and it sets the dash pattern as simply the length, in points, of the dash and the gap between the dashes.[32] Once setdash is executed, all lines drawn are in the same dashed pattern until **setdash** operator is explicitly reset.

Results: **`none`**

In these programs, **setlinewidth** and **setdash** are used to specify the width and dash pattern of the fold marks.

---

[31]For example, if the pattern is followed by a space of 10 and an offset of three, it starts with a dash of seven.

[32]The array you use may be longer than two. For example, the array [2 2 10 2 5 15] sets the dash pattern to a dash of 2, followed by a space of 2, followed by a dash of 10, followed by a space of 2, followed by a dash of 5, followed by a space of 15. The entire procedure then repeats.

string Description: This operator removes an integer from the stack, creates a string of nulls equal in length to the integer, and returns that string on the operand stack.

Arguments: `int`

Results: `string`

In these programs, string is used to define the length of a text character string. The **stroke** operator is introduced in other chapters. In this program, **stroke** makes the path of the fold mark line segments visible. A full description of **stroke** can be found on page 400.

translate Description: This operator has two versions:

Arguments (Form 1): $\mathtt{num_1}$ $\mathtt{num_2}$

This version of **translate** operator shifts the user coordinate system $\mathtt{num_1}$ units in the X direction and $\mathtt{num_2}$ units in the Y direction. The current transformation matrix is updated and the operation relocates the origin point. $\mathtt{num_1}$ and $\mathtt{num_2}$ may be either integers or real number objects.

Results (Form 1): `none`

Arguments (Form 2): $\mathtt{num_1}$ $\mathtt{num_2}$ `matrix`

This version of **translate** operator alters `matrix` by providing the transforms for shifting a user coordinate system $\mathtt{num_1}$ units in the X direction and $\mathtt{num_2}$ units in the Y direction. The current transformation matrix (CTM) is not altered and the operation has no effect on the current graphics state. $\mathtt{num_1}$ and $\mathtt{num_2}$ may be either integers or real number objects.

Results (Form 2): `matrix`

A negative 792 0 translation with a negative 90 rotation allows the use of positive X and Y coordinates for landscape viewing on a printed page. The 792 figure is derived from the length of 8.5-by-11-inch paper in point size. No adjustment is required for the Y coordinate in this instance.

b. Version 2: Text Scaled to Available Space

In this version, the text to appear on the card is scaled to fit available space. The following additional operators are introduced:

cvi

Description: The **cvi** operator removes a numeric or string object from the operand stack, converts it into an integer object, and returns an object of type integer on the stack. If the argument is an integer, **cvi** returns that value. If the argument is a real, fractional parts of the number are truncated, unless the real is too large to convert to an integer, in which case an error is generated. If the argument is a string, the characters are interpreted as a number according to PostScript syntax rules. The number obtained is evaluated as described.

Arguments: **`num`** or **`string`**

cvi operator takes either a number or a string as an argument.

Results: **`int`**

If the result of the conversion of the **`num`** or **`string`** argument is too large to convert to an integer, an error is generated.

cvr

Description: The **cvr** operator removes a numeric or string object from the operand stack, converts it into a real object, and returns that object on the stack. If the argument is a real, **cvr** returns that value. If the argument is a string, the characters are interpreted as a number according to PostScript syntax rules.

Arguments: **`num`** or **`string`**

cvr operator takes either a number or a string as an argument.

Results: **`real`**

If the result of the conversion of the **`num`** or **`string`** argument is too large to convert to a real, an error is generated.

floor

Description: This operator removes a numeric object from the stack, rounds the value down to the nearest integer value, and then returns the result onto the operand stack.

Arguments: **`num`**

`num` is the number to be floored.

Results: **`num`**

The **floor** operator function returns a number as described above.

In these programs, **cvi**, **cvr**, and **floor** are used to change the scale factor to one of a limited set.

ifelse

Description: The **ifelse** command pops three objects from the stack, evaluates the first argument and, if it is true, executes the second argument, the $\mathbf{proc_1}$ procedure. Otherwise, it executes the third argument, the $\mathbf{proc_2}$ procedure.

Arguments: $\mathbf{boolean}$ $\mathbf{proc_1}$ $\mathbf{proc_2}$

`proc` is a set of zero or more PostScript commands.

Results: **none**

Although **ifelse** operator does not directly leave results on the stack, the procedure that is executed may alter stack after the invocation of the **ifelse** procedure has completed.

neg

Description: This operator expects two numbers on the stack. They are removed and their sum is pushed onto the stack.

Arguments: **num**

num may be either an integer or a real number object.

Results: **num**

The **neg** operator function returns a number of the same type as the **num** argument.[33]

scale

Description: This operator has two versions, one that operates the current transformation matrix (CTM) and affects the user space, and the other that operates a matrix that is provided.

Arguments (Form 1): $\mathbf{num_1}$ $\mathbf{num_2}$

$\mathbf{num_1}$ and $\mathbf{num_2}$ may be either integers or real number objects and represent the X axis and the Y axis scaling factors, respectively.

Results: **none**

Arguments (Form 2): $\mathbf{num_1}$ $\mathbf{num_2}$ **matrix**

$\mathbf{num_1}$ and $\mathbf{num_2}$ may be either integers or real number objects, and represent the X axis and the Y axis scaling factors, respectively. In the matrix case, scaling is also done along the X and Y axes. Scaling does not affect the graphics state or, more importantly, alter the CTM.

Results: **matrix**

In these programs, scale is determined by the X and Y coordinates of the stringwidth. The Y coordinate is discarded. The X coordinate of the string and the space allocated for string placement determine the scale and obtain proportional spacing of the text in the designated space.

[33]If the number is the most negative number, the result is a real (otherwise the result is out of bounds of the maximum representable integer for that interpreter.)

c. Version 3: Text with a Logo

In this version, the text is scaled to a slightly narrower space to leave room for a logo, which is painted in the space. The following additional operators are used:

arc

Description: This operator expects five arguments on the stack, consisting of two coordinate values, a distance specification, and two angle values. They are removed and the current point and current path are altered according to the following interpretation of the arguments to create a line segment and a circular arc in the user space. Note any scaling transformations alter the shape that is imaged in device space, possibly causing a non-circular shape. The first and second coordinate values are X and Y offsets, respectively, relative to the current origin of the user space that represents the center of the arc. The arc has a radius equal to the distance specification. The arc starts at an angle equal to the first angle value in degrees counterclockwise from the positive X axis and ends at an angle equal to the second angle value, also in degrees counterclockwise from the positive X axis. After the **arc** operator command, the current point is equal to the arc's endpoint. The current path is the aforementioned arc if the current point is undefined or is equal to the arc's starting point. If the current point is defined and is different from the arcs starting point, a straight line segment is appended to the current path before the aforementioned arc is appended to the current path. The line segment starts at the value of the current point at the start of the **arc** operator command and terminates at the start arc's point.

Arguments: $\texttt{real}_1$ $\texttt{real}_2$ $\texttt{real}_3$ $\texttt{real}_4$ $\texttt{real}_5$

$\texttt{real}_1$ and $\texttt{real}_2$ are the X and Y coordinates relative to the origin of the user space that specify the center of the arc. $\texttt{real}_3$ represents the distance in user space units from the X and Y coordinate values represented by $\texttt{real}_1$ and $\texttt{real}_2$. $\texttt{real}_4$ and $\texttt{real}_5$ are the angles relative to the positive X axis of the user space that specify the arc's start and end points.

Results: `none`

In this program, the **arc** operator is used to paint circles for the logo.

fill

Description: The **fill** operator command paints the area enclosed by the current path with the current shade of gray. If the path is not closed, the **fill** command closes any portions of the current path that are open.

Arguments: `none`

Results: `none`

for Description: This operator expects a start value, an increment value, a final value, and a procedure on the operand stack. The procedure is executed a number of times, and each execution increments a counter variable by the value of the increment operand. The counter begins at the start value, and when it reaches the final value, the loop ends.

Arguments: $\mathbf{num_1}$ $\mathbf{num_2}$ $\mathbf{num_3}$ **{operator(s)}**

The first $\mathbf{num_1}$ is the loop counter's starting value. The second $\mathbf{num_2}$ is the loop counter's increment value, and the third operator, $\mathbf{num_3}$, is the loop counter's destination value. An operator or group of operators enclosed in the curly brackets indicates the number of times the loop executes.

Results: **none**

In this program, the **for** operator is used to paint circles of decreasing size in a bull's-eye pattern.

newpath Description: This operator initializes the current path to be empty, causing the current point to be undefined.

Arguments: **none**

Results: **none**

After the command is executed there is no path and the current point is undefined.

In this program, **newpath** is called before each circle in the logo is painted so that new circle paths are not be appended on to old ones.

2. Essential Features

Creating attractive place cards is a matter of addressing the following problems:

Landscape printing — The text of the person's name should be printed along the longest axis of the page. To accomplish this (in all versions of the program), the axes are rotated 90 degrees and the origin is translated to a new corner so that positive coordinates correspond to positions on the printable page area.

Text orientation — Once the place card is printed and folded, the text should appear right side up on both of its faces. This requires you to invert the coordinate space before the second copy of the text is painted. Inversion is accomplished (in all three versions of the program) with another rotation of the axes, followed by a translation of the origin.

Space constraints

The first version of the program prints the text in a size likely to be legible at a distance. Long strings, however, may exceed the width available on the page, requiring the program to rerun with a smaller type size. In the second and third versions of the place card program, a scale factor is calculated based on the available width and the length of the string. Scaling the coordinate space to this factor prior to painting the string guarantees the string fits.

Size consistency

Although the scale factor calculation guarantees that strings do not exceed the width of the page, its use produce strings in a wide variety of sizes. However, when you produce a large number of such cards you want a certain degree of uniformity. The second and third versions of the program seek a compromise between scaling and uniformity. This is accomplished by rounding off the scaling factor to one of a limited set.

3. Explanation of the Listings

The program listings are shown in Listing 8.1, Listing 8.2, and Listing 8.3. They correspond to the output displayed in Figure 8.1, Figure 8.2, and Figure 8.3, respectively. The first version prints the text string at two different orientations, and draws a fold mark. The second version is essentially the same except the text is scaled to fit the available space. The third version scales the text to fit a narrower area and paints a logo in the remaining space.

a. Version 1: Simplest Place Card

The first program contains two procedures. Prior to the first procedure definition, the current font is set to 100-point Helvetica-Bold, and **str1** is defined as a string variable of width 80.

Listing 8.1: Simplest Place Card

```
%!PS-Adobe-3.0 EPSF-30.
%%BoundingBox 0 0 612 797
%%Title:(Placex1)
%%CreationDate: (12/6/91)
%%EndComments
/Helvetica-Bold findfont 100 scalefont setfont
/str1 80 string def
%--------------------------Procedures-----------------------
```

```
/foldmarks {gsave 1 setlinewidth [2 4] 0 setdash
            306 0 moveto 0 72 rlineto
            306 360 moveto 0 72 rlineto
            306 720 moveto 0 72 rlineto
            stroke grestore} def

/makecard
 {
 50 150 moveto str1 show
  } def

%----------------------Main Program--------------------------

/str1 (Michael Spring) def

gsave
-90 rotate
-792 0 translate
makecard
grestore

gsave
90 rotate
0 -612 translate
makecard
grestore

foldmarks
showpage
%%EOF
```

The first procedure, **foldmarks**, sets the linewidth of the current graphics state to 1 point wide, and sets a dash pattern. It then moves to three positions on the page, and at each position (the edges and the middle), draws a dashed line 1-inch long. The procedure is bracketed between a **gsave/grestore** pair so that the line width and dash pattern does not carry over to other procedures.[34] The second procedure, **makecard**, simply moves to the coordinates (50, 150) and paints the text string defined in the program script.

The script begins by setting the value of **str1** to "Michael Spring." Following that, the graphics state is saved and the axes are rotated 90 degrees clockwise. The origin is then translated 792 units in a negative direction along the X axis. Because 792 points equals 11 inches, the origin is now at the place which would correspond to the upper left corner of the page if it were viewed in standard portrait mode. Since the axes have been rotated, positive coordinates can now be used as if the printable page area had been rotated 90 degrees counterclockwise. The **makecard** procedure moves the current point to a point a little more than 2 inches from what is now the "bottom" of the page and paints the string.

[34]Because we do not draw any other lines in this program, the precaution is unnecessary but is included as an illustration of good programming style.

Figure 8.1: Simplest Place Card

The second copy of the text string is painted next. First, the graphics state is restored, reestablishing the original coordinate system. This time the axes are rotated 90 degrees clockwise, and the origin is translated 612 units in a negative direction along the Y axis. The origin is now in what used to be the lower right corner of the page, so it is as if the printable page area were rotated clockwise 90 degrees. Again, a **gsave/grestore** pair brackets this routine, so the original coordinate system is restored after the string is painted.

The last two lines of the script paint the fold marks and eject the page.

b. Version 2: Text Scaled to Available Space

In the second version, the type size is reduced from 100 points to 72, and a procedure is introduced to scale the size to fit the available space. Initially, the scale factor is equal to the available space divided by the length of the string (the variable **width** defines the space available). The resulting value is then changed to the nearest suitable value from a limited set. The following algorithm is used: if the scale factor is greater than one it is rounded down to the nearest integer value using the **floor** operator; otherwise it is multiplied by 10, converted to an integer using **cvi**, divided by two using integer division, multiplied by 2, converted back to a real using **cvr**, and finally divided by 10 again. This latter case rounds off **sf** to even tenth (such as .2, .3, .4, etc.).

Listing 8.2: Text Scaled to Available Space

```
%!PS-Adobe-3.0 EPSF-30.
%%BoundingBox 0 0 612 797
%%Title:(Cardex2)
%%CreationDate: (12/6/91)
%%EndComments
/Helvetica-Bold findfont 72 scalefont setfont
/str1 80 string def
%--------------------------Procedures------------------------
/foldmarks {gsave 1 setlinewidth [2 4] 0 setdash
            306 0 moveto 0 72 rlineto
            306 360 moveto 0 72 rlineto
            306 720 moveto 0 72 rlineto
            stroke grestore} def

/fittext
 {
 gsave
  dup stringwidth pop width exch div /sf exch def
  sf 1 gt {sf floor /sf exch def}
          {sf 10 mul cvi 2 idiv 2 mul cvr 10 div /sf exch def} ifelse
  sf sf scale

  dup stringwidth pop 2 div neg 0 rmoveto
```

```
 0 setgray
 show
 grestore
 } def

/makecard
 {
 396 150 moveto str1 fittext
  } def

%-----------------------Main Program----------------------------

/str1 (Michael Spring) def
/width 700 def

gsave
-90 rotate
-792 0 translate
makecard
grestore

gsave
90 rotate
0 -612 translate
makecard
grestore

foldmarks
showpage
%%EOF
```

This algorithm is implemented in the **fittext** procedure. The command **/sf exch def** at the end of each procedure used by the **ifelse** operator replaces the old value of the scale factor with the new value. After the coordinate space has been scaled by **sf** in both directions, the string is centered around the current point by moving the current point to the left a distance equal to half the string width. The **setgray** operator, which precedes the **show** operator ensures the string is painted in black ink. Because this procedure includes scaling the coordinate space, it is bracketed by a **gsave/grestore** pair.

c. Version 3: Text with a Logo

Listing 8.3: Text With a Logo

```
%!PS-Adobe-3.0 EPSF-30.
%%BoundingBox 0 0 612 797
%%Title:(Cardex2)
%%CreationDate: (12/6/91)
%%EndComments
/Helvetica-Bold findfont 72 scalefont setfont
```

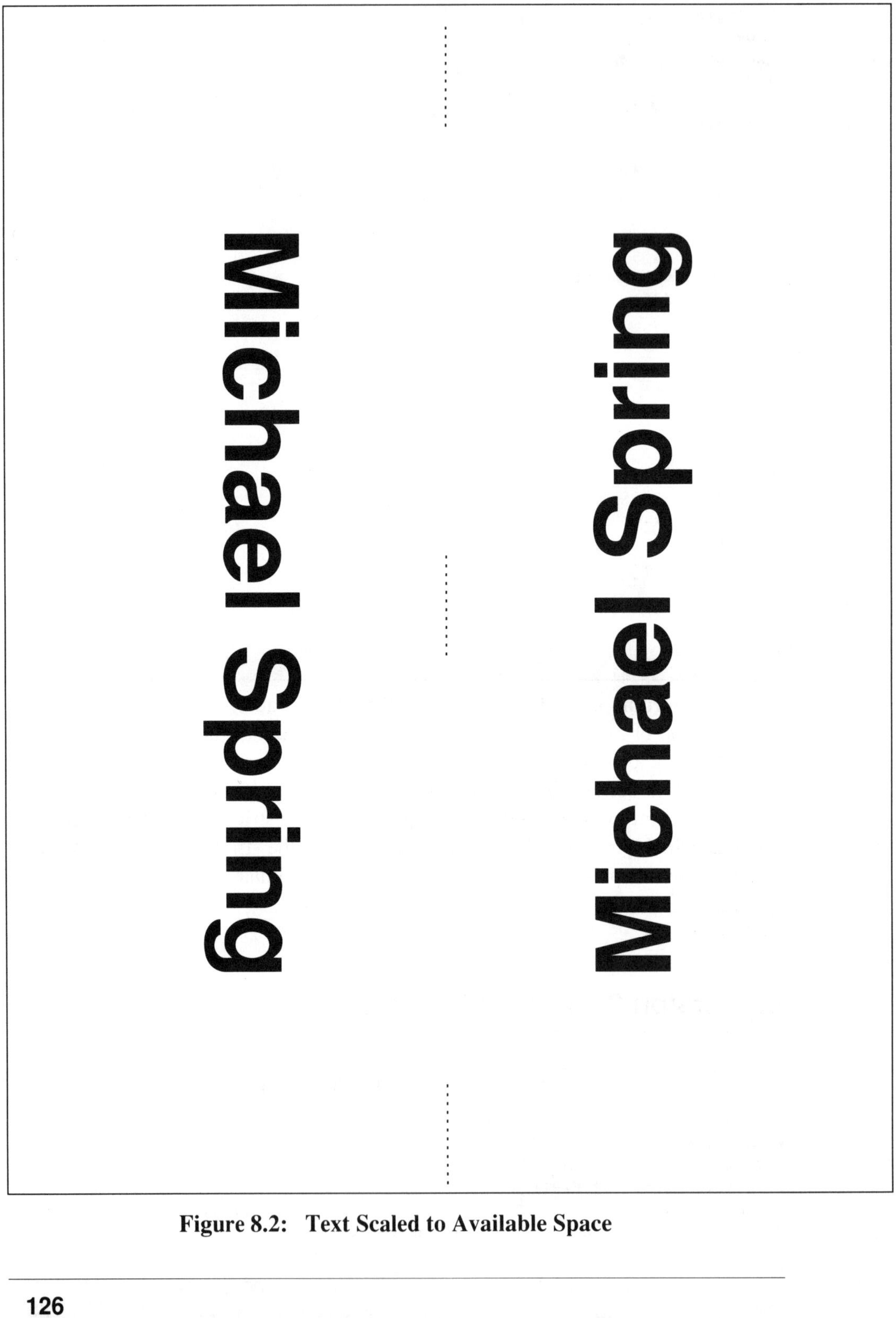

Figure 8.2: Text Scaled to Available Space

```
/str1 80 string def
%-------------------------Procedures-----------------------

/foldmarks {gsave 1 setlinewidth .5 setgray [2 4] 0 setdash
            306 0 moveto 0 72 rlineto
            306 360 moveto 0 72 rlineto
            306 720 moveto 0 72 rlineto
            stroke grestore} def

/fittext
 {
 gsave
  dup stringwidth pop width exch div /sf exch def

  sf 1 gt {sf floor /sf exch def}
         {sf 10 mul cvi 2 idiv 2 mul cvr 10 div /sf exch def} ifelse
  sf sf scale


  dup stringwidth pop 2 div neg 0 rmoveto
 0 setgray
 show
 grestore
 } def

/circle {/rad exch def
          rad 100 div setgray
          newpath 125 175 rad 0 360 arc fill} def

/makecard
 {
 500 150 moveto str1 fittext
 100 -10 1 {circle} for
  } def

%----------------------Main Program---------------------------

/str1 (Michael Spring) def
/width 500 def

gsave
-90 rotate
-792 0 translate
makecard
grestore

gsave
90 rotate
0 -612 translate
makecard
grestore

foldmarks
showpage
%%EOF
```

The third version of the program is very similar to the second. The space available (as defined by **width**) is reduced from 700 to 500, and the point around which the string is centered is moved 104 units to the right. The remainder of the new material is a procedure for drawing filled circles (**circle**) and is invoked in the **makecard** procedure. The procedure is part of a **for** loop, and each time **circle** is called, it passes the looping counter is passed as a parameter on the stack. The loop executes a total of 10 times, and so 100 is passed the first time, followed by 90, 80, 70, and so forth. The **circle** procedure sets the variable **rad** equal to the looping counter and sets the current gray level to **rad**/100. The value of **rad** is also passed to the **arc** operator as the radius of the circle. The loop draws the bull's-eye pattern depicted in Figure 8.3.

4. Problems and Modifications

The first version is awkward, because you must determine the text size and positioning coordinates by trial and error. The others are more robust, although very short strings (fewer than seven characters) end up scaled too large. An excellent modification would be to write a driver program (see Chapter 14) that can read names from a text file and produce one long PostScript program to print as many cards as there are names on the list.

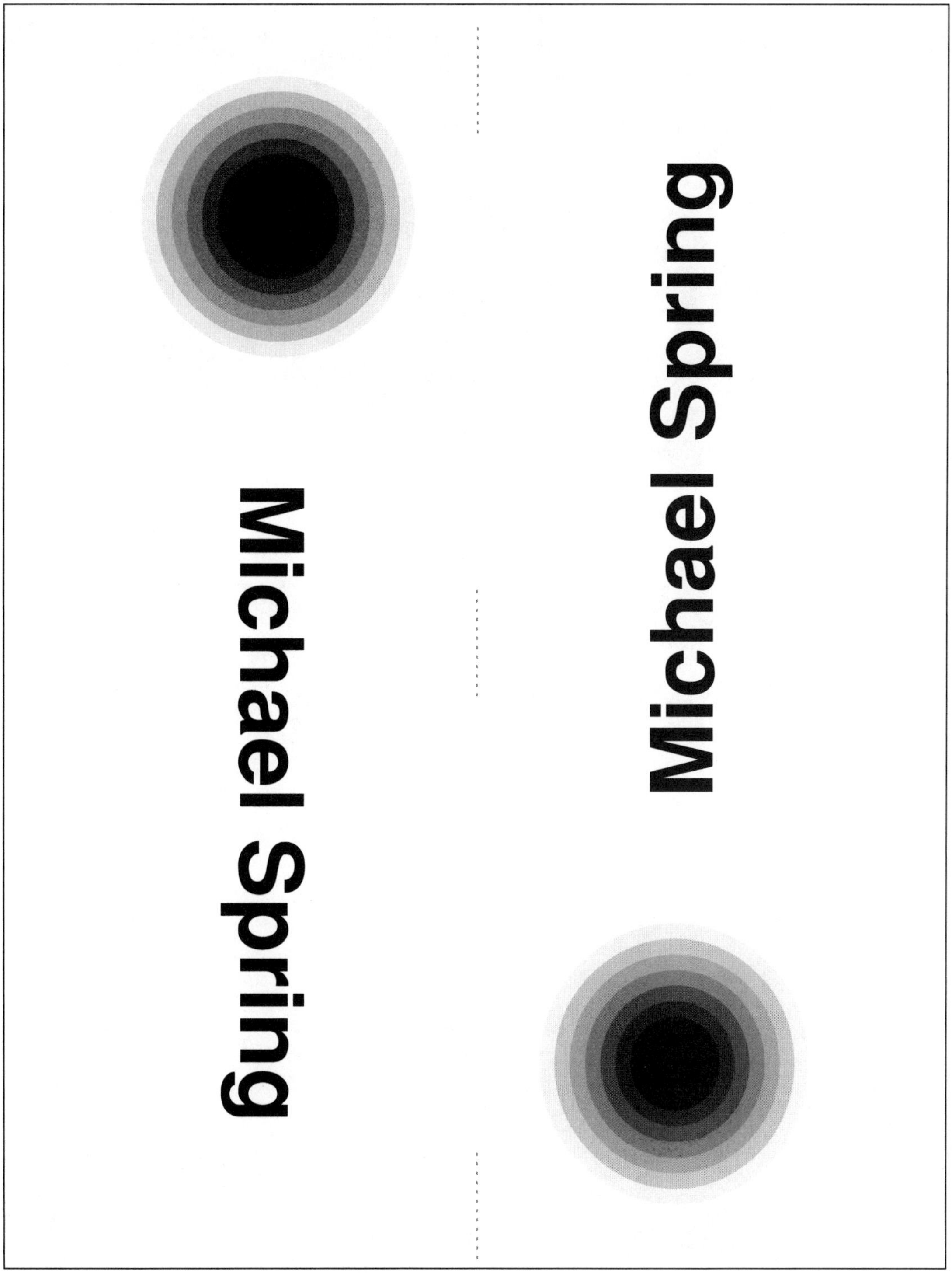

Figure 8.3: Text with a Logo

Chapter 9
Wrapping Paper

You can often use of a small piece of wrapping paper customized to the occasion and to the recipient. Similarly, there might be occasions when small pieces of wrapping paper could be tiled for a desirable effect. This chapter presents an example of using PostScript[35] to create that personalized wrapping paper.[36]

1. Objectives

This chapter will:

- Provide a PostScript program that produces personalized wrapping paper with both the occasion and person's name (or other text) that can be easily changed for any occasion or person;
- Make use of the PostScript operators;
  - **exit**
  - **kshow**
  - **loop**
  - **rotate**
  - **translate**
- Review coordinate space concepts;
- Introduce the concepts of kerning and leading.

[35]A few of the procedures in this chapter are variations of examples presented in Adobe's *PostScript Language Tutorial and Cookbook*. Specifically, it adopts the end of the line test and line spacing procedures presented in the cookbook.

[36]The wrapping paper program and chapter were developed by Roberta Pavol. Roberta has an M.S. in Information Science and consults in the business systems and desktop publishing areas.

Although the wrapping paper program itself is fairly straightforward, the concept of how the coordinate space is affected by operators such as **rotate** and **translate** can be confusing. Chapter 4 provides an introduction to the coordinate space. This program expands that introduction because it to make use a rotation to print at a 45-degree angle. Understanding how the coordinate system and the printing area are transformed helps make the process of the writing program easier.

In order to explain the PostScript code used in this example, this chapter defines the operators introduced, explains how the coordinate system can be transformed, and provides a detailed explanation of the code used in the wrapping paper PostScript program. Examining the final output, shown in Figure 9.1, should help the reader understand how to produce the final code.

2. Operator Explanations and Definitions

The operators that are used in this chapter include

- **div**
- **dup**
- **exch**
- **findfont**
- **moveto**
- **pop**
- **rotate**
- **scalefont**
- **setfont**
- **setgray**
- **show**
- **showpage**
- **sub**
- **stringwidth**
- **translate**

Check Chapter 21, if you need to review the function of these operations. The additional PostScript operators used in this program include:

loop Description: The **loop** operator repeatedly executes `proc` until the **exit** or **stop** operators are called.

Arguments: `proc`

`proc` must execute an **exit** or **stop**, or an infinite loop results.

Results: `none`

Figure 9.1: Personalized Wrapping Paper

exit

Description: This operator terminates execution of innermost loop for the procedure which contains it. Valid operator procedures for this command to be executed in are: **cshow, filnameforall, for, forall, kshow, loop, pathforall, repeat, resourceforall.**

Arguments: `none`

Results: `none`

kshow

Description: The term kshow is derived from kern-show and is designed to allow for easy kerning, or adjusting the inter-letter space. The **kshow** operator takes a procedure and a string off the stack and begins by reading the character codes in the string. It shows the first character code at the current point, updating the current point by the first character code width. It then pushes the character codes for the first and second characters onto the operand stack as integers and executes `proc`, which may perform any action but typically modifies the current point to affect the subsequent placement of the next character in the string. Basically, **kshow** operator checks for certain pairs of characters. For example, if a *T* were followed by an *o*, the *o* is kerned, or moved closer, to the *T* to give an authentic appearance.

Arguments: `proc string`

Results: `none`

3. Typesetting Concepts

The typesetting concepts of kerning and leading become more visible in this program. Understanding these two terms may help in designing a page and determining where to place the characters on a printed page.

Kerning:

To adjust the amount of space between certain pairs of characters. This can be accomplished by either increasing or decreasing the amount of space. Kerning is used primarily for purely visual or aesthetic reasons to make the text look better or to improve the text's legibility. Kerning can be either pairwise or track. Pairwise kerning adjusts the inter-letter spacing between a particular pair of letters, usually by using a table of values stored for each font. Track kerning changes the inter-letter spacing for an entire line of text relative to the point size of the font. Smaller type should be set slightly wider than normal, and large type, often called display type, should be spaced closer together.[37] The **kshow** operator addresses kerning by automatically adjusting the spacing between pairs of characters. The 10 most commonly kerned letters are

- To
- Tr
- Ta
- Yo
- YA
- WO
- WA
- P.
- TA
- PA

Leading: The distance or space between lines of text measured from baseline to baseline. This is synonymous with line spacing. This term originated from the days of metal letterpress-printing when thin strips of lead were placed between lines of type to control line spacing. At that time, leading was measured as the distance from the bottom of one line of text to the top of the next. Today, leading refers to the baseline-to-baseline distance between two lines of text.[38]

4. Coordinate Space

As discussed in Chapter 4 and shown in Figure 9.2, user space in PostScript is a grid of X and Y coordinates that continues indefinitely in all directions. The part of the page that prints, though, is contained within the following coordinate pairs: 0,0; 0,612; 612,792; and 792,0. These coordinates are the boundaries of an 8.5-by-11-inch page defined in points (72 points to an inch), and are shown as a gray box on the grid.

The command **45 rotate**, moves the coordinates you normally think of as being in the printable space. This is shown in Figure 9.3 as an unfilled box. Rotating 45 degrees counterclockwise results in more than half of page coordinates we normally think of as in the printable area being moved out of the area that will be

[37] Adobe's *PostScript Language Program Design* also provides a discussion of kerning and ligatures.

[38] Several typesetting, design, and page layout books offer descriptions of leading and the mechanics of setting type, including Adobe's *PostScript Language Program Design.*

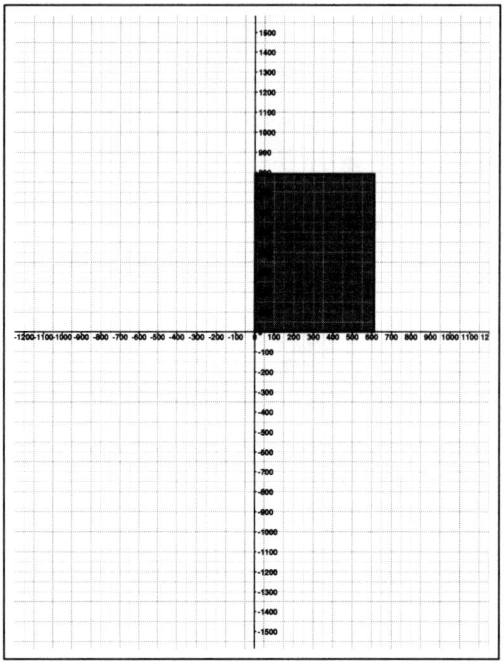

Figure 9.2: Page Coordinate System. Gray Box is Printable Page Area.

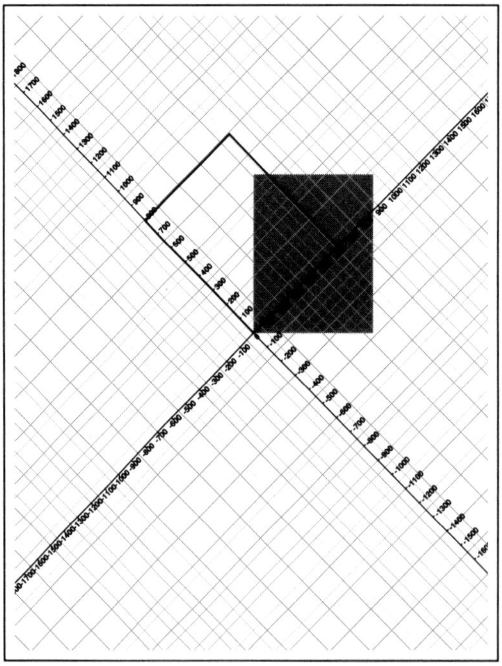

Figure 9.3: Effect on Coordinate User Space With Rotation

printed. Any objects, including text, placed in the box outside the gray printed area *will not print* when the **showpage** operator is used. Of course, we could solve our problem by simply making sure the coordinates you use are in the gray area. However, this means using both positive and negative Y coordinates.

A way to address the problem is to use the **translate** operator to move the coordinate access so the printable area is again in the positive quadrant. In this case, using **306 –350 translate** operator before the rotate moves the printable area into the positive coordinate space. Figure 9.4 now shows the origin translated to a new position and rotated so the printable area is all in the positive coordinate space.

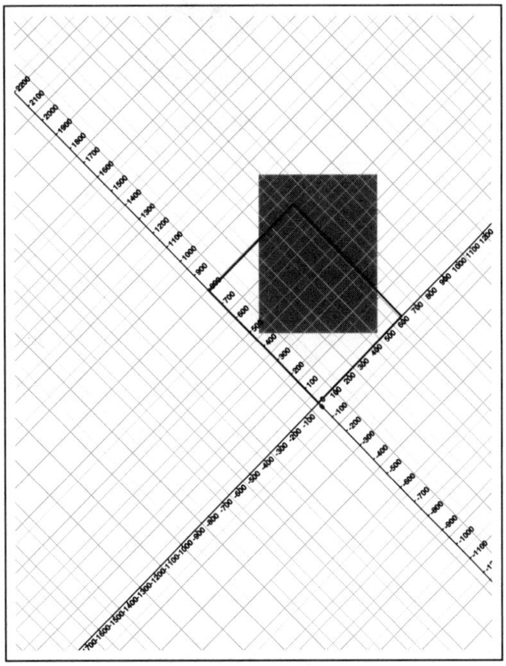

Figure 9.4: Effect on Coordinate User Space with Rotation and Translate

As you recall, rotations of 90, 180, and 270 degrees can be accompanied by a **translate** to move the printable area back to the positive quadrant easily (see Chapter 4 on page 35). Although things become more complicated when you wish to use angles other than multiples of 90 degrees, you can use such transformations to fill a page with the name and the event at a 45 degree angle to each other. As the final output of the wrapping paper shows, this creates a pleasing effect. A procedure is automatically filling the page with lines of text using automatic returns based on designated margins. You want to use a **for** loop to place the name at predetermined places on the page. An example of using the **for** operator is

```
0 10 792 {0 moveto  (Name) show} for
```

where the word “Name” appears at every 10 increments from zero to 792.

With the rotated page, to paint the name across the page by taking full advantage of the coordinate space and simply defining a larger imaging area. Do not worry about the fact that some of the text is not printed. By increasing the coordinates for the right and top margins to 1050 and 1050, the coordinate space being drawn to completely encompasses the area to be printed. The coordinate space area being drawn to in relation to the print area is shown in Figure 9.5.

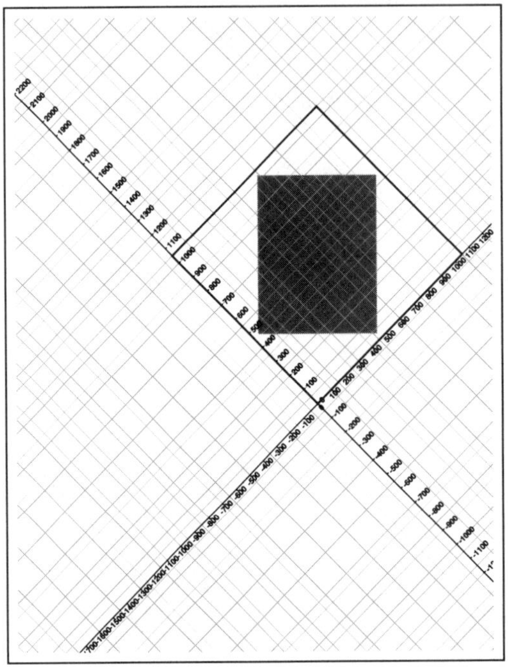

Figure 9.5: Wrapping Paper Coordinate Space/Printable Page Area

5. Program Listing Discussion

The code for the wrapping paper is shown in Listing 9.1. Its output shown in Figure 9.1 on 133. The program is split into two, practically duplicate sections to provide a clear explanation of how the text is being printed on the page. The first section fills the page with the word(s) for the occasion. This can be done within the standard margins. The second section of the program redefines the margins, translates and rotates the page, and then prints the name of the person over the occasion across the page. The page is then assembled and sent to the PostScript printer.

Listing 9.1: Listing to Produce Wrapping Paper

```
%!PS-Adobe-3.0  EPSF-30.
%%BoundingBox:  0 0 612 792
%%Title:  (Wrapping Paper)
%%Creationdate:  (10/22/91)
%%EndComments

% --------- Begin First Part of the Program --------
/TM 792 def     %Top Margin
/BM 0 def    %Bottom
/LM 0 def        %Left
/RM 612 def    %Right

/newline        %set the spacing between lines
 { currentpoint 30 sub exch pop LM exch moveto } def

/return %return linefeed
 { currentpoint pop RM gt  {newline} if } def

/done?    %stack:--- bool.
 { currentpoint exch pop BM lt } def

/fillpage            %stack: str
{ /strg exch def  {  {pop pop return} strg kshow done? {exit} if
  } loop } def

/Times-Bold findfont 20 scalefont setfont
LM TM moveto    %move to the top left margin
.8 setgray      %fill the characters with 80 percent gray
(Happy Birthday  ) fillpage

% --------- Begin Second Part of the Program --------
/TM 1050 def    %Top Margin
/BM 0 def    %Bottom
/LM 0 def        %Left
/RM 1050 def    %Right

/newline2       %set spacing between lines
  { currentpoint 80 sub exch pop LM exch moveto } def

/return2
 { currentpoint pop RM gt {newline2} if } def

/fillpage2
{ /strg exch def
   { { pop pop return2} strg kshow done? {exit} if } loop }def

/Times-Roman findfont 60 scalefont setfont
LM TM moveto    %Move to the top left corner
0 setgray       %Set the character fill to black
306 -350 translate      %Move to the right and down 350 degrees
45 rotate       %Rotate the coordinate space 45 degrees
(Jane    ) fillpage2

showpage
```

```
%%EOF
```

An examination of the code shows what is happening at each step. The first section, after the beginning comments, is:

```
/TM 792 def
/BM 0 def
/LM 0 def
/RM 612 def
```

These four lines define the page margins (top, left, right, and bottom) as literals that can be used in the program. Next, **newline** is defined to set the spacing between the lines.

```
/newline
{currentpoint 20 sub exch pop LM exch moveto} def
```

The **newline** procedure determines the X and Y coordinates of the next line of text. It takes the X and Y coordinates of the current point, pushes 20 on the stack, subtracts 20 from the Y value, and exchanges these two values on the stack (X is now on top and the remainder of the subtraction, or Y, is now under the X). The **newline** procedure then pops the top value (Y is now on top), puts the left margin (0) on the stack, exchanges the 0 (becomes the X value) with the Y value so the X value is on top and moves to new coordinate that is 20 points lower than the previous line.

```
/return
    { currentpoint pop RM gt {newline} if } def
```

The **return** procedure determines if you need to return to the beginning of the next line by calling **newline** if the right margin has been reached. Like **newline**, **return** starts with the current X and Y coordinates, pops the top value off the stack (discards the Y) so the current X position is on top of the stack, pushes the defined value for the right margin on the stack, compares it to the current X value, and puts a boolean value on the stack. If the current X value is greater than the defined value for the right margin or beyond the right edge of the page, **return** calls **newline**, which determines the new X and Y coordinates of the next line.

```
/done?
    { currentpoint exch pop BM lt } def
```

The **done?** procedure simply returns a boolean true or false if the current point is below or above the bottom margin. In terms of the stack, **done?** takes the current point, exchanges the values (X is now on top), pops the X value (Y is now on top of the stack), puts the defined value with the bottom edge of the page. If the current point is less than the bottom margin, then **done?** returns a true boolean object which stops **fillpage** from printing down the page.

```
/fillpage
  { /strg exch def
    { {pop pop return} strg kshow done? {exit} if
 } loop } def
```

The **fillpage** procedure takes a string off the stack and places it in the defined variable, **strg**. A loop starts that places a procedure and **strg** on the stack and executes **kshow**. The procedure executed between characters pops the character codes left on the stack by **kshow** off the stack and calls the **return** procedure. This continues until **done?** is true or the bottom of the page is reached.

```
/Times-Bold findfont 15 scalefont setfont
LM TM moveto
.8 setgray
(Happy Birthday   ) fillpage
```

This is the main part of the program; the previous segments defined procedures that will be called. The action here is very straightforward:

1. The font Times-Bold is called, scaled, and set to 15 point.
2. The top left corner is set as the starting point and the gray value for the text is set to .8.
3. The page is filled with the text "Happy Birthday."

A few blank spaces are inserted after the word "Birthday" in the parenthesis. Their purpose is to space the words "Happy Birthday" apart as they print across the line.

The next, or second, part of the program is simply a repeat of code from the first section.

```
/TM 1050 def
/BM 0 def
/LM 0 def
/RM 1050 def

/newline2
{ currentpoint 80 sub exch pop LM exch moveto } def

/return2
  { currentpoint pop RM gt {newline2} if } def

/fillpage2
 { /strg exch def
   { { pop pop return2} strg kshow
   done? {exit} if } loop } def

/Times-Roman findfont 60 scalefont setfont
LM TM moveto
0 setgray
306  -350 translate
45 rotate
(Jane   ) fillpage2
showpage
%%EOF
```

Here, the name of the person, celebrating the holidays is printed in larger type (60 points), on a 45 degree angle over the holiday. The differences are:

- The defined top and right margins for the coordinate user space are increased to handle the problem that occurs with coordinate rotation and translation.
- The spacing between lines increases to 80 points because the type size is now 60 points.
- The fill is set to 0, or black, for the characters.
- The origin moves to the right and down (350 –350 translate).
- The coordinate user space rotates counterclockwise 45 degrees (45 rotate).

Again, a few blank spaces are left after the person's name and the close parenthesis to put some spaces between the name as it prints across each line on the page.

The procedures remain the same but are duplicated because more leading or spacing is used between the printed lines. The type size for the name is larger than the occasion—60 versus 15—so more spacing between the lines is needed. Since 80 leading is used in printing the name, **newline2** is created that substitutes the 20 in **newline** with 80 in **newline2**. The **return2** and **fillpage2** procedures are basically the same as **return** and **fillpage**, but must call **newline2** and **return2**, respectively.

The person's name actually prints in a rotated user coordinate space that is larger than an 8.5-by-11-inch page, but the printer's print area works as a natural clipping area to trim the page. (Most laser printers have about a quarter of an inch nonprintable area around the edge of the page.)

6. Wrapping Paper Wrapup

This is one PostScript program for wrapping paper. You are encouraged to experiment with adaptations of this code to find other variations of printed wrapping paper. One important point to keep in mind: because this is a PostScript program, it can be printed on any PostScript printer, including a PostScript color printer, such as the Tektronix, NEC, or QMS. For color output, **setcolor** should be substituted for **setgray** to create colorful wrapping paper. Different combinations can be used to achieve various printed results.

Chapter 10
Greeting Card

This chapter introduces another programming project: a customized greeting card.[39] Users of graphics editors may already have experimented with the designing of personalized birthday or Christmas cards produced on an 8.5-by-11-inch sheet of paper and then folded vertically and horizontally. Creating such cards is a matter of designing two panels, one for the outside of the card and one for the inside. Typically, the outside panel is printed right side up in the lower, right hand quadrant of the page while the inside panel is printed upside down in the upper, left hand quadrant. This design produces a properly oriented card when the printed sheet is folded first horizontally (the top and bottom edges of the page meet) and then vertically (left and right edges meet).

1. Objectives

The greeting card design presented in this chapter might as easily have been designed using a drawing or painting program. However, you want to create a greeting card directly in PostScript because:

- A PostScript greeting card design can be adapted for multiple recipients and occasions simply by changing a few string constants.
- You can add sophisticated modifications through more advanced PostScript programming. You could include an image, for example, or improve the appearance of text by printing it along a path (see page 185 in Chapter 13).
- It provides an example of modular design in PostScript programming.
- It enables you to add programming "bells and whistles" the card's features:

[39]The greeting card program and chapter were developed by Kathy Vrudney.

- Painting of a border around the front panel.
- Enhancing a text string with a simple special effect (shadowing).
- Combining rotation and translation of the coordinate system to print text upside down.

2. The Use of Procedures

Like other programming languages, PostScript supports the definition of procedures. Procedures enable a program to be divided into a set of logical components or modules. Defining a procedure allows a frequently used piece of code to be execute repeatedly without being listed more than once. In PostScript, the definition of a procedure begins with the procedure name listed as a literal (i.e. preceded by a /). Following the literal name, the body of the procedure is a list of PostScript commands enclosed in curly brackets. Nowhere in the procedure definition is there a formal declaration of its parameters; arguments are passed to procedures on the operand stack, and it is the programmer's responsibility to ensure needed parameters are waiting on the stack when a procedure is invoked. It may be helpful to include a comment indicating what arguments are expected on the first line of the procedure definition. The **def** operator follows the closing curly bracket to denote the end of the procedure. Procedures are always listed before the main part of the program, because definitions must be stored in a user dictionary before they can be invoked (see Chapter 3). Procedures may be called from the main part of a program or from other procedures (as demonstrated with the procedure **clearit**). After a procedure has finished executing, control returns to the first line following the line that called the procedure.

The greeting card program has seven defined procedures. Three of them represent logical divisions of the program, and the other four are utility functions.

- **Logical divisions**

border	This procedure paints a border around the lower, right hand quadrant of the page.
front	This procedure lays down the text strings for the front panel of the card.
inside	This procedure lays down the text strings for the inside panel of the card.

- **Utility functions**

ctr	This procedure expects a string on top of the operand stack. It allows that string to

	be shown centered around the current point.
rit	This procedure is similar to **ctr**, except the string is right-justified around the current point.
shadow	This procedure expects a string on the operand stack. The string is shown in white over a gray shadow.
clearit	This utility function is defined within **border** (and thus is redefined every time **border** is invoked). Its purpose is to clear unwanted objects off the operand stack.

3. Operator Explanations

Operators used in the greeting card program include:

arcto

Description: This operator expects five arguments on the stack: four coordinate values representing two X,Y points and a distance specification representing the radius of a circle. The two points (together with the **current point**) represent a pair of intersecting line segments, each of which is tangential to a circle of the specified radius. The five arguments are removed and four coordinate values representing beginning and ending points of the the arc are placed on the stack. Also, an arc and, optionally, a straight line segment are appended to the current path. The arc starts at **(num_1, num_2)** and follows the circle's circumference between the two points of tangent, ending at **(num_3, num_4)**. If the current point is different from the first tangent point, a straight line is added to the current path from the current point to the first tangent point **(num_1, num_2)** before the arc segment is added. After the arc segment is added, the **currentpoint** is always **(num_3, num_4)**.

Arguments: **num_1 num_2 num_3 num_4 num_5**

The **currentpoint** *must be defined.* The arguments must be of type integer or real. The **currentpoint** represents the start of the first tangent line and **(num_1, num_2)** specify the end of the first tangent line. If **currentpoint** is undefined, a "nocurrentpoint" error is generated. Likewise, **(num_1, num_2)** specifies the second tangent line's start point, and **(num_3, num_4)** specifies the end point of the second tangent line. Finally, **num_5** specifies the radius of the circle in user space units. As with the **arc** operator, if scaling is specified, the shape represented in device space may not be circular.

Results: $\texttt{real}_1$ $\texttt{real}_2$ $\texttt{real}_3$ $\texttt{real}_4$

The **arcto** operator alters the **currentpath** and **currentpoint** as indicated in the description section and leaves the X and Y coordinates of the two tangent points on the stack.

repeat

Description: The **repeat** operator executes `proc` `int` times, where `int` is a non-negative number, or until the **exit** or **stop** operators are called. If the **exit** or **stop** operators are called, the **repeat** operator terminates prematurely.

Arguments: `int proc`

`proc` is a set of zero or more PostScript commands.

Results: `none`

Although **repeat** operator does not directly leave results on the stack, the procedure that is executed may alter the stack after the invocation of the **repeat** procedure has completed.

4. Explanation of the Program Listing

Listing 10.1 shows the program. A display of the output is displayed in Figure 10.1. Two comment lines, "Defined Procedures" and "Main Program," are distinguishable in the greeting card program. The labels are intended to make the procedure area and the main program area easily recognizable. A more elaborate formatting convention is introduced In Chapter 3, that includes a prologue for procedure definitions and a script constituting the main part of the program.

Listing 10.1: Greeting Card Program Listing

```
 %!PS-Adobe-3.0 EPSF-30.
%%BoundingBox: 0 0 612 792
%%Title: (Greeting Card)
%%Creationdate: (10/24/91)
%%EndComments
/Helvetica-Bold findfont
30 scalefont
setfont
%---------------------Defined Procedures----------------------

/leftm 345 def
/rightm 574 def
/centerl 462 def

/ctr {dup stringwidth pop 2 div neg 0 rmoveto} def

/rit {dup stringwidth pop neg 0 rmoveto} def

/shadow {gsave currentpoint translate
.95 -.1 0 {setgray 1 -.5 translate 0 0 moveto dup show} for
```

```
1 -.5 translate 0 0 moveto 1 setgray  show grestore} def

/border
{4 setlinewidth
    /clearit
      {4 {pop} repeat
       stroke}
     def
  334 62 moveto
  334 352 388 352 36 arcto
  clearit
  370 352 moveto
  586 352 586 298  36 arcto
  clearit
  586 320 moveto
  586 28 514 28 36 arcto
  clearit
  550 28 moveto
  334 28  334 82  36 arcto
  clearit}
def

/front
{.2 setgray
leftm 282 moveto (Birthdays) show
rightm 249 moveto (are like) rit show
centerl 216 moveto (Shadows) ctr shadow
centerl 183 moveto (they're always) ctr show
leftm 150 moveto (Coming...) show
centerl 117 moveto (or) ctr show
rightm 84 moveto (...Going) rit show
} def

/inside
 {612 792 translate
  180 rotate
  centerl 258 moveto
  .2 setgray (Fred,) ctr show
  centerl 225 moveto (I Hope the one) ctr show
  centerl 192 moveto (Shadowing) ctr shadow
  centerl 159 moveto (you is) ctr show
  centerl 126 moveto (Happy!) ctr show
}def
%--------------------Main Program------------------------------
border
front
inside
showpage
%%EOF
```

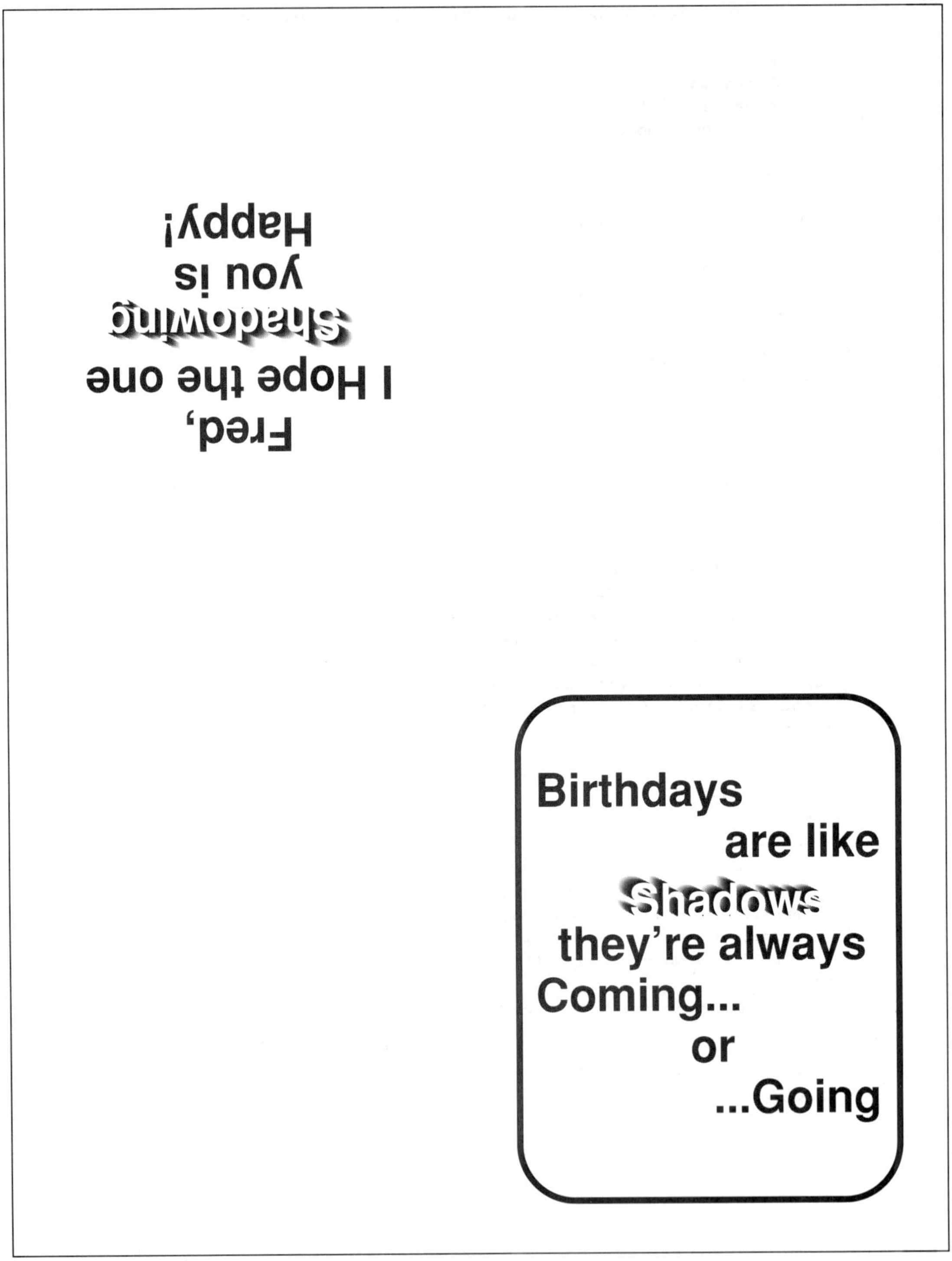

Figure 10.1: Output of Greeting Card Listing

a. General Overview

The main body of the program contains calls to each of the three major procedures (**border**, **front**, and **inside**) followed by a **showpage**. In the **border** procedure, the coordinates for the corners of the border are written directly into the code. Aided by the **clearit** procedure which disposes of extraneous objects on the stack, the **arcto** operators paint the boarder.

The **front** procedure works by moving the current point to various coordinates in the lower, right hand quadrant of the page and showing strings of text. Three utility procedures are invoked by both **front** and **inside**: the **ctr** procedure expects a string placed on the stack and that you want to show it centered around the current point. Invoking the procedure with a string on the stack moves the current point to the left a distance equaling half the length of the string. If a **show** is carried out following the **ctr** procedure, the string is shown centered around whatever point was current when the **ctr** procedure was invoked. The purpose of this utility procedure is to enable you to deal with strings relatively independent of their length. Instead of choosing a point for the left hand side of the string (based on the string length), the point for the middle of the string is designated. This makes it easier to modify the program so alternate strings can be substituted for those in the listing.

The **rit** procedure is almost identical to **ctr**, except that the current point is moved to the left the full width of the string. This positions the current point for right justification (again, independent of the string's width). The other utility procedure is **shadow**, a procedure which achieves a shadow effect for a string of text. This is accomplished by showing the string repeatedly, each showing at a slight offset from the previous, and each showing in a gradually darker shade of gray. Finally, the string is shown in white over top of the shadow.

Text in the upper left quadrant of the page must be printed upside down so it is right side up when the page is folded in half. This is accomplished by translating the origin from the lower, left corner of the page to the upper right corner of the page. The axes of the coordinate space are then rotated 180 degrees. From this point, it is possible to proceed as in the **front** procedure: X and Y coordinates are relative to a new coordinate space in which text strings are shown upside down.

b. The Procedures ctr, rit, and shadow

Both **front** and **inside** use the **ctr** and **shadow** procedures. The **ctr** procedure first works by removing the string on top of the operand stack, duplicating it, and then pushing both copies back on the stack. The **stringwidth** procedure destroys one of the copies but returns the horizontal and vertical size of the string on the stack (the vertical size of the string is unimportant and is popped off the stack immediately). What is left on the stack at this point is the string to be shown, with its horizontal size on top. The latter is divided by two (to derive a figure equal to half the string's width), and then made negative (since relative movement of the current point must be to the left). A zero is pushed over top of the halved and negated width figure and both become arguments to an **rmoveto**.

The **rit** procedure is exactly the same as **ctr**, except that the horizontal width of the string is not divided by two. Therefore, the current point is moved left by the full width of the string. Showing the string after this operation right justifies it against whatever point was current when the **rit** procedure was invoked. In the main body of the program, the constants **leftm**, **rightm**, and **centerl** are passed as parameters to both **ctr** and **rit**. These constants represent left and right margins and a center line (for a quadrant, not the whole page). They are defined at the top of the program, prior to the procedures.

The **shadow** procedure gives a text string a three-dimensional appearance. It takes a string from the operand stack and prints it several times. Each time the string is displayed, the starting position is moved slightly lower and to the right and each display is in a slightly darker shade of gray. Finally, the string is printed in white ink. The overall effect is that the string is casting a shadow.

The shadowing effect is accomplished by running a loop where, at each iteration, where the axes of the coordinate space are translated down and to the right, the gray level is decreased by a constant, and the string is duplicated and shown. After the loop finishes the axes are translated once more, the gray level is set to 1 (white ink), and the string is shown.

The first line of the **shadow** procedure contains a **gsave** and a translation of the origin to the current point. The goal is to have a base point to place the left end of the string at each iteration of the loop. The **gsave** ensures the original coordinate system can be restored at the termination of the procedure. The second line of the procedure is the loop for drawing the shadow. The first operator within the curly brackets is **setgray**, because the looping variable (always equal to the desired gray level) is pushed on the stack at each iteration of the **for** loop. Each time through the loop, the axes are translated 1 point to the right and half a point down, the current point moves to 0,0 (relative to the new origin), the string duplicates, and one copy is shown. The last line of the procedure does one more translation and movement, sets the gray level to 1, shows the string in white ink, and **grestore** restores the original coordinate system.

c. Border Procedure

The **border** procedure draws the border when called from the main program. It has a nested procedure called **clearit**. The first line in **border** sets the line width to 4/72 of an inch with the **setlinewidth** operator. The next four lines are the **clearit** procedure. The first line after the procedure definition moves the current point to 334,62. The seventh line pushes 334 and 352 onto the stack, which is the end point of the first line. The second point— 388, 352—is pushed on to the stack. Finally, 36 the radius of the curve to be drawn, is pushed on the stack. The operator in the seventh line is **arcto**, which determines the path to be drawn by removing the radius (36) and leaving the following four numbers on the stack: 352 (top), 388, 352, 334 (bottom). **Clearit** is called in the eighth line and clears the two points (four numbers) that are left on the stack. At this point, the upper left corner of the border is drawn.

Each following group of operators (**moveto**, **arcto**, **clearit**) does exactly the same as these three lines we just described. However, the coordinates are changed to continue drawing the other four corners of the border correctly.

d. Clearit Procedure

The **clearit** procedure is nested within **border** and called from within to make sure that the stack is clear before the next **arcto** is issued. The first line in **clearit** pops the top 4 elements off the stack. These are the four numbers left on the stack after the arcto operator is executed as explained in the **border** procedure above. The second line of **clearit** strokes the path the **arcto** operator designates.

e. Front Procedure

The **front** procedure places text strings in the lower right quadrant of the page (the front panel of the card). The first line of the **front** procedure sets the graphics state to a .2 gray level. The next seven lines each move to a specified point (employing defined constants for the X values) and display a string. The two left-justified strings are simply shown at the defined left margin for the panel. The centered strings are shown after the current point is moved to the centering point and the **ctr** procedure is invoked to move the current point to the left. Likewise, the right-justified strings are shown after the current point is moved to the right margin of the panel and the **rit** procedure moves the current point to the left. One of the lines is displayed using the **shadow** command rather than **show** to achieve the shadow effect.

f. Inside Procedure

The **inside** procedure is very much like the **front** procedure in that strings are displayed sequentially in a panel. The main difference between **front** and **inside** is that the latter procedure must print the strings upside down so they appear right-side-up when the card is folded. This effect easily can be accomplished by translating the origin and rotating the axes of the coordinate space. As a beneficial side effect, the new user space will enable you to reuse the margin and center line constants without redefining them.

The first line of the **inside** procedure translates the origin to 612, 792, which puts it in the upper right corner of the printable page area. The second line rotates the axes counterclockwise 180 degrees. In this new coordinate space, of positive coordinates for X and Y result in areas on the printable page area, but it is as if the page were turned upside-down relative to the previous coordinate space. The upshot is that by printing normally in what is now the "lower right quadrant" we are actually printing upside down in what had been the upper left quadrant of the page. This means the margin constants defined earlier can be reused for centering, left, and right justification without being redefined! As shown in the listing, the coordinates used to print the inside panel text are very close to those used for the outside panel text.

g. The Main Program

The main program simply calls the three main procedures in sequence (**border**, **inside**, **outside**). Structuring the program as a collection of independent modules makes it much easier to understand and modify the code.

5. Changing or Adding to the Design

There are a number of ways to improve the greeting card:

- You can change the string constants to adapt the card for different recipients and different occasions.
- You can select different fonts and experiment with the centering and justification procedures to arrange the text in different ways.
- Special effects, such as writing in a circle, can be incorporated into this card for even more dramatic effects (see Chapter 13 on page 185)
- A greeting card can even incorporate a scanned image.

Chapter 11
Keyboard Templates

This chapter describes a program to produce keyboard templates, e.g. telephone speed dial buttons, TV direct turning buttons, etc.[40] Many software packages such as Borland's QUATTRO® PRO enable you to define each of the function keys. The only problem is that it is sometimes hard to remember what meaning you assigned. This sample program provides a way of producing a template for whatever function keys you define and for whatever keyboard you use. The tool also enables programmers who produce software to make professional-looking templates for their own software.

Specifically, this project presents a PostScript program to produce keyboard templates for a laptop computer. How you can modify the program to produce templates for a variety of other uses is also presented.

1. Objectives

The objectives of this chapter are:

- To provide a function key template program that can be modified to produce an appropriate template for a variety of situations and keyboard layouts.
- To present some new PostScript operators and to provide increased familiarity of some operators that have been introduced in previous chapters. The operators important to this program include
    - **add**
    - **mul**
    - **neg**

[40]The template program and chapter were developed by Molly Sorrows. Molly's main research area is medical information systems.

- **ifelse**
- **rlineto**
- **exch**

2. Command Explanations

The operators introduced in this chapter include:

add

Description: This operator expects two numbers on the stack. They are removed and their sum is pushed onto the stack.

Arguments: `num`$_1$ `num`$_2$

`num`$_1$ and `num`$_2$ may be either integers or real number objects.

Results: `num`

The **add** operator function returns a number of type real or integer which represents the mathematical sum of the two arguments. The type is determined to be integer only if both arguments are of type integer and the result is within the range of representable integers for the PostScript interpreter. A type of real is assigned to the result if both conditions are not met, and some loss in the result's precision may occur.

closepath

Description: This operator does not use any arguments or push any results onto the stack. It is intended to provide an easy way to append a straight line segment to the current path from the current point to the point that represents the start of the current subpath. (This is especially helpful when drawing Bézier curves and arcs, where the required line segment can be tedious to calculate.)

Arguments: `none`

Results: `none`

Note that **closepath** operator terminates the current subpath. Any operator that appends to the current path begins a new subpath. If the current subpath is already closed or the current path is empty, **closepath** operator does nothing.

mul

Description: This operator expects two numbers onto the stack. They are removed and the result of multiplying the two is pushed onto the stack.

Arguments: `num`$_1$ `num`$_2$

`num`$_1$ and `num`$_2$ may be either integers or real number objects.

Results: `real`

The **mul** operator function returns a number of type integer only if both operands are integers and the result is within the representable bounds of an integer for the current PostScript interpreter.

3. Explanation of the Keyboard Template Listing

The keyboard template program is divided into three main sections. The first section contains the definition of the lookup values used in the program. The second section defines the procedures in the prologue, and the third section is the script of the program where the template is actually drawn and text placed on the page. The third section makes the program quite large; however, it is straightforward and repetitive because it draws the key and places the text on the key for each of the function keys on the template.

It is frequently difficult to get software templates that match the keyboard, especially for laptop computers. This problem is caused by the differences in key sizes and the placement of keys on the small laptop keyboards. The keyboard template program consists of calculating the correct places where keys should be drawn to correspond to the keyboard and placing the correct text in each of the keys.

The listing for the laptop keyboard template program is displayed in Listing 11.1, and its output appears in Figure 11.1. This version prints a template for WordPerfect[41] to match the keyboard layout on the Toshiba 1000LE laptop computer.

Listing 11.1: A Laptop Keyboard Template

```
%!PS-Adobe-3.0 EPSF-30.
%%BoundingBox: 0 0 612 792
%%Title: (Keyboard Template, example 2)
%%EndComments

%----- Definition of lookup values -----

/inch {72 mul} def
/kw .75 inch def                        % key width measured from keyboard
/kh .80  inch def                   % key height measured from keyboard
/kx .40 inch def
/ky .50 inch def
/ptsizek 9 def
/textsp 1.10 def
/numb 13 def


%----- Define procedures for drawing keys and printing text -----
```

[41]WordPerfect is a Registered Trademark of WordPerfect, Inc.

```
/draw_key {kx ky moveto 0 kh rlineto kw 0 rlineto 0 kh neg rlineto
           closepath stroke} def

/sel_key_text
      {dup 1 eq
         {/Times-Bold findfont ptsizek scalefont setfont put_key_text}
         { dup 2 eq
             {/Times-Italic findfont ptsizek scalefont setfont put_key_text}
             {/Times-Roman findfont ptsizek scalefont setfont put_key_text}
          ifelse}
       ifelse} def

/put_key_text { ky kh add exch textsp ptsizek mul mul sub
               kw 10 div kx add exch moveto show} def

/draw_box {kx .10 inch sub  ky .10 inch sub moveto
            kw numb mul .10 inch 2 mul add 0  rlineto
            0 kh .10 inch 2 mul add rlineto
            kw numb mul .10 inch 2 mul add neg 0 rlineto
            closepath
            stroke
          } def

%----- Draw template and text -----

-90 rotate              % draw on landscape page
-792 0 translate

1 setlinewidth          % thick line for outer box

draw_box                % draw the outer box

.5 setlinewidth                 % use thin line for key outlines

draw_key                % draw key outline starting at current point

(Shell) 1 sel_key_text  % place lines of text on key
(Thesaurus)  2 sel_key_text
(SETUP)  3 sel_key_text
(Cancel)  4 sel_key_text
(F1)  5 sel_key_text
/kx kx kw add def       % change the starting point for next key

draw_key
(Spell)  1 sel_key_text
(Replace) 2 sel_key_text
(B. SEARCH)  3 sel_key_text
(F. Search)  4 sel_key_text
(F2) 5 sel_key_text
/kx kx kw add def

draw_key
(Screen)  1 sel_key_text
(RevealCodes) 2 sel_key_text
(SWITCH) 3 sel_key_text
(Help)  4 sel_key_text
(F3)  5 sel_key_text
```

```
/kx kx kw add def

draw_key
(Move) 1 sel_key_text
(Block) 2 sel_key_text
(INDENT) 3 sel_key_text
(Indent) 4 sel_key_text
(F4) 5 sel_key_text
/kx kx kw add def

draw_key
(Text In/Out)  1 sel_key_text
(Mark Text)  2 sel_key_text
(DATE)  3 sel_key_text
(List Files)  4 sel_key_text
(F5)  5 sel_key_text
/kx kx kw add def


draw_key
(Tab Align) 1 sel_key_text
(Flush Right)  2 sel_key_text
(CENTER) 3 sel_key_text
(Bold) 4 sel_key_text
(F6)  5 sel_key_text
/kx kx kw add def

draw_key
(Footnote)  1 sel_key_text
(Math/Col.)  2 sel_key_text
(PRINT) 3 sel_key_text
(Exit)  4 sel_key_text
(F7)  5 sel_key_text
/kx kx kw add def

draw_key
(Font)  1 sel_key_text
(Style)  2 sel_key_text
(FORMAT) 3 sel_key_text
(Underline) 4 sel_key_text
(F8)  5 sel_key_text
/kx kx kw add def

draw_key
(Merge/Sort)  1 sel_key_text
(Graphics)  2 sel_key_text
(M. CODES)  3 sel_key_text
(Merge R)  4 sel_key_text
(F9) 5 sel_key_text
/kx kx kw add def

draw_key
(Macro Def.) 1 sel_key_text
(Macro)  2 sel_key_text
(RETRIEVE) 3 sel_key_text
(Save)  4 sel_key_text
(F10) 5 sel_key_text
```

```
/kx kx kw add def

draw_key
(RevealCodes)  4 sel_key_text
(F11)  5 sel_key_text
/kx kx kw add def

draw_key
(Block)  4 sel_key_text
(F12)  5 sel_key_text
/kx kx kw add def

(Ctrl)  1 sel_key_text
(Alt)  2 sel_key_text
(SHIFT)  3 sel_key_text

showpage
%%EOF
```

a. Initial definitions

The first section of the program contains the definitions of lookup values which are used throughout the program.

1. The first line defines an "inch." The procedure is **72 mul** and it converts points to inches. **72 mul** is placed with definitions rather than procedures because it is used in the definition of other lookup values. Because users are often more comfortable using inches than points, this provides the simple conversion.[42]

2. The next two lines define the width and height of each key. The key used in the example was three-fourths of an inch wide so **/kw .75 div inch def**. The **inch**, which was defined in the first line causes 72 to be placed onto the stack and multiplied by .75. The product of these two is placed back onto the stack. The operator **def** then defines **kw** as that result.

3. The key height **kh** is defined in the same manner as the key width. The literal /**kh** is placed on the stack followed by .80. The height in inches, .80, is converted to points by multiplying by 72. This final result is pushed onto the stack and assigned to **kh** by **def**.

4. The variables **kx** and **ky** are X and Y coordinates for the current key which is being drawn on the page. They are incremented during the program as each key is drawn and are used with the key width and height, **kw** and **kh**, to define each key. The last lookup value definitions are related to the text that is printed on the template.

[42]There are 72 points per inch, so multiplying a given number of inches by 72 gives the equivalent value in points.

Key	Ctrl	*Alt*	SHIFT	(unshifted)
F1	**Shell**	*Thesaurus*	SETUP	Cancel
F2	**Spell**	*Replace*	B. SEARCH	F. Search
F3	**Screen**	*RevealCodes*	SWITCH	Help
F4	**Move**	*Block*	INDENT	Indent
F5	**Text In/Out**	*Mark Text*	DATE	List Files
F6	**Tab Align**	*Flush Right*	CENTER	Bold
F7	**Footnote**	*Math/Col.*	PRINT	Exit
F8	**Font**	*Style*	FORMAT	Underline
F9	**Merge/Sort**	*Graphics*	M. CODES	Merge R
F10	**Macro Def.**	*Macro*	RETRIEVE	Save
F11				RevealCodes
F12				Block

Ctrl
Alt
SHIFT

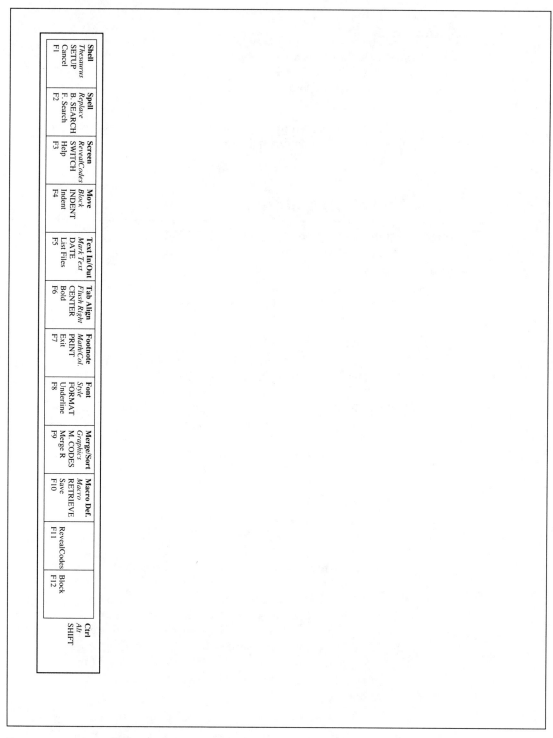

Figure 11.1: A Laptop Keyboard Template

5. The variable **ptsizek** is the point size for text that is printed on the template.
6. The variable **textsp** is used to determine the line spacing between lines of text, and it is value, 1.1, corresponding to 110 percent, is later multiplied by the point size so the text from two lines do not overlap.
7. The variable **numb** is the number of keys you define. This determines the size of the outer enclosing box.

b. Definition of procedures

The next section of the program defines four procedures: two that draw boxes for the keys and the template, and two that work to place text on the template. The first procedure draws a single key.

1. The **draw_box** procedure draws the outer box of the template with a 1/10-inch margin around the outlined set of keys.
    - The first line moves the current point to the bottom left corner of the outer box that is drawn.
        - **kx** pushes the value of **kx** (28.8 points) onto the stack.
        - The value **.10** is pushed onto the stack.
        - The **inch** procedure is defined as **{72 mul}**. When **inch** is executed, 72 is pushed on the stack, and then 72 is multiplied by the next value on the stack, .10. The result, 7.2 is placed onto the stack.
        - The **sub** operator subtracts 7.2 from the value of **kx**, and the result, 21.6 points, is pushed onto the stack.
        - The **ky** procedure pushes the value of **ky** (36 points) onto the stack.
        - The value **.10** is pushed onto the stack. Again, **inch** is executed, multiplying .10 by 72, and pushes 7.2 on to the stack.
        - The **sub** operator subtracts 7.2 from the value of **ky**, and the result, 28.8, is pushed onto the stack.
        - The operator **moveto** removes the top two values from the stack, then uses the first as the Y value and the second as the X value of the coordinates to place the current point at the new position. This places the current point 1/10 inch down and 1/10 inch to the left of the bottom left corner where the first key outline will be drawn.
    - The next line executes an **rlineto** to the bottom right corner of the outer box. There is space for **nbox = 13** keys inside the box, plus the 1/10-inch margin on each side.

- The value of **kw** is pushed onto the stack. **nbox** is pushed on to the stack. **mul** multiplies **kw**, the key width, by **nbox**, the number of keys there are space for on the template.
- The command **.10 inch 2 mul add** multiplies the 1/10-inch margin by two because there is a margin on each side. The **add** operator pushes the sum of the margin width and total key width onto the stack. This is the relative X position that is used for the **rlineto** operator.
- Next, 0 is pushed onto the stack. The **rlineto** operator is executed, moving the current point 0 units in the Y direction relative to the current point, and moving in the X direction the relative amount calculated above. The **rlineto** operator appends this section of path to the current path.

- The next line calculates the movement from the current point at the bottom right corner of the box to the upper right corner.
  - First, 0 is pushed on the stack. This is used as the relative amount to move in the X direction.
  - Next, **kh .10 inch 2 mul add** calculates the relative movement for the Y direction. Then **kh** is pushed onto the stack. The 1/10-inch size is multiplied by two because there is a top and bottom margin. The **add** operator adds the margin size to **kh**, the key height, to determine the relative Y position.
  - Next, **rlineto** moves 0 in the X direction, and the calculated amount in the Y direction and this section of path is appended to the current path.

- The next line calculates the movement from the current point at the top right corner of the box to the top left corner of the box. This requires no movement in the Y direction. In the X direction, the calculation is the same as for the first line segment, but the movement is in the opposite direction.
  - The first part of the line, **kw nbox mul .10 inch 2 mul add**, calculates the total width of the box which is being traced.
  - The operator **neg** takes the value from the top of the stack, the width of the box, and replaces it with –1 multiplied by the value. Then 0 is pushed on the stack. The **rlineto** operator moves 0 units relative to the current point in the Y direction, and moves the width of the box in the negative X direction. It appends this segment of path to the current path.

- The last lines of the procedure finish determining the path and trace the path using the current line width and set gray values.

- First, **closepath** adds the path segment from the current point at the top left corner of the box to the starting point of the current path, which was the bottom left corner of the box, to the current path.
- The **stroke** operator draws a line using the current line width and set gray or set color values to follow the current path.

2. The **draw_key** procedure assumes that **kx** and **ky** are defined and equal the bottom left corner of the box. This procedure uses the **rlineto** operator to move from the current point to each of the corners of the box will represent a key. Remember, the **rlineto** operator moves relative to the present current point.

   - **kx** and **ky** are pushed onto the stack and the **moveto** operator is executed.

   - Then, 0 is pushed onto the stack, followed by **kh**. The **rlineto** operator removes **kh** as Y and 0 as X from the stack and moves relative to the current point. Starting at the bottom left corner of the box, the first **rlineto** then moves 0 points in the X direction and **kh**, the key height, in the Y direction to form the path for the left side of the box.

   - **kw** is pushed onto the stack, followed by 0. The **rlineto** operator removes the **kw** and 0 from the stack and moves **kw**, the width of the key in the X direction, and 0 in the Y direction, to form the top of the box.

   - To form the right hand side of the box going from the top to the bottom, there is no change in the X direction, and **kh neg**, negative key height, is the relative change in the Y direction.

   - The **closepath** operator adds the section between that last point and the start of the path at the bottom left corner of the box to the current path.

   - The **stroke** operator causes that current path to be drawn.

3. The **sel_key_text** procedure determines the font to be used for the text through two nested **ifelse** operators, and then calls the **put_key_text** procedure to find the correct location for the line of text and display the text. A sample call helps show what happens when the **sel_key_text** procedure is executed; it should be clear how these procedures would work with different values. The sample line of code for this example is: **(Any Text) 2 sel_key_text**. First (Any Text) is pushed onto the stack, then the value 2 is pushed onto the stack:

`2`
`(Any Text)`

Executing **sel_key_text** does the following:

- The 2 on top of the stack indicates the line number of the text to be written on the key. The **dup** operator duplicates the 2 on top of the stack, so there are two of them. The top one is used for a boolean comparison.
- Next, 1 is pushed onto the top of the stack. The operator **eq** removes two numbers from the stack, in this case 1 and 2, and places the value **true** on the stack if they are equal, and **false** if they are not. In this example, it places **false** on the stack.
- Two procedures are pushed onto the stack.
- The **ifelse** operator removes the boolean and two procedures from the stack and causes the first procedure to be executed if the value on the stack is **true**; otherwise, the second procedure is executed. In this case the value on top of the stack is **false**, so the second procedure is executed.
- The operator **dup** duplicates the 2 that is once again on top of the stack. The top one is used for a boolean comparison.
- Next, **2** pushes the number two onto the top of the stack. The operator **eq** removes two numbers from the stack, now 2 and 2, and then places a value of **true** back onto the stack because the two numbers are equal.
- Two procedures are pushed onto the stack.
- The **ifelse** operator pops the two procedures and the boolean. The first procedure is executed this time, because the stack holds a value of true.
- The command /**Times-Italic** pushes the name of the Times-Italic dictionary onto the stack. The **findfont** operator removes that name and pushes the dictionary onto the stack. Executing **ptsizek** pushes the point size for key text, which was defined as 9, onto the stack. The **scalefont** operator scales the dictionary to 9-point, and the **setfont** operator makes 9-point Times-Italic the current font.
- At this point, the stack again appears exactly as it did when you started and is now executed.

4. The **put_key_text** procedure places the text, using the font already selected, at the appropriate place.
   - First, the value of **ky** is placed on top of the stack.
   - Executing **kh** pushes the value of kh, 58.5, onto the stack. The **add** operator removes the top two numbers **kh** and **ky**, from the stack, and places their sum back on the stack. This result is

the absolute Y position of the top of the key, which is used later to calculate where to place the text.

- The **exch** operator exchanges the top two elements on the stack so the value 2 is on top of the stack and the second element from the top is the sum of **kh** and **ky**.
- Executing **textsp** pushes the value of textsp, the text spacing (1.10), onto the stack.
- Executing **ptsizek** pushes the point size for key text (9) onto the stack.
- The **mul** operator multiplies **ptsizek** by **textsp** to give the number of points for spacing the text on the key.
- The next **mul** operator multiplies that value for the spacing by the next item down on the stack, which is the line number (in this case, 2). This result gives the number of points down from the top of the key to place the text. This result is on top of the stack, and the item below it is the sum of **kh** and **ky**.
- The **sub** operator removes the top two numbers from the stack and subtracts the top item from the one that was below it. The number of points to move down is subtracted from the position top of the keys giving the absolute Y position where the text should be printed. Now this Y position is on top of the stack. The next item down on the stack is the value of **kx**, and below that is still the actual text to be displayed—in this case, (Any Text).
- The value **kx** is on top of the stack.
- Executing **kw** pushes the value of kw onto the stack. Next, 10 is pushed onto the stack.
- The **div** operator divides the top item on the stack into the second item from the top—in this case, 10 into **kw**. The result is one-tenth of the key width.
- Executing **add** adds **kx** and one-tenth the key width. The variable **kx** is the absolute X position of the key, so the result gives a small margin inside the key and is the X position where the text will be written.
- The stack contains the X position where the text will be written on top of the stack and the Y position as the second item on the stack.
- The **exch** operator exchanges the top two items on the stack so the Y position is on top.
- Executing **moveto** removes the Y position and then the X

position from the stack, and moves the current point to those coordinates.

- The **show** operator removes the value **Any Text** from the stack and prints **Any Text** starting at the current point.

c. Main Program

The final section of the program, although long, is straightforward.

- The coordinate system is rotated and translated. This sets the page to a landscape orientation. The **–90 rotate** rotates the page in the space, and **–792 0 translate** sets the coordinates so the origin (0,0) is at the bottom left corner of the landscape page.
- Executing **1 setlinewidth** sets the thickness of lines the **stroke** operator draws.
- The **draw_box** procedure, as described in the previous section, draws the outer rectangular box of the template using definitions **kx**, **ky**, and **nbox**.
- Executing **.5 setlinewidth** specifies a thinner line to be drawn.
- The **draw_key** procedure, as described above, draws the outline of a key starting with **kx** and **ky** as the bottom left corner of the key.
- The line **(Shell) 1 sel_key_text** executes the **sel_key_text** procedure as described above. The items (Shell) and 1 are placed onto the stack. The **sel_key_text** procedure is executed, which executes a **dup** operator on line number (1), and determines the font for that line of text. Then it executes the **put_key_text** procedure, which finds the correct position for the text based on line number (1), and **kx**, and **ky**.
- The next four lines perform the same action to print lines (2) through (5) of text on the key outline for the first key. At this point, one key outline has been drawn on the template with five lines of text.
- The next line, **/kx kx kw add def**, changes the definition of **kx**, the X coordinate for the bottom left corner of the current key outline, so **kx** is defined as the X coordinate for the bottom left corner of the next key outline to be drawn to the right—that is, the current X position plus the key width (**kx + kw**). **/kx** pushes the literal, **kx**, onto the stack. Then the value of **kx** is pushed onto the stack. Next the value of kw is pushed on the stack. The **add** operator adds the values of **kx** and **kw**, and pushes the result on the stack. Then **def** is executed, which defines the literal, **kx**, as the result which was placed on the stack.

The previous items are repeated for each key outline drawn and for the text which is placed on the template. This is a little cumbersome, but it is done this way instead of in a loop so the contents of the stack remain relatively simple.

Looking at the very end of the program listing, the four lines of code starting six lines up from the bottom are slightly different from the previous blocks of code. These four lines leave out the **draw_key** procedure. This is because this does not correspond to a key; rather, it gives instruction about the use of the other keys. In looking at the output of the program, notice the text Ctrl, Alt and Shift do not have a key outline around them.

At the very bottom of the listing is the final operator, **showpage**. Remember, nothing is be printed on the page until the **showpage** operator is executed.

4. Suggestions for Modification

The easiest modification to this program is to change the text printed on the keys to match a different software program. This merely consist of editing the PostScript file and changing each of the text values.

A fairly simple modification is to adjust the program for a different computer keyboard. Many keyboards, such as the basic AT style keyboard, have 12 function keys, in three sections of four keys each. One way to accommodate this difference is to define a literal value such as smallgap to be the size of the gap between the sections of keys. Then, place an additional statement, which defines the current **kx** as **kx** plus the value of **smallgap—/kx kx smallgap add def**, between the appropriate blocks of code, such as between the sections for key numbers 4 and 5. Be sure to keep the statement that adds the key width, because you always need to move at least that much or your keys overlap.

With some thought, this program can be modified to make a template for the block of function keys found on the left hand side of some keyboards. This involves changing both the kx and ky values as the keys are drawn, and might best be done by drawing the left column of keys and then using a **translate** operator to move the coordinate axes to the right column before drawing that set.

This program could be modified to produce templates for any type of keypad. For example, it could be used to make a template for telephones with buttons for different programmed telephone numbers or even the keypad on a microwave oven.

Chapter 12
Christmas Ornament

This chapter introduces a program that produces a Christmas tree ornament.[43] The program is presented in three stages, each demonstrating features of the language and illustrating how they are used. This chapter makes extensive use of procedure definitions as a way of structuring PostScript. In the programs, 90 percent or more of the program lines are definitions. The action, or drawing the ornament is left to the last few lines. Indeed, by most accounts the program is overdefined, but it helps us make our point.

1. Objectives

The objectives of this chapter are:

- To use procedures in PostScript.
- To provide an ornament program that can be adapted for personal use.
- To demonstrate drawing circles, drawing groups of lines, stack manipulation, and axes manipulation.

2. Operator Explanations

These programs move around the page and lay down lines, arcs, and text. In some cases, manipulations are done before anything is laid down. The following sections give a summary of the PostScript operators used in the three programs:

[43]The ornament program and chapter were developed by Jeff Deppen.

a. A Bulb

This first program simply draws a bulb used for decorating a Christmas tree. The program uses only eight PostScript operators to draw the necessary circle, square, and semicircle. Most PostScript operators used in this program have been explained in earlier chapters. For complete descriptions of all of them see Chapter 21. A brief summary of how some operators participate in these programs follows:

This program uses **arc** to draw the Christmas bulb as well as the hoop on top of the bulb. The **def** operator minimizes the need for identical blocks of code in the program and to allow for easier visualization of the program's action. This program uses **moveto** to move the current point around the page in order to draw a square and **rlineto** to create the path that draws a square.

The **setgrey** operator is used to set the grey value for the arcs, lines, and the color of the square and the **stroke** operator is used to paint the path constructed by the **rlineto** operator. The fill operator is the only new operator introduced in this first program. It is used to paint the square.

fill

Description: The **fill** operator command paints the area enclosed by the current path with the current shade of gray. If the path is not closed, the **fill** command closes any portions of the current path that are open.

Arguments: `none`

Results: `none`

b. Two Christmas Tree Bulbs

The second program draws two Christmas tree bulbs opposite one another and a horizontal dashed line across the page, where the page will be folded. In addition to using all of the first program, the second program introduces five more PostScript operators. The **gsave** and **grestore** operators enable a program to capture and then later restore a captured graphics state. The **gsave/grestore** operators are very useful when used in conjunction with either the **rotate** or **translate** operators.

This program uses **gsave** to capture the graphics state before the execution of the **translate** and **rotate** operators and **grestore** to restore the original origin with no rotation.

This program uses **rotate** in conjunction with **translate** to draw the second Christmas bulb above the first bulb. The program also uses **translate** to move the origin from the lower left corner of the page to the upper right corner. The program uses **setdash** to draw the fold line. It is the only new operator introduced in this part of the program.

setdash Description: This operator expects an array and a number on the stack. They are removed and their sum is pushed onto the stack.

Arguments: `array, offset`

The top value on the stack is the offset into the dash pattern used for each line.[44] The second value is given as an array (placed between [ ]), and it sets the dash pattern as simply the length, in points, of the dash and the gap between the dashes.[45] Once setdash is executed, all lines drawn are in the same dashed pattern until **setdash** operator is explicitly reset.

Results: `none`

c. Complete Christmas Tree Bulb

Finally, the third program provides a complete Christmas tree bulb. Both sides of the bulb are drawn along with a person's name on one side and the words "Merry Christmas" with a drawing of a Christmas tree on the other side. The third program slightly modifies the second program and also introduces seven more PostScript operators. These operators, are used primarily to scale text and graphics. The operators used in this final program were all introduced in earlier chapters; see Chapter 21, for complete descriptions of the operators.

In this program, **div** is used to determine the appropriate horizontal scaling factor. The program uses **exch** to swap operands before division so the correct scaling factor is determined.

The **dup** operator duplicates the person's name so that the **stringwidth** operator has a copy of the name to measure. The **stringwidth** operator is used to calculate the horizontal width of the string; the vertical dimension is discarded. This program uses **pop** to remove the Y value returned by executing **stringwidth**.

The program uses **scale** to either expand or contract the scale so the person's name fits inside the bulb. It is also used to enlarge the drawing of the Christmas tree.

---

[44]For example, if the pattern is followed by a space of 10 and an offset of three, it starts with a dash of seven.

[45]The array you use may be longer than two. For example, the array [2 2 10 2 5 15] sets the dash pattern to a dash of 2, followed by a space of 2, followed by a dash of 10, followed by a space of 2, followed by a dash of 5, followed by a space of 15. The entire procedure then repeats.

The **show** operator prints the text in the bulb and above the fold line.

3. Explanation of the Listings

The program listings are shown in Listing 12.1, Listing 12.2, and Listing 12.3. They correspond to the output displayed in Figure 12.1, Figure 12.2, and Figure 12.3, respectively. The first program draws a single-sided Christmas tree bulb. The second program draws a two-sided bulb with a horizontal fold line in the middle of the page. And, finally, the third program draws the two-sided bulb with a person's name on one side and the words "Merry Christmas" with a Christmas tree on the other side.

a. Version 1: A Christmas Tree Bulb

The first listing consists of 33 lines of code and comments.

Listing 12.1: A Christmas Tree Bulb

```
%!PS-Adobe-3.0 EPSF-30.
%%BoundingBox: 0 0 612 792
%%Title: (Christmas Ornament example 1)
%%Creationdate: (11/10/91)
%%EndComments
/centerball
 {306 200} def
/ball
 {144 0 360 arc} def
/centersquare
 {306 340 moveto} def
/outlinesquare
 {-18   0 rlineto
    0  36 rlineto
   36   0 rlineto
    0 -36 rlineto
  -18   0 rlineto} def
/hoop
 {1 setlinewidth
  18 0 180 arc} def
/squareandhoop
 {centersquare outlinesquare stroke
  0 setgray
  centersquare outlinesquare fill
  306 376 hoop stroke} def
/drawabulb
 {4 setlinewidth
  centerball ball stroke
  squareandhoop} def
drawabulb
showpage
```

```
%%EOF
```

All but the last two lines of the program, excluding the comments, are definitions. In all there are seven definitions. The last line, a **showpage** operator, causes the page to be printed and output. Line 25, **drawabulb**, marks the starting point of the program's explanation.

The **drawabulb** procedure is defined above its use. It uses several other commands in its definition some of which are user-defined, and some of which are system-defined.

By compartmentalizing the program into seven user defined operators, the program is much easier to understand because each meaningful step is compartmentalized. Understanding that each procedure must be defined before it is used, now turn to the top of the listing.

The first definition statement in the program creates a procedure called **centerball**. The **centerball** operator is pushed onto the dictionary stack. Now any time **centerball** appears in the program from this point, the value of the key **centerball** is looked up in the dictionary stack and executed. In this case, **centerball** is defined as the values 306 and 200, so executing **centerball** causes two operands to be placed on the operand stack as shown below:

200
306

The next definition statement defines the **ball** procedure as **144 0 360 arc**. **Ball** basically draws a circle with a radius of 144 points, centered at the current point when it is executed. If no current point is defined, the result is an error.

The next operator, **centersquare**, is a **moveto** statement. The point being moved to is 306, 340. This operator moves the current point to the coordinates where a square will be drawn.

The **outlinesquare** procedure is a series of five **rlineto** operators. This operator, when executed, creates a path of a square. The square placement depends upon the current point.

The **hoop** procedure sets the line width to one and creates a path that is a half circle with a radius of 18 points, centered at the current point.

The **squareandhoop** procedure uses three of the operators defined above. The first line of **squareandhoop** causes **centersquare** to be looked up and its definition pushed onto the operand stack. As previously defined literals are encountered, their definitions are looked up and pushed onto the operand stack in a recursive manner—that is, literals are looked up and replaced by their definitions until there is nothing to look up. **Squareandhoop** causes the definitions of **centersquare** and **outlinesquare** to be pushed onto the stack and executed. These two definitions cause a square to be drawn starting at 306, 340, according to the **rlineto** statements in **outlinesquare**. The **stroke** operator then causes the square's outline to be drawn. The next line in **squareandhoop** causes the drawing color to be set to black. The next line again causes the definitions of **centersquare** and **outlinesqsuare** to be pushed onto the operand stack. This time instead of being stroked, the current path is filled with black. The **fill** operator ends the **squareandhoop** definition.

The last definition statement defines **drawabulb**. The first line sets the linewidth to four. The second line pushes the two values contained in **centerball** and then push the contents of **ball**. This lays down a circular path. The **stroke** operator then draws the circle. The last line in **drawabulb** pushes the definition of **squareandhoop** onto the stack. This will executes the **squareandhoop** lines and draws the black square and half circle on top of the ball. After the last definition statement, there are only two operators left to execute.

The **drawabulb** procedure causes the contents of its definition to be pushed onto the stack and then executed. **Showpage** prints the page. The printed page contains a one-sided Christmas tree bulb complete with the hoop on top to attach it to a tree.

b. Version 2: Two Christmas Tree Bulbs

The second program adds only two definition statements to the first program: **drawpicture** and **drawfoldline**.

The first action of **Drawpictures** is to call **drawabulb**. The next line, **gsave**, saves all of the current graphics settings. These settings are pushed onto a stack and are later reinstated with a **grestore** operator. The next line moves the origin to the coordinates 612, 792. The **rotate** operator rotates the axes 180 degrees. The **translate** and **rotate** operators make the top right corner of the page become the new lower left corner of the drawing area. Because the drawing area has been adjusted to the top right corner, **drawabulb** draws another bulb.[46] The graphics state is restored to the point that the **gsave** was last executed by **grestore**.

The second operator, **drawfoldline**, draws a horizontal line across the sheet of

[46]It should be clear at this point that the original choice of where the bulb was placed was far from arbitrary. It was carefully chosen so the center of the hook's arc is the precise center of the page.

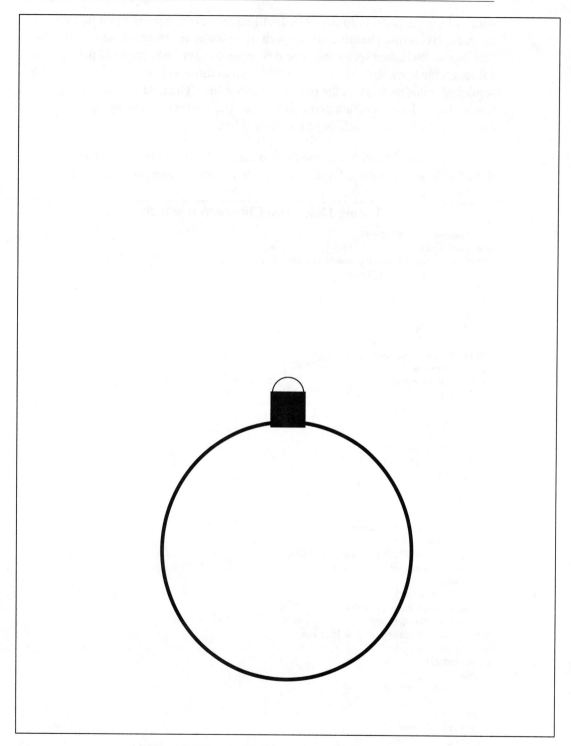

Figure 12.1: A Christmas tree Bulb

paper where the paper is folded. The first line moves the current point halfway up the page. Executing **rlineto** causes a path to be traced horizontally across the page. The line width is then set to one. The next operator, **setdash**, pops off the top two values on the stack and sets the dashed pattern to three with an offset of zero. The **stroke** operator then draws the path as a dashed line. The next line changes the font to Times-Roman with a point size of 10. The **moveto** and **show** operators cause "Fold here" to be set above the dashed line.

Given these definitions, **drawpicture** causes the two bulbs to be drawn, **drawfoldline** causes dotted line to be drawn, and **showpage** prints the page.

Listing 12.2: Two Christmas tree bulbs

```
%!PS-Adobe-3.0 EPSF-30.
%%BoundingBox: 0 0 612 792
%%Title: (Christmas Ornament example 1)
%%Creationdate: (11/10/91)
%%EndComments
%----- begin example 1 ------
/centerball
 {306 200} def
/ball
 {144 0 360 arc} def
/centersquare
 {306 340 moveto} def
/outlinesquare
 {-18   0 rlineto
    0  36 rlineto
   36   0 rlineto
    0 -36 rlineto
  -18   0 rlineto} def
/hoop
 {1 setlinewidth
  18 0 180 arc} def
/squareandhoop
 {centersquare outlinesquare stroke
  0 setgray
  centersquare outlinesquare fill
  306 376 hoop stroke} def
/drawabulb
 {4 setlinewidth
  centerball ball stroke
  squareandhoop} def
%----- begin example 2 addition -----
/drawpicture
 {drawabulb
  gsave
  612 792 translate
  180 rotate
  drawabulb
  grestore} def
/drawfoldline
 {0 396 moveto
  612 0 rlineto
```

```
  1 setlinewidth
  gsave
  [3 3] 0 setdash
  stroke
  /Times-Roman findfont 10 scalefont setfont
  10 400 moveto
  (Fold here) show
  grestore} def

drawpicture
drawfoldline
showpage
%%EOF
```

c. Version 3: A Personalized Christmas Tree Bulb

The last program adds six additional definitions to write a person's name on one side of the bulb, the words "Merry Christmas" on the other side of the bulb, and draw a Christmas tree.

The **name** variable is a string. It is this string that appears alone on one side of the bulb.

The **putname** procedure saves the current graphics state, anticipating the scale operator that will be executed. It then moves the current point to 198, 146, selects the Times-Roman font and scales it to 144 points. **Name** is then executed, causing the string to be pushed onto the operand stack. The string is then duplicated. **Stringwidth** removes the top string off the stack and computes the X and Y offsets that would occur if the string were printed under the current font and point size. Since **stringwidth** pushes first the X offset and then the Y offset, the **pop** operator is used to discard the Y offset. The top of the stack now holds the horizontal width of the string. In the next line, 216 is pushed onto the stack. (This is the width the string has to be printed to be centered on the bulb). The **exch** operator causes the exchange of two values, so 216 is divided by the width of the string. Executing **div** pops 216 and the **stringwidth** from the stack. The 216 is then divided by the width and the result is placed on top of the stack. Next, a 1 is pushed onto the stack and then the **scale** operator is executed. **Show** then draws the scaled string onto the page and **grestore** restores the graphics state. These four lines of codes accept any length string and scale it into a horizontal width of 216 points without changing the scale factor in the Y direction. This in essence squeezes or expands a string to the specified length.

The **tree** procedure is defined as a **moveto** and a series of **rlineto**s. These **rlineto**s lay down a path from a current point that resembles a Christmas tree

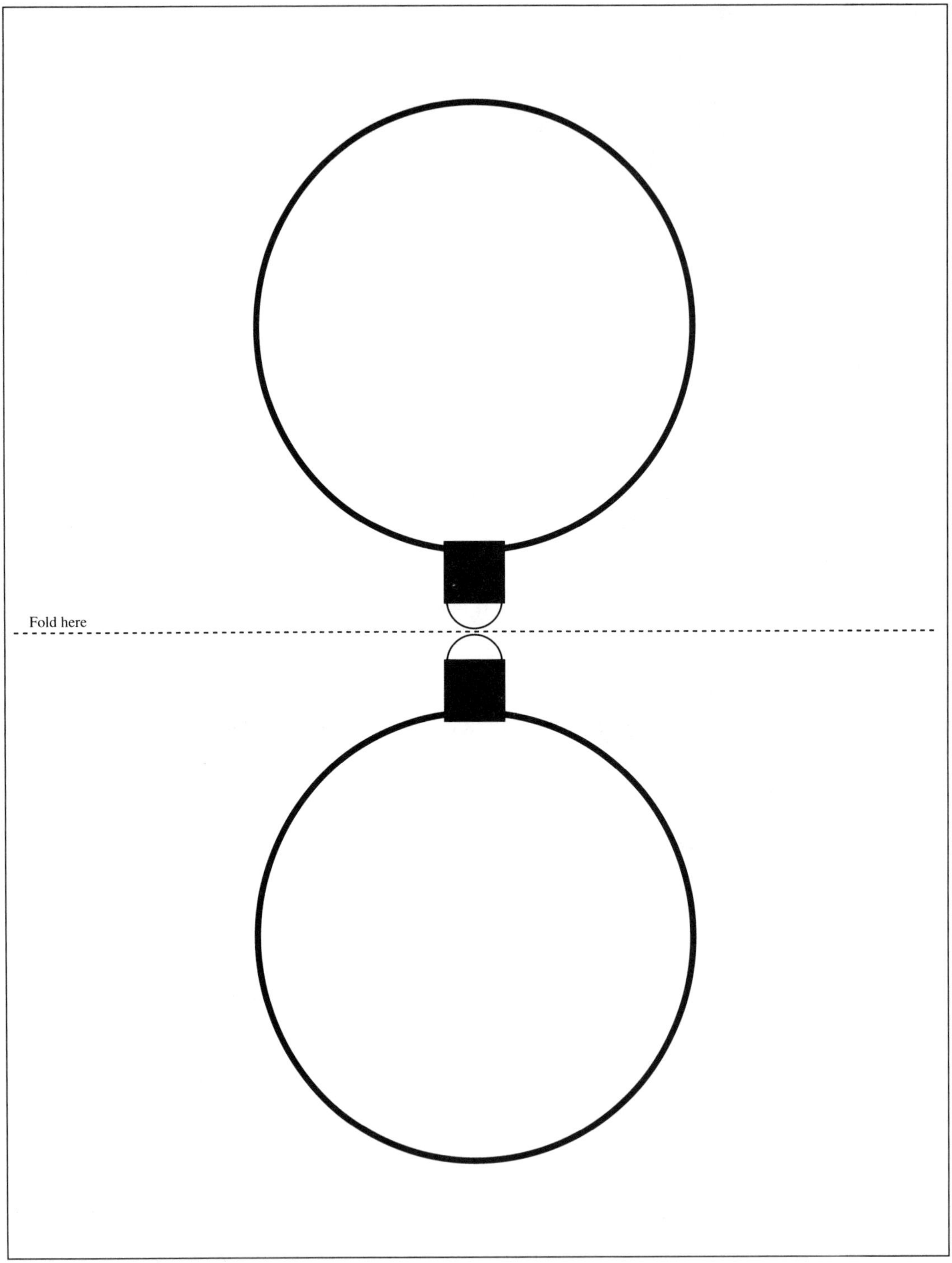

Figure 12.2: Two Christmas tree bulbs

centered on one current point. The X and Y values are kept between –1 and +1 to resemble a unitized representation of the tree. This allows the programmer to make a tree of any size by simply scaling. In this case, you want a tree that is no more than 80 points wide and 80 points high, so we will use a **40 40 scale** command.

The **drawtree** procedure saves the current graphics settings and moves the current point to the center of the ball. The **40 40 scale** command scales the axes by a factor of 40 in each direction. The next line divides 1 by 40 and sets the line width to the result. This is essential in keeping the line width to a visual width of one. This must be done because the scaling factor used above causes a line width of 1 to appear as a line width of 40. The next line of **drawtree** draws the path of the tree by calling the definition of tree. Executing **stroke** then draws the tree. The graphics settings are then restored.

The **putxmas** command sets the font to Times-Roman with a point size of 54. A **moveto** is used along with a **show** to print "Merry" onto the page. A second **moveto**, again with a **show**, prints "Christmas" on the page.

The last definition, **puttexttree**, prints the text and tree that appear within the two sides of the bulb. It has the same format as the **drawpicture** definition described in the second program. The first line of the definition, **putname**, scales and writes a defined string to the page. The graphics settings are then saved. The next two lines use a **translate** and **rotate**, as described in the last program, to re-orient the origin to the upper right corner of the page. Executing **drawtree** then draws the Christmas tree in the center of the bulb. Next, **putxmas** writes "Merry Christmas" onto the page. The graphics settings are then restored and the **puttexttree** definition ends.

The next line, **drawpicture**, draws the two sides of the bulb. The second line, **drawfoldline**, draws the fold line across the page. Next, **puttexttree** is used to write a string and "Merry Christmas" onto the bulb, along with a line drawing of a Christmas tree. The **showpage** operatorthen prints and ejects the page.

Listing 12.3: Personalized Christmas Tree Bulb

```
%!PS-Adobe-3.0 EPSF-30.
%%BoundingBox: 0 0 612 792
%%Title: (Christmas Ornament example 1)
%%Creationdate: (11/10/91)
%%EndComments

%----- begin example 1 ------
/centerball
 {306 200} def
/ball
 {144 0 360 arc} def
/centersquare
```

```
 {306 340 moveto} def
/outlinesquare
 {-18   0 rlineto
    0  36 rlineto
   36   0 rlineto
    0 -36 rlineto
  -18   0 rlineto} def
/hoop
 {1 setlinewidth
  18 0 180 arc} def
/squareandhoop
 {centersquare outlinesquare stroke
  0 setgray
  centersquare outlinesquare fill
  306 376 hoop stroke} def
/drawabulb
 {4 setlinewidth
  centerball ball stroke
  squareandhoop} def

%----- begin example 2 addition -----
/drawpicture
 {drawabulb
  gsave
  612 792 translate
  180 rotate
  drawabulb
  grestore} def
/drawfoldline
 {gsave
  0 396 moveto
  612 0 rlineto
  1 setlinewidth
  [3 3] 0 setdash
  stroke
  /Times-Roman findfont 10 scalefont setfont
  10 400 moveto
  (Fold here) show
  grestore} def

%----- begin example 3 ------
/name
 {(Jeff)} def
/putname
 {gsave
   198 146 moveto
  /Times-Roman findfont 144 scalefont setfont
  name
  dup stringwidth
  pop
  216 exch div 1 scale
  show
  stroke
  grestore} def

/tree
 {  0 -1 rmoveto
```

```
    -0.25  0 rlineto
      0  .5 rlineto
     -1  0 rlineto
    .75  .5 rlineto
     -.5  0 rlineto
      .5  .5 rlineto
   -0.25  0 rlineto
    .75  1 rlineto
    .75 -1 rlineto
   -0.25  0 rlineto
      .5 -.5 rlineto
     -.5  0 rlineto
    .75 -.5 rlineto
     -1  0 rlineto
      0 -.5 rlineto
   -0.25  0 rlineto} def

/drawtree
 {gsave
  centerball moveto
  40 40  scale
  1  40 div setlinewidth
  tree stroke
  grestore} def

/putxmas
 {/Times-Roman findfont 54 scalefont setfont
  234 268 moveto
  (Merry) show
  199 118 moveto
  (Christmas) show} def

/puttexttree
 {putname
  gsave
  612 792 translate
  180 rotate
  drawtree
  putxmas
  grestore} def

drawpicture
drawfoldline
puttexttree
showpage
%%EOF
```

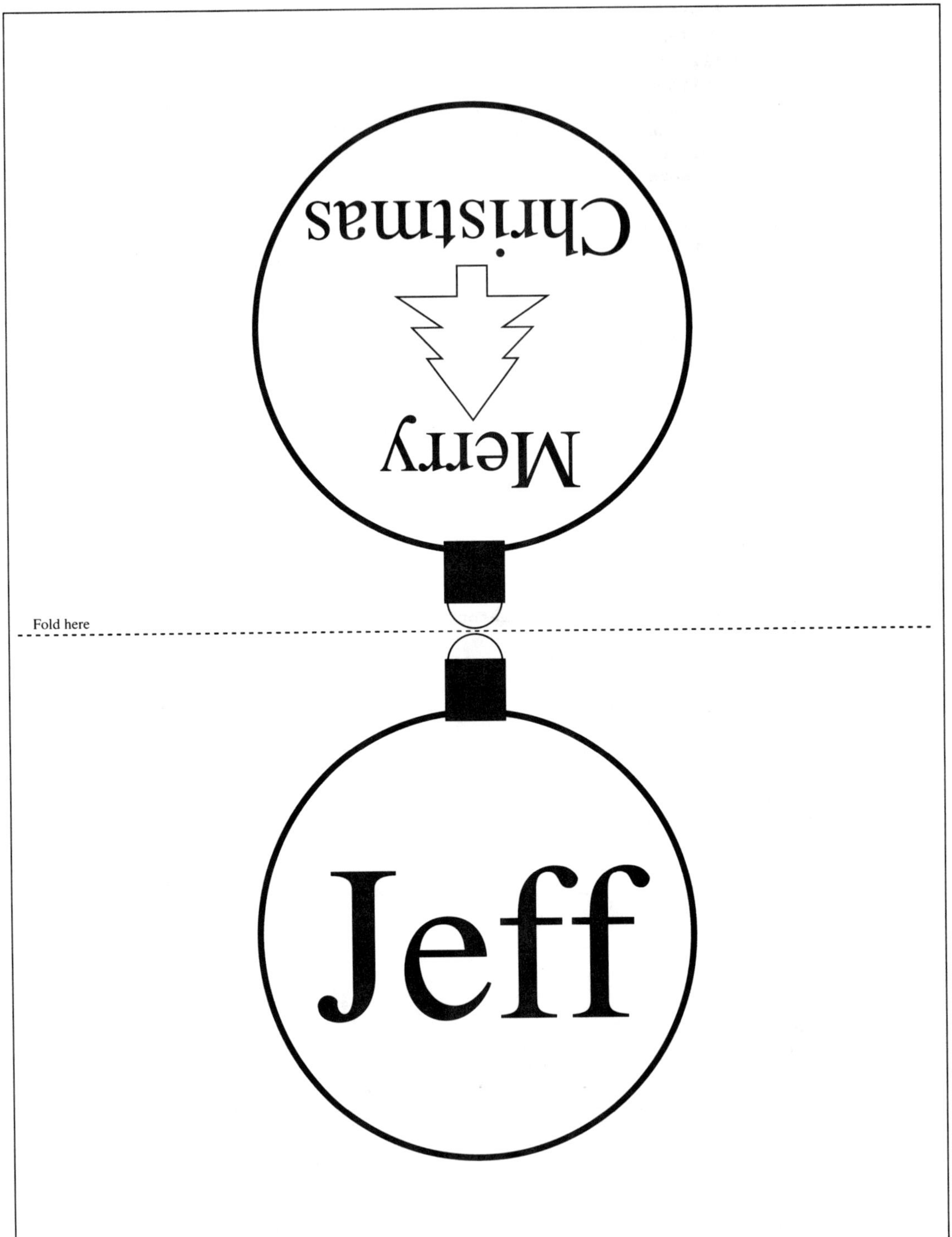

Figure 12.3: Personalized Christmas Tree Bulb

4. Possible Modifications

The three programs presented in this chapter gradually build in complexity. Although the last program is dubbed a "Complete Christmas tree bulb," the program can, by all means, be modified and improved:

- The **fill** operator can be used, in conjunction with **setgray**, to fill regions within the existing drawings. For instance, in the **drawtree** definition statement, only the tree's outline is drawn; another call to the **tree** definition and a **fill** operator darkens the entire tree. The **setgray** operator is used to select different shades of gray.
- Since the tree is drawn using **rlineto**s, another definition statement can be used to move the current point around the page and draw the tree at that point. The **scale** operator can also vary the size of the trees.
- The **ball** definition statement can be modified to draw concentric circles instead of a single circle. Furthermore, the line width can be changed with each drawing of the circle to create a bull's-eye effect.

5. Possible Errors

You may encounter particular kinds of problems when you develop programs such as those introduced in this chapter. Use these guidelines when writing programs that define new procedures:

- Always know what is on the stack. PostScript operators expect certain types of values to be on the stack when they execute. For example, a **moveto** operator requires two numeric values to be on top of the stack. If the appropriate values are not where the operator expects them to be, it generates an error and the operator is not executed.
- Even though the PostScript drawing plane allows you to move to virtually any point in the plane, only the default page is drawn when **showpage** is executed. For instance, if a line were drawn outside of the default page boundaries (0,0)–(612,792), would not appear on the printed page because it was outside the printable window. Avoid frustration by knowing where the current point is.
- Coordinate system transformations should be preceded by **gsave** and followed by a **grestore**. Some transformations are hard to recover from. This recovery is particularly difficult if you do not know the exact transformations that were previously executed. This is why it is beneficial to save the graphic settings before doing any axis transformations. For example, after a **scale** operator is executed, if the graphic settings is saved, a graphics restore negates the scaling to the settings being used prior to the last **gsave**.

- Remember, PostScript drawings are opaque. The third program draws text within a circle. This is possible because the circle is drawn before the text is written. If, however, the circle was drawn after the text was written, only the circle would be visible. This is because drawings are opaque. So if a drawing is to appear on top of another drawing, draw the smaller figure last. This way, the larger drawing does not block the smaller drawing.

Chapter 13
Poster

1. Introduction

This chapter's project is a poster: an image that can be enlarged to a size that is too big to fit on a single 8.5-by-11-inch page, and so is printed out in pieces on a series of sheets.[47] The first two versions of the program introduce the routines for producing a small image on a single sheet. The final version demonstrates how these same procedures can be used in the enlarged version.

a. Objectives

Objectives covered in this chapter include:

- Provide a poster that can be adapted to personal use;
- Demonstrate a style of PostScript programming which, although not as computationally efficient as the orthodox style, avoids some of the complexities of stack management;
- Present routines for achieving special effects, including background text, circular printing, scaling text to fit within a shape, and printing a large image over several 8.5- by-11-inch sheets;[48]
- Demonstrate an application of "clipping" in PostScript.

---

[47]The poster program and chapter were originally developed by Richard Baker, the Information Systems Manager and Community Development Director in Bethel Park, PA.

[48]The procedures for background text, circular text were adapted from Adobe Systems, Inc.'s *PostScript Language Tutorial and Cookbook*, Addison-Wesley, Reading, M.A. 1985

2. Command Explanations

There are three versions of the poster program. Explanations of the new operators introduced in this chapter are broken down according to the program version in which they appear.

a. The Simple Poster Operators

The following operators are introduced in the first version of the program:

currentpoint Description: This operator pushes two numeric objects representing the current point's the X and Y values. The values are retrieved from the active graphics state.

Arguments: `none`

Results: $\texttt{num}_1$ $\texttt{num}_2$

The **currentpoint** operator function returns two numbers of type real which represent the X and Y coordinates of the current point in the graphics state. The current point is the trailing end point of the current path. A "nocurrentpoint" error is generated if **currentpoint** is undefined.

cvi Description: The **cvi** operator removes a numeric or string object from the operand stack, converts it into an integer object, and returns an object of type integer on the stack. If the argument is an integer, **cvi** returns that value. If the argument is a real, fractional parts of the number are truncated, unless the real is too large to convert to an integer, in which case an error is generated. If the argument is a string, the characters are interpreted as a number according to PostScript syntax rules. The number obtained is evaluated as described.

Arguments: `num` or `string`

cvi operator takes either a number or a string as an argument.

Results: `int`

If the result of the conversion of the `num` or `string` argument is too large to convert to an integer, an error is generated.

forall Description: The **forall** operator executes a procedure for each element of a string or array. A procedure object is expected on top of the stack (the procedure to be executed) with the string or array underneath it. The **forall** operator pushes each string or array element onto the stack and executes a procedure. The procedure may or may not act the stack element. With strings, the stack objects are codes, or numeric values, of the characters.

Arguments (Form 1): **`array proc`**

Arguments (Form 2): **`packedarray proc`**

Arguments (Form 3): **`dict proc`**

Arguments (Form 4): **`proc proc`**

Note if the first operand in any of the forms is empty (i.e. has length zero), **forall** operator does not execute at all.

Results: **`None`**

idiv

Description: This operator removes two integers from the stack and divides the first argument by the second argument. The quotient is returned onto the operand stack.

Arguments: $\texttt{int}_1$ $\texttt{int}_2$

Results: **`int`**

The **idiv** operator function returns a number of type integer that represents the result of the division of the first argument by the second argument, with any fraction discarded.

if

Description: The **if** operator command pops two objects from the stack, evaluates the first argument and, if it is true, executes the second argument, the **`proc`** procedure.

Arguments: **`boolean proc`**

`proc` is a set of zero or more PostScript commands.

Results: **`none`**

While **if** operator is not directly leave results on the stack, the procedure that is executed may alter the stack.

kshow

Description: The term kshow is derived from kern-show and is designed to allow for easy kerning, or adjusting the inter-letter space. The **kshow** operator takes a procedure and a string off the stack and begins by reading the character codes in the string. It shows the first character code at the current point, updating the current point by the first character code width. It then pushes the character codes for the first and second characters onto the operand stack as integers and executes **`proc`**, which may perform any action but typically modifies the current point to affect the subsequent placement of the next character in the string. Basically, **kshow** operator checks for certain pairs of characters. For example, if a *T* were followed by an *o*, the *o* is kerned, or moved closer, to the *T* to give an authentic appearance.

Arguments: **`proc string`**

Results: **`none`**

loop Description: The **loop** operator repeatedly executes `proc` until the **exit** or **stop** operators are called.

Arguments: `proc`

`proc` must execute an **exit** or **stop**, or an infinite loop results.

Results: `none`

put Description: This operator has three forms:

Arguments (Form 1): `array, index, any`
Arguments (Form 2): `dict, key, any`
Arguments (Form 3): `string, index, int`

If the first operand is an `array` or `string`, **put** treats the second operand as an `index` and stores the third operand at the position the `index` identifies, counting from zero. The `index` operator must be in the range of 0 to one less than the length of the array or string. If the first operand is a dictionary, **put** uses the second operand as a key and the third operand as a value, then stores this key-value pair the `dict`. If the key exists for a key-value pair, it is overwritten. Note if the value of `array` or `dict` is in global VM and `any` is a composite object whose value is in local VM, an error occurs.

Results: `none`

b. One-Page Poster Commands

The second program introduces the following operators:

floor Description: This operator removes a numeric object from the stack, rounds the value down to the nearest integer value, and then returns the result onto the operand stack.

Arguments: `num`

`num` is the number to be floored.

Results: `num`

The **floor** operator function returns a number as described above.

c. Multi-Page Poster Commands

The third program introduces the following operators:

clip Description: This operator does not take any arguments or push any results onto the stack. However, it does alter the current path: **clip** operator takes the area of the user space considered to be inside the current path (as determined by the nonzero winding rule) and the area considered to be inside the current clipping path (as determined by the winding rule in use at the time of the clipping path's creation). It then returns a new path that, generally, is the intersection of both of these areas. It is not possible to enlarge the clipping path unless the **initclip** or **initgraphics** operators are called, both of which reset the clipping region to its initial value.

Arguments: `none`

Results: `none`

For example, if the current path describes a 2-inch-wide circle in the middle of the page then executing clip will limit the area in which new marks will be visible to that circle.

3. Modular Design and Programming Style

The programs in this chapter are modular: a series of procedures are defined prior to the execution of the main program, and those procedures are used as "building blocks." One advantage of modular design is that the definition of procedures allows chunks of PostScript code to be executed multiple times. In these programs, however, the definition of procedures serves mainly to divide the program into its logical divisions, making it easier for humans to understand and modify the code.

Procedures are executable arrays of PostScript commands that are delimited by curly brackets. Definition of a procedure takes the form **/Procedure_name {body commands} def** (i.e. a literal followed a procedure object followed by a **def** operator). Once defined, the procedure name can substitute for the body code in either the program script or in another procedure. The syntax for defining a procedure includes no provision for formal parameters: The body of the procedure is written with the assumption that necessary parameters are waiting on the stack, and it is the programmer's responsibility to ensure that appropriate parameters are at the top of the operand stack when the procedure executes.

Another characteristic of these programs designed to make comprehension easier is an unorthodox style of programming known as overdefinition for purposes of this book. Overdefinition avoids some of the rigors of stack management by defining many new variables (in a manner similar to the unstructured variable definitions of the BASIC programming language). The most computationally efficient PostScript programs store data on the operand stack and make effective use of operators like **dup**, **exch**, and **roll** to make sure data is at the top of the stack when it is needed.

The alternative to stack management is to associate each piece of data with a variable name and store that association in some dictionary on the dictionary stack. Whenever a particular value is needed, the appropriate variable is referenced in the program. Overdefining in a PostScript program necessarily decreases the program's execution the efficiency. Each time a value is assigned or reassigned to a variable, a new entry must be made in a dictionary, and each time the variable is referenced that dictionary entry must be retrieved.

4. Simple Poster

This section introduces a simplified version of the image which is used to create a poster later in the chapter. The image produced by this version, as depicted in Listing 13.1, prints on a single 8.5-by-11-inch sheet of paper. There are four main design elements to each of the poster programs presented in this chapter:

background text
: The poster programs include routines for printing a string repeatedly in a small type size so the poster's background is filled with that string. Essentially, procedures are defined that fill a single page with the string, and the rest of the poster is laid over top of that pattern.

gray circle
: The first thing to be laid over top of the background pattern is a circle filled with gray ink. Because all marks are opaque in PostScript, the circle will obscures all marks beneath it, despite the fact it is not pure black.

circular text
: Within the circle, a second string is printed around the circle's circumference. The routines for printing circular text include a function for determining which portion of the circumference is taken up by the string. Using integer division, the PostScript interpreter determines how many times the string can be displayed without overwriting an earlier copy.

central slogan
: A set of strings (stored in an array in later versions) is displayed upright and centered horizontally and vertically within the circle at the center of the image.

An illustration of output from the first version can be found in Figure 13.1.

Listing 13.1: A Simple Poster

```
%!PS-Adobe-3.0 EPSF-30.
%%BoundingBox: 0 0 612 792
%%Title: (poster example 1)
%%Creationdate: (10/31/91)
%%EndComments

%General Use Variable

/inch {72 mul} def

%Constants

/TM 11 inch def %top poster margin
/BM 0 inch def %bottom poster margin
/LM 0 inch def %left poster margin
/RM 8.5 inch def %right poster margin
/PM {4.25 inch 5.5 inch}  def %middle poster
/pi 3.1415923 def
/ptsize 50 def
/radius 200 def

%Background Printing Procedures

/newline %move to start of new line
 {currentpoint 13 sub exch pop LM exch
  moveto } def

/newlinecheck %check if to start new line
 {currentpoint pop RM gt
 {newline} if} def

/finish %check if at page bottom
 {currentpoint exch pop
  BM lt} def

/fillpage %fill page with background names
  {/fillstrg exch def
   {{pop pop newlinecheck} fillstrg kshow %move to proper position
   finish {exit} if  %if at bottom of page exit loop

      } loop
      }def

%Draw Circle Procedure

/drawcircle  %draw gray circle in center page
 {newpath
  PM  3.5 inch 0 360 arc
  closepath
 .9 setgray
 fill}
 def
```

```
%Horizontal Line Printing Procedures


/hcenter {dup stringwidth pop 2 div neg 0 rmoveto show} def


%Circular Line Printing Procedures

/circtext  %print outside circle
  { /str exch def
  /xradius radius ptsize 4 div add def
  gsave
  str calculateangle cvi 2 mul 360 exch idiv /iter exch def
  -180 rotate
  1 1 iter {pop
           str
           {/charcode exch def ( ) dup 0 charcode put circchar} forall
           } for
  grestore
  } def

/calculateangle %find half of angle
{stringwidth pop 2 div
 2 xradius mul pi mul div 360 mul} def


/circchar   %show character upright on circle clockwise
 {/char exch def
 /halfangle char calculateangle def
  gsave
  halfangle neg rotate
  radius 0 translate
  -90 rotate
  char stringwidth pop 2 div neg 0 moveto
  char show
  grestore
  halfangle 2 mul neg rotate
  } def

%Begin Program

% ------------ Fill with background Text------------------------
/Times-Bold findfont 15 scalefont setfont
LM TM moveto
.5 setgray
(Kayaking Climbing Scuba Caving Skiing Canoeing Rafting Biking )
fillpage

drawcircle


% --------------------- Circular Text ------------------------
0 setgray
/Times-Bold findfont ptsize scalefont setfont
PM translate
 (Explorer's Club of Pittsburgh  ) circtext
```

```
% --------------------- Center Slogan ----------------------
0 0 moveto
0 ptsize 1.1 mul rmoveto
(We) hcenter
0 0 moveto
(do) hcenter
0 0 moveto
0 ptsize 1.1 mul neg rmoveto
(it all) hcenter
showpage

%%EOF
```

a. Explanation of the listing

The Listing 13.1 program execution consists of running four main modules:

Print background text	The **fillpage** procedure (supported by the procedures **newline**, **newlinecheck**, and **finish**) fills the page with a string.
Draw circle	The **drawcircle** procedure draws a gray circle in the middle of the page.
Print circular text	The **circtext** procedure and its auxiliary procedures print a string repeatedly just within the circumference of the gray circle.
Print central slogan	The central slogan is printed in the middle of the circle.

Several constants are defined at the beginning of the program:

- The **TM**, **BM**, **LM** constants, and **RM** represent the top, bottom, left, and right margins of the poster when it is printed on a single page.
- The **PM** constant represents the coordinates of the middle of the poster when it is printed on a single page.
- The **pi** constant represents the value of π, which is used in calculating the angle subtended by a string.
- The **ptsize** constant represents the size of the type used for the circular text and central slogan.
- The **radius** constant represents the radius of the circle around which text is printed. Note: This is different from the radius of the gray circle underlying the circular text.

As noted, the first major division of the program is the background text module, which is accomplished in the first five lines of the program script. The

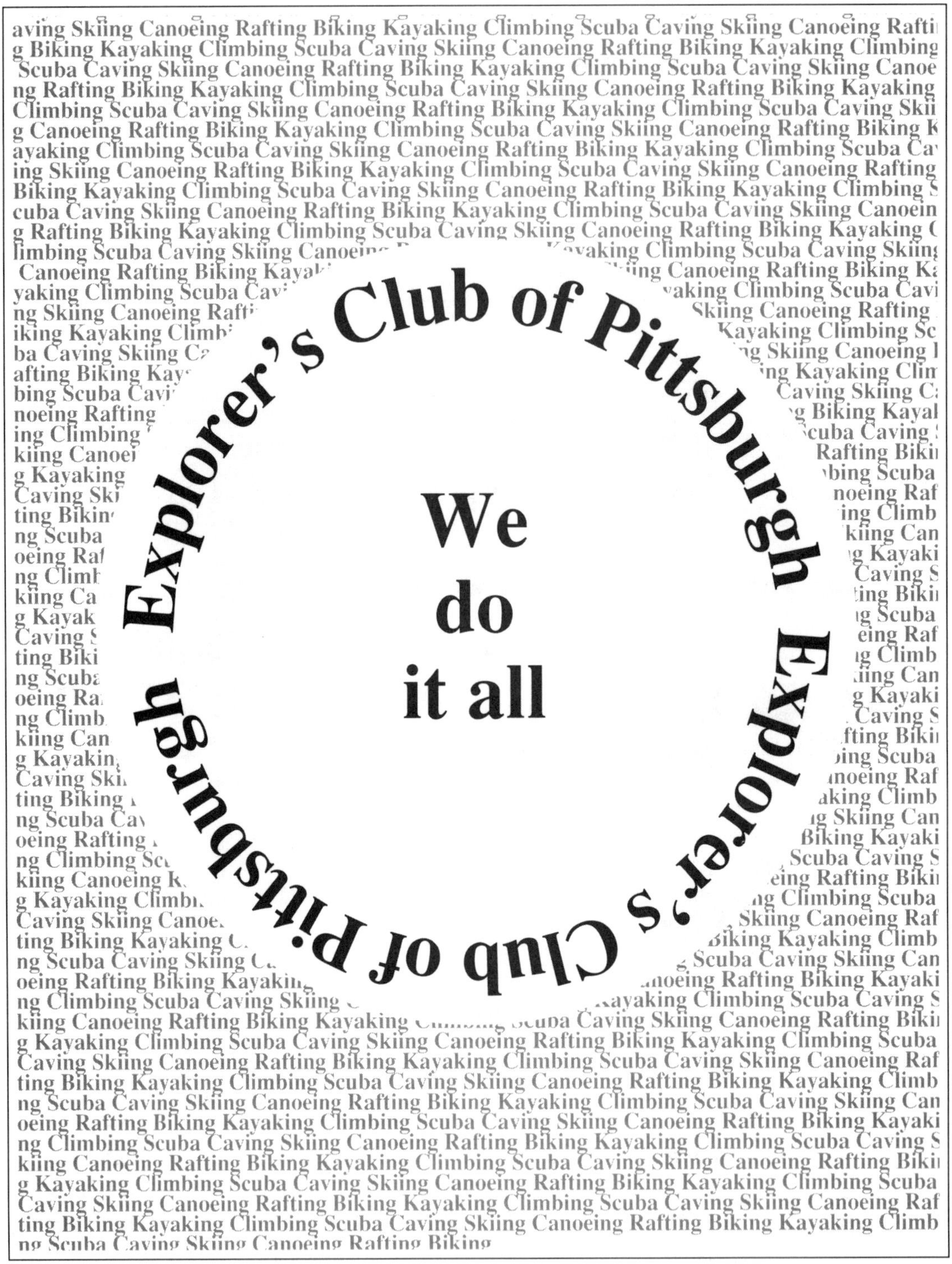

Figure 13.1: A Simple Poster

current font is set to 15-point Times-Bold, and the current color is set to a medium gray (the background text is printed in a lighter color so draw attention away from the larger text in the center). The current point is moved to the top left corner of the page, and the background string is pushed onto the operand stack. At that point, the **fillpage** page procedure is invoked.

The **fillpage** procedure works by repeatedly printing the background string at the current point, checking after each character is shown for the right and bottom margins. When the right margin is reached, the current point moves back to the left margin on a new line. If the bottom margin is reached, the procedure terminates.

The **kshow** operator is at the heart of the **fillpage** procedure. As previously explained, **kshow** takes a string and a procedure as parameters. Between the showing of each character, two characters are pushed on the stack and the procedure parameter is executed. In **fillpage**, the two characters are not needed and are therefore popped from the stack.

The **fillpage** procedure operates as follows. First, the background string is assigned to the **fillstrg** variable. Then a loop commences in which **fillstrg** is passed to **kshow** repeatedly. At each iteration of the loop, the **finish** procedure determines whether the Y coordinate of the current point is lower than the bottom margin defined for the poster; if so, the loop ends. The parameter passed to **kshow** along with **fillstrg** is a procedure which determines (after popping the unnecessary characters off the stack) whether the X coordinate of the current point is greater than the defined right margin for the poster; if so, the current point is moved down 13 points and back to the left margin. This last test is performed after each character of the background string is displayed. As a result, the string is broken at the end of each line and continues on the next line of the page.

The routine for painting the circle in the center of the page (as defined in the **drawcircle** procedure) is essentially a call to the **arc** operator, which expects the X and Y coordinates of the arc's center of curvature, a starting angle, and an ending angle on the stack (from bottom to top). Because the total angle in this case equals 360 degrees, the result is a circle. The circle is then filled with a light gray pattern.

To understand how circular text is printed, you must imagine the text sitting along the outside of the circumference of an invisible circle. The procedures for printing circular text rely on the program's capability to determine how much of a 360 degree circle is taken up by a string. This is determined by first dividing the length of the string (in points) by the length of the circle's circumference ($2\pi r$). The result of that division is the fraction of the circle subtended by that string. Multiplying that fraction by 360 gives the number of degrees for that particular string.

Use the following procedure for printing text in a circle:

1. Translate the origin to the center of the circle.
2. Rotate the axis to the starting point for the text (9 o'clock in this example).
3. For each character in the string:
    a. Calculate the angle subtended by the character.
    b. Rotate the axes clockwise by half that angle (the character is to be centered round the current X axis).
    c. Translate the origin in a straight line to the circumference of the circle.
    d. Rotate the axes 90 degrees so the character is upright.
    e. Show the character centered around what is now the Y axis.
    f. Undo the last rotation and translation, and rotate the axes by the angle subtended by the width of the character.

This sequence of steps is accomplished by the **circtext** procedure. This procedure expects the string that is to be printed around the circumference of the circle on the operand stack. The string on the stack is assigned to the **str** variable. Next, the **xradius** variableis defined as the radius of the circle plus one fourth of the type size. This **xradius** variable is used to calculate string angles rather than the original circle radius. This modification addresses the aesthetics of type placement: calculating angles with a slightly larger circle radius results in smaller angles (since the calculated circumference is longer). As a result, characters are placed closer together than they otherwise would have been. Other aesthetic issues surrounding of the central poster slogan display will be addressed with the second version of the program.

After the variables are defined, the current graphics state is saved. It is assumed the origin is at the center of the invisible circle which the text will rest. The next line assigns the number of times the string will fit around the circle without overlapping to the **iter** variable. This is accomplished by calculating the angle subtended by the string, converting that value to an integer, and dividing (using integer division) by 360. If, for example, a string takes up 160 degrees, it fits twice. If it takes up 120 degrees, it fits exactly three times.

The circular text string chosen for this poster fills up the circle nicely by printing the string twice. Obviously, if the angle subtended by the string does not divide evenly into 360, the circular text is not be perfectly symmetrical. If, for example, a string takes up 220 degrees, it is printed once, leaving the rest of the circumference empty. Perhaps the best solution to finding the perfect string length is to start with a relatively short string and then pad either end with blank spaces until you achieve a pleasing effect is achieved. For example, the string "Explorer's Club of Pittsburgh" used in this poster is padded with two blanks at the end.

After the **iter** variable is defined, the axes are rotated 180 degrees clockwise so that printing always starts at 9 o'clock on the circle. The next line begins a **for** loop, which executes once for each time the string is to be printed around the circle. First a number representing the index of the loop is popped from the stack (the **for** operator pushes it there but is not needed). The string to be printed is pushed onto the stack, followed by a procedure to be executed for each character in the string (by the **forall** operator).

The goal of the procedure passed to **forall** is to create a series of one-character strings, push each onto the stack, then invoke the **circchar** procedure. When the **forall** operator is used with a string, the characters are represented with numeric codes, so to create a one-character string, the **put** operator places the character into position zero of a null string.

The **circchar** procedure accomplishes these steps for each character in the string (the translations, rotations, and character display). Of course, these coordinate space transformations are placed between **gsave** and **grestore** operators so they are undone after each character is placed. The **calculateangle** procedure expects a string on the stack and returns the size of the angle subtended by half that string. (Note the value is multiplied by two when the full angle is needed).

The remaining procedure, **hcenter**, is simply a horizontal centering procedure used in the last part of the program script to center the lines of the central slogan. Like other string centering procedures in this book, it works by moving the current point to the left a distance equal to half the string's width. In this first version of the poster, the central slogan is printed in a fixed position at a fixed size. The next version of the program adds flexibility by scaling any slogan to fit the available space.

5. One-Page Poster

The second version of the poster program (shown in Listing 13.2) is identical to the first version except in its handling of the slogan at the center of the gray circle. The first version displays the slogan in a fixed type size. Depending on the length and number of lines in the slogan, this may not make the best use of the available space within the circle. The second version adds flexibility by defining the center slogan as an array of strings and displaying that array in a scaled coordinate space.

Listing 13.2: One-Page Poster Program

```
%!PS-Adobe-3.0 EPSF-30.
%%BoundingBox: 0 0 612 792
%%Title: (poster example 1)
%%Creationdate: (10/31/91)
%%EndComments

%General Use Variable

/inch {72 mul} def

%Constants

/TM 11 inch def %top poster margin
/BM 0 inch def %bottom poster margin
/LM 0 inch def %left poster margin
/RM 8.5 inch def %right poster margin
/PM {4.25 inch 5.5 inch}  def %middle poster
/pi 3.1415923 def
/ptsize 50 def
/radius 200 def

%Background Printing Procedures

/newline %move to start of new line
 {currentpoint 13 sub exch pop LM exch
  moveto } def

/newlinecheck %check if to start new line
 {currentpoint pop RM gt
 {newline} if} def

/finish %check if at page bottom
 {currentpoint exch pop
  BM lt} def

/fillpage %fill page with background names
  {/fillstrg exch def
   {{pop pop newlinecheck} fillstrg kshow %move to proper position
   finish {exit} if  %if at bottom of page exit loop

      } loop
      }def

%Draw Circle Procedure

/drawcircle  %draw gray circle in center page
 {newpath
  PM  3.5 inch 0 360 arc
  closepath
 .9 setgray
 fill}
 def
```

```
%Horizontal Line Printing Procedures


/hcenter {dup stringwidth pop 2 div neg 0 rmoveto show} def

/vcenter {dup length ptsize mul 2 div ptsize .8 mul sub 0 exch rmoveto}
         def

/width { /longstring 0 def
         { stringwidth
         pop
         dup
         longstring gt {/longstring exch def} {pop} ifelse} forall
         longstring} def

/height {length ptsize mul} def

%Circular Line Printing Procedures

/circtext  %print outside circle
  { /str exch def
  /xradius radius ptsize 4 div add def
  gsave
  str calculateangle cvi 2 mul 360 exch idiv /iter exch def
  -180 rotate
  1 1 iter {pop
           str
           {/charcode exch def ( ) dup 0 charcode put circchar} forall
           } for
  grestore
  } def

/calculateangle %find half of angle
{stringwidth pop 2 div
 2 xradius mul pi mul div 360 mul} def


/circchar   %show character upright on circle clockwise
 {/char exch def
 /halfangle char calculateangle def
  gsave
  halfangle neg rotate
  radius 0 translate
  -90 rotate
  char stringwidth pop 2 div neg 0 moveto
  char show
  grestore
  halfangle 2 mul neg rotate
  } def

%Begin Program

% ----------- Fill with background Text-----------------------
/Times-Bold findfont 15 scalefont setfont
LM TM moveto
.5 setgray
(Kayaking Climbing Scuba Caving Skiing Canoeing Rafting Biking )
```

```
fillpage

drawcircle


% --------------------- Circular Text -----------------------
0 setgray
/Times-Bold findfont ptsize scalefont setfont
PM translate
 (Explorer's Club of Pittsburgh  ) circtext

% --------------------- Center Slogan ----------------------
0 0 moveto
/slogan [(We) (do) (it all)] def
slogan height slogan width gt
{2 sqrt radius mul slogan height div /sf exch def}
{2 sqrt radius mul slogan width div /sf exch def} ifelse
sf sf scale
slogan
vcenter
{hcenter currentpoint pop neg ptsize 1 sf div floor add neg rmoveto}
forall
showpage

%%EOF
```

Three new procedures are included in version 2:

- The **vcenter** procedure is similar to **hcenter** except it centers an array of strings vertically instead of a single string horizontally. The procedure expects an array of strings on the stack and moves the current point vertically in a positive direction a distance equal to half the height of the array.[49]

- The **width** procedure uses a **forall** loop to iterate through an array of strings. Before the loop begins, a **longstring** variable is set to zero. This variable represents the width (in points) of the longest string in the array. Each string in the array is tested to see whether it is longer than the current value of **longstring**; if so, the value is changed. Once the loop is completed, **longstring** is equal to the width of the longest string in the array (and therefore the width of the array). This value is returned onto the operand stack.

- The **height** procedure determines the height of the string array by multiplying the length of the array (the number of strings) by the **ptsize** variable, which equals the size of the type.

---

[49]As you can see by the listing, the distance moved is actually less than half the array height by .8 times the type size. This is another type aesthetics issue because without this reduction, the centering is off for text sizes typically generated by this program. Depending on the length of the central slogan, changing the constant from .8 to some other value may improve the posters appearance.

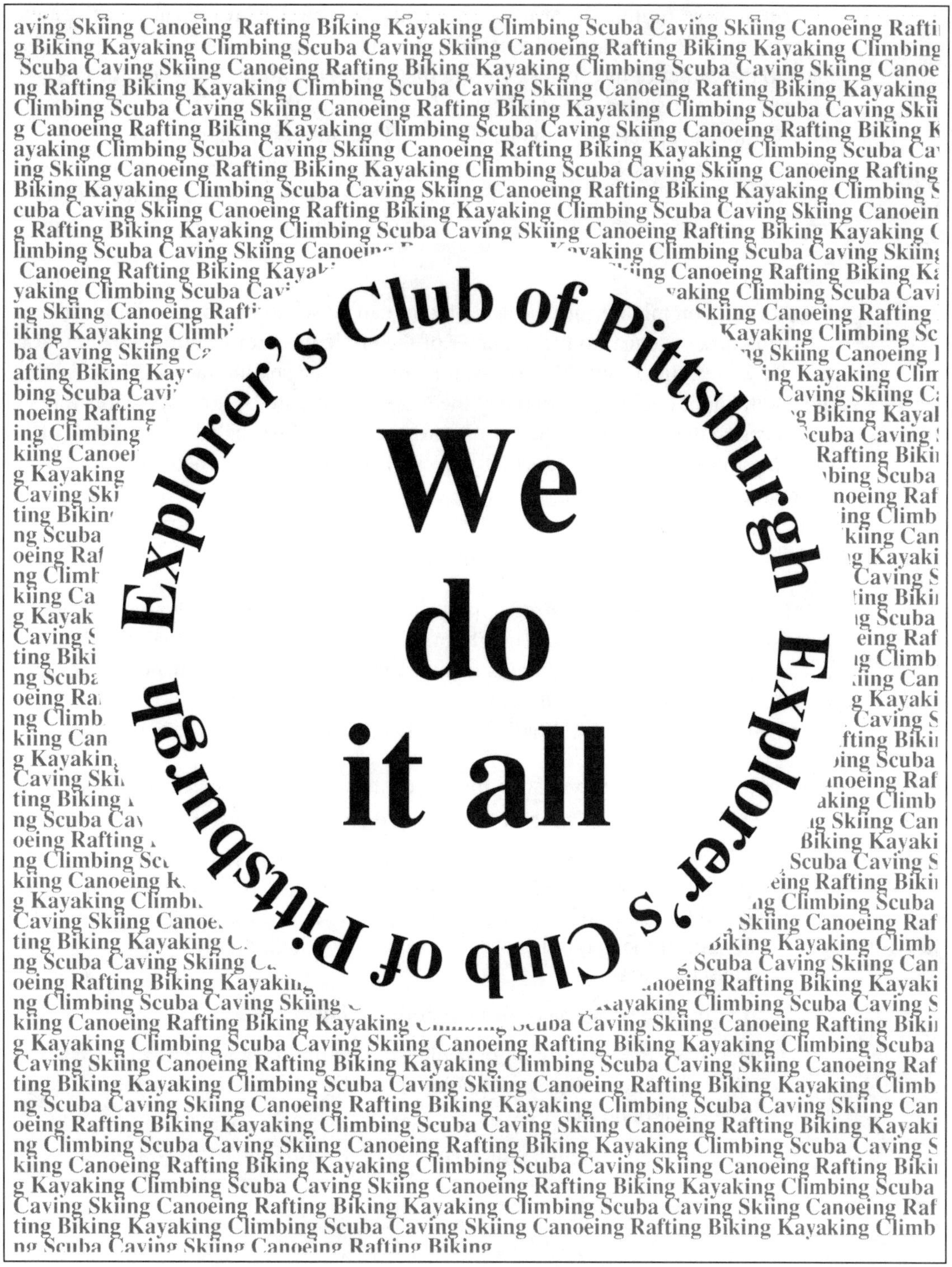

Figure 13.2: One-Page Poster Program

The revised routine for printing the central slogan displays the array of strings centered both horizontally and vertically around the origin (which has been translated to the center of the poster). Before displaying the array, however, the coordinate space is scaled so the slogan fills as much of the circle's interior as possible without overlapping with circular text. The output is illustrated in Figure 13.2. Because the text must be scaled proportionally, a single scale factor is calculated for both the X and Y axes. The scale factor is based on the size of the largest dimension of the string array (either its height or width, whichever is bigger).

At first, you might think the scale factor can be set so the longest dimension of the string array is equal to the diameter of the circle used for printing the circular text. However, this is not the case. If, for example, the scaling factor is based on the width and it could be guaranteed the longest string in the array appeares midway through the array, then the coordinate space could be scaled so the width of the array measures slightly less than the circle's diameter. But there is no guarantee—the longest string might be closer to the beginning or end of the array. Scaling based on the circle's diameter is a mistake if the longest string is displayed anywhere other than the widest part of the circle.

To ensure the slogan is sized appropriately, the scale factor is based on the longest dimension of the array (height or width) and the width of a square the circle circumscribes. This square is depicted in Figure 13.3. The diagonals of the square are diameters of the circle, which means both the height and width of the square are equal to the circle radius multiplied by the square root of two.

The revised routine for displaying the center slogan proceeds as follows:

1. Define the **slogan** variable to equal the array of strings.
2. Determine whether the height of the array is greater than the width. If it is, the scale factor, **sf**, is equal to the square root of two multiplied by the radius of the text circle and then divided by the height of **slogan**. If the height is not greater than the width, divide by the width of **slogan**.
3. **sf** scales the coordinate space in both directions.
4. The string defined as **slogan** is placed onto the stack and **vpos** is invoked to move the current point vertically so the array of strings is centered around the X axis.
5. A **forall** loop is begun, which centers each string in the array around

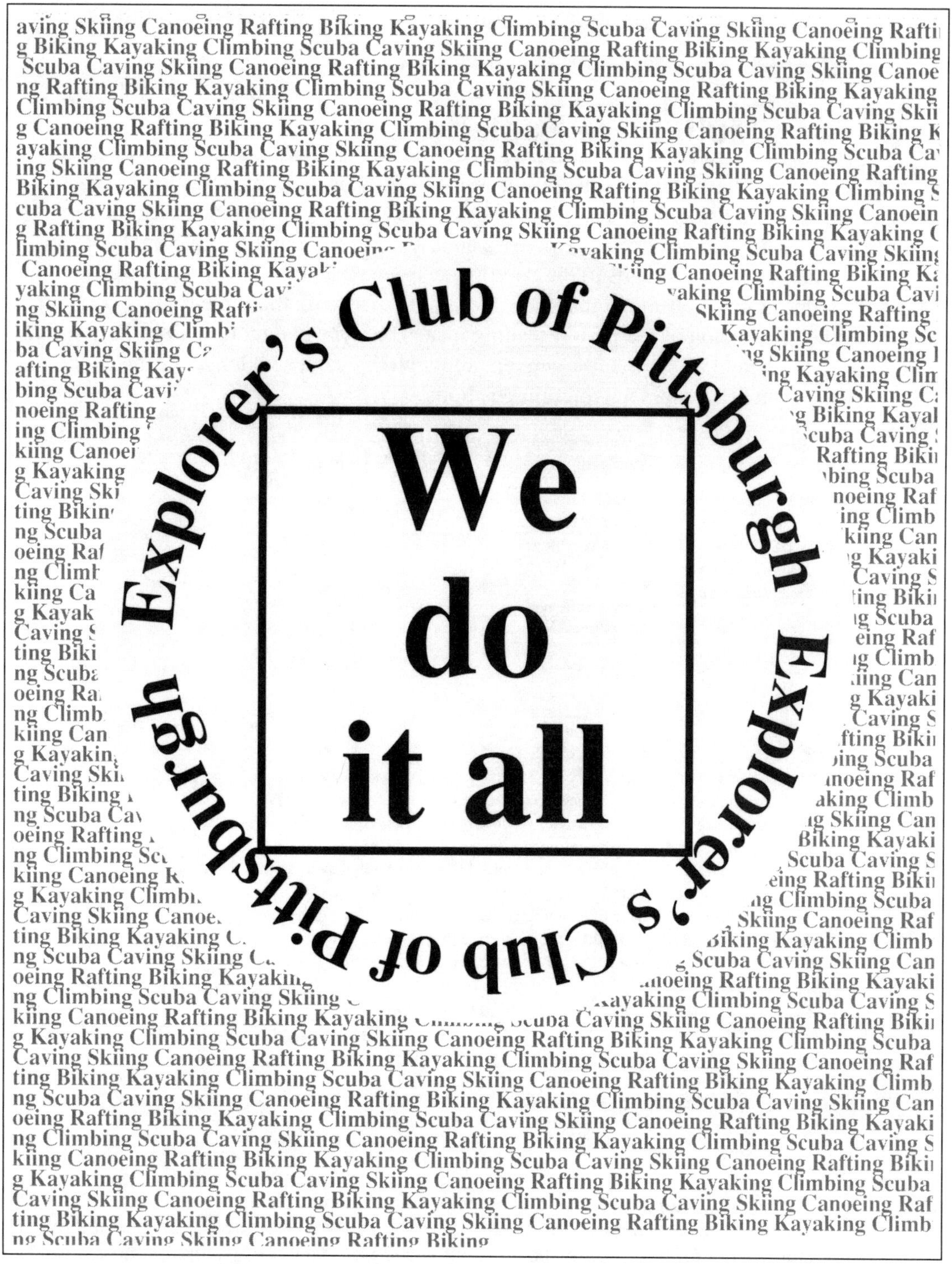

Figure 13.3: Poster with Center Slogan Scaled to Fit

the Y axis and moves the current point to the start of the next line.[50]

6. Multi-Page Poster

The final version of the poster program, Listing 13.3, enlarges the size of the image and prints it on a series of pages. Those pages can then be assembled into the completed poster. As demonstrated in the last section, the **scale** operator can change the size of units in the coordinate space so an image can be enlarged or reduced. In this section, the **scale** operator is used with the same routines used in the last version of the poster. Scaling means the type and margin sizes do not need to be changed from the last version, although the values no longer correspond to the actual type sizes and margin positions.

Listing 13.3: Multi-Page Poster Program

```
%!PS-Adobe-3.0 EPSF-30.
%%BoundingBox: 0 0 612 792
%%Title: (poster example 1)
%%Creationdate: (10/31/91)
%%EndComments

%General Use Variable

/inch {72 mul} def

%Constants

/TM 11 inch def %top poster margin (original size)
/BM 0 inch def %bottom poster margin (original size)
/LM 0 inch def %left poster margin (original size)
/RM 8.5 inch def %right poster margin (original size)
/PM {4.25 inch 5.5 inch}  def %middle poster (original size)
/LMC .5 inch def %left margin of the clipping region
/BMC .5 inch def %bottom margin of the clipping region
/PHC 10 inch def %height of the clipping region
/PWC 7.5 inch def %width of the clipping region
/pi 3.1415923 def
/ptsize 50 def % typesize at original size
/radius 200 def
/pscale 2 def % the sacle factor for the poster

%Background Printing Procedures
```

[50]The calculation of the vertical component for the **rmoveto** operator is another issue of aesthetics. The vertical distance moved is equal to the type size plus the inverse of the scale factor (rounded down), which should result in adequate interline spacing for most slogans. If the interline spacing seems off, the constant 1 used in the division operation can be increased or decreased.

```
/newline %move to start of new line
 {currentpoint 13 sub exch pop LM exch
  moveto } def

/newlinecheck %check if to start new line
 {currentpoint pop RM gt
 {newline} if} def

/finish %check if at page bottom
 {currentpoint exch pop
  BM lt} def

/fillpage %fill page with background names
  {/fillstrg exch def
   {{pop pop newlinecheck} fillstrg kshow %move to proper position
   finish {exit} if  %if at bottom of page exit loop

      } loop
      }def

%Draw Circle Procedure

/drawcircle  %draw gray circle in center page
 {newpath
  PM  3.5 inch 0 360 arc
  closepath
 .9 setgray
 fill}
 def


%Horizontal Line Printing Procedures


/hcenter {dup stringwidth pop 2 div neg 0 rmoveto show} def

/vcenter {dup length ptsize mul 2 div ptsize .8 mul sub 0 exch rmoveto}
         def

/width { /longstring 0 def
         { stringwidth
         pop
         dup
         longstring gt {/longstring exch def} {pop} ifelse} forall
         longstring} def

/height {length ptsize mul} def

%Circular Line Printing Procedures

/circtext  %print outside circle
  { /str exch def
  /xradius radius ptsize 4 div add def
  gsave
  str calculateangle cvi 2 mul 360 exch idiv /iter exch def
  -180 rotate
  1 1 iter {pop
```

```
          str
          {/charcode exch def ( ) dup 0 charcode put circchar} forall
          } for
  grestore
  } def

/calculateangle %find half of angle
{stringwidth pop 2 div
 2 xradius mul pi mul div 360 mul} def


/circchar   %show character upright on circle clockwise
 {/char exch def
 /halfangle char calculateangle def
  gsave
  halfangle neg rotate
  radius 0 translate
  -90 rotate
  char stringwidth pop 2 div neg 0 moveto
  char show
  grestore
  halfangle 2 mul neg rotate
  } def



/posterproc {
gsave
pscale PWC 8.5 inch div mul pscale PHC 11 inch div mul scale
% ----------- Fill with background Text-----------------------
/Times-Bold findfont 15 scalefont setfont
LM TM moveto
.5 setgray
(Kayaking Climbing Scuba Caving Skiing Canoeing Rafting Biking )
fillpage

drawcircle


% -------------------- Circular Text -----------------------
0 setgray
/Times-Bold findfont ptsize scalefont setfont
PM translate
 (Explorer's Club of Pittsburgh  ) circtext

% --------------------- Center Slogan ----------------------
0 0 moveto
/slogan [(We) (do) (it all)] def
slogan height slogan width gt
{2 sqrt radius mul slogan height div /sf exch def}
{2 sqrt radius mul slogan width div /sf exch def} ifelse
sf sf scale
slogan
vcenter
{hcenter currentpoint pop neg ptsize 1 sf div floor add neg rmoveto}
forall
grestore} def
```

```
%Begin Program

newpath  %draw clipping path
LMC BMC moveto
0 PHC rlineto
PWC 0 rlineto
0 PHC neg rlineto
closepath clip
LMC BMC translate %translate to correspond with clipped area
0 1 pscale 1 sub
{/rowcount exch def
 0 1 pscale 1 sub  %run for each row and column
 {/colcount exch def
 gsave
 PWC colcount mul neg
 PHC rowcount mul neg
 translate
 posterproc
 gsave showpage grestore %print page
 grestore
 }for
 }for

%%EOF
```

If you have a laser printer with large enough paper, enlarging the size of the poster is simply a matter of scaling the coordinate space at the start of the program script. For example, if both the X and Y dimensions are scaled by a factor of two, the poster image is twice as tall and twice as wide as the original. But because most PostScript devices do not print on 17-by-22-inch paper, scaling by two on a normal laser printer results in only part of the image printing—the lower left quadrant, to be precise, because that part is closest to the origin at the lower left corner of the printable page area.

A fourth of the poster image can be printed simply by scaling, revealing the strategy of how the poster image is broken down over a series of individual sheets. If the origin is moved away from the lower left corner of the printable page area, portion of the enlarged poster image that falls into the printable page area changes. As demonstrated in the last section, the origin of the coordinate space can be moved using the **translate** operator. Thus, by translating the origin multiple times and printing the enlarged image after each translation, you can produe the entire poster image.

Figure 13.4 illustrates the strategy for printing the enlarged image. The axes are scaled by a factor of two, and the origin of the coordinate space is translated in a negative direction both horizontally and vertically, so, the portion of the enlarged image falling within the printable page area corresponds to the upper right quadrant of the image.

Theoretically, the entire image (no matter how large it has been scaled) can be

Figure 13.4: Enlarged Poster With Translation of Origin

mapped onto a set of pages with a series of such translations. There is one complicating factor, however. Because no laser printer can print to the very edge of the paper, it typically leaves a about a half inch of white border on all sides. Printers with limited memory may leave a larger border. It is necessary to accommodate this limitation by reducing the scaling factor and incorporating the size of the imaging area into the strategy for translating the origin. The final version of the poster program works as follows:

1. Borders for a clipping region are defined, creating a window to the printable page area that is smaller than an 8.5-by-11-inch page. The **clip** operator makes this window the current clipping path, and any marks falling outside that region are not visible. Essentially, the size of the printable page area is reduced to accommodate the laser printer's limits.

2. An **pscale** integer variable is defined as the scaling factor for the poster. For example, setting **pscale** equal to two produces a poster that is two sheets high and two sheets wide; defining **pscale** as three produces a 3 × 3 poster, and so forth. The actual poster image must be scaled by slightly less than **pscale** because the printable page area has been reduced. In the horizontal direction:

   $$\text{the scaling factor} = \textbf{pscale} \times \frac{w}{8.5}$$

   where w equals the width of the clipping region. In the vertical distance:

   $$\text{the scaling factor} = \textbf{pscale} \times \frac{h}{11}$$

   where h equals the height of the clipping region.

3. The enlarged image must be printed a number of times equal to the number of "tiles" (**pscale**^{2}), with a translation after each piece has been printed. This is accomplished with a pair of nested **for** loops, the outer one iterating up to the number of "rows" and the inner one looping within each row up to the number of "columns." Because the poster is scaled proportionally, both the number of rows and the number of columns is the same (**pscale**).

There are few changes to the code between the second and third versions of the program. At the top of the listing, the new **LMC**, **BMC**, **PHC**, and **PWC** variables represent the left and bottom margins, and the height and width of the clipping region. These can be adjusted to reduce or enlarge the size of the white border around each "tile." The **pscale** variable is the scaling factor for the poster, with a value of two for a four-sheet poster.

The script from the second version of the program is changed to a procedure called **posterproc** with the following changes:

- A **gsave** and **grestore** is placed at the start and end of the procedure to avoid carrying over any scaling into the script.
- The image is scaled according to the formula listed above.
- The **showpage** operator is removed.

The script of third version begins with constructing a rectangular path equal to the dimensions of the desired clipping region and invocating the **clip** operator, which adds that path to the current clipping path. This reduces the size of the printable page area. The origin of the coordinate space is then translated to **LMC**, **BMC**, and the nested **for** loops begun. The outer loop iterates up to the number of rows (starting at zero) and the inner loop up to the number of columns. At each iteration, the origin is translated in a negative direction equaling **PWC** times the column count along the X axis and **PHC** times the row count along the Y axis. To keep the effects of these translations from being cumulative, they are bracketed by **gsave** and **grestore**. After each translation the **posterproc** procedure is invoked, followed by **showpage**. The **showpage** is also between a **gsave/grestore** pair to avoid resetting the clipping region.

7. Further Modifications

You are encouraged to experiment with different strings for the background text, circular text, and center slogan. As discussed, the numeric constants governing horizontal centering, interletter, and interline spacing may need to be adjusted, depending on the size of the text. The clipping region is defined to leave a half inch margin around each tile. By increasing the size of the clipping region, a smaller border (and thus a larger image) can be produced.

Part 3
Simple PostScript Drivers

Some of the most interesting things that can be done with PostScript can only be accomplished when a program is written to produce the PostScript code. This allows the user to provide only the changed information while the program takes care of the detailed and repetitive calculations. A program that controls a device is called a driver.

The first chapter in this section introduces the concept of a device driver. A general overview of the functionality of a device driver is presented along with examples of actual code. This is followed by a chapter that provides some additional information of fonts. Following this are five more chapters that introduce simple driver programs in one or more languages. The simplest versions are presented in BASIC, the next most sophisticated in Pascal, and the most sophisticated in C. Most of the programs can be cross translated without too much work, as they contain only the barest essentials in terms of code.

We caution the user that the goal of keeping the programs simple has resulted in very little user interface code—the programs are not bulletproofed. Take care in using the programs to enter information correctly. If you don't, the program will either not produce the PostScript code file, or it will produce it incorrectly. The versions of these programs that we actually use are 2 to 3 times longer than the versions presented here. This additional code is concerned with things like text editors, interface bulletproofing, and WYSIWYG[51] displays. The interested reader will find that the programs are generally so constructed that this kind of code can be easily added.

[51] What You See Is What You Get

Chapter 14
Drivers

1. Introduction

The preceding chapters provide an introduction to PostScript, how it works, and the effects you can accomplish with it. The projects have demonstrated how it is possible for expensive graphics editors to flow text along a curve or rotate a shape by an arbitrary angle. PostScript is a powerful language, that is not difficult to program in; nevertheless, in reading through these chapters and trying out the examples, you may have wondered whether stack juggling and axis spinning is worth the effort. While PostScript is not all difficult to learn, you probably do not want to do your resume directly in PostScript. A word processing application could create the necessary output more easily. This chapter introduces techniques for writing driver programs in conventional programming languages. In particular, you will learn some simple rules to use in developing more complex projects.

2. Drivers

Word processors and graphic editors that output to laser printers are examples of PostScript drivers. It may be helpful to think of a driver program as an automobile driver or chauffeur. There are two ways having a chauffeur drive you around can be easier than driving yourself in two ways:

- A chauffeur can execute a complex series of operations with just a simple command from you. For example, you can tell a chauffeur, "Drive me from the hotel to the airport." You could do the driving yourself, but the chauffeur allows you to turn your attention to (presumably) more important matters.

- A chauffeur frees you from worrying about the details of the specific vehicle in which you are riding. You count on the chauffeur to carry out the same instructions whether the limousine has manual or automatic transmission, regular or power steering, or whether it is a limousine or a pickup truck.

There are different kinds of printer driver programs, but all of them aim to achieve goals analogous to this comparison. Suppose graphics editor users wants to draw a line between two points on a page. They may know that the line is ultimately realized as hundreds of toner dots on paper, but after drawning the line on the screen (or specified coordinates for the end points), the driver is expected to take responsibility for ensuring the printer puts each dot in the right place. You should be able to specify parameters such as line thickness once, and then count on the driver to keep that parameter as a default. The graphic being produced may eventually be printed on more than one type of printer, but the job of the printer driver is to make sure a command (such as one for drawing a line) is translated into whatever device-specific operations are appropriate.

Some printer drivers accomplish this device independence by keeping tables of primitive commands for each type of printer they "know." One advantage of working with PostScript is that the language itself is designed to be device-independent, which means that handling device-specific details is the PostScript interpreter's job. Writing a PostScript driver involves achieving the first of the two goals listed above: how to produce a long string of PostScript code based on high-level interaction with the user. A driver program may be given a user interface which although not as elaborate as a word processor is, enables you to concentrate on the task at hand rather than on PostScript language details. In fact, a well-written driver can be used by someone who has little knowledge of PostScript.

None of the projects in the preceding chapters are longer than a couple dozen lines of code. They demonstrate how you can achieve striking graphic effects using only a few PostScript commands, but they should also give a sense of how complex a multi-page project can be and how difficult it would be to code page after page of PostScript by hand. Earlier chapters have shown how you can reduce complexity by the definition in the prologue of procedures, which can then be used repeatedly in the program script. The next series of projects achieve even greater complexity by having a program written in BASIC, Pascal, or C to produce the script code automatically, based on input from the user.

A chauffeur needs skill and knowledge in driving and navigation if he is to get you from point A to point B based on your command. By the same token, it is often necessary to equip a PostScript driver with a PostScript interpreter's knowledge to handle calculations that the output device would otherwise compute. The most radical example would be for the driver program to maintain detailed graphics state information such as the current coordinate system, dictionary, and clipping path. Most applications can avoid representing those details explicitly by writing strong procedures for the prologue. However, it is not unusual for a driver to keep track of what the current font is, what page is being worked on, and where the marks are being placed on the page. Programming this kind of information into a driver may seem like reinventing the wheel, but there are some very practical reasons for this approach:

- Although it is now economically feasible for each person in a work environment to have a CPU on his or her desk, laser printers are usually shared resources. For that reason it is efficient to shift the burden of processing from the printer back to the PC so you do not tie up the printer. Thanks to PostScript, printers can handle complex calculations, but it is often better to leave them to the driver program.

- The formatting conventions for structured PostScript encourage straightforward rather than sophisticated code because their agenda is clarity rather than efficiency. For example, you could write a very small PostScript program that runs in a loop and produces a different page of output at each iteration by changing parameters (perhaps at random!) each time. But if you decide you like a particular page, there might be no way to separate the particular code that produced that image. So, as discussed in Chapter 3, one of the demands of structured PostScript is that each page should be independent.

The initial versions of the driver program in this chapter defer some calculations to the PostScript interpreter. Later versions employ font information from font metric files to demonstrate how you can determine such information prior to executing the PostScript program.

3. How to Program a Driver

There are a few basic steps to writing a PostScript driver:

1. Any text or image can be thought of as a collection of objects. Even if you are not working in an object-oriented programming language, you will want to identify the basic objects that will appear on the page. These objects may be shapes, paragraphs, lines, lines of text, or individual words.

2. The next step is to write the PostScript procedures that constitute the program prologue. As demonstrated in earlier chapters, procedures defined in the prologue act as the basic building blocks which are assembled in the program script. Most procedures correspond to objects identified in the previous step. For example, there might be procedures to draw a particular shape at a particular orientation, procedures to box a text string, and so forth.

3. Write the primitive functions into a data file. This file copied into the prologue of each output from the driver program.

4. Write the driver code itself. It should have three parts:
   - One part to take care of setup chores such as opening files, reading data into arrays, and copying the PostScript prologue to the output file.
   - Another part of the program should handle interaction with the user and create the driver's internal representation of what is to be printed. At its simplest, this step could consist solely of collection of parameters to be passed to PostScript procedures in the output script.
   - The final part of the program should write the script, sending procedure calls to the output in the appropriate sequence, with string and numeric I/O functions to write in operands at the appropriate places.

4. Building a PostScript Driver

The best way to illustrate the concepts of the last section is with examples of PostScript driver programs for creating small posters. The programs in this section are written in Pascal. Each accepts one or more strings and creates an ASCII file of PostScript commands as output. The listings omit constant, type, variable, function, and procedure definitions, but those omitted elements are explained in the accompanying description. The programs' input and output are fairly robust, but not bullet proof; they presuppose, for example, that parentheses and control characters are not part of input strings. Functions to verify user input should be easy to write.

a. A Very Simple Driver

The first version, Listing 14.1, is a very simple kind of driver. You enter a string at a prompt, and the program produces a four-line PostScript program as output. In the output program, a type style and size is selected, the current point is placed half way up the page at a spot one inch from the left margin, and the user's string is shown at that point, followed by a **showpage**. This is not an earth-shattering reduction in complexity compared to coding in PostScript by hand, but it illustrates the basic function of a PostScript driver. The output from the first version is shown in Listing 14.2. The output from executing that output is illustrated in Figure 14.1.

Listing 14.1: A Simple Driver

```
Program Driver1(Input, Output);

{CONST, Type, Var, Function, and Procedure Definitions ommitted}

Begin
  Setup; {Open output file, etc.}

  Write('Enter a string ->');
  Readln(stringvar);

  Writeln(outfile,'%!');
  Writeln(outfile,'/Helvetica findfont 20 scalefont setfont');
  Writeln(outfile,'72 396 moveto');
  Writeln(outfile,'(' + stringvar + ') show showpage');

  Cleanup; {close the output file, etc.}
End. {Program}
```

Listing 14.2: PostScript Output from a Simple Driver

```
%!
/Helvetica findfont 20 scalefont setfont
72 396 moveto
(Mary had a little lamb) show showpage
```

There are two procedures which are part of every example in this section. The **Setup** and **Cleanup** procedures initialize all variables, read data from external files, and preparation of the output file. Listings for **Setup** and **Cleanup** are omitted, but both are fairly straightforward. In all but the last version of the driver **Setup** simply opens an output text file and assigns that file to the **outfile** variable which is of type **text**. **Cleanup** simply closes that same file.[52]

[52] Here are the listings for **Setup** and **Cleanup**. Different versions of Pascal vary slightly in the syntax for opening and closing text files. Assuming most readers work on PCs, the following procedures are consistent with Borland's Turbo Pascal:

```
Procedure Setup;
  Begin
    assign(outfile, 'output.ps');
    rewrite(outfile);
  End; {Procedure}

Procedure Cleanup;
  Begin
    close(outfile);
  End; {Procedure}
```

Figure 14.1: Output from a Simple Driver

b. Adding Variability

The second version of the program, Listing 14.3, adds a layer of complexity by making the driver output variable in length. The program runs in a repeat loop, and accepts strings from the user until a blank line is entered. After each string is input, a PostScript command is written to the output file to show the string and move the current point. This version also illustrates graphics state information incorporated in the driver program: the **Vpos** variable keeps track of the vertical position of the next string to be displayed. At each iteration of the loop, **Vpos** is decreased by 22 (1.1 times the type size) in keeping with a common guideline for calculating the spacing between lines of text.

Listing 14.3: Driver Outputting Multiple Strings

```
Program Driver2(Input, Output);

{CONST, Type, Var, Function, and Procedure Definitions ommitted}

Begin
  Setup; {Open output file, etc.}

  Writeln(outfile,'%!');
  Writeln(outfile,'/Helvetica findfont 20 scalefont setfont');
```

```
  Writeln(outfile,'72 396 moveto');

  Vpos := 396;

  Repeat
    Write('Enter a string ->');
    Readln(stringvar);
    Writeln(outfile,'(' + stringvar + ') show');
    Vpos := Vpos - 22;
    Write(outfile, '72 ');
    Write(outfile, Vpos);
    Writeln(outfile, ' moveto')
  Until stringvar = '';

  Writeln(outfile, 'showpage');

  Cleanup; {close the output file, etc.}
End. {Program}
```

c. Expanding the Prologue

The third version, shown in Listing 14.4, illustrates how PostScript procedure definitions can be output as building blocks for the script. Two additional lines at the start of the output are the definition for a procedure called **ctrstr**, which is a string centering procedure.[53] In this version of the program, the horizontal component of the display point for each string is changed from 76 (one inch from the left) to 306 (half way across the page). The **ctrstr** procedure centers a string around the current point, which in this case centers it horizontally on the page. When the script is written to the output file, the **show** operators of the previous version are replaced by **ctrstr** operators.

Listing 14.4: Driver Outputting Multiple Strings with Horizontal Centering

```
Program Driver3(Input, Output);

{CONST, Type, Var, Function, and Procedure Definitions ommitted}

Begin
  Setup; {Open output file, etc.}

  Writeln(outfile,'%!');
  Writeln(outfile,'/ctrstr {dup stringwidth pop 2 div');
  Writeln(outfile, '0 exch sub 0 rmoveto show} def');
```

[53]The string centering procedure works by making a duplicate of the string, calculating its width, and then moving the current point to the left a distance of half the length of the string.

```
  Writeln(outfile,'/Helvetica findfont 20 scalefont setfont');
  Writeln(outfile,'306 396 moveto');

  Vpos := 396;

  Repeat
    Write('Enter a string ->');
    Readln(stringvar);
    Writeln(outfile,'(' + stringvar + ') ctrstr');
    Vpos := Vpos - 22;
    Write(outfile, '306 ');
    Write(outfile, Vpos);
    Writeln(outfile, ' moveto')
  Until stringvar = '';

  Writeln(outfile, 'showpage');

  Cleanup; {close the output file, etc.}
End. {Program}
```

d. Calculation by the Driver

In the fourth version of the driver, Listing 14.5, first notice the string variable is replaced by an array of strings. This gives you the option of centering the output vertically as well as horizontally. In the first repeat loop, you use enter strings into an array one at a time until a blank line terminates the loop. You are then given the option of centering the output vertically. If you choose not to center the **Vpos** variable is set to 396 (as in previous versions). But if you choose is to center the output, the **index** variable, which is equal to the number of strings in the array, is multiplied by 22 (1.1 times the type size) and then divided by two. The current point is then moved vertically by that distance. The overall effect is to move the current point above the vertical center of the page a distance equal to half the height of the output. This version illustrates how calculation that the PostScript interpreter might otherwise handle can be worked out by the driver program in advance of execution. The **ctrstr** procedure can be rewritten to take care of both horizontal and vertical centering by accepting an array of strings on the operand stack. However, you avoid writing a much more complex PostScript procedure without adding to the driver program's complexity. The output from the driver is shown in Listing 14.6. The result of executing that output is illustrated in Figure 14.2.

Listing 14.5: Driver for Vertical and horizontal centering

```
Program Driver4(Input, Output);

{CONST, Type, Var, Function, and Procedure Definitions ommitted}

Begin
  Setup; {Open output file, etc.}

  Writeln(outfile,'%!');
  Writeln(outfile,'/ctrstr {dup stringwidth pop 2 div');
  Writeln(outfile, '0 exch sub 0 rmoveto show} def');
  Writeln(outfile,'/Helvetica findfont 20 scalefont setfont');

  index := 0;

  Repeat
    index := index + 1;
    Write('Enter a string ->');
    Readln(sarray[index]);
  Until sarray[index] = '';

  Write('Center vertically? (Y/N)');
  Readln(response);
  If response = 'Y' then Vpos := 396 + (index/2 * 22)
                          else Vpos := 396;

  index := 1;

  Repeat
    Write(outfile, '306 ');
    Write(outfile, Vpos :3 :0);
    Writeln(outfile, ' moveto');
    Writeln(outfile,'(' + sarray[index] + ') ctrstr');
    Vpos := Vpos - 22;
    index := index + 1;
  Until sarray[index] = '';


  Writeln(outfile, 'showpage');

  Cleanup; {close the output file, etc.}
End. {Program}
```

Listing 14.6: Outputting with Multiple Strings and Horizontal Centering

```
%!
/ctrstr {dup stringwidth pop 2 div
0 exch sub 0 rmoveto show} def
/Helvetica findfont 20 scalefont setfont
306 451 moveto
(Mary had a little lamb) ctrstr
306 429 moveto
(its fleece was white as snow) ctrstr
```

```
306 407 moveto
(and everywhere that Mary went) ctrstr
306 385 moveto
(the lamb was sure to go) ctrstr
showpage
```

5. Font Metric Files: Providing More Information to the Driver

The last version of the driver is able to accomplish some prior calculations based on a very simple piece of information: the type size is 20 point. However, there are other calculations that can make the driver more powerful, but it ca not accomplish them without more detailed information about the output. Suppose, for example, you enter a string that is too wide for an 8.5-by-11-inch page. The string centering function still works, causing equal portions of the left and right sides of the string to be cut off when the page is printed. If the driver has a way to calculate the width of the string during the user interaction, it can notify you that the string is too wide to appear. It might give you the option of changing the string or reducing the size of the type. The final version of the driver program is not this sophisticated, but this section introduces font metric files to provide the kind of information necessary for these kinds of improvements.

The final version of the driver, Listing 14.7, achieves the same effects as the previous version. However, in this version, the calculations of the driver program are more complex and rely on information stored in font metric files. In the fifth version, the **ctrstr** PostScript procedure is eliminated and calculation for the strings' horizontal position is turned over to the driver. At each iteration of the second repeat loop, the real valued variable **Hpos** is set to a value equal to 306 minus half the width of the string, as calculated by a function called **stringwidth**. This achieves the same effect as the **cs** PostScript Procedure, which was used in the previous versions. The listing for **stringwidth** is omitted from Listing 14.7 and is included in Listing 14.8.

Listing 14.7: Horizontal centering via string width calculation

```
Program Driver5(Input, Output);

{CONST, Type, Var, Function, and Procedure Definitions ommitted}

Begin
  Setup; {Open output file, etc.}

  Writeln(outfile,'%!');
  Writeln(outfile,'/Helvetica findfont 20 scalefont setfont');
```

Mary had a little lamb
its fleece was white as snow
and everywhere that Mary went
the lamb was sure to go

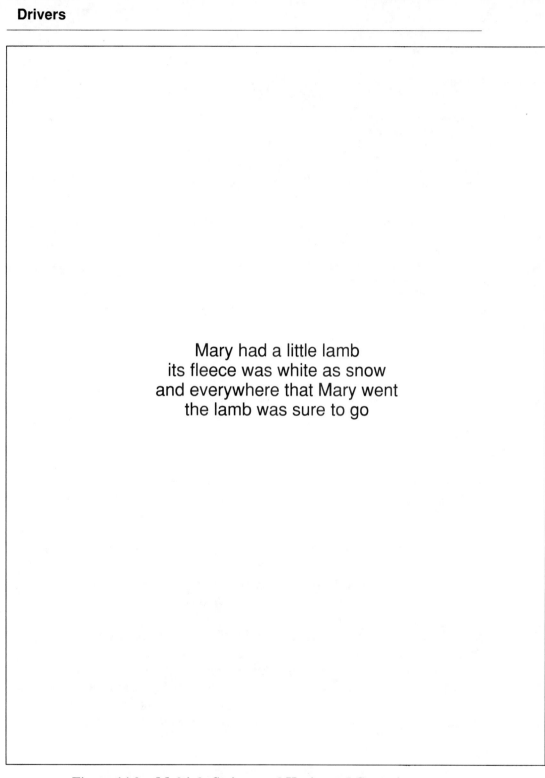

Figure 14.2: Multiple Strings and Horizontal Centering

```
  index := 0;

  Repeat
    index := index + 1;
    Write('Enter a string ->');
    Readln(sarray[index]);
  Until sarray[index] = '';

  Write('Center vertically? (Y/N)');
  Readln(response);
  If response = 'Y' then Vpos := 396 + (index/2 * 22)
                          else Vpos := 396;

  index := 1;

  Repeat
    Hpos := 306 - (stringwidth(sarray[index])/2);
    Write(outfile, Hpos :3 :0);
    Write(outfile, ' ');
    Write(outfile, Vpos :3 :0);
    Writeln(outfile, ' moveto');
    Writeln(outfile,'(' + sarray[index] + ') show');
    Vpos := Vpos - 22;
    index := index + 1;
  Until sarray[index] = '';


  Writeln(outfile, 'showpage');

  Cleanup; {close the output file, etc.}
End. {Program}
```

In order to calculate the width of the strings, the function presented in Listing 14.8 needs to know the widths of the characters that make up the string (which in this case are in the Helvetica font). Width information is an example of data that is available in font metric files such as the Adobe font metric (AFM) and Adobe composite font metric (ACFM) files, specifications for which are available from the Adobe Systems Developers' Association. AFM and ACFM files contain width information for the various fonts, as well as additional information such as kerning data. However, the example in this chapter uses a simplified file which pairs characters with an integer representing the width of that character in thousandths of an em-space (see Listing 14.9 for an extract). An em-space is a value equal to the type size in points. So, if 20-point type is used, an em-space is equal to 20 points. Measuring the character width in fractions of an em-space makes the width value independent of the type size. So although a driver needs a metric file for each font, it does not need separate files for each size.

Listing 14.8: Function to calculate width of a string

```
{Calculate the width of the string in points}
Function stringwidth(the_string:string): real;
  Var
    a_char:char;
    numchars,loop:integer;
    the_width:real;
  begin
    the_width := 0;
    numchars := length(the_string);
    for loop := 1 to numchars do
      the_width := the_width + farray[ord(the_string[loop])];
    the_width := (the_width * 20)/1000;
    stringwidth := the_width;
  end; {function stringwidth}
```

The **Setup** procedure in the fifth version of the driver does more than simply open the output file. The values stored in the font metric file are read into a one-dimensional array (**farray**). The index of **farray** begins at 32, not 0, so the index of the array corresponds to the ASCII value of the character whose width value is stored. This permits the **stringwidth** procedure to call **ord(the_string[loop]**) to retrieve the width value of each character in the string. After these values are summed, the result is multipied by 20 (the point size) and divided by 1,000 to get the width of the string in points.

Listing 14.9: Excerpt from a simplified font metric file

```
V 667
W 944
X 667
Y 667
Z 611
[ 278
\ 278
] 278
^ 469
_ 556
` 222
a 556
b 556
c 500
d 556
e 556
f 278
g 556
```

6. Further Improvements

There are a number of ways the driver program presented in this chapter can be more sophisticated.

- The font can be chosen from a menu rather than being hard coded. Of course, a metric file for each font has to be maintained.

- The point size of the string can be entered by the user rather than being hard coded. The I/O functions would have to be robust enough to check for negative or non-numeric values.

- A conditional statement can test whether the length of the string exceeds the width of the page (612 points). If so, a **maxsize** function can calculate the maximum point size as follows:

```
the_width := 0;
numchars := length(the_string);
for loop := 1 to numchars do
the_width := the_width +
       the_font[ord(the_string[loop])];
maxsize := 612,000/the_width;
```

- You can have the option of printing the poster in landscape mode. This requires writing **rotate** and **translate** operators to the output file.

Chapter 15
Fonts

This book makes a number of references to the proper placement and rendering of characters, special effects that can be achieved with characters, and other font-related issues. The full story of fonts, font types, and font dictionary composition would take a separate book. However, there are effects you can achieve without understanding all the nuances of PostScript fonts. These include accessing accented characters or outlining a character path rather than filling it. The introduction provided here is cursory. Interested readers should refer to the *PostScript Reference Manual* and the *Adobe Type 1 Font Format* for more information. The chapter begins with definitions. In the next section, utility programs are provided to help in working with fonts. The Adobe Font Metric files are briefly introduced, and the font files used in the driver chapters are described. A brief mention about the encoding options that allow for a wide selection of accented characters is made in the final section.

1. Definitions

Technically, a font is the complete set of characters of one size in one style. A Times-Roman 18-point Bold font is different from its 19-point font or from the Italic font of the same family. The set of fonts for a given style, i.e Times-Roman, or Palatino, or Helvetica, is known as a font family. "Palatino" defines the font family, and 18-point Palatino Italic, 22-point Palatino Bold, and 23 1/2-point Palatino BoldItalic are different fonts withing the font family. In traditional printing, this distinction between fonts was very real—either you had the font or you did not. With modern technology, the distinctions have blurred. Most systems work from different designs for each style—bold, italic, etc.—but scale all the different sizes from one mathematical model. Some systems even develop bold and italic from a single model of the Roman font. In these systems, the term "font" encompasses not only the traditional meaning, but also everything up to a font family. Generally speaking, we use font to refer to all sizes of a given style. The code shown in Listing 15.1 causes most printers to produce a listing of the fonts that exist on the printer.

Listing 15.1: Program to List Fonts Available on a Printer

```
%!PS-Adobe-3.0 EPSF-30.
%%BoundingBox: 0 0 612 792
%%Title: (Font List: Prints out all available fonts)
%%Creationdate: (11/26/91--08:00)
%%EndComments
% Prints out all available fonts
/Helvetica findfont
12 scalefont setfont
/astring 80 string def
/writefont
        {pop astring cvs  dup stringwidth pop
        exch show neg -14 rmoveto}
        def

100 700 moveto
FontDirectory {writefont} forall
showpage
%%EOF
```

Each printer varies, and although there are more accurate and sophisticated ways to get a listing, this is satisfactory for your purposes. The approach takes the FontDirectory array, which defines the fonts available in virtual memory, and prints a list of them. We found the following fonts on the printer in our office:

- NewCenturySchlbk-Italic
- Bookman-LightItalic
- Helvetica
- Courier-Bold
- Helvetica-Narrow-Bold
- Courier-BoldOblique
- Times-Italic
- Times-Bold
- NewCenturySchlbk-Roman
- Helvetica-Narrow-Oblique
- Bookman-DemiItalic
- Symbol
- Bookman-Demi
- Helvetica-BoldOblique
- Bookman-Light
- Helvetica-Oblique
- AvantGarde-Book
- AvantGarde-DemiOblique
- AvantGarde-BookOblique
- AvantGarde-Demi
- Helvetica-Narrow

- ZapfChancery-MediumItalic
- Courier-Oblique
- NewCenturySchlbk-BoldItalic
- Helvetica-Bold
- Times-Roman
- Times-BoldItalic
- Helvetica-Narrow-BoldOblique
- NewCenturySchlbk-Bold
- Palatino-Bold
- Courier
- Palatino-Italic
- Palatino-Roman
- Palatino-BoldItalic
- ZapfDingBats

Typography's long history has given us many terms to describe the appearance and characteristics of fonts. Traditionally, a character was engraved on a metal block. In modern terms, the dimensions that completely enclose a character are the character's bounding box. The character origin is a point on the base line that is used as a reference location for drawing the character. The X width is the distance from the origin of a given character to the origin of the next character. Most users are familiar typewriter or monospaced fonts found on typewriters and generally do not the consider typographic or proportionally spaced fonts used for typesetting. If you type text on typewriter, you probably notice each character is the same width; the *l* in "Hello" takes up the same amount of line space as the capital *H* does. That is a "monospaced" font. The alternative is a "proportionally" spaced font, which books use. Look at this "M" and this "i" in this. The "M" is wider than the "i." The widths for the characters in the Helvetica font are printed above the characters in Figure 15.1. More is explained in the section on font metrics.

2. Character Manipulations

Because characters in PostScript are defined in terms of a series of lines and curves that are normally connected and filled with "black ink," it is possible to use the basic character forms to achieve special effects. One effect is outlining characters rather than filling them in, as is normally the case. The code is shown in Listing 15.2. and the resulting graphic is depicted in Figure 15.2. The **show** operator that is normally used with a string is replaced by a boolean and the **charpath** operator. The boolean should be false if the path that outlines the characters is to be stroked. It should be true if the path is to be used for filling or clipping, as shown in Figure 15.3.

Times-Roman 18 point

Code	Width	Character	Name
32	0.25		space
33	0.332	!	exclam
34	0.408	"	quotedbl
35	0.499	#	numbersign
36	0.499	$	dollar
37	0.833	%	percent
38	0.777	&	ampersand
39	0.332	’	quoteright
40	0.332	(	parenleft
41	0.332	)	parenright
42	0.499	*	asterisk
43	0.563	+	plus
44	0.25	,	comma
45	0.332	-	hyphen
46	0.25	.	period
47	0.277	/	slash
48	0.5	0	zero
49	0.5	1	one
50	0.5	2	two
51	0.5	3	three
52	0.5	4	four
53	0.5	5	five
54	0.5	6	six
55	0.5	7	seven
56	0.5	8	eight
57	0.5	9	nine
58	0.278	:	colon
59	0.278	;	semicolon
60	0.564	<	less
61	0.564	=	equal
62	0.564	>	greater
63	0.443	?	question
64	0.92	@	at
65	0.722	A	A
66	0.667	B	B
67	0.667	C	C
68	0.722	D	D
69	0.61	E	E
70	0.555	F	F
71	0.722	G	G
72	0.722	H	H
73	0.333	I	I
74	0.388	J	J
75	0.722	K	K
76	0.61	L	L
77	0.889	M	M
78	0.722	N	N
79	0.722	O	O
80	0.555	P	P
81	0.722	Q	Q
82	0.667	R	R
83	0.555	S	S
84	0.61	T	T
85	0.722	U	U
86	0.722	V	V
87	0.944	W	W
88	0.722	X	X
89	0.722	Y	Y
90	0.61	Z	Z
91	0.333	[	bracketleft
92	0.278	\	backslash
93	0.333	]	bracketright
94	0.468	^	asciicircum
95	0.5	_	underscore
96	0.333	‘	quoteleft
97	0.443	a	a
98	0.5	b	b
99	0.443	c	c
100	0.5	d	d
101	0.443	e	e
102	0.333	f	f
103	0.5	g	g
104	0.5	h	h
105	0.278	i	i
106	0.278	j	j
107	0.5	k	k
108	0.278	l	l
109	0.777	m	m
110	0.5	n	n
111	0.5	o	o
112	0.5	p	p
113	0.5	q	q
114	0.333	r	r
115	0.388	s	s
116	0.278	t	t
117	0.5	u	u
118	0.5	v	v
119	0.722	w	w
120	0.5	x	x
121	0.5	y	y
122	0.443	z	z
123	0.48	{	braceleft
124	0.2	|	bar
125	0.48	}	braceright
126	0.54	~	asciitilde

Figure 15.1: Character Widths for Helvetica 18 Point Font

Listing 15.2: Outlined Characters

```
%!PS-Adobe-3.0 EPSF-30.
%%BoundingBox: 0 0 612 792
%%Title: (Stroking using Charpath)
%%Creationdate: (11/27/91:08:00)
%%EndComments
/Helvetica-Bold findfont 100 scalefont setfont

50 200 moveto
(PostScript) false charpath stroke
showpage
%%EOF
```

Figure 15.2: Outlined Characters

Another dramatic effect possible in PostScript is created by using character outline to clip an underlying graphic or image. In Figure 15.3, the word PostScript is shown with two different patterns behind it: horizontal lines and a starburst. The figure was produced by the code found in Listing 15.3. Note that in this case, the boolean value preceding **charpath** is "true." Also, to draw the second "PostScript" and the horizontal lines, it is necessary to issue the **initclip** operator, which returns the clipping path to the default clipping path. Otherwise, anything drawn where the second graphic was drawn cannot be seen.

Listing 15.3: Characters as Clip Path for Special Effects

```
%!PS-Adobe-3.0 EPSF-30.
%%BoundingBox: 0 0 612 792
%%Title: (Clipping using Charpath)
%%Creationdate: (11/27/91--08:30)
%%EndComments
/Helvetica-Bold findfont 100 scalefont setfont
1 setlinewidth 0 setgray


/point {50 500} def
point moveto
(PostScript) dup stringwidth pop 2 div /cstr exch def true charpath clip
0 50 1000
```

```
        {point exch cstr add exch moveto
        dup 1000 exch sub exch rlineto }
for
-1000 50 0
        {point exch cstr add exch moveto
        dup 1000 add  rlineto }
for
stroke

initclip

/point {50 200} def
point moveto
(PostScript) true charpath clip
point moveto
-50 5 100{point 3 2 roll add moveto 500 0 rlineto} for
stroke

initclip

showpage
%%EOF
```

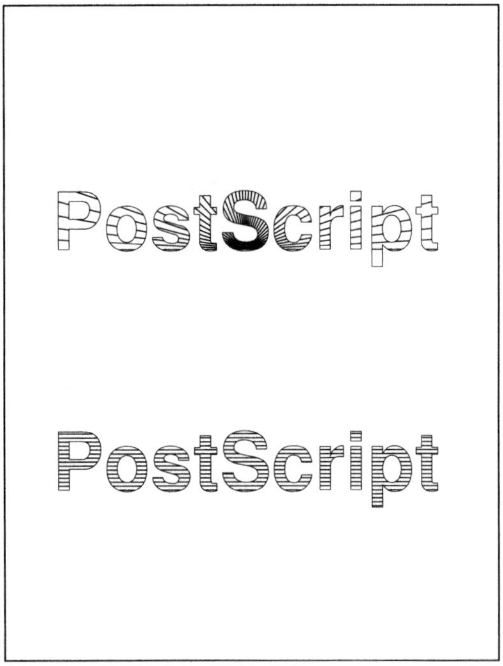

Figure 15.3: Characters as Clip Path for Special Effects

3. Font Metric Files

It is often necessary for an application to calculate the width of a text string before it is sent to the printer. This is the case when you want to know if a given string fits on a nametag or when you develop a graphics editor that shows the user what he gets when the page is printed—a WYSIWYG display. This information is obtained from some form of font metric file. An overview of a Adobe Font Metric (AFM) File an application might use is shown in Listing 15.4.

Listing 15.4: Excerpts from an Adobe Font Metric File

```
 StartFontMetrics 2.0
Comment Copyright (c) 1984 Adobe Systems Incorporated.  All Rights Reserved.
Comment Creation Date:Sun Feb 8 18:48:01 PST 1987
FontName Helvetica
EncodingScheme AdobeStandardEncoding
FullName Helvetica
FamilyName Helvetica
Weight Medium
ItalicAngle 0.0
IsFixedPitch false
UnderlinePosition -97
UnderlineThickness 73
Version 001.002
Notice Helvetica is a registered trademark of Allied Corporation.
FontBBox -174 -220 1001 944
CapHeight 729
XHeight 525
Descender -219
Ascender 729
StartCharMetrics 228
............

EndCharMetrics
StartKernData
StartKernPairs 105

.........

EndKernPairs
EndKernData
StartComposites 58

..........

EndComposites
EndFontMetrics
```

The listing shows the general information. The spaces indicate where information on the characters, kern pairs, and composite characters fits. Samples of this information are shown in Listing 15.5, Listing 15.6, and Listing 15.7, respectively.

Listing 15.5: Character Information Excerpts from an AFM File

```
StartCharMetrics 228
C 32 ; WX 278 ; N space ; B 0 0 0 0 ;
C 33 ; WX 278 ; N exclam ; B 124 0 208 729 ;
..........

C 42 ; WX 389 ; N asterisk ; B 40 452 343 740 ;
C 43 ; WX 584 ; N plus ; B 50 -10 534 474 ;
C 44 ; WX 278 ; N comma ; B 87 -150 192 104 ;
C 45 ; WX 333 ; N hyphen ; B 46 240 284 313 ;
C 46 ; WX 278 ; N period ; B 87 0 191 104 ;
C 47 ; WX 278 ; N slash ; B -8 -21 284 708 ;
C 48 ; WX 556 ; N zero ; B 43 -23 507 709 ;
C 49 ; WX 556 ; N one ; B 102 0 347 709 ;
C 50 ; WX 556 ; N two ; B 34 0 511 710 ;
.......

C 56 ; WX 556 ; N eight ; B 37 -23 513 709 ;
C 57 ; WX 556 ; N nine ; B 38 -23 509 709 ;
C 58 ; WX 278 ; N colon ; B 110 0 214 525 ;
C 59 ; WX 278 ; N semicolon ; B 110 -150 215 516 ;
C 60 ; WX 584 ; N less ; B 45 -10 534 474 ;
C 61 ; WX 584 ; N equal ; B 50 112 534 352 ;
C 62 ; WX 584 ; N greater ; B 50 -10 539 474 ;
C 63 ; WX 556 ; N question ; B 77 0 509 738 ;
C 64 ; WX 1015 ; N at ; B 34 -146 951 737 ;
C 65 ; WX 667 ; N A ; B 17 0 653 729 ;
C 66 ; WX 667 ; N B ; B 79 0 623 729 ;
C 67 ; WX 722 ; N C ; B 48 -23 677 741 ;
C 68 ; WX 722 ; N D ; B 89 0 667 729 ;
.......

C 87 ; WX 944 ; N W ; B 22 0 929 729 ;
C 88 ; WX 667 ; N X ; B 22 0 649 729 ;
C 89 ; WX 667 ; N Y ; B 13 0 661 729 ;
C 90 ; WX 611 ; N Z ; B 28 0 583 729 ;
C 91 ; WX 278 ; N bracketleft ; B 64 -214 250 729 ;
C 92 ; WX 278 ; N backslash ; B -8 -20 284 729 ;
C 93 ; WX 278 ; N bracketright ; B 23 -215 209 729 ;
C 94 ; WX 469 ; N asciicircum ; B 44 333 425 713 ;
C 95 ; WX 556 ; N underscore ; B -22 -175 578 -125 ;
C 96 ; WX 222 ; N quoteleft ; B 65 459 158 708 ;
C 97 ; WX 556 ; N a ; B 42 -23 535 540 ;
C 98 ; WX 556 ; N b ; B 54 -23 523 729 ;
C 99 ; WX 500 ; N c ; B 31 -23 477 540 ;
C 100 ; WX 556 ; N d ; B 26 -23 495 729 ;
C 101 ; WX 556 ; N e ; B 40 -23 513 541 ;
C 102 ; WX 278 ; N f ; B 18 0 258 733 ; L i fi ; L l fl ;
..........

C 119 ; WX 722 ; N w ; B 6 0 708 525 ;
C 120 ; WX 500 ; N x ; B 17 0 473 525 ;
C 121 ; WX 500 ; N y ; B 20 -219 478 525 ;
C 122 ; WX 500 ; N z ; B 31 0 457 525 ;
C 123 ; WX 334 ; N braceleft ; B 43 -214 276 731 ;
```

```
C 124 ; WX 260 ; N bar ; B 100 -215 160 729 ;
C 125 ; WX 334 ; N braceright ; B 29 -214 262 731 ;
C 126 ; WX 584 ; N asciitilde ; B 75 267 508 438 ;
C 161 ; WX 333 ; N exclamdown ; B 121 -214 205 525 ;
C 162 ; WX 556 ; N cent ; B 52 -120 510 628 ;
C 163 ; WX 556 ; N sterling ; B 26 -21 535 726 ;
C 164 ; WX 167 ; N fraction ; B -174 -21 336 708 ;
C 165 ; WX 556 ; N yen ; B 11 0 545 710 ;
.......

C 232 ; WX 556 ; N Lslash ; B 0 0 552 729 ;
C 233 ; WX 778 ; N Oslash ; B 30 -23 744 742 ;
C 234 ; WX 1000 ; N OE ; B 43 -20 959 739 ;
C 235 ; WX 365 ; N ordmasculine ; B 40 301 324 741 ;
C 241 ; WX 889 ; N ae ; B 34 -20 845 546 ;
C 245 ; WX 278 ; N dotlessi ; B 94 0 178 525 ;
C 248 ; WX 222 ; N lslash ; B 0 0 212 729 ;
C 249 ; WX 611 ; N oslash ; B 18 -27 529 548 ;
C 250 ; WX 944 ; N oe ; B 40 -22 899 540 ;
C 251 ; WX 611 ; N germandbls ; B 126 -20 566 729 ;
EndCharMetrics
```

The values are specified in the character coordinate system (1000 units per em). For example, in the line:

```
C 65; WX 667; N A; B 17 0 653 729;
```

C 65 represents the decimal value of the PostScript character code—65 is an **A**. WX 667 represents the width of the character—here, 667 represents 667 thousandths of an em, where an em is a distance equal to the point size of the font. So for a 1-point font, an A is .667 points wide. For a 2-point font, an A is 2*.667 points wide or 1.334 points wide. For a 10-point font, an A is 6.67 points wide, etc. The N entry tells you the name of the 65th character—"A," and the last information tells you the bounding box, or extent of the character from the character origin in thousandths of ems.

Listing 15.6: Kern Pair Excerpts from an AFM File

```
 StartKernData
StartKernPairs 105

KPX A y -18
KPX A w -18
KPX A v -18
KPX A space -55
KPX A quoteright -74
KPX A Y -74
KPX A W -37
KPX A V -74
KPX A T -74

......

KPX Y v -55
```

```
KPX Y u -55
KPX Y space -18
KPX Y semicolon -65
KPX Y q -92
KPX Y period -129
KPX Y p -74
KPX Y o -92
KPX Y i -37
KPX Y hyphen -92
KPX Y e -92
KPX Y comma -129
KPX Y colon -55
KPX Y a -74
KPX Y A -74

......

KPX y period -74
KPX y comma -74
EndKernPairs
EndKernData
```

The information in Listing 15.6 shows a few pairs of letters that are kerned in PostScript. KPX A Y –74 informs you that when a capital A is followed by a capital Y, the Y is to be moved back 74/1,000 of an em space.

Listing 15.7: Composite Character Excerpts from an AFM File

```
 StartComposites 58
CC Zcaron 2 ; PCC Z 0 0 ; PCC caron 139 199 ;
CC zcaron 2 ; PCC z 0 0 ; PCC caron 83 0 ;
CC Scaron 2 ; PCC S 0 0 ; PCC caron 167 199 ;
CC scaron 2 ; PCC s 0 0 ; PCC caron 83 0 ;
CC Ccedilla 2 ; PCC C 0 0 ; PCC cedilla 207 0 ;
..........

CC ntilde 2 ; PCC n 0 0 ; PCC tilde 117 0 ;
CC Otilde 2 ; PCC O 0 0 ; PCC tilde 222 199 ;
CC otilde 2 ; PCC o 0 0 ; PCC tilde 111 0 ;
CC Aring 2 ; PCC A 0 0 ; PCC ring 167 199 ;
CC aring 2 ; PCC a 0 0 ; PCC ring 111 0 ;
EndComposites
EndFontMetrics
```

The information in Listing 15.7 shows a few pairs of letters that can be combined to form composite characters.

```
CC otilde 2 ; PCC o 0 0 ; PCC tilde 111 0 ;
```

informs you there is a composite character known as otilde that is made up of two characters. The first Part of the Composite Character (PCC) is an "o" and it is offset 0x 0y. The second PCC is a tilde that is offset 111 times from its normal position and 0y.

Font information can be generated from the PostScript font dictionaries, as shows in Figure 15.4.

Times-Roman 18 point

	0	1	2	3	4	5	6	7	8	9	A	B	C	D	E	F
00	NULL	NULL	NULL	NULL	NULL	NULL	NULL	NULL	NULL	NULL	NULL	NULL	NULL	NULL	NULL	NULL
10	NULL	NULL	NULL	NULL	NULL	NULL	NULL	NULL	NULL	NULL	NULL	NULL	NULL	NULL	NULL	NULL
20	0.25 space	0.332 ! exclam	0.408 " quotedbl	0.499 # numbersign	0.499 $ dollar	0.833 % percent	0.777 & ampersand	0.332 ’ quoteright	0.332 (parenleft	0.332) parenright	0.499 * asterisk	0.563 + plus	0.25 , comma	0.332 - hyphen	0.25 . period	0.277 / slash
30	0.499 0 zero	0.499 1 one	0.499 2 two	0.499 3 three	0.499 4 four	0.499 5 five	0.499 6 six	0.499 7 seven	0.499 8 eight	0.499 9 nine	0.277 : colon	0.277 ; semicolon	0.563 < less	0.563 = equal	0.563 > greater	0.444 ? question
40	0.921 @ at	0.722 A A	0.666 B B	0.666 C C	0.722 D D	0.61 E E	0.555 F F	0.722 G G	0.722 H H	0.332 I I	0.388 J J	0.722 K K	0.61 L L	0.889 M M	0.722 N N	0.722 O O
50	0.555 P P	0.722 Q Q	0.666 R R	0.555 S S	0.61 T T	0.722 U U	0.722 V V	0.944 W W	0.722 X X	0.722 Y Y	0.61 Z Z	0.332 [bracketleft	0.277 \ backslash	0.332] bracketright	0.469 ^ asciicircum	0.499 _ underscore
60	0.332 ‘ quoteleft	0.444 a a	0.499 b b	0.444 c c	0.499 d d	0.444 e e	0.332 f f	0.499 g g	0.499 h h	0.277 i i	0.277 j j	0.499 k k	0.277 l l	0.777 m m	0.499 n n	0.499 o o
70	0.499 p p	0.499 q q	0.332 r r	0.388 s s	0.277 t t	0.499 u u	0.499 v v	0.722 w w	0.499 x x	0.499 y y	0.444 z z	0.479 { braceleft	0.199 | bar	0.479 } braceright	0.54 ~ asciitilde	NULL
80	NULL	NULL	NULL	NULL	NULL	NULL	NULL	NULL	NULL	NULL	NULL	NULL	NULL	NULL	NULL	NULL
90	NULL	NULL	NULL	NULL	NULL	NULL	NULL	NULL	NULL	NULL	NULL	NULL	NULL	NULL	NULL	NULL
A0	NULL	0.332 ¡ exclamdown	0.499 ¢ cent	0.499 £ sterling	0.167 ⁄ fraction	0.499 ¥ yen	0.499 ƒ florin	0.499 § section	0.499 ¤ currency	0.179 ' quotesingle	0.444 “ quotedblleft	0.499 « guillemotleft	0.332 ‹ guilsinglleft	0.332 › guilsinglright	0.555 ﬁ fi	0.555 ﬂ fl
B0	NULL	0.499 – endash	0.499 † dagger	0.499 ‡ daggerdbl	0.25 · periodcentered	NULL	0.452 ¶ paragraph	0.349 • bullet	0.332 ‚ quotesinglbase	0.444 „ quotedblbase	0.444 ” quotedblright	0.499 » guillemotright	1.0 … ellipsis	1.0 ‰ perthousand	NULL	0.444 ¿ questiondown
C0	NULL	0.332 ` grave	0.332 ´ acute	0.332 ˆ circumflex	0.332 ˜ tilde	0.332 ¯ macron	0.332 ˘ breve	0.332 ˙ dotaccent	0.332 ¨ dieresis	NULL	0.332 ˚ ring	0.332 ¸ cedilla	NULL	0.332 ˝ hungarumlaut	0.332 ˛ ogonek	0.332 ˇ caron
D0	1.0 — emdash	NULL	NULL	NULL	NULL	NULL	NULL	NULL	NULL	NULL	NULL	NULL	NULL	NULL	NULL	NULL
E0	NULL	0.889 Æ AE	NULL	0.275 ª ordfeminine	NULL	NULL	NULL	NULL	0.61 Ł Lslash	0.722 Ø Oslash	0.889 Œ OE	0.309 º ordmasculine	NULL	NULL	NULL	NULL
F0	NULL	0.666 æ ae	NULL	NULL	NULL	0.277 ı dotlessi	NULL	NULL	0.277 ł lslash	0.499 ø oslash	0.722 œ oe	0.499 ß germandbls	NULL	NULL	NULL	NULL

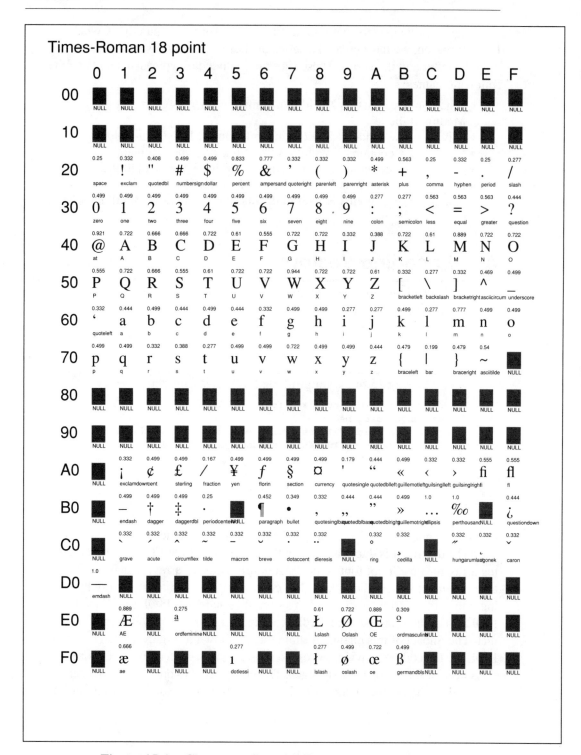

Figure 15.4: Character Set with Standard Encoding

When writing drivers, we seldom find a need for more than the X width data. For this reason, we have created a series of files from the AFM files that contain only the letter and the width. These files are included on your disk and have the following names:

- zcha_l_r.fxw contains X width information for ZapfChancery-MediumItalic
- helv_b_r.fxw contains X width information for Helvetica-Bold
- tiro_l_r.fxw contains X width information for Times-Roman
- tiro_b_i.fxw contains X width information for Times-BoldItalic
- pala_b_r.fxw contains X width information for Palatino-Bold
- pala_b_i.fxw contains X width information for Palatino-BoldItalic

4. Encoding Vectors

Accented characters tend to be the bane of many academics who work with laser printers. From the PostScript point of view, it is actually rather simple. The basic code to define a new font with a full range of accented characters is shown in Listing 15.8.

Listing 15.8: Changing the Standard Encoding Vector

```
 /Helvetica findfont % any font will do
dup length dict begin
        {1 index /FID ne {def} {pop pop} ifelse} forall
        /Encoding ISOLatin1Encoding def
        currentdict
        end
/HelveticaIL1 exch definefont pop
```

This code is explained in the *PostScript Language Reference Manual, Second Edition*, on pp. 275–277. Basically, a font dictionary is placed on the dictionary stack (**findfont**). It is duplicated, with the exception of the FID. The default encoding array for PostScript font is the "StandardEncoding" array, which is defined in the systemdict system dictionary. The code changes the encoding array by redefining it to another array also found in systemdict, namely "ISOLatin1Encoding." ISOLatin1Encoding, like StandardEncoding, is a built-in array be found in systemdict. The impact of this change is dramatic, as shown in Figure 15.5. The ISOLatin1Encoding provides access to most of the accented character combinations needed for European languages. The characters beyond the normal set are accessed by the escape character and octal notation or by the hex string notation.

TR-Accents18 point

	0	1	2	3	4	5	6	7	8	9	A	B	C	D	E	F
00	NULL	NULL	NULL	NULL	NULL	NULL	NULL	NULL	NULL	NULL	NULL	NULL	NULL	NULL	NULL	NULL
10	NULL	NULL	NULL	NULL	NULL	NULL	NULL	NULL	NULL	NULL	NULL	NULL	NULL	NULL	NULL	NULL
20	0.249 space	0.332 ! exclam	0.407 " quotedbl	0.499 # numbersign	0.499 $ dollar	0.832 % percent	0.777 & ampersand	0.332 ’ quoteright	0.332 (parenleft	0.332) parenright	0.499 * asterisk	0.563 + plus	0.249 , comma	0.563 − minus	0.249 . period	0.277 / slash
30	0.499 0 zero	0.499 1 one	0.499 2 two	0.499 3 three	0.499 4 four	0.499 5 five	0.499 6 six	0.499 7 seven	0.499 8 eight	0.499 9 nine	0.277 : colon	0.277 ; semicolon	0.563 < less	0.563 = equal	0.563 > greater	0.443 ? question
40	0.92 @ at	0.721 A A	0.666 B B	0.666 C C	0.721 D D	0.61 E E	0.555 F F	0.721 G G	0.721 H H	0.332 I I	0.388 J J	0.721 K K	0.61 L L	0.888 M M	0.721 N N	0.721 O O
50	0.555 P P	0.721 Q Q	0.666 R R	0.555 S S	0.61 T T	0.721 U U	0.721 V V	0.943 W W	0.721 X X	0.721 Y Y	0.61 Z Z	0.332 [bracketleft	0.277 \ backslash	0.332] bracketright	0.468 ^ asciicircum	0.499 _ underscore
60	0.332 ‘ quoteleft	0.443 a a	0.499 b b	0.443 c c	0.499 d d	0.443 e e	0.332 f f	0.499 g g	0.499 h h	0.277 i i	0.277 j j	0.499 k k	0.277 l l	0.777 m m	0.499 n n	0.499 o o
70	0.499 p p	0.499 q q	0.332 r r	0.388 s s	0.277 t t	0.499 u u	0.499 v v	0.721 w w	0.499 x x	0.499 y y	0.443 z z	0.479 { braceleft	0.199 | bar	0.479 } braceright	0.54 ~ asciitilde	NULL
80	NULL	NULL	NULL	NULL	NULL	NULL	NULL	NULL	NULL	NULL	NULL	NULL	NULL	NULL	NULL	NULL
90	0.277 ı dotlessi	0.332 ` grave	0.332 ´ acute	0.332 ˆ circumflex	0.332 ˜ tilde	0.332 ¯ macron	0.332 ˘ breve	0.332 ˙ dotaccent	0.332 ¨ dieresis	NULL	0.332 ˚ ring	0.332 ¸ cedilla	NULL	0.332 ˝ hungarumlaut	0.332 ˛ ogonek	0.332 ˇ caron
A0	0.249 space	0.332 ¡ exclamdown	0.499 ¢ cent	0.499 £ sterling	0.499 ¤ currency	0.499 ¥ yen	0.199 ¦ brokenbar	0.499 § section	0.332 ¨ dieresis	0.759 © copyright	0.275 ª ordfeminine	0.499 « guillemotleft	0.563 ¬ logicalnot	0.332 - hyphen	0.759 ® registered	0.332 ¯ macron
B0	0.4 ° degree	0.563 ± plusminus	0.299 ² twosuperior	0.299 ³ threesuperior	0.332 ´ acute	0.499 µ mu	0.452 ¶ paragraph	0.249 · periodcentered	0.332 ¸ cedilla	0.299 ¹ onesuperior	0.309 º ordmasculine	0.499 » guillemotright	0.749 ¼ onequarter	0.749 ½ onehalf	0.749 ¾ threequarters	0.443 ¿ questiondown
C0	0.722 À Agrave	0.722 Á Aacute	0.722 Â Acircumflex	0.722 Ã Atilde	0.722 Ä Adieresis	0.722 Å Aring	0.888 Æ AE	0.666 Ç Ccedilla	0.61 È Egrave	0.61 É Eacute	0.61 Ê Ecircumflex	0.61 Ë Edieresis	0.332 Ì Igrave	0.332 Í Iacute	0.332 Î Icircumflex	0.332 Ï Idieresis
D0	0.722 Ð Eth	0.722 Ñ Ntilde	0.722 Ò Ograve	0.722 Ó Oacute	0.722 Ô Ocircumflex	0.722 Õ Otilde	0.722 Ö Odieresis	0.563 × multiply	0.721 Ø Oslash	0.722 Ù Ugrave	0.722 Ú Uacute	0.722 Û Ucircumflex	0.722 Ü Udieresis	0.722 Ý Yacute	0.555 Þ Thorn	0.499 ß germandbls
E0	0.444 à agrave	0.444 á aacute	0.444 â acircumflex	0.444 ã atilde	0.444 ä adieresis	0.444 å aring	0.666 æ ae	0.444 ç ccedilla	0.444 è egrave	0.444 é eacute	0.444 ê ecircumflex	0.444 ë edieresis	0.277 ì igrave	0.277 í iacute	0.277 î icircumflex	0.277 ï idieresis
F0	0.499 ð eth	0.499 ñ ntilde	0.499 ò ograve	0.499 ó oacute	0.499 ô ocircumflex	0.499 õ otilde	0.499 ö odieresis	0.563 ÷ divide	0.499 ø oslash	0.499 ù ugrave	0.499 ú uacute	0.499 û ucircumflex	0.499 ü udieresis	0.499 ý yacute	0.499 þ thorn	0.499 ÿ ydieresis

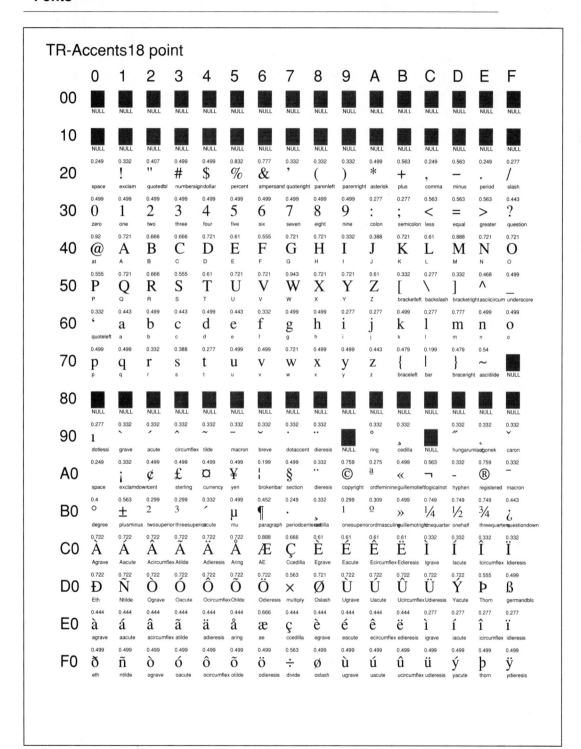

Figure 15.5: Character Set with ISO Latin Encoding

Chapter 16
Drivers for a Greeting Card

This chapter introduces a series of programs in BASIC, Pascal, and C that produce greeting cards. In each of these sections, one or more programs are discussed. The BASIC driver provides a careful line-by-line explanation of a simple program that allows you to input an event and a message that outputs to a card. The Pascal driver begins with a very simple program along much the same lines. It proceeds to a driver that has a nicer interface. All these programs are suitable for creating a single card, which can then be duplicated.

The last section presents three C drivers. In the C versions, a series of more advanced features is introduced. The information to be placed on the main body of the card may be read from a file created by a text editor, or it may be entered interactively. This is true for all three versions. All three versions also use information about the width of each character to calculate line width before the PostScript code is written. The second and third version provide for some simple special effects to be indicated in the text file or through the input. (Basically, you can specify whether the line should be flush left, centered, or centered and shadowed.) Finally, the third version enables you to specify the base card and then add personal messages to each card as they are written to the file. The program takes care of wrapping lines, based on the font width information command..

1. Greeting Card Driver: BASIC

In this section, a BASIC[54] program is the driver to create the PostScript code to produce a greeting card. Using a driver simplifies code creation as you respond to prompts for the variable data. This card is a modified version of the one

[54]The BASIC code was tested with BASICA V3.3, GW-BASIC 3.20, QuickBASIC V4.0, and QBASIC V1.0.

presented in the Greeting Card examples, shown in Chapter 10, "Greeting Card." The greeting card shown in Figure 16.4 is appropriate for many user-selected occasions. The inside of the card may be personalized.

a. Building the Driver

Prologue

The prologue, Listing 16.1, is the section of the PostScript program that remains unchanged. The driver creates this part of the PostScript file first.

Listing 16.1: PostScript Prologue

```
%!PS-Adobe-3.0 EPSF-30.
%%BoundingBox: 0 0 612 792
%%Title: (Greeting Card)
%%EndComments
/ctr {dup stringwidth pop 2 div neg 0 rmoveto show} bind def
/clearit    {4 {pop} repeat     stroke} bind def
/font {/Helvetica-Bold findfont exch scalefont setfont} bind def
/inside{/Times-BoldItalic findfont 20 scalefont setfont
        306 720 translate
        180 rotate }def
/Border {4 setlinewidth
         334  62 moveto  334 352 388 352 36 arcto clearit
         360 352 moveto  586 352 586 298 36 arcto clearit
         586 320 moveto  586  28 514  28 36 arcto clearit
         550  28 moveto  334  28 334  82 36 arcto clearit   } def
%--------------Main---------------------------------------%
Border
```

The **ctr** procedure centers its argument and is explained in Chapter 6. **Clearit** is explained in Chapter 10. **Font** is similar to the font procedure used in Chapter 6, but the size is the only argument needed because Helvetica-Bold is the default font. This procedure is added because of the many font-size changes on the outside of the card. The **inside** procedure sets the font and size for the inside of the card and does the translation and rotation to allow writing of the inside card. The **border** procedure draws the box around the front of the card.

After the procedures are defined, the first line of the main program is listed. All user-specified lines are appended to this prologue.

The BASIC program segment, Listing 16.2, opens the prologue file, **card_b1.psp**, and creates a new file, **card.eps**. Each line of the prologue file is read, then printed to the PostScript output file. After all prologue lines are copied, the file is closed. The output file is ready for the variable data.

Listing 16.2: BASIC Prologue Code

```
810 OPEN "card_b1.psp" FOR INPUT AS #1
820 OPEN "card.eps" FOR OUTPUT AS #2
830 WHILE NOT (EOF(1))
840   LINE INPUT #1, C$
850   PRINT #2, C$
860 WEND
870 CLOSE #1
```

The Front

The occasion is the focus for the front of the card. You select the occasion and it is printed repeatedly. The first printing is a small font in light gray. As the word is repeated, it prints in a larger font and a darker gray.

You must supply the name of the occasion. The size of the string for the occasion must be limited. Since no allowance is made for changing font sizes, a string that is too long exceeds the box. Eleven letters are allowed. Too many letters reduces the size of the final repetition and ruins the card's appearance.

The BASIC code, Listing 16.3, prompts you to input an occasion of 11 characters or less. Suggestions are provided. Strings longer than 11 characters are disallowed and you are forced to provide another input.

Listing 16.3: Occasion Input Code

```
310 CLS
320 PRINT "Enter the occasion for the card.  You are limited to 11"
330 PRINT "characters.  Suggestions:  Anniversary...Get Well......"
340 PRINT "Birthday...Graduation...New Home...New Baby"
350 INPUT "Enter the occasion==>>>";OCCASION$
360 IF LEN(OCCASION$)>11 THEN 310
```

The output-generating code, Listing 16.4, initializes **gray** to .36, **font** to 4 and **Y** to 322. These are the initial arguments to **setcolor**, **setfont** and the Y position for **moveto**. A loop writes 20 lines of code to the output file, Listing 16.5. The value of **gray** decreases by .04 each time through the loop, so it becomes black at the loops final execution. The font size is increased by 4 points each time through the loop. The distance for Y axis movement is controlled by the font size of the next line to be printed, with an extra 6 points for larger fonts. The **occasion** variable, is written by line 950.

The selection of factors for font size, the Y distance, and the change in gray is based on font size. The smallest font size is almost too small and light to read. The largest font fills the box horizontally when the maximum number of letters is used. You want a common increment for all factors is desired to allow the loop to calculate and write the code.

Listing 16.4: Occasion Output Code

```
900 GRAY = .36
910 FONT = 4
920 Y = 322
930 FOR I = 1 TO 10
940 PRINT #2, GRAY; " setgray "; FONT; " font"
950 PRINT #2, "460 "; Y; " moveto ("; OCCASION$; ") ctr"
960 GRAY = GRAY - .04
970 FONT = FONT + 4
980 IF FONT < 20 THEN Y = Y - FONT ELSE Y = Y - (FONT + 6)
990 NEXT I
```

The output, Listing 16.5, these program segments generate has 10 pairs of lines. The first line sets the gray color and supplies a numeric argument to **font**. The **font** is defined in the prologue, Listing 16.1, to simplify the many size changes required. The second line moves the current point to the lower quarter of the page. It is centered at the proper line position. The occasion becomes the argument to the **ctr** procedure. See Listing 16.1.

Listing 16.5: PostScript Segment 1 Generated

```
 .36  setgray  4  font
460  322  moveto (Anniversary) ctr
 .32  setgray  8  font
460  314  moveto (Anniversary) ctr
 .28  setgray  12  font
460  302  moveto (Anniversary) ctr
 .24  setgray  16  font
460  286  moveto (Anniversary) ctr
 .2  setgray  20  font
460  260  moveto (Anniversary) ctr
 .1600001  setgray  24  font
460  230  moveto (Anniversary) ctr
 .1200001  setgray  28  font
460  196  moveto (Anniversary) ctr
 8.000006E-02  setgray  32  font
460  158  moveto (Anniversary) ctr
 4.000006E-02  setgray  36  font
460  116  moveto (Anniversary) ctr
 5.960464E-08  setgray  40  font
460  70  moveto (Anniversary) ctr
```

The Inside

The inside message may be personalized, or it may simply be a message or verse. Four lines are allowed for the message. The line length and the font style and size are fixed. Two signature lines are provided.[55]

[55]An empty **ctr** argument should not be given to PostScript. An aborted program may result.

The code shown in Listing 16.6 provides an example. The length of the line is checked. A line that is too long is rejected and a new entry is requested. The message is stored in an array.

Listing 16.6: Message Input Code

```
420 CLS
430 PRINT "Enter the message for the inside of the card"
440 PRINT "You may enter 4 message lines and 2 signature lines"
450 PRINT "For Example:"
460 PRINT "Uncle Ben"
470 PRINT "May you spend"
480 PRINT "many happy years"
490 PRINT "in you new home."
500 PRINT "Love"
510 PRINT "Chris and Jenny"
520 PRINT:PRINT:PRINT"Enter one line at a time"
530 FOR A=1 TO 6
540 IF A=5 THEN PRINT "Remember, these are signature lines"
550 PRINT "Line #";A;
560 INPUT MESSAGE$(A)
570 IF LEN(MESSAGE$(A))>26 THEN PRINT "26 characters only!":GOTO 540
580 NEXT A
```

After the message array is entered and the data is verified, the remainder of the file is printed. The verification code, Listing 16.7, prints the data for you to check. If the data is not acceptable, pressing the space bar signals that you want to reenter it.

Listing 16.7: Input Verification Code

```
640 CLS
650 A$ = ""
660 LOCATE 22, 1
670 PRINT "The data you entered is shown above.  To change it,"
680 PRINT "press the space bar.  To accept as shown, press enter."
690 FOR B = 1 TO 6
700 LOCATE (6 + B * 2), 40 - INT(LEN(MESSAGE$(B)) / 2)
710 PRINT MESSAGE$(B)
720 NEXT B
730 PRINT "The occasion is : "; OCCASION$
740 C$ = INKEY$
750 IF C$ = "" THEN 740
760 IF C$ = " " THEN A$ = " "
```

The BASIC module to print the message, Listing 16.8, begins with the call to the procedure inside line 1,000. The starting Y position for the message lines is initialized. A loop, 1,020 through 1,050, is used to print the message lines. The center of the inside quarter is 153. One additional point allows a small adjustment for the fold. The final segment prints the showpage and EOF statements. This ends the PostScript file, and line 1,080 closes it.

Listing 16.8: Message Output Code

```
1000 PRINT #2, "inside"
1010 Y = 250
1020 FOR I = 1 TO 6
1030 PRINT #2, "154 "; Y; " moveto ("; MESSAGE$(I); ") ctr"
1040 IF I = 4 THEN Y = Y - 55 ELSE Y = Y - 40
1050 NEXT I
1060 PRINT #2, "showpage"
1070 PRINT #2, "%%EOF"
1080 CLOSE #2
```

The generated PostScript code is illustrated in Listing 16.9. The **inside** procedure establishes a new font and performs the rotation-translation for the inside. Each line of output prints one message line with uniform spacing. Extra space separates the signature lines from the message.

Listing 16.9: PostScript Segment 2 Generated

```
inside
154  250  moveto (MOTHER and DAD) ctr
154  210  moveto (We hope this anniversary) ctr
154  170  moveto (brings you all the joy and) ctr
154  130  moveto (happiness you gave to us) ctr
154  75  moveto (Love from all of us) ctr
154  35  moveto (Don, Jan, Bob, Dee & Larry) ctr
showpage
%%EOF
```

b. Putting It All Together

The program is structured modularly. All the routines discussed must be called as subroutines; the BASIC code to call the subroutines is illustrated in Listing 16.10. Each routine is called in turn. The routine to specify the message is continued until the verification routine allows the program to continue.

Listing 16.10: Subroutine Control

```
190 GOSUB 290: REM get occasion
200 A$ = " "
210 WHILE A$ = " "
220 GOSUB 400: REM get message
230 GOSUB 640: REM verify input
240 WEND
250 GOSUB 800: REM open files and write prologue
260 GOSUB 890: REM write user input to PostScript file
270 GOTO 1430
1430 END
```

The final result of the driver program execution is shown in Listing 16.11 and illustrated in Figure 16.1.

Listing 16.11: Example of Driver Output File

```
%!PS-Adobe-3.0 EPSF-30.
%%BoundingBox: 0 0 612 792
%%Title: (Greeting Card)
%%EndComments
/ctr {dup stringwidth pop 2 div neg 0 rmoveto show} bind def
/clearit     {4 {pop} repeat     stroke} bind def
/font {/Helvetica-Bold findfont exch scalefont setfont} bind def
/inside{/Times-BoldItalic findfont 20 scalefont setfont
        306 720 translate
        180 rotate }def
/Border {4 setlinewidth
         334  62 moveto  334 352 388 352 36 arcto clearit
         360 352 moveto  586 352 586 298 36 arcto clearit
         586 320 moveto  586  28 514  28 36 arcto clearit
         550  28 moveto  334  28 334  82 36 arcto clearit   } def
%--------------Main-------------------------------------%
Border
 .36  setgray  4  font
460  322  moveto (Anniversary) ctr
 .32  setgray  8  font
460  314  moveto (Anniversary) ctr
 .28  setgray  12  font
460  302  moveto (Anniversary) ctr
 .2400001  setgray  16  font
460  286  moveto (Anniversary) ctr
 .2000001  setgray  20  font
460  260  moveto () ctr
 .1600001  setgray  24  font
460  230  moveto (Anniversary) ctr
 .1200001  setgray  28  font
460  196  moveto (Anniversary) ctr
 8.000006E-02  setgray  32  font
460  158  moveto (Anniversary) ctr
 4.000006E-02  setgray  36  font
460  116  moveto (Anniversary) ctr
 5.960465E-08  setgray  40  font
460  70  moveto (Anniversary) ctr
inside
154  250  moveto (MOTHER and DAD) ctr
154  210  moveto (We hope this anniversary) ctr
154  170  moveto (brings you all the joy and) ctr
154  130  moveto (happiness you gave to us.) ctr
154  75  moveto (Love from all of us) ctr
154  35  moveto (Don, Jan, Bob, Dee & Larry) ctr
showpage
%%EOF
```

Don, Jan, Bob, Dee & Larry
Love from all of us
happiness you gave to us.
brings you all the joy and
We hope this anniversary
MOTHER and DAD
Anniversary
Anniversary
Anniversary
Anniversary
Anniversary
Anniversary
Anniversary
Anniversary
Anniversary

Figure 16.1: Example of Driver Output

c. Suggested Enhancements

Several additional enhancements are suggested, such as those shown in Listing 16.12. Color is a nice feature, and program line 110 sets colors for you. Refer to the reference manual to choose other color combinations or eliminate the line for monochrome systems.

Lines 120–180 provide a brief introduction to the driver, followed by a pause to allow you to read the text. The length of the pause may be adjusted by altering the upper limit of the **for** loop in line 170 to suit the system you are using.

Listing 16.12: Introduction to the Driver

```
110 COLOR 14, 1, 9

120 CLS
130 LOCATE 10, 1
140 PRINT TAB(10); "This program creates a greeting card. Follow"
150 PRINT TAB(10); "directions carefully.  You are asked to enter"
160 PRINT TAB(10); "an occasion and a 6 line message."
170 FOR I = 1 TO 3500: NEXT I
180 CLS
```

The comma is a delimiter in BASIC. If a string is entered that includes commas, BASIC flashes the "Redo from start" message to the screen. A message warning about this can be added to the prompt, but the prompt then becomes more complex and less user-friendly. More complete input routines are shown in subsequent drivers.

Several additional fonts are suitable for the card and a menu that allows you to select different fonts would be appropriate.

2. Greeting Card Driver: Pascal

This section's aim is to create a PostScript greeting card program using a driver program written in Pascal. There are two versions of the driver; the first contains simple prompts for you to follow, with limited directions and no screen formatting. The second version gives more explicit directions, formats the input screens in a more attractive manner, and does more error checking with the input. Both versions interact with you by prompting for the information needed to write the PostScript greeting card program.

a. Files Used and Created

Files are read, written, and created during the execution of both drivers. Both files that are opened are listed in the **Const** of the Pascal programs and are assigned the **infile** and **outfile** variables.

The **infile** variable is used to read the file **card_p1.psp**. This file contains a segment of PostScript code known as the prologue which remains unchanged regardless of input. This file is read and then written to the file with the variable name **outfile**. This is the beginning of the PostScript program the Pascal program creates. The prologue file is illustrated in Listing 16.13.

Listing 16.13: Prologue File

```
%!PS-Adobe-3.0 EPSF-30.
%%BoundingBox: 0 0 612 792
%%Title:(Greeting Card)
%%EndComments
%------------------------Procedures-----------------------
/ctr {dup stringwidth pop 2 div neg 0 rmoveto show} bind def
/clearit {4 {pop} repeat  stroke} bind def
/font{/Helvetica-Bold findfont exch scalefont setfont}
 bind def
/inside{/Times-BoldItalic findfont 20 scalefont setfont
       306 720 translate
       180 rotate }def
/Border {4 setlinewidth
       334 62 moveto 334 352 388 352 36 arcto clearit
       360 352 moveto 586 352 586 298 36 arcto clearit
       586 320 moveto 586 28 514 28 36 arcto clearit
       550 28 moveto 334 28 334 82 36 arcto clearit }def
%-------------------------MAIN------------------------
Border
```

As mentioned, the **outfile** variable is used to refer to the PostScript program that is being created.

This program's actual file name is **greetout.eps** As the Pascal driver is executed, it adds lines to the prologue, completing the PostScript greeting card program. The PostScript file that is created after the Pascal driver has been executed is illustrated in Listing 16.14.

Listing 16.14: PostScript Program Produced by the Pascal Driver

```
%!PS-Adobe-3.0 EPSF-30.
%%BoundingBox: 0 0 612 792
%%Title:(Greeting Card)
%%EndComments
%------------------------Procedures-----------------------
/ctr {dup stringwidth pop 2 div neg 0 rmoveto show} bind def
```

```
/clearit {4 {pop} repeat  stroke} bind def
/font{/Helvetica-Bold findfont exch scalefont setfont}
 bind def
/inside{/Times-BoldItalic findfont 20 scalefont setfont
       306 720 translate
       180 rotate }def
/Border {4 setlinewidth
       334 62 moveto 334 352 388 352 36 arcto clearit
       360 352 moveto 586 352 586 298 36 arcto clearit
       586 320 moveto 586 28 514 28 36 arcto clearit
       550 28 moveto 334 28 334 82 36 arcto clearit }def
%-------------------------MAIN------------------------
Border
 3.6000000000E-01 setgray 4 font
460 322 moveto (BIRTHDAY) ctr
 3.2000000000E-01 setgray 8 font
460 314 moveto (BIRTHDAY) ctr
 2.8000000000E-01 setgray 12 font
460 302 moveto (BIRTHDAY) ctr
 2.4000000000E-01 setgray 16 font
460 286 moveto (BIRTHDAY) ctr
 2.0000000000E-01 setgray 20 font
460 260 moveto (BIRTHDAY) ctr
 1.6000000000E-01 setgray 24 font
460 230 moveto (BIRTHDAY) ctr
 1.2000000000E-01 setgray 28 font
460 196 moveto (BIRTHDAY) ctr
 8.0000000000E-02 setgray 32 font
460 158 moveto (BIRTHDAY) ctr
 4.0000000000E-02 setgray 36 font
460 116 moveto (BIRTHDAY) ctr
 3.9790393203E-13 setgray 40 font
460 70 moveto (BIRTHDAY) ctr
inside
154 250  moveto(This is Your)ctr
154 210  moveto(Special Day)ctr
154 170  moveto(We Hope it is Filled)ctr
154 130  moveto(with Happiness)ctr
154 90  moveto(Best Wishes)ctr
154 50  moveto(John and Mary)ctr
%%EOF
```

b. Version 1 of the Greeting Card Driver

There are two versions of the Pascal Driver included in this chapter. Version 1 is illustrated in Listing 16.15. It is a simple program with as few user prompts as possible but its lack of instructions and screen organization makes it less enjoyable to use than Version 2.

Listing 16.15: Version 1: Pascal Driver for Greeting Card Program

```
Program makecard(Input, Output);

USES CRT;

Const
     infile = 'card_p1.psp';
     outfile = 'shortout.eps';

Var inf:text;
    outf:text;
    poststring: string[62];
    cardtype: string[20];
    firline: string[25];
    linetrack: integer;
    InsideY: integer;
    line1: string[25];
    line2: string[25];
    line3: string[25];
    line4: string[25];
    line5: string[25];
    line6: string[25];
    fontsize: integer;
    color: real;
    x: integer;
    y: integer;
    linenum: integer;
    dif: integer;

Procedure Setup;
Begin
   assign(outf, outfile);
   rewrite(outf);
   assign(inf,infile);
   reset(inf);
   While NOT EOF(inf) Do
     Begin
       Readln(inf,poststring);
       Writeln(outf,poststring);
     End;
End;{Procedure}

Procedure Welcome;
Begin
Writeln('This program makes a greeting card from');
Writeln('user input.  The outside is the Occasion line');
Writeln('which is one line of 11 characters. The inside');
Writeln('is 6 lines, 20 characters long.  Four are the');
Writeln('message lines and the last two are the closing.');
Writeln('Enter the occasion for the front of your card');
Readln(cardtype);

 Repeat
  If (length(cardtype) > 11) then
   Begin
```

```
    Writeln('Line too long. Re-enter the text');
    Readln(cardtype);
   End;
 Until length(cardtype) <= 11;
 Clrscr;
End;{Procedure}


Procedure GetCardFront;
Begin
  color := 0.36;
  fontsize := 4;
  y := 322;
  x := 460;
  linenum := 1;
  dif := 4;
  Repeat
    Writeln(outf,color,' setgray ',fontsize,' font');
    Writeln(outf,x,' ',y,' moveto (',cardtype,') ctr');
    linenum := linenum + 1;
    if linenum = 5 then
     dif := dif + 10
    else
     dif := dif + 4;
    y := y - dif;
    fontsize := fontsize + 4;
    color := color - 0.04;
  Until y = 20;
End;{Procedure}

Procedure Checkline;
Begin
Repeat
 Writeln('The length of line ', linetrack,' is longer than 20');
 Write('Please retype the line ====>  ');
 Readln(firline);
Until length(firline) <= 20;
End;{Procedure}

Procedure InsideText;
Begin
Repeat
  Writeln('Enter line ',linetrack,' for the card.');
  Readln(firline);
  If length(firline) > 20 then
  Checkline;

  CASE linetrack of
    1:
     Begin
      line1 := firline;
     End;
    2:
     Begin
      line2 := firline;
     End;
    3:
```

```
     Begin
      line3 := firline;
     End;
    4:
     Begin
      line4 := firline;
     End;
    5:
     Begin
      line5 := firline;
     End;
    6:
     Begin
      line6 := firline;
     End;
 ELSE
 End;
 linetrack := linetrack + 1;
Until linetrack = 7;
End;{Procedure}

Procedure Cleanup;
Begin
 Close(outf);
 Close(inf);
End;{Procedure}

Procedure WriteOut;
Begin
InsideY := 250;

Writeln(outf,'inside');
Writeln(outf,'154 ',InsideY,'  moveto(',line1,')ctr');
InsideY := InsideY - 40;
Writeln(outf,'154 ',InsideY,'  moveto(',line2,')ctr');
InsideY := InsideY - 40;
Writeln(outf,'154 ',InsideY,'  moveto(',line3,')ctr');
InsideY := InsideY - 40;
Writeln(outf,'154 ',InsideY,'  moveto(',line4,')ctr');
InsideY := InsideY - 40;
Writeln(outf,'154 ',InsideY,'  moveto(',line5,')ctr');
InsideY := InsideY - 40;
Writeln(outf,'154 ',InsideY,'  moveto(',line6,')ctr');
InsideY := InsideY - 40;
Writeln(outf,'%%EOF');
End;{Procedure}

{------------------MAIN--------------------------}

Begin
     Clrscr;
     linetrack := 1;
     Setup;
     Welcome;
     GetCardFront;
     InsideText;
     WriteOut;
```

```
     Cleanup;
End.{Main}
```

Setup is called from main and opens files for input and output. **Setup** reads the prologue file, **card_p1.psp**, and writes it to the PostScript output file, **greetout.eps**. **Setup** remains the same in both the short and the long version of the driver. The variables are:

- **outf**: The variable for the **outfile** constant, which is **greetout.eps**, the PostScript file being created. The prologue file is written to the outfile by this variable.
- **inf**: The variable for the **infile** constant, which is **card_p1.psp** or the prologue file. The prologue file is written this variable.
- **poststring**: The variable to read each line of the prologue file and to write out each line to the PostScript file. Writing out the prologue to the PostScript file is accomplished by using a **While/Do** loop. This loop continually reads one line of the prologue file and writes the line to the PostScript file until the end of file character is read.

Welcome is called from **Main**, clears the screen, gives the user minimal instructions for input, then prompts you for the text for the front of the card. The input is held in the **cardtype** variable. The **Welcome** procedure also does error checking in a **Repeat/Until** loop to check the length of the input. If the input is too long, the loop allows you to reenter the input.

GetCardFront is called from **Main** and writes the lines 19 through 36 out to the PostScript file. The **Repeat/Until** loop, in the Pascal driver writes these lines, and the variables enclosed in the loop handles the increments and decrements. This procedure's purpose is to print the lines out to the PostScript file that prints the text for the front of the card. The **writeln** lines in the **Repeat/Until** loop are the lines written out to the PostScript file. These PostScript lines print the card's occasion nine times while consecutively moving down the card. With each move, the font size is incremented and the gray shade is decremented. The variables used to accomplish this are:

1. **color**: the variable that holds the gray shade. It is initialized at .36 and decremented by .04 on each pass through the loop, which increases the darkness of the text on the front of the card.
2. **fontsize**: the size of the font. The font is initialized to 4. It is incremented by 4 each pass through the loop. The **font** procedure names, finds, and sets the font.
3. **x**: the X coordinate for the **moveto** operator. The X coordinate is initialized to 460, and it remains at that value throughout the procedure so the text always starts at the same point on the X axis.
4. **y**: the Y coordinate for the **moveto** operator. This variable is decremented by the **dif** variable each pass through the loop. This

is so the text moves down the Y axis each consecutive time it is printed. The **y** variable is used as a control in the loop in that once **y** is equal to 20, the looping stops and the procedure ends.

5. **linenum**: counts the lines to be printed by the PostScript code. Each time the line of text for the front of the card is printed, the current point moves down the Y axis. At one point, you want a larger gap for appearance's sake and this appears after a fifth line has been printed. This is why **dif** is incremented by 10 after **linenum** equals 5, but only after line five.
6. **dif**: is the difference of the differences plus four of each consecutive **y**. It is used to give **y** the proper decrement. This is confusing but for example: the first **y** equals 322 and the second **y** equals 314. They have a difference of 8. The second **y**, 314, and the third **y**, 302, have a difference of 12. The third **y**, 302, and the fourth **y**, 286, have a difference of 16. Therefore, there is a difference of four between each consecutive difference of **y**. **Y** is initialized at 322 and **dif** is initialized at 4. Because **dif** is incremented by four and **y** is decremented by **dif**, 4's range remains correct during each pass through the loop.

Notice in the PostScript file that every two lines are similar to the previous two except the numeric values are incremented or decremented consistently. The first line in each set of two sets the gray scale, and calls the **font** procedure from above to name, scale and set the font. The second line in each two sets of the PostScript file place and center the text on the front of the card by calling the **ctr** procedure.

Checkline is called from **InsideText** and checks the length of the text input for the inside of the card. If the line you enter is longer than 15 characters, you are prompted to re-enter the line.

InsideText is called from **Main** and its function is to have you enter input for the inside of the card by the **Repeat/Until** loop. The lines of text are also entered into individual variables by the **CASE** statement.They are written out to the PostScript file later in the **Writeout** procedure.

Cleanup is called from **Main** and closes all files that have been opened.

WriteOut is called from **Main** and writes lines 37 through 44 out to the PostScript file. These lines in the PostScript file write the inside text of the card. They first call **inside**, which is a PostScript procedure that changes the font and its size. The succeeding lines move the current point and print the text after it is centered by calling the **ctr** procedure. The variables in the Pascal driver for the **WriteOut** procedure are:

1. **InsideY**: the Y coordinate for the **moveto** operator. It is initialized at 250 and decremented by 40 after each **Writeln** statement.

2. **line1...line6**: the text lines for the inside of the greeting card. Every time a line of text is entered in the **InsideText** procedure, the line of text is also entered consecutively into a line variable through the **case** statement in the **InsideText** procedure.

The main body of the Pascal greeting card driver first version is simple because it clears the screen, initializes the **linetrack** variable to 1, and calls each procedure one time. The output for the **greetout.eps** PostScript file creates is illustrated in Figure 16.2.

c. Version 2 of the Greeting Card Driver

The second version of the driver, illustrated in Listing 16.16 is visually more attractive because it has input screens and interacts with you much more efficiently. The additional procedures in the driver are to accommodate you for input. Of the following eight defined procedures, **GetCardFront** and **WriteOut** are the only two that actually build PostScript code in the PostScript file. This is true in both versions of the driver.

Listing 16.16: Enhanced Pascal Driver for Greeting Card Program

```
Program makecard(Input, Output);

USES CRT;

Const
    infile = 'card_p1.psp';
    outfile = 'greetout.eps';

Type
    holdtype = array[1..33] of char;

Var inf:text;
    outf:text;
    poststring: string[62];
    holdspaces:holdtype;
    cardtype: string[20];
    firline: string[25];
    linetrack: integer;
    InsideY: integer;
    line1: string[25];
    line2: string[25];
    line3: string[25];
    line4: string[25];
    line5: string[25];
    line6: string[25];
    fontsize: integer;
    color: real;
    x: integer;
    y: integer;
```

This is Your
Special Day
We Hope it is Filled
with Happiness
Best Wishes
John and Mary
BIRTHDAY
BIRTHDAY
BIRTHDAY
BIRTHDAY
BIRTHDAY
BIRTHDAY
BIRTHDAY
BIRTHDAY

Figure 16.2: Output of Initial Version

```
   linenum: integer;
   dif: integer;
   redo: string[1];


Procedure Setup;
Begin
 assign(outf, outfile);
 rewrite(outf);
 assign(inf,infile);
 reset(inf);
 While NOT EOF(inf) Do
  Begin
    Readln(inf,poststring);
    Writeln(outf,poststring);
  End;
End;{Procedure}

Procedure Welcome;
Begin
 CLRSCR;
 Writeln('----------------------------------------------------');
 Writeln('      WELCOME TO THE GREETING CARD PROGRAM');
 Writeln('----------------------------------------------------');
 Writeln('');
 Writeln('This program will allow you to make a greeting card.');
 Writeln('The front of the card has the occasion for the card.');
 Writeln('The occasion can be only 11 characters and is entered');
 Writeln('by the user. For example, Christmas or New Baby could');
 Writeln('could be entries for the occasion.');
 Writeln('');
 Writeln('The inside will contain 4 lines, 15 characters or less');
 Writeln('and 2 closing lines.  The first closing line may be');
 Writeln('Best Wishes, Best of Luck, etc. The second closing line');
 Writeln('is for your name.');
 Writeln('');
 Writeln('The backspace key may be used to delete letters.');
 Writeln('However, the user cannot correct a line once it is');
 Writeln('finished until the program allows the user to do so');
 Writeln('by way of a prompt.');
 Writeln('');
 Writeln('');
 Write('Enter the Occasion for the front of your card ----> ');
 Readln(cardtype);

 Repeat
 If (length(cardtype) > 11) then
 Begin
  Writeln('');
  Writeln('The Occasion you entered is more than 11 characters');
  Write('long, please re-enter the Occasion ---->');
  Readln(cardtype);
 End;
 Until length(cardtype) <= 11;
 Clrscr;
End;{Procedure}
```

```
Procedure GetCardFront;
Begin
 color := 0.36;
 fontsize := 4;
 y := 322;
 x := 460;
 linenum := 1;
 dif := 4;
 Repeat
  Writeln(outf,color,' setgray ',fontsize,' font');
  Writeln(outf,x,' ',y,' moveto (',cardtype,') ctr');
  linenum := linenum + 1;
  if linenum = 5 then
  dif := dif + 10
  else
  dif := dif + 4;
  y := y - dif;
  fontsize := fontsize + 4;
  color := color - 0.04;
 Until y = 20;
End;{Procedure}


Procedure Checkline;
Begin
Repeat
 If length(firline) > 20 then
 Begin
  Writeln('The length of line ', linetrack,' is longer than 20');
  Write('Please retype the line ====>  ');
  readln(firline);
 End;
Until length(firline) <= 20;
End;{Procedure}


Procedure Screen2;
Begin
 Writeln('----------------------------------------------------------');
 Writeln('  INSIDE TEXT FOR THE  "',cardtype, '" GREETING CARD');
 Writeln('----------------------------------------------------------');
 Writeln('');
 If linetrack = 5 then
  Writeln('       ****** ENTER YOUR CLOSING LINE ******');
 If linetrack = 6 then
  Writeln('           ****** ENTER YOUR NAME ******');
 If linetrack <= 4 then
  Writeln('  Enter line ',linetrack,' of the inside of your card.');
 Writeln('');
 Writeln('');
 If linetrack = 1 then
  Write('          ');
End;{Procedure}


Procedure CenterScreenText (textin:string);
```

```
Var Space:char;
    index:integer;
    center:integer;
    l:integer;

Begin
 l := 0;
 space := ' ';
 index := 0;
 Repeat
  holdspaces[index] := space;
  index := index + 1;
 Until index = 27;
 index := 0;
 l := length(textin);
 center := (54 - l) DIV 2;
 While index <> center do
  Begin
   holdspaces[index] := space;
   Write(holdspaces[index]);
   index := index + 1;
  End;
End;{Procedure}


Procedure InsideText;
Begin
 Repeat
  If linetrack > 1 then
  Begin
   Clrscr;
   Screen2;
  End;

  If linetrack = 2 then
  Begin
   Writeln('          ',line1);
   Write('          ');
  End;

  If linetrack = 3 then
  Begin
   Writeln('          ',line1);
   Writeln('          ',line2);
   Write('          ');
  End;

  If linetrack = 4 then
  Begin
   Writeln('          ',line1);
   Writeln('          ',line2);
   Writeln('          ',line3);
   Write('          ');
  End;

  If linetrack = 5 then
  Begin
```

```
 Writeln('          ',line1);
 Writeln('          ',line2);
 Writeln('          ',line3);
 Writeln('          ',line4);
 Writeln('');
 Write('            ');
End;

If linetrack = 6 then
Begin
 Writeln('          ',line1);
 Writeln('          ',line2);
 Writeln('          ',line3);
 Writeln('          ',line4);
 Writeln('');
 Writeln('          ',line5);
 Write('            ');
End;

If linetrack = 7 then
Begin
 CenterScreenText (line1);
 Writeln(line1);
 CenterScreenText(line2);
 Writeln(line2);
 CenterScreenText(line3);
 Writeln(line3);
 CenterScreenText(line4);
 Writeln(line4);
 Writeln('');
 CenterScreenText(line5);
 Writeln(line5);
 CenterScreenText(line6);
 Writeln(line6);
End;

Readln(firline);
Checkline;

CASE linetrack of
  1:
   Begin
    line1 := firline;
   End;
  2:
   Begin
    line2 := firline;
   End;
  3:
   Begin
    line3 := firline;
   End;
  4:
   Begin
    line4 := firline;
   End;
  5:
```

```
      Begin
       line5 := firline;
      End;
     6:
      Begin
       line6 := firline;
      End;
   ELSE
   End;
   linetrack := linetrack + 1;
  Until linetrack = 8;
End;{Procedure}


Procedure Cleanup;
Begin
 Close(outf);
 Close(inf);
End;{Procedure}


Procedure CheckInsideText;
Begin
 Writeln('This is the text centered. Satisfied? Type "Y"');
 Writeln('If you are not satisfied, type "N" ');
 Write('Enter N or Y here ---->');
 Readln(redo);

 If (redo <> 'Y')then
 Begin
 If (redo <> 'y')then
 Begin
 If (redo <> 'N')then
 Begin
 If (redo <> 'n') then
 Begin
  Writeln('The character you entered is not an answer.');
  Write('Please re-enter your answer ---->');
  Readln(redo);
 End;
 End;
 End
 End;

 If (redo = 'N') OR (redo = 'n') then
 Begin
  linetrack := 1;
  Clrscr;
  Screen2;
  InsideText;
  CheckInsideText;
End;

 If (redo = 'Y') OR (redo = 'y') then
 Begin
  Writeln('');
  Writeln('Hope you like your card! ');
```

```
  Writeln('');
 End;
End;{Procedure}

Procedure WriteOut;
Begin
 InsideY := 250;
 Writeln(outf,'inside');
 Writeln(outf,'154 ',InsideY,'  moveto(',line1,')ctr');
 InsideY := InsideY - 40;
 Writeln(outf,'154 ',InsideY,'  moveto(',line2,')ctr');
 InsideY := InsideY - 40;
 Writeln(outf,'154 ',InsideY,'  moveto(',line3,')ctr');
 InsideY := InsideY - 40;
 Writeln(outf,'154 ',InsideY,'  moveto(',line4,')ctr');
 InsideY := InsideY - 40;
 Writeln(outf,'154 ',InsideY,'  moveto(',line5,')ctr');
 InsideY := InsideY - 40;
 Writeln(outf,'154 ',InsideY,'  moveto(',line6,')ctr');
 InsideY := InsideY - 40;
 Writeln(outf,'%%EOF');
End;{Procedure}

{------------------MAIN---------------------------}

Begin
  linetrack := 1;
  Setup;
  Welcome;
  GetCardFront;
  Screen2;
  InsideText;
  CheckInsideText;
  WriteOut;
  Cleanup;
End.{Main}
```

- **Setup** is the same as in the first version and provides the same function.
- **Welcome**, which is called from **Main**, is expanded in the second version to print out an attractive screen and give you more detailed directions. It still prompts you for the text for the front of the card and does error checking.
- **GetCardFront** is the same as in the first version and provides the same function.
- **Checkline**'s code is the same as in the first version and serves the same function.
- **Screen2** is called from **Main**, **InsideText**, and **CheckInsideText**, and sets up an attractive screen for your input. It also prompts you for each line of inside text.

- **CenterScreenText** is called from **InsideText** and centers all the text for the inside of the card on the screen so you can preview may view how the text is formatted at output.
- **InsideText** is called from **Main** and **CheckInsideText**. The additional code of the **if** statements keeps the screen attractive during user input. The screen is cleared, the **Screen2** procedure is called, and the screen is then rebuilt according to which lines of text have been entered. This provides you with a clear view of each line of text that has been entered without extraneous prompt commands.
- **CheckinsideText** is called from **Main** and from within itself. It prompts you after all input and centering is complete to see if you are pleased with the input. If you want to change the input, the procedure calls **Screen2** and **InsideText**. If the input is correct, the message "Hope you like your card!" is written on the screen.
- **WriteOut** performs the same function as it did in Version 1.

The main body of Version 2 is simple because it initializes linetrack to 1 and calls all the procedures except **CenterScreenText** and **Checkline**. These two procedures are called from within other procedures. The output from Version 2 of the driver is the PostScript file shown in Listing 16.17.

Listing 16.17: Output produced by Version 2 of the program

```
%!PS-Adobe-3.0 EPSF-30.
%%BoundingBox: 0 0 612 792
%%Title:(Greeting Card)
%%EndComments
%-------------------------Procedures------------------------
/ctr {dup stringwidth pop 2 div neg 0 rmoveto show} bind def
/clearit {4 {pop} repeat  stroke} bind def
/font{/Helvetica-Bold findfont exch scalefont setfont}
 bind def
/inside{/Times-BoldItalic findfont 20 scalefont setfont
       306 720 translate
       180 rotate }def
/Border {4 setlinewidth
       334 62 moveto 334 352 388 352 36 arcto clearit
       360 352 moveto 586 352 586 298 36 arcto clearit
       586 320 moveto 586 28 514 28 36 arcto clearit
       550 28 moveto 334 28 334 82 36 arcto clearit }def
%--------------------------MAIN-------------------------
Border
 3.6000000000E-01 setgray 4 font
460 322 moveto (NEW YEAR) ctr
 3.2000000000E-01 setgray 8 font
460 314 moveto (NEW YEAR) ctr
 2.8000000000E-01 setgray 12 font
460 302 moveto (NEW YEAR) ctr
 2.4000000000E-01 setgray 16 font
460 286 moveto (NEW YEAR) ctr
```

```
 2.0000000000E-01 setgray 20 font
460 260 moveto (NEW YEAR) ctr
 1.6000000000E-01 setgray 24 font
460 230 moveto (NEW YEAR) ctr
 1.2000000000E-01 setgray 28 font
460 196 moveto (NEW YEAR) ctr
 8.0000000000E-02 setgray 32 font
460 158 moveto (NEW YEAR) ctr
 4.0000000000E-02 setgray 36 font
460 116 moveto (NEW YEAR) ctr
 3.9790393203E-13 setgray 40 font
460 70 moveto (NEW YEAR) ctr
inside
154 250  moveto(May the Incoming)ctr
154 210  moveto(Year Bring You)ctr
154 170  moveto(Peace Health &)ctr
154 130  moveto(Happiness)ctr
154 90  moveto(Happy New Year!)ctr
154 50  moveto(Sandy and Joe)ctr
%%EOF
```

The output from executing this file is illustrated in Figure 16.3.

d. Suggested Enhancements

Here are some suggestions to further enhance the greeting card driver:

- Allow users to choose their own font in both the outside and inside rather than hard coding the font.
- Users may want to choose the number of lines to be entered inside, although you would have to set a limit for spacing reasons. However, once the number of lines is chosen, the driver can vertical centering rather than locking it a certain number of lines so vertical centering is hard coded.
- Have user enter their own text on the front and the inside of the card rather than confining them to one saying on the front.
- Let users input the point size for the font. A procedure to check the point size against the font type was to be implemented with this enhancement.
- The second version can be redone using graphics screens instead of the text-formatted screens.

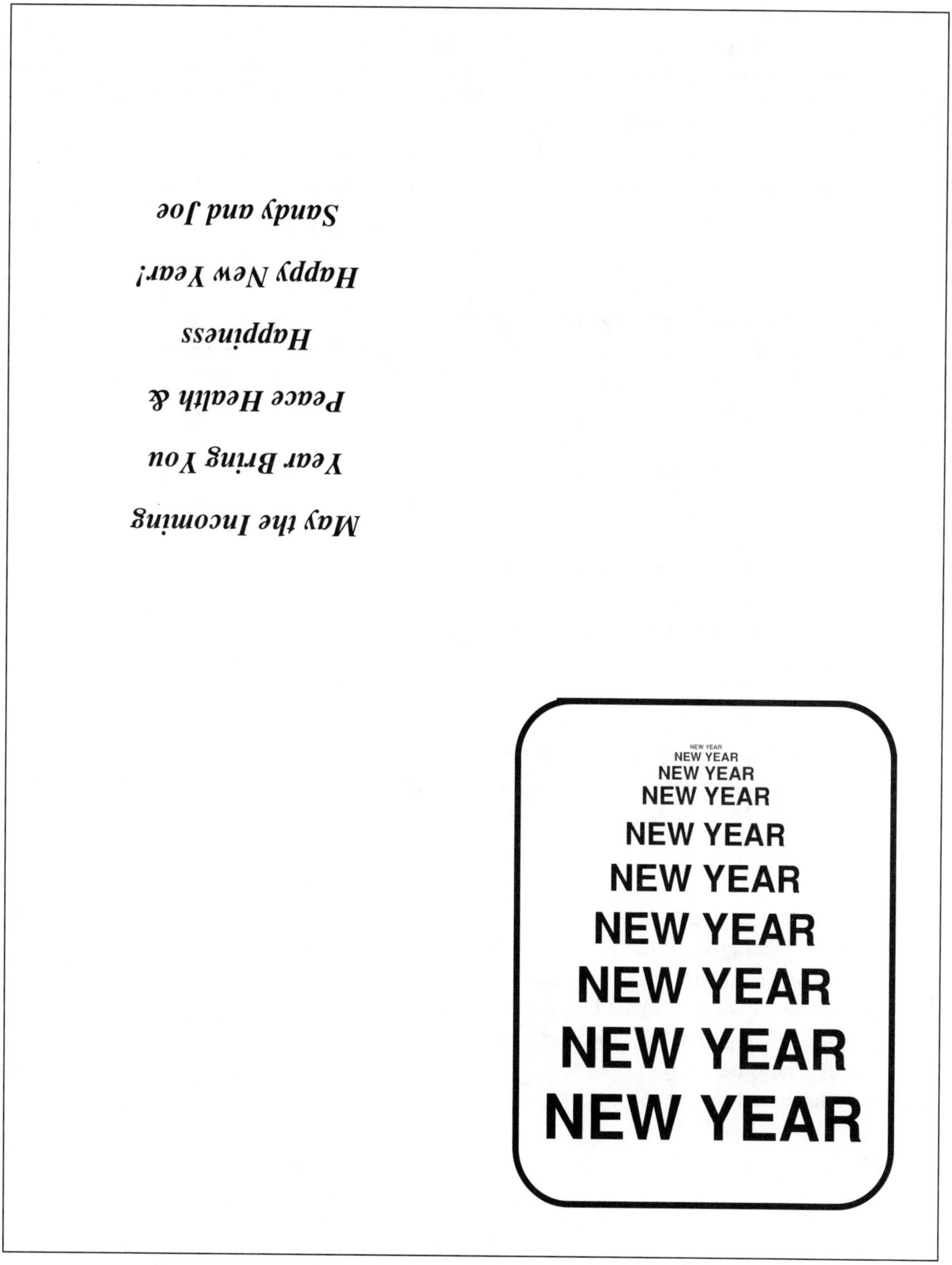
May the Incoming
Year Bring You
Peace Health &
Happiness
Happy New Year!
Sandy and Joe
NEW YEAR
NEW YEAR
NEW YEAR
NEW YEAR
NEW YEAR
NEW YEAR
NEW YEAR
NEW YEAR
NEW YEAR
NEW YEAR

Figure 16.3: Output created by the Enhanced Driver

3. Greeting Card Driver: C

This section introduces a PostScript driver program that produces greeting cards. The language is Turbo C but few Turbo C functions are used, so minimal code changes are required to run this program on other systems. The program is presented in three stages, each stage introducing various, user-defined functions that enhance the greeting card.

a. Program Specifications

Before describing how the programs work, first it is necessary to define what they should do.

Simple Greeting Card

The first program's objective is to generate, a simple greeting card on a sheet of paper. The simple greeting card contains text only on the outside cover and inside right flap. Also, each face that displays text contains eight centered lines of 18-point type. You define the font style at program run time. In the case of the inside face, the eighth line is reserved for program user's name, which is printed in Times-BoldItalic font with a point size of 18. You generate the rest of the text to appear on the card.

Greeting Card with Formatting

The objective output of the second program is similar to the the first program, except three simple formatting commands are supported. These three formatting operations are centered-shadowed text, left-justified text and centered text.

Complete Greeting Card

The output of the final program is the same as the second program output, except a personal note is written on the greeting card's inside left flap. The text written here is in ZapfChancery-MediumItalic with a point size of 12 except for the first line which is 15 points. Also, the text of the personal note is left-justified and automatically line-wrapped. So, for instance, lines of any length fit into the inside left flap of the greeting card.

b. Explanation of the Listings

The first version of the C driver for a card introduces the majority of the code. This code, which is explained in detail, is presented in Listing 16.18.

Listing 16.18: Simple Greeting Card Generator

```
#include "stdio.h"
#include "conio.h"
#include "dos.h"
#include "string.h"
#include "stdlib.h"

void top_menu();
char font_menu();
void setup_font_file ();
char text_menu();
void readintext();
void printname();
void openhelveticabold();
void opentimes();
void openzapt();
void openpalatino();
void openpalatinobi();
void opentimesbi();
void clean(char oneline[80]);
void readinwidths ();
float computewidth (char oneline[80]);
float center (char oneline[80]);

FILE *fontfile, *textfile, *psfile;
char name[30], typeface[60];
int widarray [100];

main ()
{ char choice;
  clrscr();
  printf("\nThis program produces greeting cards\n");
  printf("Some preliminary information isrequired first\n");
  setup_font_file ();
  printf("\nPlease enter the name to sign the card with: ");
  fflush (stdin); gets (name);
  readintext();
  printname();
  fprintf (psfile, "showpage");
  fclose (psfile);
}

char font_menu()
{ char choice;
  printf("\n\nPlease select the font for the printing of the text:");
  printf("\n\t1 - Helvetica Bold");
  printf("\n\t2 - Times Roman");
  printf("\n\t3 - Zapf Chancery Italic");
  printf("\n\t4 - Palatino Bold Italic");
```

```
  printf("\n\t5 - Times Roman Bold Italic");
  printf("\nEnter the number of your choice : ");
  fflush(stdin); choice = getch();
  return (choice);
}

void setup_font_file ()
{ char choice;
  choice = font_menu();
  switch (choice)
  { case '1' : {
        strcpy (typeface,"/Helvetica-Bold");
        openhelveticabold();
        break;
          }
    case '2' : {
        strcpy (typeface,"/Times-Roman");
        opentimes();
        break;
          }
    case '3' : {
        strcpy (typeface,"/ZapfChancery-MediumItalic");
        openzapt();
        break;
          }
    case '4' : {
        strcpy (typeface,"/Palatino-BoldItalic");
        openpalatinobi();
        break;
          }
    case '5' : {
        strcpy (typeface,"/Times-BoldItalic");
        opentimesbi();
        break;
          }
  }
strcat(typeface," findfont 18 scalefont setfont\n");
readinwidths();
}


char text_menu()
{ char choice;
  psfile = fopen ("card.ps","w");
  fprintf(psfile,"%!PS-Adobe\n");
  fprintf(psfile,"%s\n",typeface);
  do { printf ("\nHow will data be input?");
          printf("\n\t1. Input text from a file.");
          printf("\n\t2. Input text interactively.");
          printf("\nChoice : ");
       choice = getch();
  } while ((choice != '1') && (choice != '2'));
  return (choice);
}

void readintext ()
{ char oneline[80], filename[80],choice;
```

```
int numblanks, counter, pagenumber, numberoflines, toobig;
float x,y,changeiny;

toobig = 0;
choice = text_menu();
pagenumber=0;
switch (choice)

{ case '1' : { clrscr();
        gotoxy (1,1); printf("Enter the name of the text file: ");
     fflush (stdin); gets (filename);
     if ((textfile = fopen (filename,"r")) == NULL)
          { clrscr(); printf("File does not exist!");}
     else {
     do
        {pagenumber++;
         switch(pagenumber)
         { case 1 : {numberoflines = 8;
           fprintf(psfile,"gsave\n306 0 translate\n");
           break;}
           case 2 : {numberoflines = 7;
           fprintf(psfile,"grestore\n");
           fprintf(psfile,"gsave\n306 792 translate\n");
           fprintf(psfile,"180 rotate\n");
           break;}
         }
         numblanks = 0; counter = 0; y=353.0; changeiny = 35.0;
         do
           {counter++; y-=changeiny;
            fflush(stdin); fgets(oneline,80,textfile);
            clean(oneline);
            if (strlen(oneline)==0)
         numblanks++;
            else if (numblanks < 2)
         { x = center (oneline);
           fprintf (psfile,"%f %f moveto (%s) show\n",
                 x,y,oneline);}
         } while ((counter<numberoflines)&&(numblanks<2));
         if (counter == numberoflines)
           { fgets(oneline,80,textfile);
        fgets(oneline,80,textfile);
           }
     } while ((pagenumber<2)&&(!feof(textfile));}
     break;
         }

  case '2' : { do
        {pagenumber++;
         clrscr();
         switch(pagenumber)
         { case 1 : {gotoxy (36,1); printf("Cover Page");
           gotoxy(1,2); numberoflines=8;
           fprintf(psfile,"gsave\n306 0 translate\n");
           break;}
           case 2 : {gotoxy (36,1); printf("Inside Right Flap");
           gotoxy (1,2); numberoflines=7;
           fprintf(psfile,"grestore\n");
```

```
              fprintf(psfile,"gsave\n306 792 translate\n");
              fprintf(psfile,"180 rotate\n");
              break;}
            }
            counter = 0; y=353.0; changeiny = 35.0;
            do
              {counter++; y-= changeiny;
              do
              {printf("Enter line #%d : ",counter);
               fflush(stdin); gets(oneline);
               if (strlen (oneline) !=0)
            { if (18*computewidth(oneline) > 306.0)
                { printf ("Line is too long!");
                  toobig = 1;
                }
              else
                toobig = 0;
              if (!toobig)
                { x = center (oneline);
                  fprintf (psfile, "%f %f moveto",x,y);
                  fprintf (psfile, " (%s) show\n",oneline);
                }
            }
              } while (toobig);
            } while (counter<numberoflines);
        } while (pagenumber < 2);
        break;
            }
  }
}

void clean (char oneline [80])
{ int i;
  for (i=0;i<=strlen(oneline);i++)
    if (oneline[i] == '\n') oneline[i] = '\0';
}

void readinwidths ()
{ int i;
  char alpha[10];

  i = 0;
  rewind (fontfile);
  while (!feof(fontfile))
  {
    fgets(alpha, 10, fontfile);
    widarray[i++]=atoi(alpha+1);
  }
fclose(fontfile);
}

float computewidth (char oneline [80])
{ int ordvalue, wstring, j;
  float tw;

  tw = 0;
  wstring = strlen (oneline);
```

```
    for (j=0;j<wstring;j++)
      {ordvalue = oneline [j];
          tw = tw + widarray [ordvalue - 32];
      }
    tw = (tw/1000);
    return tw;
}

float center (char oneline [80])
{ float width,x;
  width = computewidth(oneline);
  x = (306.0 - (18.0*width))/2.0;
  return x;
}

void openhelveticabold()
{ fontfile = fopen ("helv_b_r.fxw","r");}

void opentimes()
{ fontfile = fopen ("tiro_l_r.fxw","r");}

void openzapt()
{ fontfile = fopen ("zcha_l_r.fxw","r");}

void openpalatino()
{ fontfile = fopen ("palab_r.fxw","r");}

void openpalatinobi()
{ fontfile = fopen ("palab_i.fxw","r");}

void opentimesbi()
{ fontfile = fopen ("tiro_b_i.fxw","r");}

void printname ()
{ float tw;
  opentimesbi();
  readinwidths();
  tw = computewidth (name);
  fprintf (psfile, "/Times-BoldItalic findfont 18 scalefont setfont\n");
  fprintf (psfile, "%f 33 moveto (%s) show\n",(275.0-(18.0*tw)), name);
}
```

Simple Greeting Card

The objective of this program is to accept text and, after some computations, print it out to a PostScript program. This first program accomplishes the requirements by using 16 functions. The purpose and motivations of each function is discussed in the order they are encountered, starting with the main function.

For these functions to be carried forward, the driver needs information regarding character widths. This information is obtained from font width files. The files used in this book are greatly simplified versions of the Adobe Font Metric Files. See page 227 in Chapter 15 for more information on the font files.

The program also uses ASCII text stored in a file to produce the text on the card rather than inputting the information manually. The contents of the file are

```
'Twas the night
before Christmas.
And all thru
the house,
not a creature
was stirring.
Not even a mouse . . .



But if you can
hear a mouse,
give us a call.
We can make your
Holidays quiet again.
```

The **main** function undertakes control of the overall program and consists of six parts. First, the screen is cleared and some information is printed. Second, font information is obtained via **setup_font_file** which uses the **font_menu** function which allows you to select one of the five fonts. After execution, **setup_font_file** fills a string variable, **typeface**, to the appropriate PostScript operator that selects the font chosen. Third, the program obtains the name to be used as a signature for the cards. Fourth, the text is read either from a file or interactively—this is where most of the work takes place. Fifth, the signature line is actually placed in the code. Sixth, and last, the **showpage** operator is written to the file and the file is closed.

The **font_menu**, **setup_font_file**, and **text_menu** functions are straightforward.

The **readintext** function enables you to enter text either from a text file or interactively. Once you make your choice, an integer variable, **pagenumber**, is initialized to 0. This variable keeps track of which part of the card is currently being written to. So, for instance, if **pagenumber** is equal to 1, the current part of the card being written to is the cover. If **pagenumber** is 2, the current part of the card is the inside right flap. After **pagenumber** is initialized, a case statement is used to accept text depending which input mode you selected.

Case 1 of the case statement reads in text from a file. You are is prompted for the drive and file name that contains the text. The text file pointer is called **textfile**. Next, a **do** loop repeats until either all the text for both parts of the card is read, **pagenumber** is less than two, or the end of the input file is reached. If none of these conditions are true, the loop is entered.

The first thing that happens within the **do** loop is a case statement. This case statement is based which page is currently active. If the first page is active the appropriate PostScript operators that move are written to **psfile**. the origin to the middle of the bottom of the page. Also, if **pagenumber** is 1, the **numberoflines** variable is set to 8. This variable denotes how many lines of text are allowed on the current page. If, however, **pagenumber** is 2, PostScript operators that move the origin to the top middle of the page and rotate the axis 180 degrees are written in **psfile**. Also, **numberoflines** is set to 7. After this case statement is passed, some variable initializations are encountered.

Numblanks keeps track of how many back-to-back blank lines are encountered in the text file. This variable is a flag to signify when to start writing on the next part of the card.

The next variable initialized is **counter**. **Counter** keeps track of how many lines have been read from the text file. This also serves as a flag to signify when to stop writing for one part of the card and begin writing to another part. **Counter** is compared to the **numberoflines** variable to test if the allowed number of lines/card part has been met.

The next two variables, **y** and **changeiny**, are initialized to 353.0, and 35.0 respectively. These two variables are responsible for determining the Y location the line is written to. Each time a line is written to **psfile**, **changeiny** decrements **y**. These signify the last of the four variable initializations. The next statement encountered is another **do** loop.

This **do** loop reads in all text associated with the current part of the card, given by **pagenumber**. The loop reads in from **textfile** until either two blank lines or **numberoflines** are read. If either of these two conditions are met, reading the text for the current part of the card is considered complete. As each line is read from **textfile**, its width, in points, is computed and the appropriate X value is be returned from the function center, so the X corresponds to the X location that causes the line to be centered within a column 306 points wide. Once the X value is computed, a PostScript operator that moves the current point to the computed X and Y value and shows the string is written to **psfile**. This process is repeated until either all text file is read, or enough of it has been read to generate the card. This marks the end of the first case statement. Interactive text is gathered in much the same way, except you are given the opportunity to reenter a line that is too long to fit within on part of the card. Once all text is read in and printed out to **psfile**, the **readintext** function passes control back to **main** function.

Three functions, **readinwidths**, **computewidth**, and **center**, are closely related and work together to make **readintext** work. **Readinwidths** opens a font width file and reads the width of the characters into an integer array, **widarray**, So the widths of all the characters in the chosen font set are known to the program. **Widarray** is defined as a global variable so all functions within the program are able to access it.

Computewidth takes a given string and calculates its width based on the width of the characters. It works by knowing that each character has a particular order in the ASCII set. A space is the 32nd character, "A" is number 65, "B" is number 66, etc. The width information in the font file is listed in this order. The integer value of a character is equal to its ordinal value in the ASCII set. Since you read in the font files beginning with the 32nd character—a space, you know the width of any character is the value of **widarray**[char-32]. The total of these values divided by 1,000 is the width of a string in 1 point size. The width in 20-point size is the 1 point size multipled by 20. This activity is carried out by the **center** function which calculates half of the amount of white space around the string. The width of the string is subtracted from the width of the column, and the result is divided by 2. This tells you where to place the string relative to the left margin if you want it to appear centered.

The **printname** function moves to the bottom of the current card "part" and right-justifies name, which was interactively entered earlier, then shows it. The font style chosen for the name is hard-coded into the program as Times-Bold Italic at 18 points. After **printname** executes, control goes back to the **main** function.

The program's output is shown in Listing 16.19. The result of running the program is shown in Figure 16.4.

Listing 16.19: Output of Simple Greeting Card Generator

```
%!PS-Adobe
/Helvetica-Bold findfont 18 scalefont setfont

gsave
306 0 translate
87.488998 318.000000 moveto ('Twas the night) show
76.482002 283.000000 moveto (before Christmas.) show
102.995995 248.000000 moveto (And all thru) show
107.990997 213.000000 moveto (the house,) show
93.483002 178.000000 moveto (not a creature) show
99.981003 143.000000 moveto (was stirring.) show
60.966003 108.000000 moveto (Not even a mouse . . .) show
grestore
gsave
306 792 translate
180 rotate
93.491997 318.000000 moveto (But if you can) show
92.474998 283.000000 moveto (hear a mouse,) show
94.463997 248.000000 moveto (give us a call.) show
73.971001 213.000000 moveto (We can make your) show
62.973000 178.000000 moveto (Holidays quiet again.) show
/Times-BoldItalic findfont 18 scalefont setfont
121.477995 33 moveto (Acme Exterminators) show
showpage
```

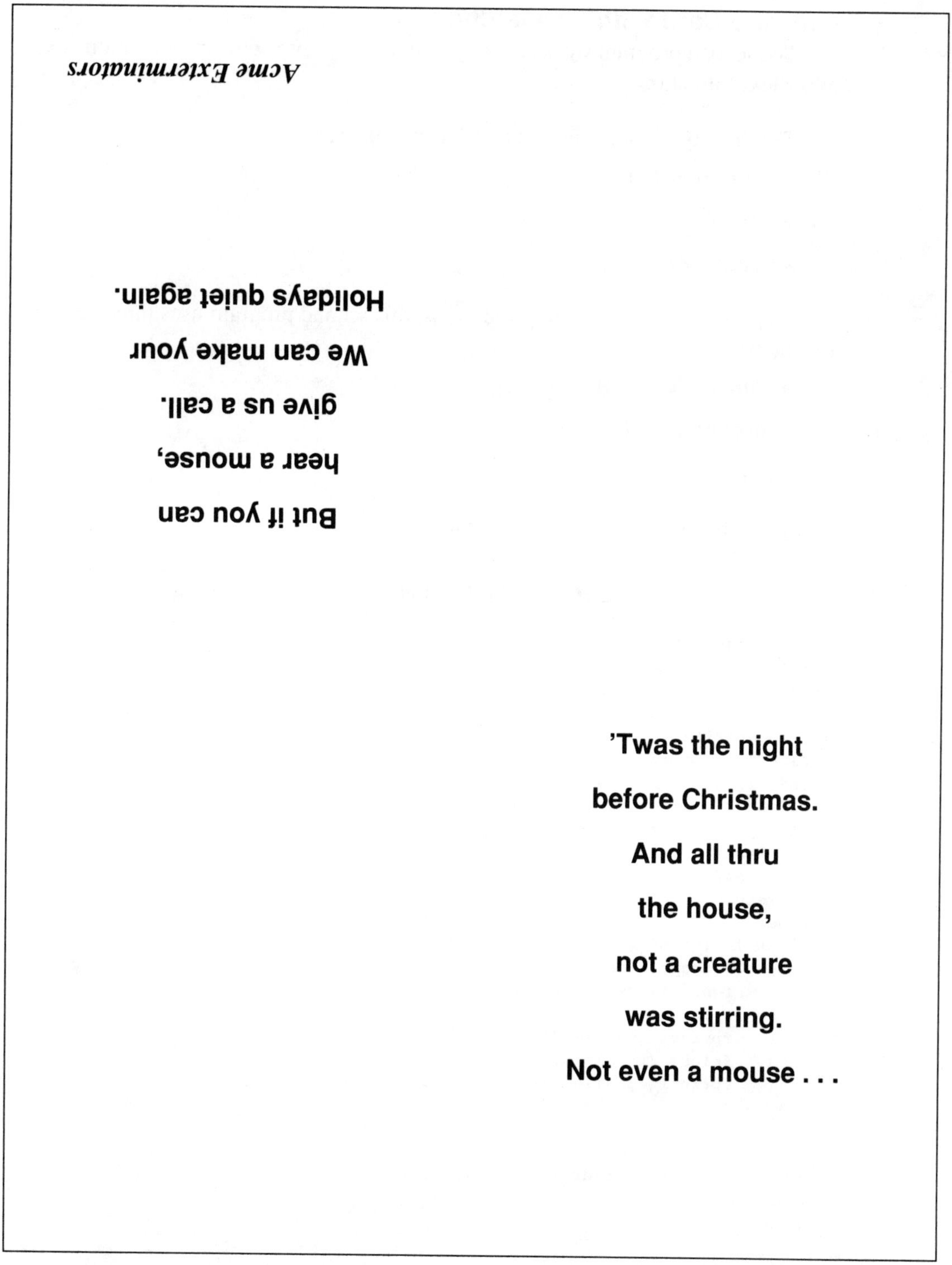
'Twas the night
before Christmas.
And all thru
the house,
not a creature
was stirring.
Not even a mouse . . .
But if you can
hear a mouse,
give us a call.
We can make your
Holidays quiet again.
Acme Exterminators

Figure 16.4: Output of Simple Greeting Card PostScript Program

Greeting Card With Formatting

The second program works exactly like the first with some modifications to allow text formatting.

The three types of supported text formatting are

- left justification
- centering
- shadow text

To provide these formatting functions, this second program uses three new functions;

- **appendfile( )**
- **formattedtext( )**
- **leftshift( )**

These functions are shown in Listing 16.20.

Listing 16.20: Additional Code for Formatting

```
int appendfile();
void formattedtext (char line [80], float y);
void leftshift (char line [80]);

int appendfile ()
{ FILE *psfile_aux;
  char line [80];
  psfile = fopen ("card.ps","w");
  if ((psfile_aux = fopen ("card_c2.psp","r")) == NULL)
    {clrscr();
     printf ("The file \"card_c2.psp\" is not in current directory.");
     return (0);}
  else
    {while (!feof (psfile_aux))
          {strcpy(line,"");
          fgets (line,80,psfile_aux);
          fputs (line,psfile);}
          fprintf (psfile,"\n");
          fclose (psfile_aux);
          fprintf (psfile,"%s\n",typeface);
          }
}

void formattedtext (char line [80], float y)
{ char format;
  float x;

  format = line [0];
  leftshift (line);
  switch (format)
```

```
  { case 'S' : { x = center (line);
         fprintf (psfile,"%f %f moveto (%s) shadow\n",x, y, line);
         break;}
     case 'L' : { fprintf (psfile,"36 %f moveto (%s) show\n", y, line);
         break;}
     default  : { x = center (line);
         fprintf (psfile,"%f %f moveto (%s) show\n", x, y, line);
         break;}
  }
}

void leftshift (char line [80])
{ int i;
  for (i=0; i<strlen(line); i++)
    line [i] = line [i+1];
}
```

The first function, **appendfile**, is executed in the main function immediately after the default font file is declared. Basically, **appendfile** reads an external file named **CARD_C2.PSP**, and copies its contents into the beginning of **psfile**, **CARD.PS**. The contents of **CARD_C2.PSP** contains the header line for the PostScript file

```
%!PS-Adobe
```

and the definition of the **shadow** literal; the file contents are shown in Listing 16.21. By using **appendfile** to define **shadow** at the top of **psfile**, this program can follow any string that is to be displayed in shadow format with the word "shadow," since the PostScript program already contain the **shadow** definition.

Listing 16.21: Prologue for the Card file

```
%!PS-Adobe
/shadow {gsave currentpoint translate
.95 -.1 0 {setgray 1 -.5 translate 0 0 moveto dup show } for
1 -.5 translate 0 0 moveto 1 setgray show grestore} def
```

The second function, **formattedtext**, accepts a string of 80 characters in length, as well as the Y position where the string will be displayed. Next, **formattedtext** strips off the first character of the string and places the character into the **format** variable. Next, the function **leftshift** is invoked. **Leftshift** then moves all the characters in the string to the left by one place, effectively removing the extra formatting character from the beginning of the string. Once **leftshift** is executed, the **format** variable is compared in a case statement.

If **format** equals to "S", the string is displayed centered and in shadow text. A call to **center** returns the starting X value. Next, PostScript operators that move to the X and Y location and then print out the string according to the definition of **shadow** are printed to **psfile**.

If **format** equals “L,” the string is displayed left-justified. Because the string is left-justified, the starting X value is be equal to the left margin, which is 36 points. PostScript operators to move to an X value of 36 and the current Y, then simply show the string are written to **psfile**.

The last case is “default.” Default displays a string centered and at the current Y location. (If you want centering, a “C” should be in the beginning of the string to avoid losing the first character of the string. If the you should forget to enter a formatting character, an appropriate PostScript file is still generated minus the first character.) This is the last function introduced by the second program. The following text file was used with the program:

```
L'Twas the night
Lbefore Christmas.
LAnd all thru
Lthe house,
Lnot a creature
Lwas stirring.
SNot even a mouse . . .



CBut if you can
Chear a mouse,
Cgive us a call.
SWe can make your
SHolidays quiet again.
```

The result of running the second program using this data is shown in Listing 16.22 and Figure 16.5.

Listing 16.22: Output of Greeting Card with Formatting Generator

```
%!PS-Adobe
/shadow {gsave currentpoint translate
.95 -.1 0 {setgray 1 -.5 translate 0 0 moveto dup show } for
1 -.5 translate 0 0 moveto 1 setgray show grestore} def

/Helvetica-Bold findfont 18 scalefont setfont

gsave
306 0 translate
36 318.000000 moveto ('Twas the night) show
36 283.000000 moveto (before Christmas.) show
36 248.000000 moveto (And all thru) show
36 213.000000 moveto (the house,) show
36 178.000000 moveto (not a creature) show
36 143.000000 moveto (was stirring.) show
60.966003 108.000000 moveto (Not even a mouse . . .) shadow
grestore
gsave
306 792 translate
```

```
180 rotate
93.491997 318.000000 moveto (But if you can) show
92.474998 283.000000 moveto (hear a mouse,) show
94.463997 248.000000 moveto (give us a call.) show
73.971001 213.000000 moveto (We can make your) shadow
62.973000 178.000000 moveto (Holidays quiet again.) shadow
/Times-BoldItalic findfont 18 scalefont setfont
121.477995 33 moveto (Acme Exterminators) show
showpage
```

Complete Greeting Card

This final program is comprised of the entire second program plus an additional function, called **personalinfo**, shown in Listing 16.23.

Listing 16.23: New Functions for the Final Greeting Card Generator

```
int personalinfo ()
{ int i, linenumber=0;
  float xlocation, ylocation;
  char oneline [80], filename [80] , choice;
  clrscr();
  fprintf (psfile, "gsave\n");
  fprintf (psfile, "612 792 translate\n180 rotate\n");
  fprintf(psfile,"/ZapfChancery-MediumItalic ");
  fprintf(psfile, " findfont 15 scalefont setfont\n");
  printf("\nGreeting:  ");
  gets(oneline);
  clean (oneline);
  if (strlen(oneline)<=1) return(0);
  fprintf(psfile,"36 318 moveto (%s) show\n",oneline);
  fprintf(psfile,"/ZapfChancery-MediumItalic findfont 12");
  fprintf(psfile," scalefont setfont\n");
  xlocation = 36.0; ylocation = 305.0;
  fprintf(psfile,"%f %f moveto (",xlocation,ylocation);
  printf("\nInside left text.\n\n");
  do{
    linenumber++;
    gets(oneline);
    fprintf(psfile, " ");
    clean (oneline);
    for (i=0; i<strlen(oneline);i++)
         {
         if (ylocation >= 36.0)
        if (xlocation < 200)
          {fprintf(psfile,"%c",oneline[i]);
         xlocation += 12*(widarray[oneline[i]-32])/1000;}
        else
          if (oneline[i] != 32)
       {fprintf(psfile,"%c",oneline[i]);
          xlocation += 12*(widarray[oneline[i]-32])/1000;}
          else
       {xlocation = 36.0; ylocation -= 13.0;
        fprintf(psfile,") show\n");
        fprintf(psfile,"%f %f moveto (",xlocation,ylocation);}
```

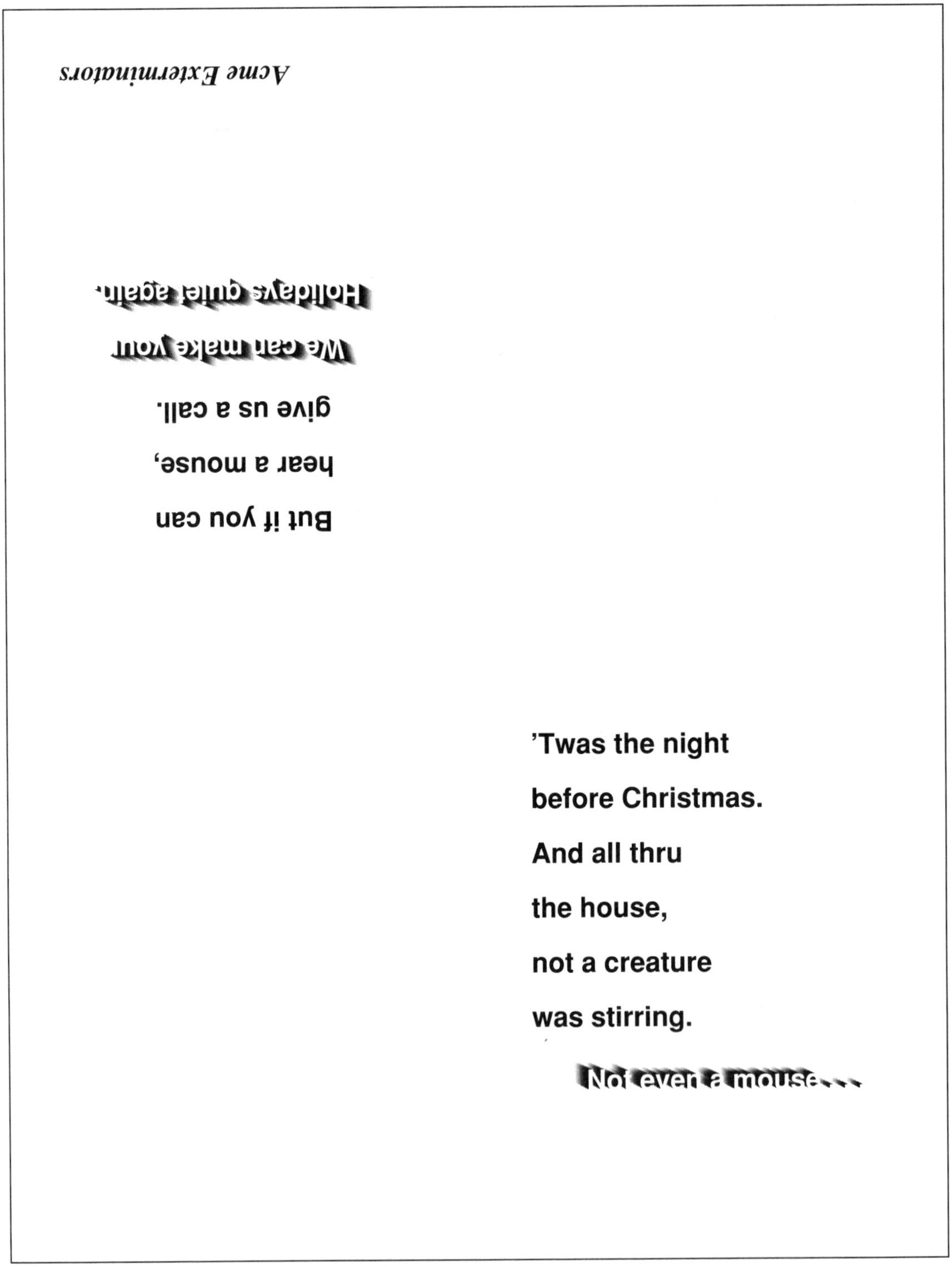
Acme Exterminators
Holidays quiet again.
We can make you
give us a call.
hear a mouse,
But if you can
'Twas the night
before Christmas.
And all thru
the house,
not a creature
was stirring.
Not even a mouse...

Figure 16.5: Output of Greeting Card with Formatting PostScript Program

```
        }
  }while (strlen(oneline)>1);
  fprintf(psfile,") show\n");
  fprintf(psfile,"grestore\n");
return(linenumber);
}
```

The **personalinfo** function displays text on the inner left flap of the card. In the process of writing text, **personalinfo** does two things:

- first line enhancement and line wrapping.

To see more easily what **personalinfo** does, a sequential trace through the function is necessary.

After initial variable declarations, two **print** statements print the PostScript operators that move the origin to the upper right corner of the page and then rotate it 180 degrees to **psfile**.

Next, the PostScript operators that change the font to ZapfChancery with point size 15 are written to **psfile**. The word "Greeting" is written out and the font is changed to 10 point. This is the font style and size that accounts for the body of the text. After this, two variables are initialized.

The first variable, **xlocation**, is initialized to 36.0. This represents the left margin. The second variable, **ylocation**, is initialized to 305.0, which represents the starting Y location where text is to be written. The **xlocation** variable changes each time a character is written to **psfile**, whereas the **ylocation** variable changes each time a line is written to **psfile**.

Next, a **while** loop is encountered that executes until a blank line is entered.

Inside the while loop is a for loop that goes through **oneline** one character at a time. To get a better understanding of what goes on within this for loop, you need a trace needed. The first statement encountered is an **if** statement. This **if** checks to see if the current **ylocation** is above 36.0, the lower bounds of the card. If **ylocation** is less than 36.0, nothing is printed to **psfile**; otherwise, another **if** statement is encountered. This next **if** statement checks to see if **xlocation** is less than 200. If the condition is true, the character is written to **psfile** and the **xlocation** is incremented by the characters width, in points. Otherwise, the character is checked to see if it is a space. If the character is not a space, the character is written out and **xlocation** is incremented. If the character is a space, **xlocation** is set to 36.0 and **ylocation** is decremented by 13. Next a right parentheses followed by a **show** are written to **psfile**. A PostScript command is then written to **psfile** that causes a **moveto** to **xlocation** and **ylocation**, followed by a left parenthesis. This process is repeated until the **for** loop is finished; then a new line is read in and the process is repeated until all of **personalfile** has been read.

Once a blank line is reached, a trailing right parenthesis followed by a **show** is written out to **psfile** to complete the final **show X**.

To enable you to write multiple copies of cards the work done in the first two programs is encapsulated as a definition in **main( )**, and a loop is added enables you to keep adding cards until you enter a blank line instead of a name, indicating you are done. The modifications to **main( )** are shown in Listing 16.24.

Listing 16.24: Changes for the Final Version

```
main ()
{ char choice;
  int more;
  clrscr();
  printf("\nThis program produces greeting cards\n");
  printf("Some preliminary information is required first\n");
  setup_font_file ();
  appendfile();
  printf("\nPlease enter the name to sign the card with: ");
  fflush (stdin); gets (name);
  fprintf(psfile, "\n/maincard {\n");
  readintext();
  printname();
  fprintf(psfile, "\n} def\n");
  openzapt();
  readinwidths();
  do{
        fprintf(psfile, "\n\nmaincard\n");
        more = personalinfo();
        fprintf (psfile, "showpage");
        }while (more);
  fclose (psfile);
}
```

The results of running the final program are shown in Listing 16.25 and in Figure 16.6. The complete program is shown in Listing 16.26.

Listing 16.25: Output of Complete Greeting Card Generator

```
%!PS-Adobe
/shadow {gsave currentpoint translate
.95 -.1 0 {setgray 1 -.5 translate 0 0 moveto dup show } for
1 -.5 translate 0 0 moveto 1 setgray show grestore} def


/maincard {
/Helvetica-Bold findfont 18 scalefont setfont
gsave
306 0 translate
36 318.000000 moveto ('Twas the night) show
36 283.000000 moveto (before Christmas.) show
36 248.000000 moveto (And all thru) show
36 213.000000 moveto (the house,) show
```

```
36 178.000000 moveto (not a creature) show
36 143.000000 moveto (was stirring.) show
60.966003 108.000000 moveto (Not even a mouse . . .) shadow
grestore
gsave
306 792 translate
180 rotate
93.491997 318.000000 moveto (But if you can) show
92.474998 283.000000 moveto (hear a mouse,) show
94.463997 248.000000 moveto (give us a call.) show
73.971001 213.000000 moveto (We can make your) shadow
62.973000 178.000000 moveto (Holidays quiet again.) shadow
/Times-BoldItalic findfont 18 scalefont setfont
121.477995 33 moveto (Acme Exterminators) show
grestore
} def


maincard
gsave
612 792 translate
180 rotate
/ZapfChancery-MediumItalic findfont 15 scalefont setfont
36 318 moveto (Dear Mr. Dubin:) show
/ZapfChancery-MediumItalic findfont 12 scalefont setfont
36 305 moveto ( We very much enjoyed getting all the bugs out) show
36 292 moveto (of your programs and would be more than happy) show
36 279 moveto (to help you get them out of your house as well.) show
36 266 moveto ( Have a very happy and rewarding holidays) show

grestore
showpage

maincard
gsave
612 792 translate
180 rotate
/ZapfChancery-MediumItalic findfont 15 scalefont setfont
36 318 moveto (Dr. Shirey) show
/ZapfChancery-MediumItalic findfont 12 scalefont setfont
36 305 moveto ( We have enjoyed helping you to get the bugs) show
36 292 moveto (out of your programs and would welcome the) show
36 279 moveto (chance to help in the removal of any bats that) show
36 266 moveto (have lodged in your belfry) show

grestore
showpage

maincard
gsave
612 792 translate
180 rotate
/ZapfChancery-MediumItalic findfont 15 scalefont setfont
showpage
```

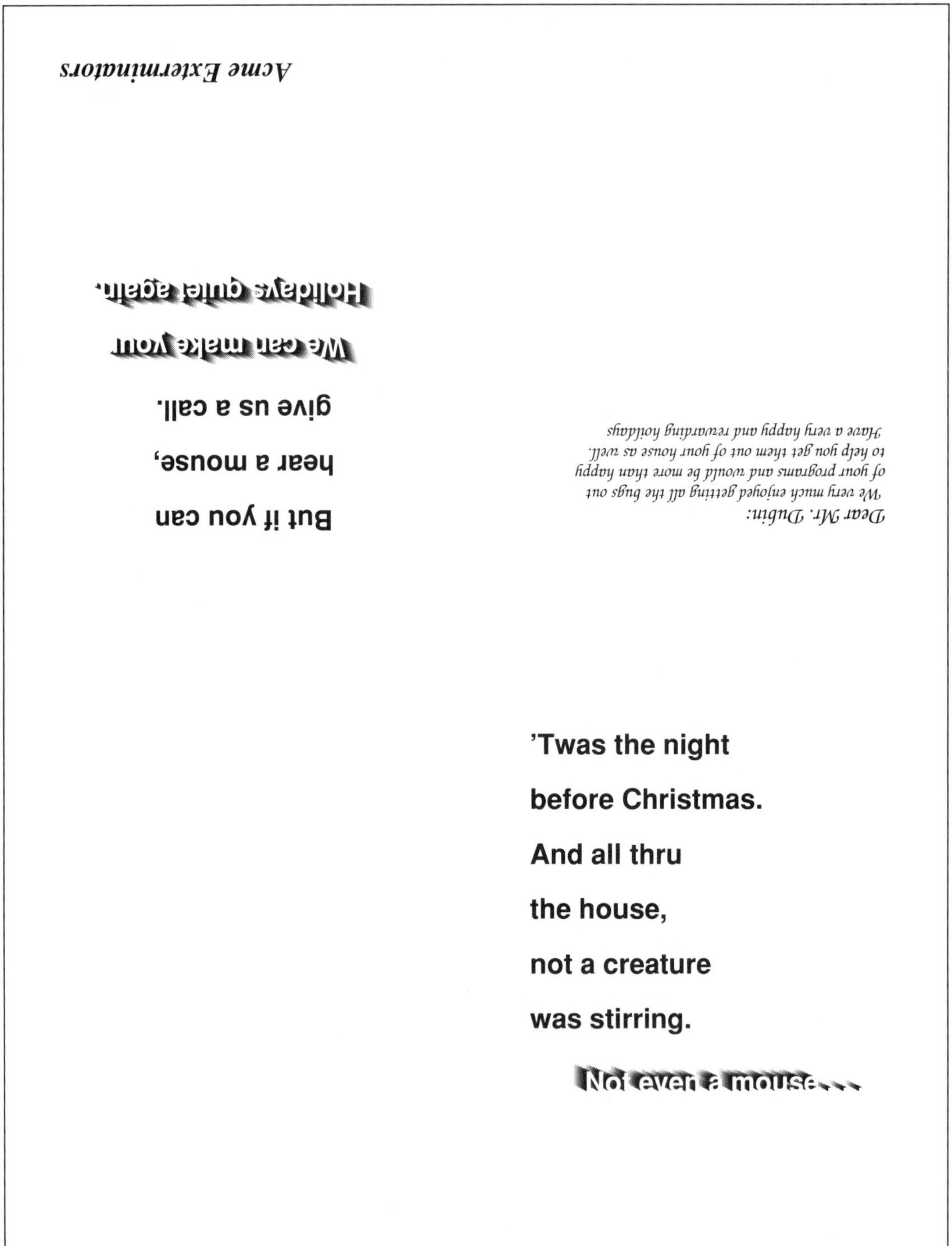

Acme Exterminators
Holidays quiet again.
We can make you
give us a call.
hear a mouse,
But if you can
Dear Mr. Dubin:
We very much enjoyed getting all the bugs out
of your programs and would be more than happy
to help you get them out of your house as well.
Have a very happy and rewarding holidays
'Twas the night
before Christmas.
And all thru
the house,
not a creature
was stirring.
Not even a mouse...

Figure 16.6: Output of One Page

Listing 16.26: Complete Greeting Card Generator

```
#include "stdio.h"
#include "conio.h"
#include "dos.h"
#include "string.h"
#include "stdlib.h"

void top_menu();
char font_menu();
void setup_font_file ();
char text_menu();
void readintext();
void printname();
void openhelveticabold();
void opentimes();
void openzapt();
void openpalatino();
void openpalatinobi();
void opentimesbi();
void clean(char oneline[80]);
void readinwidths ();
float computewidth (char oneline[80]);
float center (char oneline[80]);
int appendfile();
void formattedtext (char line [80], float y);
void leftshift (char line [80]);
int personalinfo ();

FILE *fontfile, *textfile, *psfile;
char name[30], typeface[60];
int widarray [100];

main ()
{ char choice;
  int more;
  clrscr();
  printf("\nThis program produces greeting cards\n");
  printf("Some preliminary information isrequired first\n");
  setup_font_file ();
  appendfile();
  printf("\nPlease enter the name to sign the card with: ");
  fflush (stdin); gets (name);
  fprintf(psfile, "\n/maincard {\n");
  readintext();
  printname();
  fprintf(psfile, "\n} def\n");
  openzapt();
  readinwidths();
  do{
        fprintf(psfile, "\n\nmaincard\n");
        more = personalinfo();
        fprintf (psfile, "showpage");
        }while (more);
  fclose (psfile);
}
```

```
char font_menu()
{ char choice;
  printf("\n\nPlease select the font for the printing of the text:");
  printf("\n\t1 - Helvetica Bold");
  printf("\n\t2 - Times Roman");
  printf("\n\t3 - Zapf Chancery Italic");
  printf("\n\t4 - Palatino Bold Italic");
  printf("\n\t5 - Times Roman Bold Italic");
  printf("\nEnter the number of your choice : ");
  fflush(stdin); choice = getch();
  return (choice);
}

void setup_font_file ()
{ char choice;
  choice = font_menu();
  switch (choice)
  { case '1' : {
          strcpy (typeface,"/Helvetica-Bold");
          openhelveticabold();
          break;
            }
    case '2' : {
          strcpy (typeface,"/Times-Roman");
          opentimes();
          break;
            }
    case '3' : {
          strcpy (typeface,"/ZapfChancery-MediumItalic");
          openzapt();
          break;
            }
    case '4' : {
          strcpy (typeface,"/Palatino-BoldItalic");
          openpalatinobi();
          break;
            }
    case '5' : {
          strcpy (typeface,"/Times-BoldItalic");
          opentimesbi();
          break;
            }
  }
strcat(typeface," findfont 18 scalefont setfont\n");
readinwidths();
}

char text_menu()
{ char choice;
    do { printf ("\nHow will data be input?");
          printf("\n\t1. Input text from a file.");
          printf("\n\t2. Input text interactively.");
          printf("\nChoice : ");
        choice = getch();
  } while ((choice != '1') && (choice != '2'));
  return (choice);
}
```

```
void readintext ()
{ char oneline[80], filename[80], choice;
  int numblanks, counter, pagenumber, numberoflines, toobig;
  float x,y,changeiny;

  toobig = 0;
  choice = text_menu();
  pagenumber=0;
  switch (choice)

  { case '1' : { clrscr();
       gotoxy (1,1); printf("Enter the text drive and filename : ");
       fflush (stdin); gets (filename);
       if ((textfile = fopen (filename,"r")) == NULL)
         { clrscr(); printf("File name does not exist!");}
       else {
       do
         {pagenumber++;
          switch(pagenumber)
          { case 1 : {numberoflines = 8;
                    fprintf (psfile,"%s\n",typeface);
            fprintf(psfile,"gsave\n306 0 translate\n");
            break;}
            case 2 : {numberoflines = 7;
            fprintf(psfile,"grestore\n");
            fprintf(psfile,"gsave\n306 792 translate\n");
            fprintf(psfile,"180 rotate\n");
            break;}
          }
          numblanks = 0; counter = 0; y=353.0; changeiny = 35.0;
          do
            {counter++; y-=changeiny;
             fflush(stdin); fgets(oneline,80,textfile);
             clean(oneline);
             if (strlen(oneline)==0)
          numblanks++;
             else if (numblanks < 2)
               formattedtext (oneline, y);
          } while ((counter<numberoflines)&&(numblanks<2));
          if (counter == numberoflines)
            { fgets(oneline,80,textfile);
         fgets(oneline,80,textfile);
            }
       } while ((pagenumber<2)&&(!feof(textfile)));}
      break;
          }

   case '2' : { do
         {pagenumber++;
          clrscr();
          switch(pagenumber)
          { case 1 : {gotoxy (36,1); printf("Cover Page");
            gotoxy(1,2); numberoflines=8;
                   fprintf (psfile,"%s\n",typeface);
            fprintf(psfile,"gsave\n306 0 translate\n");
            break;}
            case 2 : {gotoxy (36,1); printf("Inside Right Flap");
```

```
            gotoxy (1,2); numberoflines=7;
            fprintf(psfile,"grestore\n");
            fprintf(psfile,"gsave\n306 792 translate\n");
            fprintf(psfile,"180 rotate\n");
            break;}
          }
          counter = 0; y=353.0; changeiny = 35.0;
          do
            {counter++; y-= changeiny;
            do
         {printf("Enter line #%d : ",counter);
          fflush(stdin); gets(oneline);
          if (strlen (oneline) !=0)
            { if (18*computewidth(oneline) > 306.0)
                { printf ("Line is too long!");
             toobig = 1;
                }
              else
                toobig = 0;
              if (!toobig)
                formattedtext (oneline, y);
            }
            } while (toobig);
         } while (counter<numberoflines);
        } while (pagenumber < 2);
        break;
          }
  }
}

void clean (char oneline [80])
{ int i;
  for (i=0;i<=strlen(oneline);i++)
    if (oneline[i] == '\n') oneline[i] = '\0';
}

void readinwidths ()
{ int i;
  char alpha[10];

  i = 0;
  rewind (fontfile);
  while (!feof(fontfile))
  {
    fgets(alpha, 10, fontfile);
    widarray[i++]=atoi(alpha+1);
  }
 fclose(fontfile);
}

float computewidth (char oneline [80])
{ int ordvalue, wstring, j;
  float tw;

  tw = 0;
  wstring = strlen (oneline);
  for (j=0;j<wstring;j++)
```

```
    {ordvalue = oneline [j];
        tw = tw + widarray [ordvalue - 32];
    }
  tw = (tw/1000);
  return tw;
}

float center (char oneline [80])
{ float width,x;
  width = computewidth(oneline);
  x = (306.0 - (18.0*width))/2.0;
  return x;
}

void openhelveticabold()
{ fontfile = fopen ("helv_b_r.fxw","r");}

void opentimes()
{ fontfile = fopen ("tiro_l_r.fxw","r");}

void openzapt()
{ fontfile = fopen ("zcha_l_r.fxw","r");}

void openpalatino()
{ fontfile = fopen ("pala_b_r.fxw","r");}

void openpalatinobi()
{ fontfile = fopen ("pala_b_i.fxw","r");}

void opentimesbi()
{ fontfile = fopen ("tiro_b_i.fxw","r");}

void printname ()
{ float tw;
  opentimesbi();
  readinwidths();
  tw = computewidth (name);
  fprintf (psfile, "/Times-BoldItalic findfont 18 scalefont setfont\n");
  fprintf (psfile, "%f 33 moveto (%s) show\n",(275.0-(18.0*tw)), name);
  fprintf (psfile, "grestore");
}



int appendfile ()
{ FILE *psfile_aux;
  char line [80];
  psfile = fopen ("card.ps","w");
  if ((psfile_aux = fopen ("card_c2.psp","r")) == NULL)
    {clrscr();
     printf ("The file \"card_c2.psp\" is not in current directory.");
     return (0);}
  else
    {while (!feof (psfile_aux))
         {strcpy(line,"");
         fgets (line,80,psfile_aux);
         fputs (line,psfile);}
```

```
          fprintf (psfile,"\n");
          fclose (psfile_aux);
          }
}

void formattedtext (char line [80], float y)
{ char format;
  float x;

  format = line [0];
  leftshift (line);
  switch (format)
  { case 'S' : { x = center (line);
        fprintf (psfile,"%f %f moveto (%s) shadow\n",x, y, line);
        break;}
    case 'L' : { fprintf (psfile,"36 %f moveto (%s) show\n", y, line);
        break;}
    default  : { x = center (line);
        fprintf (psfile,"%f %f moveto (%s) show\n", x, y, line);
        break;}
  }
}

void leftshift (char line [80])
{ int i;
  for (i=0; i<strlen(line); i++)
    line [i] = line [i+1];
}


int personalinfo ()
{ int i, linenumber=0;
  float xlocation, ylocation;
  char oneline [80], filename [80] , choice;
  clrscr();
  fprintf (psfile, "gsave\n");
  fprintf (psfile, "612 792 translate\n180 rotate\n");
  fprintf(psfile,"/ZapfChancery-MediumItalic");
  fprintf(psfile, " findfont 15 scalefont setfont\n");
  printf("\nGreeting:  ");
  gets(oneline);
  clean (oneline);
  if (strlen(oneline)<=1) return(0);
  fprintf(psfile,"36 318 moveto (%s) show\n",oneline);
  fprintf(psfile,"/ZapfChancery-MediumItalic findfont 12");
  fprintf(psfile," scalefont setfont\n");
  xlocation = 36.0; ylocation = 305.0;
  fprintf(psfile,"%f %f moveto (",xlocation,ylocation);
  printf("\nInside left text.\n\n");
  do{
    linenumber++;
    gets(oneline);
    fprintf(psfile, " ");
    clean (oneline);
    for (i=0; i<strlen(oneline);i++)
          {
          if (ylocation >= 36.0)
```

```
        if (xlocation < 200)
          {fprintf(psfile,"%c",oneline[i]);
         xlocation += 12*(widarray[oneline[i]-32])/1000;}
        else
          if (oneline[i] != 32)
       {fprintf(psfile,"%c",oneline[i]);
          xlocation += 12*(widarray[oneline[i]-32])/1000;}
          else
       {xlocation = 36.0; ylocation -= 13.0;
        fprintf(psfile,") show\n");
        fprintf(psfile,"%f %f moveto (",xlocation,ylocation);}
          }
  }while (strlen(oneline)>1);
  fprintf(psfile,") show\n");
  fprintf(psfile,"grestore\n");
return(linenumber);
}
```

c. Possible Modification

This above program can obviously be modified in numerous ways. Some suggested modifications:

- Include images. It would be nice to incorporate a picture of the family when sending out, holiday greeting cards.
- Include borders. Adding borders to a card makes it much more attractive.

d. Possible Errors

The major problems you could encounter while developing the programs in this chapter deal more with the host language than the generated PostScript code. So, be forewarned; know what is going on in your program. If the program is understood, the generated PostScript should function as planned. All it takes is preplanning to write a useful PostScript driver program. Have fun!

Chapter 17
Drivers for a Certificate

This chapter introduces a series of programs in BASIC, Pascal, and C that produce certificates. The BASIC driver provides a careful line-by-line explanation of a simple program that allows you to input an event and a message that is output to a certificate. The Pascal driver begins with a very simple program along much the same lines.[56] The last section presents a C driver.[57]

1. Certificate Driver: BASIC

a. Introduction

In this section, a BASIC[58] program is the driver to create the PostScript code to produce a certificate. The certificate is the final version of the one presented in Chapter 6. This driver allows you to create multiple certificates.

[56]The model certificate, BASIC driver, and the supporting section were developed by Janice Zappone. The Pascal driver and supporting materials were developed by Kathy Vrudney.

[57]The C driver for the certificate is based a program by Michael Spring. Jeff Deppen revised and cleaned that code, and developed the supporting materials.

[58]The BASIC code was tested with BASICA V3.3, GW-BASIC 3.20, QuickBASIC V4.0, and QBASIC V1.0.

b. Creating the Driver

The PostScript file has two parts: one part is fixed and unchanging (the prologue): the other is custom-created for a particular user.

The Prologue

The program statements in the prologue, Listing 17.1, are examined in detail in Chapter 6. After the procedures are defined, a medallion is created in the center of the certificate. CERTIFICATE of RECOGNITION is printed and the signature lines are drawn. The scroll work is completed around the edges and, finally, a bold frame line is laid down. The PostScript file is ready for awardee, reason, and date.

Listing 17.1: PostScript Prologue File

```
%%!PS-Adobe-3.0  EPSF-30.
%%BoundingBox: 0 0 612 792
%%EndComments
/font {findfont exch scalefont setfont} bind def
/center {dup stringwidth pop  2 div neg 0 rmoveto} bind def
/landscape {612 0 translate 90 rotate} bind def
/portrait {796 0 translate 90 rotate} bind def
/corner {0 0 36 90 360 arc stroke}bind def
/scroll {newpath 0 36 translate 0 0 36 90 270 arc stroke} bind def
/box {newpath 72 72 moveto 0 648 rlineto 468 0 rlineto
      0 -648 rlineto   closepath} bind def
/main{
gsave
box clip  newpath
306 396 translate  .98 setgray  5 setlinewidth
  2 {30 {0 0 moveto  40 40 80 -40 432 0 curveto 360 30 div rotate
        }repeat
       -1 1 scale
    }repeat  stroke
1 setgray  0 0 8 0 360 arc fill
grestore
gsave
landscape
70/ZapfChancery-MediumItalic font  396 460  moveto
(CERTIFICATE) center show
26/ZapfChancery-MediumItalic font  396 415  moveto
(of) center show
70/ZapfChancery-MediumItalic font  396 360  moveto
(RECOGNITION) center show
24/ZapfChancery-MediumItalic font  396 190  moveto
(______________ ______________ ______________) center show
396 160 moveto
(______________ ______________ ______________) center show
396 130  moveto
(______________ ______________ ______________) center show
grestore
gsave
  5 setlinewidth  .9 setgray
```

```
  2{gsave  72 72 translate  corner  0 36 576 {scroll} for
    grestore
    landscape
    gsave  72 72 translate corner 0 36 396 {scroll} for
    grestore
    portrait
   }repeat
grestore
7 setlinewidth box stroke}def
Main
landscape
```

The BASIC program must open the prologue file and the PostScript output file. You may create multiple certificates with one execution of the BASIC program so unique file names must be established for the individual certificates. Simple code to do this is illustrated in Listing 17.2. Several rules are given and only file names of legal length are permitted. Listing 17.3 shows the code to open the prologue file and the named file. All lines of the file are copied and the prologue file is closed.

Listing 17.2: File Name Selection

```
390 CLS
400 LOCATE 13, 1
410 PRINT "Enter a name for the file. It must be 8 characters "
420 PRINT " or less.  Do select a name to identify the"
430 PRINT " certificate, such as the last name of the awardee. "
440 INPUT "Filename===>>>"; filename$
450 IF LEN(filename$)>8 THEN GOTO 390
```

Listing 17.3: File Creation

```
1050 OPEN "certpro.ps" FOR INPUT AS #1
1060 OPEN  FILENAME$ + ".eps" FOR OUTPUT AS #2
1070 WHILE NOT (EOF(1))
1080   LINE INPUT #1, C$
1090   PRINT #2, C$
1100 WEND
1110 CLOSE #1
```

The rest

Three pieces of data must be obtained: the name of the certificate's recipient, the reason for the award, and the date. The date can be retrieved from the system with the **Date$** function, but generally, certificates are not awarded the day they are created.

The name of the awardee is requested and stored in the **names$** variable, as shown in Listing 17.4. The date is obtained by the code shown in Listing 17.5.

Listing 17.4: Awardee Name Input

```
490 CLS
500 LOCATE 15, 1
510 PRINT "Enter the name of the certificate recipient."
520 PRINT "32 characters or less.  ex.  John Black"
530 INPUT "Name===>>>"; names$
540 IF LEN(names$) > 32 THEN 530
```

Listing 17.5: Date Input

```
750 CLS
760 LOCATE 15, 1
770 PRINT "Enter the date for the certificate presentation."
780 PRINT "For example,  September 4  1992"
790 INPUT "Date===>>>"; crtdate$
```

Explanation of the certificate requires more manipulation—see Listing 17.6. The reason is entered as a string of up to 130 characters in length. This must be split into two lines for printing the certificate. The string is obtained in lines 620 and 630. The midpoint is determined. From the midpoint, the string is searched toward the beginning until a space is found. Everything to the left of the space is placed in the first segment, with the balance in the second segment.

Listing 17.6: Reason for Certificate

```
580 CLS
590 LOCATE 15, 1
600 PRINT "Enter a reason or explanation for the certificate."
610 PRINT "ex. 'for loyal service' up to 130 characters "
620 INPUT "Reason===>>>";REASON$
630 IF REASON$>130 THEN 620
650 REM  this module splits reason into 2 lines
660 LINESIZE = INT(LEN(REASON$) / 2)
670 WHILE MID$(REASON$, LINESIZE, 1) <> " "
680 LINESIZE = LINESIZE - 1
690 WEND
700 REASON1$ = MID$(REASON$, 1, LINESIZE - 1)
710 REASON2$ = MID$(REASON$, LINESIZE + 1, LEN(REASON$))
```

At this point in the code, data input is complete and the data is printed for verification, as shown in the code in Listing 17.7. If it is not acceptable, the input routines are repeated.

Listing 17.7: Verification Routine

```
850 CLS
860 A$ = ""
870 LOCATE 22, 1
880 PRINT "The data you entered is shown above.  To change it,"
890 PRINT "press the space bar.  To accept it, press enter."
900 LOCATE 10, 40 - INT(LEN(NAMES$) / 2)
910 PRINT NAMES$
920 LOCATE 13, 40 - INT(LEN(REASON1$) / 2)
930 PRINT REASON1$
940 LOCATE 15, 40 - INT(LEN(REASON2$) / 2)
950 PRINT REASON2$
960 LOCATE 17, 40 - INT(LEN(CRTDATE$) / 2)
970  PRINT CRTDATE$
980 C$ = INKEY$
990 IF C$ = "" THEN 980
1000 IF C$ = " " THEN A$ = " "
1010 CLS
1020 RETURN:    REM end subroutine to verify input
```

After the input data is verified, the output file is written. The routine in Listing 17.8 is straightforward. The fonts are fixed. The variable data is inserted into the arguments and the file is printed.

Listing 17.8: Printing Variable Data

```
1140 PRINT #2, "landscape"
1150 PRINT #2, "24/Helvetica-Bold font  396 290 moveto"
1160 PRINT #2, "("; NAMES$; ") center show"
1170 PRINT #2, "24/ZapfChancery-MediumItalic font 396 245 moveto"
1180 PRINT #2, "("; REASON1$; ") center show"
1190 PRINT #2, "24/ZapfChancery-MediumItalic font 396 225 moveto"
1200 PRINT #2, "("; REASON2$; ") center show"
1210 PRINT #2, "12/ZapfChancery-MediumItalic font 396 110 moveto"
1220 PRINT #2, "("; CRTDATE$; ") center show"
1230 PRINT #2, "showpage"
1240 PRINT #2, "%%EOF"
1250 CLOSE #2
```

The output produced by this BASIC code is shown in Listing 17.9.

Listing 17.9: Personalized Output

```
24/Helvetica-Bold font  396 290 moveto
(Old Man River) center show
24/ZapfChancery-MediumItalic font  396 245 moveto
(For service above and beyond the call of) center show
24/ZapfChancery-MediumItalic font  396 225 moveto
(duty in the pursuit of truth, beauty, and wisdom) center show
12/ZapfChancery-MediumItalic font  396 110 moveto
(January 1, 1992) center show
showpage
```

```
%%EOF
```

c. Putting It All Together

Multiple certificates may be generated with this driver. At least one is produced before you are prompted to continue. The modular code is linked with a subroutine control module, Listing 17.10. Each of the routines examined must conclude with a **return** statement to send control back to the control module.

Listing 17.10: Subroutine Control Module

```
210 ANSWER$ = "Y"
220 WHILE ANSWER$ = "Y" OR ANSWER$ = "y"
230  A$ = " "
240  WHILE A$ = " "
250    GOSUB 380: REM get filename
260    GOSUB 480: REM get name
270    GOSUB 570: REM get reason for certificate
280    GOSUB 740: REM get date
290    GOSUB 850: REM verify input
300  WEND
310  GOSUB 1040: REM open files and write prologue
320  GOSUB 1130: REM write user input to PostScript file
330 CLS
340 INPUT "Create more certificates?  y/n "; ANSWER$
350 WEND
360 GOTO 1600
```

The complete listing generated by the driver is shown in Listing 17.11. The listing contains the same code as was explained in Chapter 6, but in a different order.

Listing 17.11: Driver Output

```
%%!PS-Adobe-3.0  EPSF-30.
%%BoundingBox: 0 0 612 792
%%Endcomments
/font {findfont exch scalefont setfont} bind def
/center {dup stringwidth pop  2 div neg 0 rmoveto} bind def
/landscape {612 0 translate 90 rotate} bind def
/portrait {796 0 translate 90 rotate} bind def
/corner {0 0 36 90 360 arc stroke}bind def
/scroll {newpath 0 36 translate 0 0 36 90 270 arc stroke} bind def
/box {newpath 72 72 moveto 0 648 rlineto 468 0 rlineto
      0 -648 rlineto   closepath} bind def
/main{
gsave
box clip  newpath
306 396 translate  .98 setgray  5 setlinewidth
  2 {30 {0 0 moveto  40 40 80 -40 432 0 curveto 360 30 div rotate
```

```
        }repeat
       -1 1 scale
    }repeat  stroke
1 setgray  0 0 8 0 360 arc fill
grestore
gsave
landscape
70/ZapfChancery-MediumItalic font  396 460  moveto
(CERTIFICATE) center show
26/ZapfChancery-MediumItalic font  396 415  moveto
(of) center show
70/ZapfChancery-MediumItalic font  396 360  moveto
(RECOGNITION) center show
24/ZapfChancery-MediumItalic font  396 190  moveto
(______________ ______________ ______________) center show
396 160 moveto
(______________ ______________ ______________) center show
396 130  moveto
(______________ ______________ ______________) center show
grestore
gsave
  5 setlinewidth  .9 setgray
  2{gsave  72 72 translate  corner  0 36 576 {scroll} for
    grestore
    landscape
    gsave  72 72 translate corner 0 36 396 {scroll} for
    grestore
    portrait
   }repeat
grestore
7 setlinewidth box stroke}def

main
landscape
24/Helvetica-Bold font  396 290 moveto
(Old Man River) center show
24/ZapfChancery-MediumItalic font  396 245 moveto
(For service above and beyond the call of) center show
24/ZapfChancery-MediumItalic font  396 225 moveto
(duty in the pursuit of truth, beauty, and wisdom) center show
12/ZapfChancery-MediumItalic font  396 110 moveto
(January 1, 1992) center show
showpage
%%EOF
```

Execution of the driver output produces the certificate illustrated in Figure 17.1.

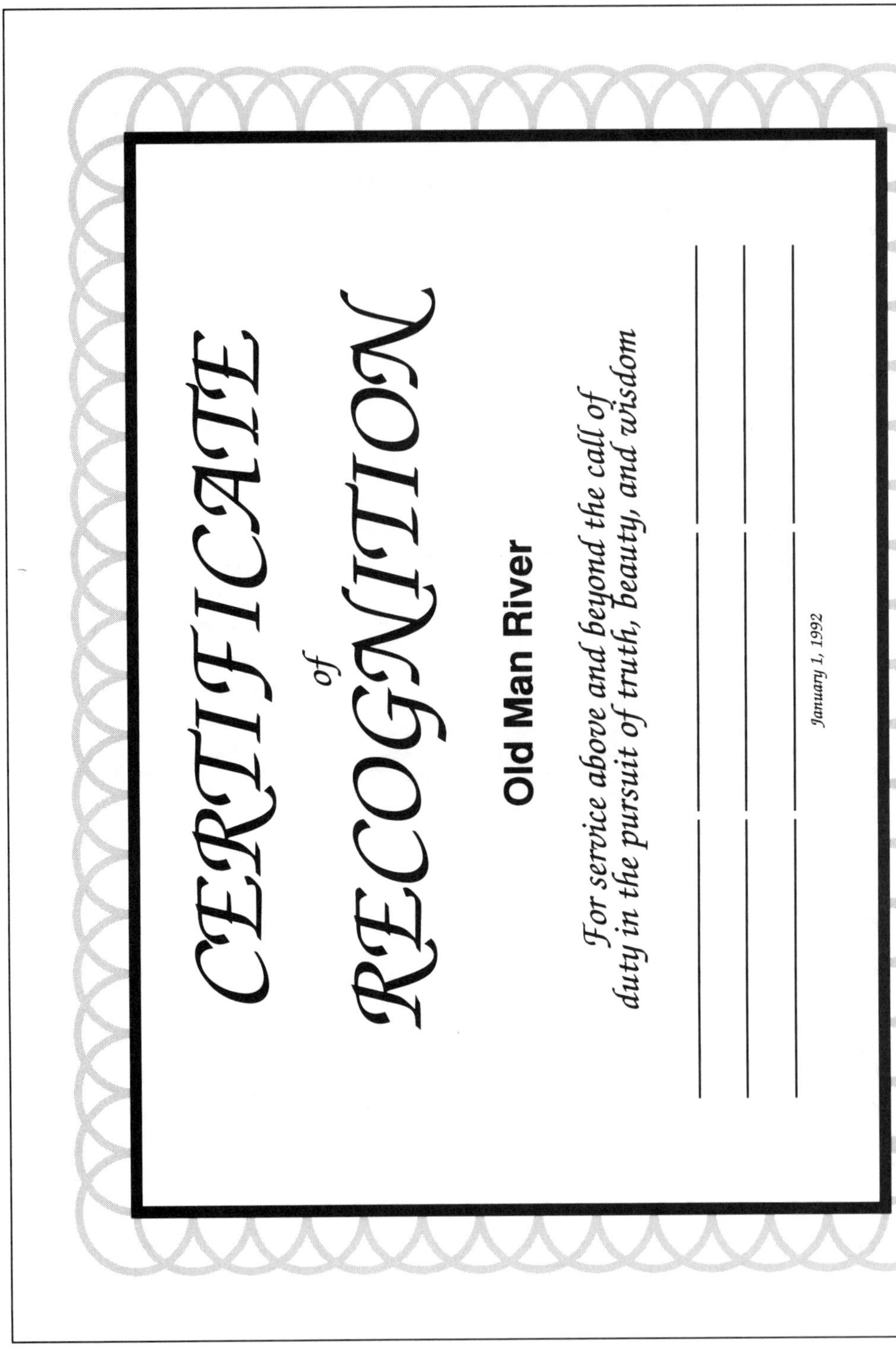

Figure 17.1: PostScript File Output

d. Suggested Enhancements

If you use a color monitor, the display should appear in color. Line 130 in Listing 17.12 sets the color display. Check the system manual for alternate colors.

A brief introduction is helpful for any program. The introduction in lines 160–180 previews the program. The loop in line 190 keeps the message on the screen for a short period. This pause may be altered by adjusting the top number of the **for** loop to suit the system running the program.

Listing 17.12: Enhancements

```
130 COLOR 14, 1, 9
140 CLS
150 LOCATE 10, 1
160 PRINT TAB(10); "  This program creates a certificate.  Follow"
170 PRINT TAB(10); "directions carefully.  You are asked to enter"
180 PRINT TAB(10); "an name, purpose or description, and a date."
190 FOR I = 1 TO 3500: NEXT I
```

The BASIC statements used to specify the character string for awardee, reason, and date are straightforward and easy to use. However, they are not very forgiving if something is wrong. For instance, if commas are placed in the dates as they normally are, BASIC makes you "Redo from start." The string must be enclosed in quotes to include commas. When long lines of data are entered, it is difficult to determine how many character have been typed.

An input routine that accepts strings of any length with any characters is beneficial. The routine shown in Listing 17.13 accepts any characters. The length of the string to be entered is displayed visually with stars for the correct number of characters. Correction is limited to the Backspace key. If you are inexperienced, this routine is useful.

Listing 17.13: String Input Routine

```
1280 REM subroutine for to all input routines. Enter with row &
1290 REM column to display in r,c and string size in maxsize
1300 LOCATE 22, 1
1310 PRINT "Use the BACKSPACE KEY ONLY to make corrections "
1320 LOCATE R, C
1330 FOR I = 1 TO MAXSIZE
1340   PRINT "*";
1350 NEXT I
1360 LOCATE R, C
1370 ROW = R
1380 B$ = ""
1390 FOR I = 1 TO MAXSIZE
1400 IF I = 81 THEN ROW = ROW + 1
1410  A$ = INKEY$
```

```
1420   IF A$ = "" THEN 1410
1430   IF A$ <> CHR$(8) THEN 1530
1440     IF (I = 1) AND (ROW = R) THEN 1410
1450     I = I - 1
1460     IF I = 80 THEN ROW = ROW - 1: C = 80
1470     B$ = MID$(B$, 1, LEN(B$) - 1)
1480     IF I <> 80 THEN C = POS(0) - 1
1490     LOCATE ROW, C
1500     PRINT "*";
1510     LOCATE ROW, C
1520     GOTO 1410
1530   IF A$ <> CHR$(13) THEN 1560
1540     I = MAXSIZE
1550     GOTO 1580
1560   B$ = B$ + A$
1570   PRINT A$;
1580 NEXT I
1590 RETURN: REM end subroutine to get input
```

To use the routine, replace the lines that get the input and check size with the location and size of the star display, call the subroutine, and transfer the generic string into the current string variable. This is done with lines 440, 450 and 460 in Listing 17.14. Refer to the original file name routine in Listing 17.2; that routine is used for any data entry, it it should be used for.

Listing 17.14: Using the String Input Routine

```
390 CLS
400 LOCATE 13, 1
410 PRINT "Enter a name for the file. It must be 8 characters "
420 PRINT " or less.  Do select a name to identify the"
430 PRINT " certificate, such as the last name of the awardee. "
440 R = 17: C = 1: MAXSIZE = 8
450 GOSUB 1280
460 FILENAME$ = B$
```

One useful improvement is a variable number of signature lines. Not every organization has nine members; This certificate was designed for school board members to present to retiring employees. A change requires removing the signature lines from the prologue. For example, with little modification to the prologue and driver code, the program could produce certificates with either 3, 6, or 9 signature lines.

2. Certificate Driver: Pascal

The program presented in this section produces the same certificate the BASIC driver creates. You may change the number of signature lines on this version. In addition, the verification routine allows the user to selectively edit the input data instead of completely reentering. Multiple certificates may be created with one execution of the program, and a list with the awardee and the file name is printed to the screen and, optionally, to the printer. The prologue file for this driver, Listing 17.15, should be named **cert_p1.psp**. The Pascal program was tested on Borland's Turbo Pascal V5.0 and Microsoft's QuickPascal V5.0.

Listing 17.15: Prologue for the Pascal Driver

```
%!PS-Adobe-3.0  EPSF-30.
%%BoundingBox: 0 0 612 792
%%Endcomments
/font {findfont exch scalefont setfont} bind def
/center {dup stringwidth pop  2 div neg 0 rmoveto} bind def
/landscape {612 0 translate 90 rotate} bind def
/portrait {796 0 translate 90 rotate} bind def
/corner {0 0 36 90 360 arc stroke}bind def
/scroll {newpath 0 36 translate 0 0 36 90 270 arc stroke} bind def
/box {newpath 72 72 moveto 0 648 rlineto 468 0 rlineto
      0 -648 rlineto   closepath} bind def
/main{
gsave
box clip  newpath
306 396 translate  .98 setgray  5 setlinewidth
  2 {30 {0 0 moveto  40 40 80 -40 432 0 curveto 360 30 div rotate
        }repeat
       -1 1 scale
    }repeat  stroke
1 setgray  0 0 8 0 360 arc fill
grestore
gsave
landscape
70/ZapfChancery-MediumItalic font  396 460  moveto
(CERTIFICATE) center show
26/ZapfChancery-MediumItalic font  396 415  moveto
(of) center show
70/ZapfChancery-MediumItalic font  396 360  moveto
(RECOGNITION) center show
grestore
gsave
  5 setlinewidth  .9 setgray
  2{gsave  72 72 translate  corner  0 36 576 {scroll} for
    grestore
    landscape
    gsave  72 72 translate corner 0 36 396 {scroll} for
    grestore
    portrait
   }repeat
grestore
7 setlinewidth box stroke}def

main
```

a. Explanation of the Listing

The full listing of the Pascal driver is depicted in Listing 17.16. The program begins with four type definitions: **filetype**, **linetype**, **datetype**, and **nametype**. Each is a string type representing a parameter of the certificate being created. The **VAR** section of the program lists **nametype** array for the awardees, **linetype** array for the signature lines, a **datetype** for the date, and two variables of **linetype** for the reason. As with the other drivers, the program's goal is to elicit this information from you and integrate it into a PostScript program similar to that presented in Chapter 6,

Listing 17.16: The Pascal Certificate Driver

```
Program Certdriv(input,output,infile,outfile);
uses crt,printer;
Const
lines='  ______________';
TYPE
 filetype=string[14];
 linetype=string[65];
 datetype=string[18];
 nametype=string[32];
VAR
 Awardee: array [1..20] of nametype;
 filename:array[1..20]of filetype;
 sig:array[1..3]of linetype;
 date:datetype;
 reason1,reason2:linetype;
 infile,outfile:text;
 finished:boolean;
 Count:integer;

 Procedure Initialize(VAR i:integer);
  Begin
   clrscr; gotoxy(1,15);
   Writeln('This program will creates a certificate.  Follow');
   Writeln('directions carefully.  You are asked to enter');
   Writeln('a name, a purpose or description, a date and');
   Writeln('the number of people who will sign the certificate.');
   Writeln('You may create as many certificates as you wish.');
   Writeln('Each will be saved in separate file.');
   Delay(2000);
   finished:=false;
   i:=1;
 End;

 Procedure Getname(VAR filename:filetype);
 Var  name:nametype;
      limit,size:integer;
      lastname:string[20];
 Begin
  Clrscr; gotoxy(1,15);
  Writeln('Enter the name of the certificate awardee.');
```

```
  Readln(name);
  Awardee[count]:=name;
  lastname:='';
  For size:= length(name) downto 1 do
   if name[size]<>' '
        then lastname:= name[size]+lastname
          else size:=1;
  filename:='';
  if length(lastname)>8 then limit:=8 else limit:=length(lastname);
  for size:=1 to limit do filename:=filename+lastname[size];
  filename:= filename+'.ps'
 End; {procedure}

 Procedure Setup(filename:filetype);
 Begin
  Assign(infile,'cert_p1.psp');    Reset(infile);
  Assign(outfile,filename);          Rewrite(outfile);
 End;{procedure}

 Procedure Cleanup;
 Begin
  Close(infile); Close(outfile)
 End; {procedure}

 Procedure Getreason(VAR str1,str2:linetype);
 Var
 Reason:string[130];
 half,i,size:integer;

 Begin
  Clrscr; gotoxy(1,15);
  writeln('Enter a reason or explanation for the certificate');
  writeln('For example,  "For Loyal Service"');
  writeln('You may use a maximum of 130 characters');
  Readln(reason);
  size:=length(reason);
  half:=(size+1) div 2 + 1;
  str1:='';
  str2:='';
  Repeat
  half:=half-1;
  until reason[half]=' ';
  For i:=1 to half do  str1 :=str1+reason[i];
  For i:=half+1 to size do str2 := str2 + reason[i];
 End; {procedure}

 Procedure Getdate(Var date:datetype);
 Begin
  Clrscr; gotoxy(1,15);
  writeln('Enter the date for the certificate');
  writeln('For example,  "February 2, 1992"');
  readln(date);
 End;  {procedure}

 Procedure Getsig;
 Var   linewidth,linenum,Number,i:integer;
 Begin
```

```
 Clrscr; gotoxy(1,15);
 for i:=1 to 3 do sig[i]:='';
 writeln('How many signatures will be on the certificate.');
 writeln('There is a maximum of nine allowed.');
 Readln(number);
 linenum:=1;
 linewidth:=0;
 if number <=3
    then begin
       sig[1]:=' ';
       sig[3]:=' ';
       for i:=1 to number do sig[2]:=sig[2]+lines;
    end {then}
    else begin
       for i:=1 to number do
        begin
        sig[linenum]:=sig[linenum] + lines;
        linewidth:=linewidth +15;
        if linewidth>40
          then begin
            linenum:= linenum + 1;
            linewidth:=0;
          end; {then linewidth}
        end; {for i}
    end; {else}
End; {procedure}

Procedure Verify;
VAR  answer:string[1];
      choice:char;
  Procedure writeit;
   Begin
    clrscr;
    writeln('You have entered the following data: ');writeln;
    writeln(Awardee[count]);
    writeln(Reason1);
    writeln(Reason2);
    writeln(sig[1]);
    writeln(sig[2]);
    writeln(sig[3]);
    writeln(date);
    writeln;writeln;
   end; {procedure writeit}

  Procedure menu;
   Begin
   writeln('You may change the following;');
   Writeln('A   Awardee');
   Writeln('R   Reason');
   Writeln('D   Date');
   Writeln('S   Signatures');
   Writeln('E   Exit');
   Writeln;Writeln('Enter your choice ');
   Readln(choice);
   case choice of
     'A','a': begin
              cleanup;
```

```
                getname(filename[count]);
                setup(filename[count]);
                end; {case A}
        'R','r': getreason(reason1,reason2);
        'D','d': getdate(date);
        'S','s': getsig;
        'E','e': finished:=true;
      end;{case}
    end; {procedure menu}

 Begin  {procedure verify}

 clrscr;
  answer:='';
  writeit;
  writeln;writeln('If you wish to change your data, press "c", then
enter');
  Readln(answer);
  if (answer='c') or (answer= 'C')
   then begin
    Menu;
    Repeat
     writeit;
     menu;
    until finished;
   end; {then}
 End;  {procedure}

 Procedure Copyprolog;
 Var
 line:string[80];
 Begin
 While not eof(infile) do
  begin
   readln(infile,line);
   writeln(outfile,line);
  end; {while}
 End; {procedure}

 Procedure Writebalance;
 Begin
  Writeln(outfile,'landscape');
  writeln(outfile,'24/Helvetica-Bold font  396 290 moveto');
  writeln(outfile,'(',Awardee[count],') center show');
  writeln(outfile,'24/ZapfChancery-MediumItalic font  396 245 moveto');
  writeln(outfile,'(',Reason1,') center show');
  writeln(outfile,'396 225 moveto');
  writeln(outfile,'(',Reason2,') center show');
  writeln(outfile,'396 190 moveto');
  writeln(outfile,'(',sig[1],') center show');
  writeln(outfile,'396 160 moveto');
  writeln(outfile,'(',sig[2],') center show');
  writeln(outfile,'396 130 moveto');
  writeln(outfile,'(',sig[3],') center show');
  writeln(outfile,'12/ZapfChancery-MediumItalic font  396 110 moveto');
  writeln(outfile,'(',date,') center show');
 End;  {procedure}
```

```
Procedure CheckforMore(var finished:boolean;VAR count:integer);
Var answer:char;
begin
 {clrscr;}
 write('Are there more certificates to process? y/n  ');
 Readln(answer);
 if (answer = 'Y') or (answer='y')
 then begin
          finished:=false;
          count:=count+1;
      end  {then}
 else finished := true;
end; {procedure}

Procedure Report(count:integer);
VAR   i:integer;
      answer:char;
Begin
  clrscr;
  Writeln('Filenames     Awardee');Writeln;
  for i:=1 to count do writeln(filename[i],'     ',Awardee[i]);
  writeln;write('Would you like a printed list? y/n ');
  Readln(answer);
  if (answer='Y')or (answer='y')
       then begin
        clrscr; gotoxy(1,20);
        writeln('Press enter when printer is ready......');
        readln(answer);
        Writeln(lst,'Filenames     Awardee');Writeln;
        for i:=1 to count do writeln(lst,filename[i],'
',Awardee[i]);
       end;{then}
 End; {procedure}

Begin    {                 Main              }
Initialize(count);
Repeat
  Getname(filename[count]);
  Setup(filename[count]);
  Getreason(reason1,reason2);
  Getdate(date);
  Getsig;
  Verify;
  Copyprolog;
  Writebalance;
  Cleanup;
  CheckforMore(finished,count);
until finished;
Report(count);
End.
```

The Pascal driver includes 12 procedures:

Setup and **Cleanup** — These are similar to those in the driver introduction chapter, except **setup** assigns a variable to the **outfile** variable based on the awardee's last name. (See the **getname** procedure.)

Initialize — The procedure introduces the program, sets certificate number (**count**) to one, and sets the loop control **finished** to false.

Getname — This procedure accepts the name of the recipient (**awardee[count]**) and sets the file name for the output (**filename**). The procedure separates last name from the rest of the name by searching backwards for a space. If the last name is less than eight characters, it uses the entire name, but if greater than eight characters, it truncates the last name for DOS.

Getreason — This procedure accepts an input string of 130 characters and divides it approximately in half, searching for a space prior to the halfway point. The two strings are stored in **reason1** and **reason2**. (See BASIC certificate driver section for an analogous routine.)

Getdate — This procedure accepts a string for the date to appear on the certificate. It is stored in the **date** variable of **datetype** type. (See BASIC certificate driver chapter for an analogous routine.)

Getsig — This is an enhancement to the BASIC driver's routine. It allows you to state the number of signature lines needed. If there are three or less, the lines are placed in the center of the reserved space. If there are more than three, the top lines are filled first, then the second, then the third. Three signatures are allowed on each line. The **sig** array variables stores the strings for the signature lines.

Verify — This is an enhancement to the BASIC driver. You may choose from a menu which (if any) of the entered data needs to be changed.

Copyprolog — This procedure copies the contents of the prologue file to the output.

Writebalance — The procedure writes the variable data to the output file.

CheckforMore — This procedure determines if you want to create additional certificates. If so, it increments the counter (**count**). If no more certificates are to be produced, then the boolean **finish** variable is set to true.

Report This procedure prints a list of the awardees and the file names to the screen, and enables you to print the list to the printer.

b. Suggested Enhancements

One simple enhancement to the Pascal driver is to make it easy to keep the date and reason constant while changing only the names of the awardees. The program can then be enhanced by letting the user enter names either interactively or from a file.

3. Certificate Driver: C

This section introduces a PostScript driver program that produces a certificate using Turbo C.

a. Program Specification

The goal of this program is to display a certificate in landscape format, with eight lines of text horizontally centered at predetermined Y values. The program reads in from a file, **cert_c1.txs**, six strings that make up the main text of the certificate. The first two strings represent the organization and the third through the sixth provide the message, with the assumption the third precedes the name and the fourth through sixth follow it. The date is automatically taken from a PC. Also, the certificate will draws a fancy background and border. This program, in achieving the graphical effects, makes extensive use of code in a prologue file called **cert_c1.psp**.

The program enables you to select the font for the name and date.

b. Explanation of the Listing

The driver program is displayed in Listing 17.19 at the end of the section. The PostScript output of that program is shown in Listing 17.17. And, finally, the output of the PostScript program is illustrated in Figure 17.2.

Listing 17.17: Output of Certificate Generator

```
%!PS-Adobe-3.0  EPSF-30.
%%BoundingBox: 0 0 612 792
/bcir {-12 -12 rmoveto 24 0 rlineto 0 24 rlineto -24 0
rlineto closepath fill} def
/bcir2 {-12 -12 rmoveto 24 0 rlineto 0 24 rlineto -24 0
rlineto closepath stroke} def
/bbox {0 -10 rmoveto 10 10 rlineto -10 10 rlineto -10 -10
rlineto closepath fill} def
/bbox2 {0 -10 rmoveto 10 10 rlineto -10 10 rlineto -10 -10
rlineto closepath stroke} def

/border{
-90 rotate -792 0 translate
0 setgray 9 setlinewidth
72 72 moveto 648 0 rlineto 0 468 rlineto -648 0 rlineto
closepath stroke
.7 setgray 2 setlinewidth
72 72 moveto bcir 720 72 moveto bcir
72 540 moveto bcir 720 540 moveto bcir
0 setgray
72 72 moveto bcir2 720 72 moveto bcir2
72 540 moveto bcir2 720 540 moveto bcir2
.7 setgray 4 setlinewidth
72 72 moveto 648 0 rlineto 0 468 rlineto -648 0 rlineto
closepath stroke
1 setgray
72 72 moveto bbox 720 72 moveto bbox
72 540 moveto bbox 720 540 moveto bbox
0 setgray 1 setlinewidth
72 72 moveto bbox2 720 72 moveto bbox2
72 540 moveto bbox2 720 540 moveto bbox2
} def

/landscape {612 0 translate 90 rotate} bind def
/portrait {796 0 translate 90 rotate} bind def
/corner {0 0 36 90 360 arc stroke}bind def
/scroll {newpath 0 36 translate 0 0 36 90 270 arc stroke} bind def
/box {newpath 72 72 moveto 0 648 rlineto 468 0 rlineto
      0 -648 rlineto   closepath} bind def

/background{
gsave
box clip  newpath
306 396 translate  .98 setgray  5 setlinewidth
  2 {30 {0 0 moveto  40 40 80 -40 432 0 curveto 360 30 div rotate
        }repeat
       -1 1 scale
    }repeat  stroke
1 setgray  0 0 8 0 360 arc fill
grestore
gsave
  5 setlinewidth  .9 setgray
  2{gsave  72 72 translate  corner  0 36 576 {scroll} for
    grestore
```

```
    landscape
    gsave  72 72 translate corner 0 36 396 {scroll} for
    grestore
    portrait
   }repeat
grestore
border}def
```

```
background
/Palatino-BoldItalic findfont 18 scalefont setfont
323 100 moveto
(December 20, 1991) show
332 270 moveto
(Karen Bluestein) show
/Times-Roman findfont 27 scalefont setfont
133 475 moveto
(Department of Graphic Design and Mathemetics) show
315 425 moveto
(Hayden Books) show
/ZapfChancery-MediumItalic findfont 18 scalefont setfont
266 320 moveto
(Be it known to all who witness this that) show
263 225 moveto
(is accorded the status of an honorary guru) show
230 190 moveto
(in the PostScript course of study by Hayden Books) show
236 155 moveto
(and is accorded all the rights and privileges thereof) show
showpage
```

As hinted earlier, this program generates a certificate by relying on many input/output functions. To follow the progression of the program, it is necessary to start with the **main** function and trace through the functions that are encountered.

Appendfile immediately opens two files. The first file, **certpro** (which contains the PostScript code for generating the background and border), is opened for reading, and the second, **psfile**, is opened for writing. These two file pointers correspond to the disk filenames **cert_c1.psp** and **certif.ps**. Next, **certpro** is reset and a **while** loop begins to copy **certpro**, one line at a time, into **psfile**. Once **certpro** contents have been transferred into **psfile**, **certpro** is closed, **appendfile** is completed, and control reverts back to the **main** function. The contents of our prologue file are shown in Listing 17.18:

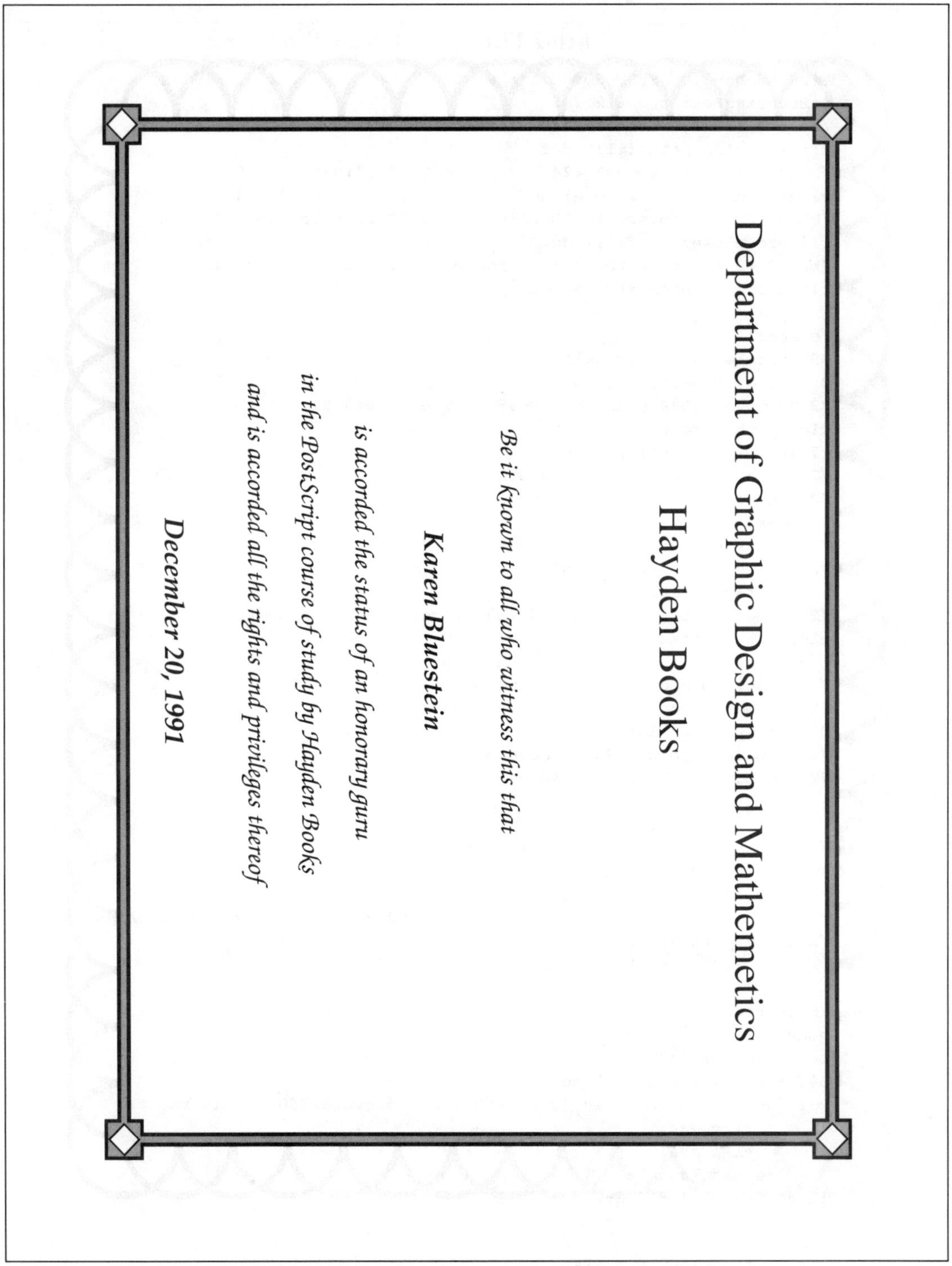

Figure 17.2: Output of Certificate PostScript Program

Listing 17.18: Certificate Prologue

```
%!PS-Adobe-3.0  EPSF-30.
%%BoundingBox: 0 0 612 792
/bcir {-12 -12 rmoveto 24 0 rlineto 0 24 rlineto -24 0
rlineto closepath fill} def
/bcir2 {-12 -12 rmoveto 24 0 rlineto 0 24 rlineto -24 0
rlineto closepath stroke} def
/bbox {0 -10 rmoveto 10 10 rlineto -10 10 rlineto -10 -10
rlineto closepath fill} def
/bbox2 {0 -10 rmoveto 10 10 rlineto -10 10 rlineto -10 -10
rlineto closepath stroke} def

/border{
-90 rotate -792 0 translate
0 setgray 9 setlinewidth
72 72 moveto 648 0 rlineto 0 468 rlineto -648 0 rlineto
closepath stroke
.7 setgray 2 setlinewidth
72 72 moveto bcir 720 72 moveto bcir
72 540 moveto bcir 720 540 moveto bcir
0 setgray
72 72 moveto bcir2 720 72 moveto bcir2
72 540 moveto bcir2 720 540 moveto bcir2
.7 setgray 4 setlinewidth
72 72 moveto 648 0 rlineto 0 468 rlineto -648 0 rlineto
closepath stroke
1 setgray
72 72 moveto bbox 720 72 moveto bbox
72 540 moveto bbox 720 540 moveto bbox
0 setgray 1 setlinewidth
72 72 moveto bbox2 720 72 moveto bbox2
72 540 moveto bbox2 720 540 moveto bbox2
} def

/landscape {612 0 translate 90 rotate} bind def
/portrait {796 0 translate 90 rotate} bind def
/corner {0 0 36 90 360 arc stroke}bind def
/scroll {newpath 0 36 translate 0 0 36 90 270 arc stroke} bind def
/box {newpath 72 72 moveto 0 648 rlineto 468 0 rlineto
      0 -648 rlineto   closepath} bind def

/background{
gsave
box clip  newpath
306 396 translate  .98 setgray  5 setlinewidth
  2 {30 {0 0 moveto  40 40 80 -40 432 0 curveto 360 30 div rotate
        }repeat
       -1 1 scale
    }repeat  stroke
1 setgray  0 0 8 0 360 arc fill
grestore
gsave
  5 setlinewidth  .9 setgray
  2{gsave  72 72 translate  corner  0 36 576 {scroll} for
    grestore
```

```
        landscape
        gsave  72 72 translate corner 0 36 396 {scroll} for
        grestore
        portrait
      }repeat
grestore
border}def
```

After the prologue is appended, you are prompted to select the fonts for name and date will be printed. Once a font is chosen, a PostScript operator to open that font is copied into the **typeface** string variable. Later, the width file indicated by the **fchoice** variable is opened and the width data read in.

The **getname** function prompts you to enter the name to display on the certificate. The name is placed into the **name** global variable.

Readintext opens the disk file **cert_c1.txs** and assigns to it the **textfile** file pointer. **Textfile** is then read sequentially six times. Each line is cleaned by the **clean** function. This "cleaning" replaces the trailing "\n" with a "\0" so unwanted carriage returns do not make it into the generated PostScript file. The text file is then closed. The text file we used is

```
Department of Graphic Design and Mathemetics
Hayden Books
Be it known to all who witness this that
is accorded the status of an honorary guru
in the PostScript course of study by Hayden Books
and is accorded all the rights and privileges thereof
```

The **get_date** function, prompts the system for the current date, and based that information, assigns **month**. the appropriate string representation of the current month to a global variable, **month**. Once **month** is filled, the function ends.

Readinwidths reads into a global integer array, **widarray**, the font widths of all the characters that are in the active font file, which is pointed to by **fontfile**. After the widths are read in, control goes back to the **main** function.

The **printoutfile** function accounts for the majority of the certificate generator's output. The first line in **printoutfile** calls the function **center** and passes it the string and the point size at which the string is to be printed.

In **center**, **computewidth** calculates the width, of the string in points, A value, **x**, is then calculated that, given the string's width, would horizontally centers the string over a space of 792 points. This **x** value is then returned through the **center** function.

Now, picking up where we left off in the **printoutfile** function, the desired **x** starting value to print the date is computed and returned by **center**. Next, a PostScript **moveto** operator is written to **psfile** with the X value just computed and a Y value of 80. Then a PostScript command that shows the month string followed by the day and year is written to **psfile**.

The next line finds the appropriate X value so that name is centered. The PostScript command is written to **psfile** to **moveto** the computed X and a Y value of 270. Next, a line that shows the name is written to **psfile**. Next, the **opentimes** function closes and reopens **fontfile**.

Because a new font is being used, **readinwidths** is called to place the current widths into **widarray**. Next, the PostScript commands to change the font to Times-Roman with point size 27 is written to **psfile**. After this, two series of **center** and **print** statements are used to print the first two lines read from the text file to a computed X location and the desired Y location. The **fontfile** is then closed again and reopened by **openzapt**.

Readinwidths is called again and the PostScript command to change the font to ZapfChancery-MediumItalic, font size 18, is written to **psfile**. Next, a series of **center**s and **print**s are used to print out the second through sixth lines. After the fourth line has been written out to **psfile**, a **showpage** is written to **psfile** and control reverts back to the **main** function.

Back in the **main** function, you are given the choice of creating another certificate or exiting. After exiting, you now have a PostScript program that creates one or more certificates.

c. Possible Modifications

Some possible modifications:

- Recode the program so it can be more interactive. This gives the user the freedom to create a different certificate each time the program is run without having to first create and memorize files and their names.
- Incorporate your own graphics into the certificate.

d. Complete Listing

Listing 17.19: Certificate Generator

```
#include "stdio.h"
#include "conio.h"
#include "dos.h"
#include "string.h"
#include "stdlib.h"

void name_font(char fchoice);
void readintext();
void get_date();
void getname();
void printoutfile();
void openhelveticabold();
void opentimes();
void openzapt();
void openpalatino();
void openpalatinobi();
void opentimesbi();
void clean(char oneline[80]);
void readinwidths ();
float computewidth (char oneline[80]);
float center (char oneline[80], float ptsize);
void appendfile();

FILE *fontfile, *textfile, *psfile;
char name[30], typeface[60], font[30], typeofcert[80], line[6][80],
        month [80];
struct date today;
int widarray [100];

main ()
{ char choice,fchoice;
  appendfile();
  clrscr();
  printf("\nSelect the font for the name and date:");
  printf("\n\t1 - Helvetica Bold");
  printf("\n\t2 - Times Roman");
  printf("\n\t3 - Zapf Chancery Italic");
  printf("\n\t4 - Palatino Bold Italic");
  printf("\n\t5 - Times Roman Bold Italic");
  printf("\nEnter the number of your choice : ");
  fflush(stdin); fchoice = getch();
  do {
    getname();
    readintext();
    get_date();
    name_font(fchoice);
    printoutfile();
    printf("\n Type C to Create Another Certificate? ");
    printf(" (Any other character to quit)");
    choice = toupper(getch());
    } while(choice=='C');
  fclose (psfile);
}
```

```
void name_font(char fchoice)
{
  switch (fchoice)
  { case '1' : {strcpy (font,"HelveticaB");
      strcpy (typeface,"/Helvetica-Bold");
      openhelveticabold();
      break;
          }
    case '2' : {strcpy (font,"Times");
      strcpy (typeface,"/Times-Roman");
      opentimes();
      break;
          }
    case '3' : {strcpy (font,"Zapf");
      strcpy (typeface,"/ZapfChancery-MediumItalic");
      openzapt();
      break;
          }
    case '4' : {strcpy (font,"PalatinoBI");
      strcpy (typeface,"/Palatino-BoldItalic");
      openpalatinobi();
      break;
          }
    case '5' : {strcpy (font,"TimesBI");
      strcpy (typeface,"/Times-BoldItalic");
      opentimesbi();
      break;
          }
  }
strcat(typeface," findfont 18 scalefont setfont\n");
readinwidths();
}

void readintext()
{ int i;
  textfile = fopen ("cert_c1.txs","r");
  for (i=0;i<6;i++)
        {fgets (line[i],80,textfile);
        clean (line[i]);}
  fclose (textfile);
}

void get_date()
{ getdate (&today);
  switch (today.da_mon)
  { case 1 : {strcpy (month,"January "); break;}
    case 2 : {strcpy (month,"February "); break;}
    case 3 : {strcpy (month,"March "); break;}
    case 4 : {strcpy (month,"April "); break;}
    case 5 : {strcpy (month,"May "); break;}
    case 6 : {strcpy (month,"June "); break;}
    case 7 : {strcpy (month,"July "); break;}
    case 8 : {strcpy (month,"August "); break;}
    case 9 : {strcpy (month,"Septemeber "); break;}
    case 10 : {strcpy (month,"October "); break;}
    case 11 : {strcpy (month,"November "); break;}
    case 12 : {strcpy (month,"December "); break;}
```

```
  }
}

void getname ()
{ printf ("\nEnter name to appear on certificate : ");
  fflush (stdin);
  gets (name);
}

void printoutfile()
{ float x,y;
  int i;
  char temp[10];
  fprintf (psfile, "\n\nbackground\n");
  fprintf (psfile, typeface);
  strcat(month, itoa(today.da_day,temp,10));
  strcat(month, ", ");
  strcat(month, itoa(today.da_year,temp,10));
  x = center (month, 18.0);
  fprintf (psfile, "%f 100 moveto\n",x);
  fprintf(psfile,"(%s) show\n", month);
  x = center (name, 18.0);
  fprintf (psfile, "%f 270 moveto\n", x);
  fprintf (psfile,"(%s) show\n",name);

  opentimes();
  readinwidths ();
  fprintf(psfile, "/Times-Roman");
  fprintf(psfile," findfont 27 scalefont setfont\n",psfile);
  for (i=0;i<2;i++)
        {y=475.0-(i*50);
        x = center (line[i], 27.0);
        fprintf (psfile,"%f %f moveto (%s) show\n", x, y, line[i]);}

  openzapt();
  readinwidths();
  fprintf(psfile, "/ZapfChancery-MediumItalic");
  fprintf(psfile," findfont 18 scalefont setfont\n",psfile);
  for (i=2;i<6;i++)
        {if (i==2) y=320.0; else y=260.0-((i-2)*35);
        x = center (line[i], 18.0);
        fprintf (psfile,"%f %f moveto (%s) show\n", x, y, line[i]);}
  fputs ("showpage\n",psfile);
}

void clean (char oneline [80])
{ int i;
  for (i=0;i<=strlen(oneline);i++)
    if (oneline[i] == '\n') oneline[i] = '\0';
}
void readinwidths ()
{ int i;
  char alpha[10];

  i = 0;
  rewind (fontfile);
  while (!feof(fontfile))
```

```
  {
    fgets(alpha, 10, fontfile);
    widarray[i++]=atoi(alpha+1);
  }
fclose(fontfile);
}

void appendfile()
{ FILE *certpro;
  char oneline [80];

  certpro = fopen ("cert_c1.psp","r");
  psfile = fopen ("certif.ps","w");

  rewind (certpro);
  while (!feof(certpro))
  { fflush (stdin);
    fgets (oneline,80,certpro);
    clean (oneline);
    fprintf (psfile,"%s\n",oneline);
  }
  fclose (certpro);
}

float computewidth (char oneline [80])
{ int ordvalue, wstring, j;
  float tw;
  tw = 0;
  wstring = strlen (oneline);
  for (j=0;j<wstring;j++)
    {ordvalue = oneline [j];
        tw = tw + widarray [ordvalue - 32];
    }
  tw = (tw/1000);
  return tw;
}

float center (char line[80], float ptsize)
{ float width,x;

  width = computewidth(line);
  x = (792.0 - (ptsize*width))/2.0;
  return x;
}


void openhelveticabold()
{ fontfile = fopen ("helv_b_r.fxw","r");}

void opentimes()
{ fontfile = fopen ("tiro_l_r.fxw","r");}

void openzapt()
{ fontfile = fopen ("zcha_l_r.fxw","r");}

void openpalatino()
{ fontfile = fopen ("pala_b_r.fxw","r");}
```

```
void openpalatinobi()
{ fontfile = fopen ("pala_b_i.fxw","r");}

void opentimesbi()
{ fontfile = fopen ("tiro_b_i.fxw","r");}
```

Chapter 18
Drivers for a Poster

Chapter 13 presented a series of PostScript programs for printing multi-page posters. This chapter introduces programs in Pascal[59] and C[60] that produce a different style of poster; instead of scaling a one-page image to some multiple of 8.5 by 11, these driver programs enable you to specify the desired height and width, and place text lines of varying sizes on the poster within the limits of the height and width. Like the C driver programs for the greeting cards (Chapter 3), these programs use character-width information (read from font metric files) to perform calculations before the PostScript code is written.

1. Poster Driver: Pascal

The first version of the poster driver is written in the Macintosh version of Borland's Turbo Pascal. However, none of the Mac toolbox routines are used, and the program's interface is entirely text-based. The program listing can be found in Listing 18.3 on page 332. Sample output from the program can be found in Listing 18.1, a reduced display is depicted in Figure 18.1. Explanation of Listing 18.3 follows a review of the multi-page printing routine below.

---

[59]The initial code for the Pascal version of the poster driver was developed by Roberta Pavol and David Dubin based on an earlier version by Michael Spring.

[60]The initial code for the C version of the poster driver was developed by Sang Yoon from code in Pascal by Michael Spring.

a. Review of Multi-page Printing

Chapter 13, describes a method that prints image that is too large to be printed on one page over several pages. PostScript code for the third version of the poster in Chapter 13 implements this algorithm, which can be summarized as follows:

1. Define a clipping region for each page of the poster. Because PostScript output devices can not print to the edge of the page, a rectangular region (equal, in our examples, to the size of a page with half-inch margins on all sides) is defined for the size of each "tile" of the poster. The current clipping path is set to this region, and the dimensions of the window determine how far the origin is translated on each iteration of the loop described in the following steps.

2. Place the code for producing the large image in a procedure. The procedure is invoked a number of times equal to the number of tiles on which it will be printed. Each time the procedure is invoked, the origin of the coordinate space must be translated (see Chapter 4) so a different piece of the image falls onto the printable page area. As discussed in Chapter 13, the origin is translated in a negative direction along both axes.

3. Create a procedure which accepts the image procedure as a parameter on the operand stack. Variables are set to the number of columns and rows for the poster (columns × rows = number of tiles). The procedure runs a nested loop—the outermost one looping through each row, and the inner one through each tile in the row. At each iteration of the inner loop, the origin is translated from its original position in a negative direction along each axis. The distance translated along the horizontal axis is equal to the current column number times the width of the clipping window. The distance translated along the vertical axis is equal to the row number times the height of the clipping window. Prior to each translation, the graphics state is saved so the original origin position can be restored. Right after each translation, the large image procedure is invoked. The current page is then ejected and the graphics state is restored.

Listing 18.1: Output from a Sample Run of the Pascal Driver

```
%!PS-Adobe
/printposter
 {/rows exch def
  /columns exch def
  /bigpictureproc exch def

  newpath
   leftmargin botmargin moveto
   0 pageheight rlineto
   pagewidth 0 rlineto
   0 pageheight neg rlineto
```

```
  closepath clip

  leftmargin botmargin translate

  0 1 rows 1 sub
   {/rowcount exch def
    0 1 columns 1 sub
     {/colcount exch def
      gsave
       pagewidth colcount mul neg
        pageheight rowcount mul neg
        translate

       bigpictureproc
       gsave showpage grestore

       grestore
     } for
   } for
 } def

/inch {72 mul} def

/leftmargin .5 inch def
/botmargin .5 inch def
/pagewidth 7.5 inch def
/pageheight 10 inch def


/sign
 { gsave
  /Helvetica-Bold findfont
     55.00 scalefont setfont
        80.0       986.8 moveto
   (Spring's Garden Gnome Emporium) show
  /Helvetica-Bold findfont
     40.00 scalefont setfont
       341.1       930.2 moveto
   (Semi-Annual 50% off) show
  /Helvetica-Bold findfont
    360.00 scalefont setfont
        59.9       558.2 moveto
   (SALE) show
  /Helvetica-Bold findfont
     40.00 scalefont setfont
       325.5       410.2 moveto
   (Now through Saturday) show
  newpath
   leftmargin botmargin moveto
   0    1386.0000 rlineto
      1026.0000 0 rlineto
   0    1386.0000 neg rlineto
  closepath
  gsave
   54 setlinewidth stroke
  grestore
  10 setlinewidth 1 setgray stroke
```

```
  grestore
 } def
{sign} 2 2 printposter
```

This algorithm is implemented in the **printposter** procedure which is shown in both the prologue file, in Listing 18.2, and the PostScript output in Listing 18.1.[61] The first three lines of this procedure remove two numbers and a procedure from the operand stack and define them as variables. As you can see in the listings, the numeric operands are the number of rows and columns to be printed and the procedure produces the enlarged image. The next six lines of the procedure define the clipping window for each tile of the poster. The **leftmargin**, **botmargin**, **pagewidth**, and **pageheight** variables are used rather than numeric constants so they can be easily modified if a smaller or larger clipping window is desired. After the origin of the coordinate space is translated to the lower left corner of the clipping window, the next 14 lines implement the looping algorithm described earlier. Note a **gsave/grestore** pair brackets the **showpage** operator. This avoids redefining the clipping window after it is reset by each **showpage**. The remaining lines of the PostScript prologue define the dimensions of the clipping window.

Listing 18.2: The Prologue File for the Pascal Driver

```
%!PS-Adobe
/printposter
 {/rows exch def
  /columns exch def
  /bigpictureproc exch def

  newpath
   leftmargin botmargin moveto
   0 pageheight rlineto
   pagewidth 0 rlineto
   0 pageheight neg rlineto
  closepath clip

  leftmargin botmargin translate

  0 1 rows 1 sub
   {/rowcount exch def
    0 1 columns 1 sub
     {/colcount exch def
      gsave
       pagewidth colcount mul neg
        pageheight rowcount mul neg
        translate

       bigpictureproc
       gsave showpage grestore
```

[61] Chapter 14 explains driver programs' use of prologue or header files.

```
      grestore
    } for
  } for
} def

/inch {72 mul} def

/leftmargin .5 inch def
/botmargin .5 inch def
/pagewidth 7.5 inch def
/pageheight 10 inch def
```

b. Explanation of the Listing

As you see in Listing 18.1, the portion of the output the driver program actually creates is the **sign** procedure and a one line script which passes as a parameter to **printposter**. Most of the **sign** procedure code is concerned with moving to various coordinates and **show**ing strings at various sizes. The last lines draw a double border by stroking a thin, white line over a thick, black line. It is the driver printer's job to accomplish the following objectives in writing the **sign** procedure and the script:

- Calculate the coordinates at which the strings must be displayed, based on the dimensions of the poster and the size of the type you choose.

- Calculate the number of rows and columns for the poster, and the corners and line widths for the border. These are based on the poster dimensions you supply.

In addition to these objectives listed, the poster driver informs you when type size choices exceed the dimensions of the poster, and enables you to interactively make changes to text and type size.

The Pascal driver program consists of 10 procedures and functions:

upper — This function changes lowercase characters to uppercase. It allows you to select options at decision points without holding down the shift key.

readcharinfo — This procedure reads character width information from a font metric file and stores it in an array. See Chapters 14 and 15 for a detailed discussion of font metric files.

choosefont — This procedure prompts you to choose a font for the poster. It then invokes **readcharinfo** for the appropriate font metric file.

Figure 18.1: Sample Output of the Pascal Driver

chooseoutfile This procedure prompts you for the name of the output file, rewrites that file, and writes the contents of the prologue file (**post_p1.psp**) to the output file.

dimensions This procedure translates the poster height and width you specify into rows and columns that can be passed as parameters to **printposter**.

maxspace This procedure calculates the maximum space available for text, based on the dimensions of the poster and the height and width of the clipping window. Recall that each tile must be smaller than an 8.5-by-11-inch page because PostScript output devices can not print to the very edge of the page.

currentstats This procedure prints the strings that currently comprise the poster and their sizes to the console. It also lists how much space and how many lines remain.

inputtext This procedure accepts the lines of text from you and prompts for each lines type size. The lines of text are stored in the **postertext** array. If showing the string at the specified size exceeds the height or width of the poster, you are given the option of selecting a different size or entering a different string. The **calcmaxpoint** procedure is used to calculate the maximum point size for a given string.

calcmaxpoint This procedure calculates the maximum point size for the current line of the poster. First, the width values for each of the characters in the string are added together. This sum divides the maximum width in points (as determined by **maxspace**) times 1000. Recall that the width values for each character are in thousandths of a point, assuming a 1-point high font.

codeposter This procedure creates the PostScript code for the **sign** procedure and the one line script. The calculations of the **x_val**, **y_val**, **xborder**, and **yborder** variables are of primary interest. The **x_val** variable is the horizontal coordinate for the current poster line and is equal to the width of the poster in points, minus the width of the line, divided by two. Using this value as the X coordinate assures the string is centered horizontally. The **y_val** variable is the vertical coordinate for the current poster line and is equal to the previous **y_val** value minus the height of the current line. The initial value for this variable is equal to the height of the poster minus the height of the border (and some additional white space). The **xborder** and **border** variables represent the rightmost and upper coordinates for the double border, respectively. They are equal to the maximum width/height of the poster plus the width of the border.

c. Complete Listing of the Pascal Driver

Listing 18.3: The Pascal Poster Driver

```
Program makeposter(input,output);
{*********************** DECLARATIONS *****************************}




const  maxlinelen=255;
       paperheight=10;
       paperwidth=7.5;         borderwidth=0.75;
       ptsperinch=72;
       maxlinenum=50;
       numdiffchar=100;        bordwidthpts=54;

type   filestr=string[30];
       linestr=string[maxlinelen];
       fontstr=string[50];
       sstring = string[80];{type for dos directory call}

       charrec=record                 {record for character values}
           charid:char;
           widthvalue:longint;
           end;

       textlinerec=record                       {record for poster lines}
           inputline:linestr;                   {line text}
           pointsize:real;                      {point size}
           sumcharvalue:longint;                {sum of character values}
           end;

       charinforay=array[1..numdiffchar] of charrec;
       postertextray=array[1..maxlinenum] of textlinerec;

var    charfile,dividefile,postfile             :text;
       height,width,maxwidth,maxheight,
       maxwidthpts,maxheightpts,maxptsz,
       totptsused,ptsleft                       :real;
       rows,columns,numlines,i,count,j,
       index                              :longint;
       charfilename,dividename,outfilename      :filestr;
       codeline,inputline                       :linestr;
       postertext                               :postertextray;
       charinfo                                 :charinforay;
       found,continue,morelines,new,quit        :boolean;
       contresp,fontpick,lineresp,ans           :char;
```

```
      fontname                              :fontstr;

{********************* PROCEDURES ******************************}

function upper(inchar:char):char;
  begin
    if (ord(inchar) >= 97) and (ord(inchar) <= 122) then
      upper := chr(ord(inchar) - 32)
    else
       upper := inchar;
  end; {function}

{*******************************************************************
Reads the font file and put the characters and values into
an array of records
*******************************************************************}
procedure readcharinfo;
begin
count:=0;
while not eof(charfile) do
        begin
        count:=count+1;
        with charinfo[count] do readln(charfile,charid,widthvalue);
        end;
end;

{****************************************************************
Allows the user to chose the font for the poster.
It needs to be modified with the addition of fonts
****************************************************************}
procedure choosefont;
var done:boolean;
     n,m:integer;
begin
done:=false;
while not done do
        begin
clearscreen;
writeln('Font Options:');
        m:= 4;

writeln('    Times-Roman');
writeln('    Palatino-Bold');
writeln('    Helvetica-Bold');


write('Enter the first letter of your choice: ');
        ans := upper(readchar);
 writeln;
        case ans of
            'T': begin
                                    charfilename:='tiro_l_r.fxw';
                                    fontname:='Times-Roman';
                                    done:=true
                                  end;
            'P': begin
                                    charfilename:='pala_b_r.fxw';
```

```
                              fontname:='Palatino-Bold';
                              done:=true
                             end;
          'H': begin
                              charfilename:='helv_b_r.fxw';
                              fontname:='Helvetica-Bold';
                              done:=true
                              end;
          otherwise  begin

 writeln('Invalid Choice, please use the first letter of a font file');
   writeln;
                write('Press Return to Continue...');
                readln;
                end;
        end;    {CAse}
        end;    {while}

reset(charfile,charfilename);     {open font file}
readcharinfo;                     {read width info}
close(charfile);                  {close font file}
end;

{*********************************************************************
This procedure allows the user to chose the name of the output file
*********************************************************************}
procedure chooseoutfile;
begin
write('Filename for code: ');
readln(outfilename);
if (length(outfilename)<3) then outfilename:='CON';
rewrite(postfile,outfilename);     {open output file}
reset(dividefile,dividename);    {open divide code file}
{put divide code in output file}
while not eof(dividefile) do
        begin
        for i:=1 to maxlinelen do codeline[i]:=chr(32);
        readln(dividefile,codeline);
        writeln(postfile,codeline)
        end;
close(dividefile);
end;
{*********************************************************
Gets the height and width for the poster and
translates them into the number of 8 1/2 by 11 sheets needed
*********************************************************}
procedure dimensions;
begin
writeln('Setting Poster Size ');
write('Enter height of poster in inches:  ');
readln(height);
write('Enter width of poster in inches:  ');
readln(width);
{The rows and columns are rounded up}
rows:=trunc(height/paperheight + 0.9999);
columns:= trunc(width/paperwidth + 0.9999);
end;
```

```
{****************************************************************
Calculates the maximum amount of vertical and horizontal
space for the text of the poster.  The clipping region and
border widths are taken into account
****************************************************************}
procedure maxspace;
begin
maxwidth:=width-(2*borderwidth);
maxwidthpts:=maxwidth*ptsperinch;
maxheight:=height-(2*borderwidth);
maxheightpts:=maxheight*ptsperinch
end;

{*****************************************************************
Print out information about the poster
*****************************************************************}
procedure currentstats;
begin
clearscreen;
writeln('LINE SIZE WIDTH(pts)  TEXT...(first 60 characters)');
for i:=1 to index do
        with postertext[i] do
        begin
        writeln(i:2,'  ',pointsize:4:0,' ',
                sumcharvalue*pointsize/1000:6:0,
                '          ',copy(inputline,1,60));
        end;
writeln;
writeln('POSTER STATS:');
writeln('Poster Height: ',maxheightpts:9:1,' pts');
writeln('Poster Width:  ',maxwidthpts:9:1,' pts');
writeln('Space Left:    ',(maxheightpts-totptsused):9:1,' pts');
writeln('Max lines left: ',maxlinenum-index);
end;
{*********************************************************
Allows the input the text of the poster one
line at a time.  It checks that the lines
will fit vert and horiz and provides menus for the user
according to the status of the line.
Uses sub procedure calcmaxpoint to figure line width
*********************************************************}
procedure inputtext;
var more:char;
widthofline:real;

           {* * * * * * * * * * * * * * * * * * * * * * * * * * *
             This procedure searches for each character of the
             input line in the array containing the values for
             the characters.  It adds the values for all the
             lines and calculates the maximum point size that
             is allowed for the line to fit
             * * * * * * * * * * * * * * * * * * * * * * * * * *}
        procedure calcmaxpoint;
        var top,bottom,mid:longint;
        begin
        with postertext[index] do
           begin
```

```
            sumcharvalue:=0;
            for j:=1 to length(inputline) do {do a binary search for}
                begin                    {each character}
                top:=count;
                bottom:=1;
                found:=false;
                while (not found) and (top>=bottom) do
                    begin
                    mid:=(top + bottom) div 2;
                    if (inputline[j] = charinfo[mid].charid) then
                         found:=true
                    else
                         if (inputline[j] < charinfo[mid].charid) then
                             top:=mid-1
                         else
                             bottom:=mid + 1
                    end; {while}
                if (found) then
                   sumcharvalue:=sumcharvalue + charinfo[mid].widthvalue;
                end;{of for}
            maxptsz:=(1000 * maxwidthpts)/sumcharvalue;  {max point size}
            ptsleft:=maxheightpts-totptsused;    {vertical points left}
            {Checks to see if line will fit.
            If will not fit vertically, 2/3 of the
            vertical points leftis max point size}
            if ((maxptsz > ptsleft)) or
                   ((maxptsz+(maxptsz/3)) > ptsleft) then
                         maxptsz:=ptsleft-(ptsleft/3);
        end{with}
    end;{internal procedures calcmaxpoint}

begin
totptsused:=0;index:=0;
currentstats;
index:=index+1;
repeat
write('Enter line number ',index,':');
readln(postertext[index].inputline);
if postertext[index].inputline = ''
        then postertext[index].inputline := '  ';
calcmaxpoint;
repeat
write('Enter pt size(Max =',(maxptsz - 1):4:0,') for line',index,': ');
readln(postertext[index].pointsize);
{checks to see if line fits horizontally}
widthofline:=(postertext[index].sumcharvalue/1000) *
                postertext[index].pointsize;
if (widthofline > maxwidthpts) then
           begin
            writeln('Line number ',index,' is too long');
            writeln('Hit E to edit, enter to change point size:');
            ans := upper(readchar);
            writeln;
            if (ans='E')  then begin
              write('Enter line number ',index, ':');
              readln(postertext[index].inputline);
              if postertext[index].inputline = '' then
```

```
                postertext[index].inputline := '  ';
                calcmaxpoint; end else
                  begin
                    postertext[index].inputline:=
                      postertext[index].inputline;
                    calcmaxpoint;
                    widthofline:=(postertext[index].sumcharvalue/1000) *
                      postertext[index].pointsize;
                     end;
                  end;
               {checks to see if line fits vertically}
          if ((totptsused+(postertext[index].pointsize*1.3))>maxheightpts)
                  then
                  begin
                   writeln('Line is taller than the available space');
                  end;
        until (widthofline< maxwidthpts) and
              ((totptsused+(postertext[index].pointsize*1.3))<maxheightpts);
totptsused:=totptsused + (1.3 * postertext[index].pointsize);
currentstats;
writeln;
write('Hit enter to input another line,  S to stop');
more := upper(readchar);
writeln;
if (more <> 'S') then index:=index+1;
if (index > maxlinenum) then
        begin
writeln('You have reached the maximum lines');
        end;
until (more = 'S') or (index > maxlinenum);
end;
{**************************************************************
Defines the PostScript code for the poster and sends
the code to the output file specified by the user
**************************************************************}
procedure codeposter;
var  linewidth,whitespace,x_val,y_val,yborder,xborder:real;
begin
writeln(postfile,'/sign');
writeln(postfile,' { gsave');
whitespace:=maxheightpts-totptsused;  {extra space for top and bottom}
y_val:=((height-borderwidth)*ptsperinch)-whitespace/2;  {initial y value}
for i:=1 to index do      {positon the remaining lines}
       begin
       writeln(postfile,'   /',fontname,' findfont ');
       writeln(postfile,postertext[i].pointsize:10:2,' scalefont setfont');
       linewidth:=(postertext[i].sumcharvalue/1000)*postertext[i].pointsize;
       x_val:=(width*ptsperinch-linewidth)/2;        {center line}
       y_val:=y_val-postertext[i].pointsize;
       writeln(postfile,'   ',x_val:10:1,' ',y_val:10:1,' moveto');
       writeln(postfile,'    (',postertext[i].inputline,') show');
       y_val:=y_val-postertext[i].pointsize*0.3;
       end;
writeln(postfile,'  newpath');                     {define border}
writeln(postfile,'   leftmargin botmargin moveto');
yborder:=bordwidthpts + maxheightpts;
writeln(postfile,'   0 ',yborder:12:4,' rlineto');
```

```
xborder:=bordwidthpts + maxwidthpts;
writeln(postfile,'    ',xborder:12:4,' 0 rlineto');
writeln(postfile,'    0 ',yborder:12:4,' neg rlineto');
writeln(postfile,'  closepath');
writeln(postfile,'  gsave');
writeln(postfile,'    ',bordwidthpts,' setlinewidth stroke');
writeln(postfile,'  grestore');
writeln(postfile,'  10 setlinewidth 1 setgray stroke');
writeln(postfile,'  grestore');
writeln(postfile,' } def');
writeln(postfile,'{sign} ',columns,' ',rows,' printposter');
writeln('The Code for the poster has been placed in ',outfilename);
end;



Begin                   {begin main}
continue:=true;
new:=false;                       {initialize variables}
quit:=false;
dividename:='post_p1.psp';

writeln('POSTER PROGRAM');
writeln('This program produces posters.');
writeln;writeln('The posters are coded in PostScript and sent to an');
writeln('output file of you choice.');
writeln;writeln('To obtain a poster, you must send the resulting file');
writeln('to a printer supporting PostScript.');
writeln;writeln('The poster can be any size,');
writeln('but line are limited to ',maxlinelen,' characters.');
writeln('Posters are limited to ',maxlinenum,' lines.');
writeln;
write('Hit any key to continue...');
ans:= upper(readchar);
writeln;
ans:='Y';

while (ans='Y') do
      begin
      choosefont;
      dimensions;                  {poster dimensions}
      maxspace;                    {max vertical and horizontal space}
      inputtext;
      chooseoutfile;
      codeposter;                {put poster code in output file}
      close(postfile);
      write('Create another poster?(Yes or No) ');
      ans := upper(readchar);
      writeln;
      end;


end.
```

2. Poster Driver: C

The first version of the poster driver is written in the DOS version of Borland's Turbo C. Like the Pascal version, the interface is completely generic. The program listing can be found in Listing 18.4. The algorithm used is the same as described in the previous section for the Pascal version. As shown here, the C functions correspond one-for-one with the Pascal procedures. The C version also uses **post_p1.psp**, the same prologue file read by the Pascal driver.

Listing 18.4: The C Poster Driver

```
/********************************************************************/
/This program creates PostScript code for a poster,*/
/*and sends it to an output file specified by the user.*/
/*In order to obtain a copy of the poster,*/
/*the output file must be sent to a printer supporting PostScript.*/
/*The program assumes that the printer uses 8 1/2" by 11" paper.*/
/*The sheets produced to make the poster will have a clipping*/
/*boundary that must be trimmed so that sheets can be*/
/*fastened together.*/

/*All posters will have a border.*/
/*Because the poster is made to fit on a number of sheets,*/
/*the actual size may be larger than the specified size.*/
/*Trim the sheets to the specified size. */
/*The program allows for upto 50 lines of 254 characters each.*/
/*Each line may be of different point size.*/
/*INPUT FILES USED:*/
/*i) The file "post_p1.psp" contains the PostScript code*/
/*to divide a poster into 8 1/2" by 11" sheets */
/*and is used as an input file.  The code in*/
/*this file is simply read in and then written to*/
/*the beginning of the poster output file.*/

/*ii) Files of the sort "tiro_l_r.fxw" contain */
/*    width information for characters according to */
/*    the font (ie. Times-Roman).*/
/*
/*    The font files must be of the format:*/

/*c v */
/* c v */
/*...*/

/*Where 'c' is the character and v is the width value.*/
/*The characters must be in ascending order according */
/*to their ASCII values because a binary search is*/
/*performed on the list of characters in the function,*/
/*void calc_max_point().*/

/*****************************************************************/

#include <stdio.h>
```

```
#include <ctype.h>
#include <string.h>
#include <stdlib.h>
#include <math.h>
#include <float.h>

#define max_line_len 225
#define paper_height 10
#define paper_width 7.5
#define border_width 0.75
#define pts_per_inch 72
#define border_width_pts 54
#define max_line_num 50
#define num_diff_char 100

typedef char file_string[30];
typedef char line_string[max_line_len];

typedef struct {
   char char_id;
      int width_value;
            } char_rec;

typedef char_rec  char_info_array[num_diff_char];

typedef struct {
      line_string input_line;
      float point_size;
      int sum_char_value;
               } text_line_rec;

typedef text_line_rec  poster_text_array[max_line_num];

FILE *fopen(), *char_file, *divide_file, *post_file;

float height=11.0, width=8.5, max_width, max_height,
      max_width_pts, max_height_pts, max_pt_size,
      total_pts_used, pts_left;

int rows, columns, num_lines, i, j,
    count, index, space;

file_string  char_filename, out_filename;
line_string  code_line, input_line, font_name;

poster_text_array  poster_text;
char_info_array    char_info;

int  found, more_lines;

void read_char_info();
void choose_font();
void choose_outfile();
void dimensions();
void max_space();
void current_stats();
void calc_max_point();
```

```
void input_text();
void code_poster();


main()
{
   clrscr();
   printf("This program produces posters\n\n");
   printf("The posters are coded in PostScript and sent to an\r\n");
   printf("output file of your choice.\n\n");
   printf("The poster can be any size,\n");
   printf("but lines are limited to %d characters\r\n", max_line_len);
   printf("posters are limited to %d lines\r\n", max_line_num);
   printf("Press any key to continue...");getch();
   choose_font();
   dimensions();
   max_space();
   input_text();
   choose_outfile();
   code_poster();
   fclose(post_file);
}


void read_char_info()
{       char dummy;

   count = 0;
   while (!feof(char_file))
   { count++;
     fscanf(char_file, "%c %d%c",
        &char_info[count].char_id,
        &char_info[count].width_value, &dummy);
   }
}


void choose_font()
{
   int done;
   int n, m,answer;

   done = 0;
   while (!done)
   {   clrscr();
      printf("\nFont Options:");
      printf("Times-Roman, Palatino-Bold Helvetica-Bold");
      printf("\nEnter the first letter of your choice: ");
      answer = toupper(getch());
      switch (answer)
      {   case 'T': strcpy(char_filename,"tiro_l_r.fxw");
              strcpy(font_name, "Times-Roman");
              space = 250;
              done = 1;
              break;
        case 'P': strcpy(char_filename, "pala_b_r.fxw");
              strcpy(font_name, "Palatino-Bold");
```

```
                space = 250;
                done = 1;
                break;
          case 'H': strcpy(char_filename, "helv_b_r.fxw");
                strcpy(font_name, "Helvetica-Bold");
                space = 250;
                done = 1;
                break;
          default : printf("Invalid choice, ");
                printf("please use the first letter of a font file/n");
                printf("Press RETURN to continue...");
                answer = getch();
       }
   }
   clrscr();

   char_file = fopen(char_filename, "r");
   read_char_info();
   fclose(char_file);
}


void choose_outfile()
{
   printf("\nFilename for output code: ");
   scanf("%s", out_filename);
   if (strlen(out_filename)<3) strcpy(out_filename, "CON");

   post_file = fopen(out_filename, "w+");
   divide_file = fopen("post_p1.psp", "r");

   while (fgets(code_line, max_line_len, divide_file))
   {   fputs(code_line, post_file);
      for (i=0; i<=max_line_len-1; i++)
         code_line[i] = ' ';
   }
   fclose(divide_file);
}


void dimensions()
{    clrscr();
   printf("Setting Poster Size ");
   printf("\n\tEnter height of poster in inches: ");
   scanf("%f", &height);
   printf("\n\tEnter width of poster in inches: ");
   scanf("%f", &width);

   rows =  ceil(height/paper_height);
   columns = ceil(width/paper_width);
   clrscr();
}


void max_space()
{
   max_width = width - (2 * border_width);
```

```
   max_width_pts = max_width * pts_per_inch;
   max_height = height - (2 * border_width);
   max_height_pts = max_height * pts_per_inch;
}


void current_stats()
{
   printf("\nPOSTER STATS >>>");
   printf("\nHeight:%8.1fpts  ", max_height_pts);
   printf("Width: %8.1fpts  ", max_width_pts);
   printf("Space Left: %8.1f pts\n",
             (max_height_pts - total_pts_used));
   if (index>0)
   {printf("\nSUMMARY OF LINES ENTERED >>>>>");
   printf("\nLINE SIZE  WIDTH(pts)   TEXT...(first 60 characters)\n");
   for (i=1; i<=index; i++)
      printf("%2d  %4.0f %6.0f         %s\n",
        i, poster_text[i].point_size,
        poster_text[i].sum_char_value*poster_text[i].point_size/1000,
        poster_text[i].input_line);
   }
}


void calc_max_point()
{
   int top, bottom, middle;
   div_t  x;

   poster_text[index].sum_char_value = 0;
   for (j=0; j<=strlen(poster_text[index].input_line); j++)
   {   top = count;
      bottom = 1;
      found = 0;
      while (!found && top>=bottom)
      {   x = div(top+bottom, 2);
         middle = x.quot;
         if (poster_text[index].input_line[j]==char_info[middle].char_id)
            found = 1;
         else
            if (poster_text[index].input_line[j]<char_info[middle].char_id)
               top = middle - 1;
            else
               bottom = middle + 1;
      }
      if (found)
         poster_text[index].sum_char_value+=char_info[middle].width_value;
      else
         if (poster_text[index].input_line[j] == ' ')
            poster_text[index].sum_char_value += space;
   }
   max_pt_size = (1000*max_width_pts)/poster_text[index].sum_char_value;
   pts_left = max_height_pts - total_pts_used;

   if (max_pt_size>pts_left || (max_pt_size+(max_pt_size/3))>pts_left)
      max_pt_size = pts_left - pts_left / 3;
```

```
}


void input_text()
{
   float width_of_line;
   char c;
   int pos, answer;

   total_pts_used = 0;
   index = 0;
   current_stats();
   do
   {    index++;
      printf("\nEnter line %2d: ", index);
      pos = 0; c = '\0';
      while((c = getche()) != '\r')
         poster_text[index].input_line[pos++] = c;
      calc_max_point();

      do
      {   printf("\nEnter pt size(Max =%4.0f) for line %2d: ",
               max_pt_size, index);
         scanf("%f", &poster_text[index].point_size);
         width_of_line = (poster_text[index].sum_char_value/1000)
                  * poster_text[index].point_size;

         if (width_of_line > max_width_pts)
         {   printf("\nLine number %2d is too long", index);
            printf("\nEnter a smaller point size:");
         }
         if ((total_pts_used+(poster_text[index].point_size*1.3))
                  > max_height_pts)
         {   printf("Line is taller than the available space");
         }
      } while ((width_of_line > max_width_pts) ||
         ((total_pts_used+(poster_text[index].point_size*1.3))
                  > max_height_pts));

      total_pts_used += 1.3 * poster_text[index].point_size;
      current_stats();

      printf("\n'E' to Enter another line,anything else to quit");
      answer = toupper(getch());
      if (answer == '\r') index++;
      if (index > max_line_num)
      {   printf("\nYou have reached the maximum lines");
      }
   } while ((answer == 'E') && (index < max_line_num));
}


void code_poster()
{
   float  line_width, white_space,
          x_val, y_val, xborder, yborder;
```

```
   fprintf(post_file, "/sign\n");
   fprintf(post_file, "{ gsave\n");

   white_space = max_height_pts - total_pts_used;
   y_val = ((height - border_width) * pts_per_inch) - white_space / 2;

   for (i=1; i<=index; i++)
   {   fprintf(post_file, "  /%s findfont \n", font_name);
      fprintf(post_file, "%10.2f scalefont setfont\n",
                   poster_text[i].point_size);
      line_width = (poster_text[i].sum_char_value / 1000.0)
                       * poster_text[i].point_size;
      x_val = (width * pts_per_inch - line_width) / 2.0;
      y_val -= poster_text[i].point_size;

      fprintf(post_file, "  %10.1f %10.1f moveto\n", x_val, y_val);
      fprintf(post_file, "  (%s) show\n", poster_text[i].input_line);

      y_val -= poster_text[i].point_size * 0.3;
   }
   fprintf(post_file, "  newpath\n");
   fprintf(post_file, "   leftmargin botmargin moveto\n");

   yborder = border_width_pts + max_height_pts;
   fprintf(post_file, "   0 %12.4f rlineto\n", yborder);
   xborder = border_width_pts + max_width_pts;
   fprintf(post_file, "   %12.4f 0 rlineto\n", xborder);
   fprintf(post_file, "   0 %12.4f neg rlineto\n", yborder);
   fprintf(post_file, "  closepath\n");
   fprintf(post_file, "  gsave\n");
   fprintf(post_file, "   %d setlinewidth stroke\n", border_width_pts);
   fprintf(post_file, "  grestore\n");
   fprintf(post_file, "  10 setlinewidth 1 setgray stroke\n");
   fprintf(post_file, "  grestore\n");
   fprintf(post_file, " } def\n");
   fprintf(post_file, "{sign} %d %d printposter", columns, rows);
   printf("The code for the poster has been placed in \"%s\"",
               out_filename);
}
```

a. Explanation of the Listing

The C driver program consists of 10 functions:

read_char_info — This function corresponds to **readcharinfo** in the Pascal version. It reads width information about characters out of a metric file into an array.

choose_font — This function prompts you to choose a font for the poster. It corresponds to **choosefont** in the Pascal version.

choose_outfile — This is the prompt and setup for the output file. It corresponds to the **chooseoutfile** procedure in the Pascal version.

dimensions — This corresponds to the procedure of the same name in the Pascal version.

max_space — This function calculates the maximum space available for lines of text on the poster. It corresponds to the **maxspace** procedure in the Pascal version.

current_stats — Like the **currentstats** procedure in the Pascal version, this function prints information about the current state of the poster to the console.

calc_max_point — This function corresponds to the **calcmaxpoint** procedure in the Pascal version.

input_text — Like the **inputtext** procedure in the Pascal driver, this function prompts you for lines of text and type sizes.

code_poster — This function creates the output code for the poster like **codeposter** in the Pascal version.

main — This is the main body of the driver.

3. Further Enhancements

The advantage of creating posters with these drivers is that maximum text size can be determined in advance rather than through trial and error. More sophisticated poster drivers could create the kind of special text effects used for the poster in Chapter 13. For example, a driver producing a poster with circular text could determine how many times a string would fit around a circle, and how much extra space would be left on the circumference after the last copy is painted before creating the code. The driver could allow modification of the string, its size, or the radius of the circle, just as the drivers in this chapter permit changes to the size of the type.

Chapter 19
Name Tag Driver in C

1. Introduction

a. Explanation

This chapter demonstrates three versions of a name tag driver written in Turbo C.[62] The first version discussed, the simplest of the three, takes name tag information from an ASCII file, adds a tag title, and outputs a PostScript file. The PostScript file contains the information for printing the name tags on labels. The second version adds an interactive option that permits you to produce the name tag information execution of the C program. The last version creates a PostScript file thah prints background text on the labels in addition to the individual tag information.

The code contained in this chapter uses simple C commands, requiring only a rudimentary understanding of the C language. At the end of the chapter are enhancement suggestions that skilled C programmers will find easy to integrate into the program.

[62]The *name tag driver* is based on a program originally developed by Michael Spring. Molly Sorrows and Richard Baker revised and cleaned the program, and worked out the initial supporting documentation found here.

b. Objectives

The objectives of this chapter are

- To illustrate three versions of a PostScript driver written using simple C commands;
- To provide a name tag program that can be adapted to personal use;
- To show C procedures that allow for batch and interactive input;
- To illustrate the use of font width files in PostScript.

2. Building a Simple Name Tag Driver

The first version of this program, Listing 19.1, takes name tag information from an ASCII file and outputs a PostScript file for printing labels. Before this program is executed, you must prepare an ASCII file containing all the name tag information. The ASCII file should contain each name with two corresponding text lines. The input file format is: Each line of text for a given name tag is separated by a comma, and the end of the information for a given name tag is indicated by a semicolon. Save and name this file for recall execution of the C program.

The first version listing contains the complete code to execute the C program. The program has three parts, as discussed in Chapter 14: setup functions, interface functions, and PostScript creation function.

Listing 19.1: Version 1: Simple Name Tag Driver

```
#include <stdio.h>
#include <ctype.h>
#include <conio.h>
#define TRUE 1
#define FALSE 0
#define MAXLINES 3

FILE *ofp,*ifp;

main()
{
  char infname[80], outfname[80];     /* input & output file names */

  cprintf("\r\nThis program creats a postscript file ");
  cprintf("which will print nametags.");
  cprintf("\r\nThe program reads the information for ");
  cprintf("the nametags from a text file.");
  cprintf("\r\nInput file format is: each line of text ");
  cprintf("for a given nametag is ");
  cprintf("\r\n   separated by a comma, and the end of ");
  cprintf("information for a given ");
```

```
  cprintf("\r\n   nametag is indicated by a semicolon.  ");
  cprintf("CR's are permitted anywhere.");

  cprintf("\r\n\r\nOutput filename (<CR> for default-print.ps):");
  if (! getstr(outfname, 1)) strcpy(outfname,"print.ps");
  if ((ofp=fopen(outfname,"w")) == NULL)
    {
    cprintf("\r\nCould not open %s for write. Exiting program.",
              outfname);
    exit(0);
    }

  labelsetup();

  do
    {
    cprintf("\r\nEnter name of file with data:  ");
    getstr(infname, 1);
    }
  while ((ifp=fopen(infname,"r")) == NULL);

  do_tags();
  fclose(ifp);
  fclose(ofp);
  return;
}

/*==============================================================
  Function labelsetup: creates initial defines for all labels;
  Returns: void
  ==============================================================*/
labelsetup()
{
  int mtfs;
  char s1[100];

  fprintf(ofp,"%!PS-Adobe-2.0\n");
  fprintf(ofp,"/outline {newpath 5 -5 moveto 235 -5 lineto ");
     fprintf(ofp,"235 130 lineto 5 130 lineto closepath \n");
  fprintf(ofp,".5 setgray 5 setlinewidth stroke} def\n");
  fprintf(ofp,"/centershow {0 setgray dup stringwidth pop \n");
  fprintf(ofp,"240 exch sub 2 div yval moveto show} def\n");

  cprintf("\r\nTitle for tag (name of event): ");
  if (getstr(s1, 0))
    {
    mtfs=320/strlen(s1);
    if (mtfs>34) mtfs=34;
    fprintf(ofp, "/mtfont { /Helvetica-Bold findfont %2d ",mtfs);
       fprintf(ofp, "scalefont setfont } def\n");
    fprintf(ofp,"/ytitle %3d def\n",(91-(mtfs/3)));
    fprintf(ofp,"/maintitle {mtfont (%s) centershow} def\n",s1);
    }
  return;
}

/*==============================================================
```

```
  Function do_tags: determines position for printing each nametag
  Returns: void
  ==============================================================*/
do_tags()
{
  int k=1;
  fprintf(ofp, "57 90 translate\n");    /* starting pos. on page*/
  while (one_tag())
    {
    switch (k)
      {
        case 4:
                fprintf(ofp,"250 -486 translate\n");
                k++;
                break;
        case 8:
                fprintf(ofp," showpage \n 57 90 translate\n");
                k=1;
                break;
        default:
                fprintf(ofp,"0 162 translate\n");
                k++;
                break;
      }
    }
  fprintf(ofp,"showpage\n");
  return;
}

/*=================================================================
  Function one_tag: reads in text from input file and writes the
                    postscript to print the tags to output file;
  Returns: 0 if end of file, non zero if not eof.
  ==============================================================*/
one_tag()
  {
  char c;
  int i=0, j=0, m=0;
  int y;
  int finished=FALSE;
  char names[MAXLINES][100];
  char fonts[MAXLINES][50] =
           { "Helvetica-Bold",
             "Helvetica-Bold",
             "Helvetica-Bold"};
  int  ptsize[MAXLINES] =
           { 18,
             12,
             12};

  while (! finished)
    {
    if (! feof(ifp))
      {
      c = fgetc(ifp);
      switch (c)
        {
```

```
        case 13: break;           /* ignore CR when reading file */
        case 10: break;           /* ignore LF when reading file */
        case ';':
          names[i++][j] = 0;
          finished = TRUE;
          break;
        case ',':
          names[i++][j] = 0;
          j=0;
          if (i>=MAXLINES) finished=TRUE;
          break;
        default:
          names[i][j++] = c;
          break;
        }
      }
    else
      {
      finished = TRUE;
      }
    }

   /* write out the strings in the array */

  y=64;
  if (i>0)
    {
    fprintf(ofp,"/yval ytitle def\n");
    fprintf(ofp,"outline maintitle\n");

    while (m<i)
    {
    fprintf(ofp,"/%s findfont %d scalefont setfont\n",
                 fonts[m], ptsize[m]);
    fprintf(ofp,"/yval %d def\n", y=y-ptsize[m]*1.10);
    fprintf(ofp,"(%s) centershow\n", names[m++]);
    }
    }
  if (feof(ifp)) return(0);
  else return(1);
}

/*================================================================
  Function getstr: accepts input from user for a string;
       isfilename = 1 if the string is a filename, otherwise, 0.
  Returns: number of characters in string;
  ==============================================================*/
int getstr(instring, isfilename)
char instring[];
int isfilename;
{
  char c;
  int j=0;
  putch(219);gotoxy(wherex()-1,wherey());
  while((c=getch()) != 13)            /* 13 = Carriage Return */
    {
    if((c==0)&&(kbhit))
```

```
      {
      c=getch();
      continue;
      }
    if((c==8)&&(j>0))                    /* 8 = backspace */
      {
      j--;
      putch(' ');
      gotoxy(wherex()-2,wherey());
      }
    if (isfilename)
      {
      if ((isalnum(c)) ||
               (c==46) ||                /* 46 = period */
               (c==95) ||                /* 95 = underscore */
               (c==92) ||                /* 92 = backslash */
               (c==58))                  /* 58 = colon */
        {
        putch(c);
        instring[j++]=c;
        }
      }
    else
      {
      if (c != 8)
        {
        putch(c);
        instring[j++] = c;
        }
      }
    putch(219);
    gotoxy(wherex()-1,wherey());
    }
  instring[j]='\0';
  gotoxy(wherex(),wherey());putch(' ');
  strcpy(instring,instring);
  return(j);
}
```

a. Setup Functions

The first section takes care of the setup chores and is required in all versions of the program.[63] This setup section starts by using the **#include** command to include the required header files and **#define** to define various constants. The **file** command declares pointers to the input and output files.

The first line of the **main** function defines string variables that contain the

[63]The exact syntax may vary for various versions of C. The commands contained in this chapter are consistent with Borland's Turbo C.

input and output file names. The next five lines output directions to your screen regarding the use of the program.

The setup procedures remain the same for all versions of the program. Listings for the later versions only reference this information.

b. User Interface Functions

You are prompted for an output file name or to press return to use the default file name, **print.ps**. The **getstr** function is called to get a file name from you. The **getstr** function has two arguments, a string that you enter in the function and the constant 1 if the string is a file name or the constant 0 if it is not. If no file name is entered, the function returns 0 and the default file name is used. The second if statement opens the file for writing. If the file cannot be opened, the program notifies you and aborts.

After establishing the output file, the **labelsetup** function is called. This function obtains the title that is printed on all name tags and writes out several PostScript procedure definitions to use in writing the labels. The PostScript procedures are defined using operators that should be familiar to you. The **outline** procedure creates a gray shaded line around the name tag. The **centershow** procedure centers a string on the label.

The **getstr** function is called to get the title for the name tags. The parameter 0 indicates the string is not a file name and therefore can contain spaces. The next six lines of code in the **labelsetup** function output PostScript procedures to print the title in the proper font and point size. This is accomplished by dividing the distance across the label in points by the title string length. If the result is less than 34, a point size of 34 is used; otherwise the computed result is used. The **mtfont** PostScript procedure defines the title font definition. The **ytitle** procedure defines the base line of the text. Last, the **maintitle** procedure uses the other procedures to print the tag title when called later in the PostScript output file.

The last interface function in the **main** function obtains the name of the input file. A **do while** loop continues to prompt you for a file name until a readable file is entered.

c. Final PostScript Creation Functions

The last section creates the rest of the PostScript output by calling the **do_tags** function. The **do_tags** function determines the position for printing each label, and calls the **one_tag** function to read in the text and output PostScript commands for printing each name tag. The **do_tags** function first writes PostScript code to translate the origin to the first label position on the image page. It then calls the **one_tag** function, which places the information for the first label on the page.

A **while** loop is then executed based on the value returned by the **one_tag** function. The **one_tag** function gets the next label information if it exists or else returns 0. A return of 0 terminates the **while** loop.

The **one_tag** function starts by defining three strings: the text of name tag information, fonts to use and point sizes to use. The names and fonts arrays are two-dimensional. A **while** loop continues until all the information for one tag is read in, or the end of the input file is reached. A case statement within the **while** loop checks each of the characters read in from the input file. If a carriage return or line feed is present, it is not added to the string, and the next character is evaluated. If a semicolon is read, indicating the end of the input for a tag, the **finished** variable is set to true and the loop terminates. If a comma is read, then the end of the string has been reached. If the first dimension of the names array is equal to **MAXLINES**, the **finished** variable is set to true, indicating the maximum number of lines permitted for a tag has been reached. In all other cases, the character read in is added to the names array at the proper position, and the loop continues until it reaches a comma or semicolon.

Once the information is read in for a tag, the PostScript commands to print the tag are written to the output file. This is accomplished by proceeding line by line through the names array and writing the proper name tag information or title for the tag using the correct fonts and point sizes. Each line is centered on the tag using the **centershow** procedure. If the end of the input file is reached, the **one_tag** function returns 0; otherwise it returns 1. As mentioned, this value determines whether the **while** loop's contents are executed.

The **switch** statement inside the **while** loop prints the information for each label on the appropriate label space. The counter keeps track of the label position on the page. Printing starts at the bottom left corner of the page. If the label is at the top of the page (i.e. counter equals 4), the PostScript command to translate the origin to the bottom of the next label column is written to the output file. If the label is the last one on the page (i.e. counter equals 8), the PostScript commands to show the page and translate the origin to the first label for the next page are written to the output file. The counter is then set to 1. In all other cases, the translation establishes the position for the next label by moving the origin up the height of one label, within the label column. This loop continues until the input file is at the end of the file.

d. Output Results

A sample PostScript file created using Version 1 of the program is shown in Listing 19.2.

Listing 19.2: Version 1 Output Listing

```
%!PS-Adobe-2.0
/outline {newpath 5 -5 moveto
235 -5 lineto 235 130 lineto 5 130 lineto closepath
.5 setgray 5 setlinewidth stroke} def
/centershow {0 setgray dup stringwidth pop
240 exch sub 2 div yval moveto show} def
/mtfont { /Helvetica-Bold findfont 34 scalefont setfont } def
/ytitle  82 def
/maintitle {mtfont (Sample Tags) centershow} def
57 90 translate
/yval ytitle def
outline maintitle
/Helvetica-Bold findfont 18 scalefont setfont
/yval 44 def
(Person's Name) centershow
/Helvetica findfont 12 scalefont setfont
/yval 30 def
(Title One) centershow
/Helvetica findfont 12 scalefont setfont
/yval 16 def
(Title Two) centershow
0 162 translate
/yval ytitle def
outline maintitle
/Helvetica-Bold findfont 18 scalefont setfont
/yval 44 def
(Mr. Example) centershow
/Helvetica findfont 12 scalefont setfont
/yval 30 def
(University of Pittsburgh) centershow
/Helvetica findfont 12 scalefont setfont
/yval 16 def
(Postscript Expert) centershow
0 162 translate
showpage
```

The result of printing this sample file to a laser printer is illustrated in Figure 19.1.

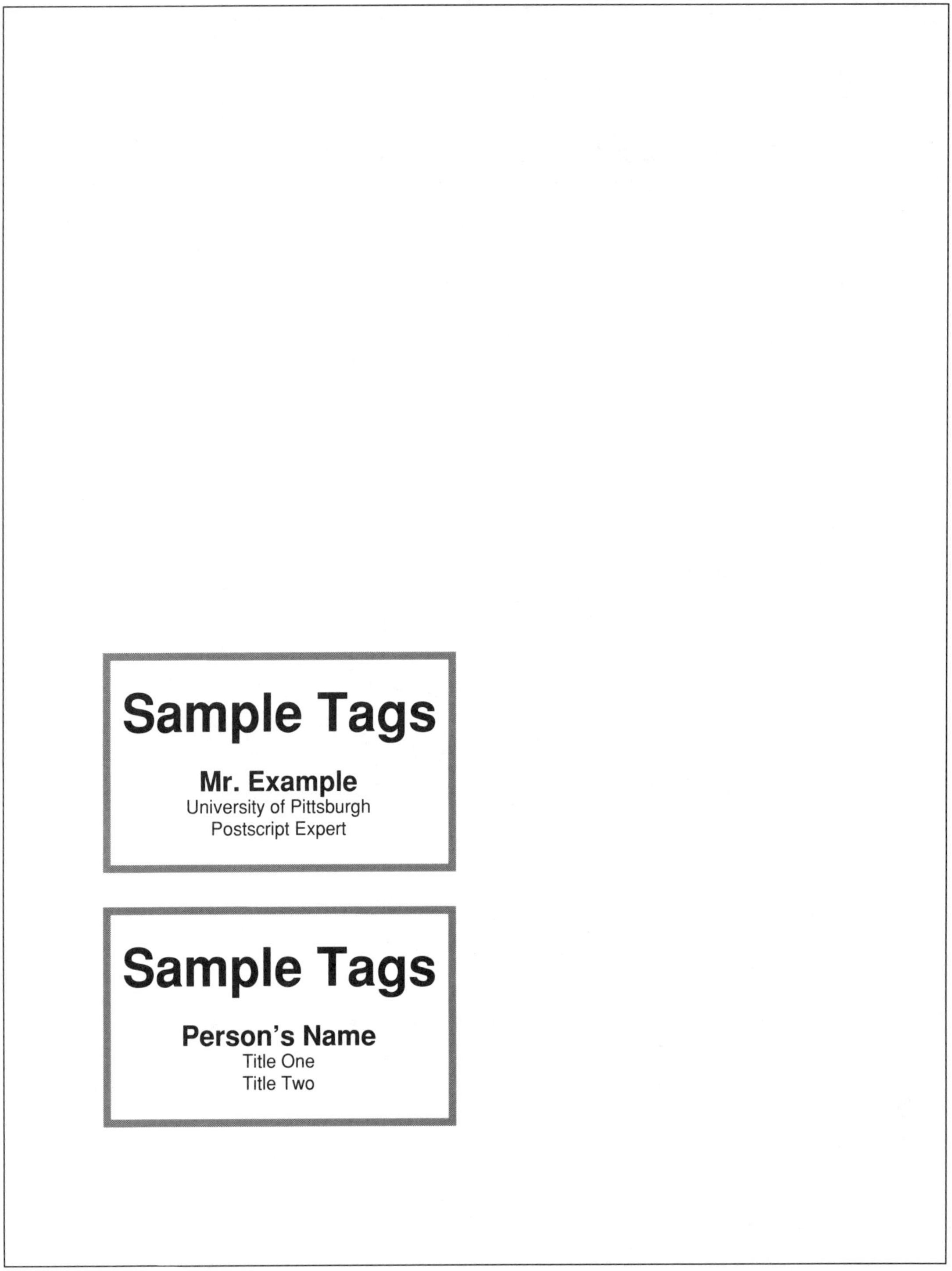

Figure 19.1: Printed Output of Version 1

3. Version 2: Adding an Interactive Procedure

The second version of this driver enables you to choose between using a file to read in the text for the name tags, (as in Version 1), or entering the text interactively. A boolean variable, **interactive**, is used to indicate which method you selected. The definitions of several variables—for example, the names, fonts, and point size arrays are moved from the **one_tag** function and defined as globals since they will now be used in several procedures.

The major change for this version takes place in what was the **one_tag** function. In Version 1, the first part of the function read in text from a file, and the second part wrote the PostScript code to print that text. The part that reads in text is now split out from this function. The original code for reading in text from a file is put in the **get_file_text** function. A new function called **get_user_text** is created that reads in the text from an interactive session with the user. The code for these changes is in Listing 19.3.

In **one_tag** function, a simple conditional statement determines whether to call **get_file_text** or **get_user_text**, depending on the value of the **interactive** boolean. Each of these functions returns the number of lines entered or –1 to indicate either the end of file or the end of interactive data entry; this value is stored in the variable lines, which determine whether PostScript code is written to the output file.

The **get_file_text** function is not discussed further here. Because it is essentially the same as the code from Version 1.

The **get_user_text** function prompts you to enter text for each line of a single name tag, up to the value of **MAXLINES**. A null string on line 1 for a name tag indicates no more name tags will be entered, in which case the function returns –1.

The appropriate PostScript procedures and text strings are then written to the output file from the **one_tag** function, as in the first version.

Listing 19.3: Listing of New Code in Version 2

```
one_tag()
  {
  int lines=0;
  int m=0;
  int y=64;

  if (!interactive) lines=get_file_text();
  else lines=get_user_text();

  if (lines>0)
    {
    fprintf(ofp,"/yval ytitle def\n");
```

```
    fprintf(ofp,"outline maintitle\n");
    }
  while (m<lines)
    {
    fprintf(ofp,"/%s findfont %d scalefont setfont\n",
                fonts[m], ptsize[m]);
    fprintf(ofp,"/yval %d def\n", y=y-ptsize[m]*1.10);
    fprintf(ofp,"(%s) centershow\n", names[m++]);
    }
  if (lines == -1) return(0);
  else return(1);
  }


int get_user_text()
  {
  char c;
  int finished=FALSE;
  int i=0;

  while (!finished)
    {
    if (i==0) cprintf("\r\nEnter line %d, or CR if done: ",i+1);
    else cprintf("\r\nEnter line %d, CR for none: ",i+1);
    if ((getstr(names[i],0)<1) && (i==0)) finished=TRUE;
    else
      {
      if (++i>=MAXLINES) finished=TRUE;
      }
    }
    if (i>0) return(i);
    else return(-1);
  }
```

The printed results of this version appear the same as in the first version, given the same label information. The difference lies only in the choice of input methods.

4. Version 3: Printing Background Text and Using Font Metrics Files

Two major modifications are made in this version: you enter text string is and print it as background text on each of the labels, and font widths files are used to determine the maximum possible point size for the text strings to be printed on the name tags. Because these two topics are somewhat separate, they are presented separately here.

a. Background Printing

The procedure created for printing the background text is similar to the one used in the wrapping paper and poster PostScript chapters (see Chapters 9 and 13). You are encouraged to review these chapters if the code is unfamiliar. The code used for writing the background text is given in Listing 19.4.

Listing 19.4: Listing of Code for Printing Background Text

```
/* global definition */
struct line_attrib {char fontname[50];
                    char fontfile[50];
                    long int ptsize;};

struct line_attrib background=
          { "Helvetica-Bold", "helv_b_r.fxw", 6L};


/************************************************************
   In function labelsetup, the following lines were added
   to determine the background string for the nametags and
   to define the necessary postscript procedures.
 ************************************************************/

  cprintf("\r\n Enter background string for tag: ");
  getstr(s1,0);

  fprintf(ofp,"/newline {currentpoint 8 sub exch ");
  fprintf(ofp,"pop 5 exch moveto} def\n");
  fprintf(ofp,"/chknewline {currentpoint pop 230 gt ");
  fprintf(ofp,"{newline} if } def\n");
  fprintf(ofp,"/done {currentpoint exch pop -4 lt } def\n");
  fprintf(ofp,"/strg ( %s ) def\n",s1);
  fprintf(ofp,"/fillbox { /%s findfont %ld \n",
             background.fontname, background.ptsize);
  fprintf(ofp,"scalefont setfont 0 121 moveto\n");
  fprintf(ofp,"{ {pop pop chknewline} strg kshow done\n");
  fprintf(ofp,"{exit} if } loop } def\n");

  fprintf(ofp,"/whitebox {newpath 15 10 moveto\n");
  fprintf(ofp,"225 10 lineto 225 65 lineto 15 65 lineto \n");
  fprintf(ofp,"closepath 1 setgray fill 0 setgray newpath \n");
  fprintf(ofp,"15 10 moveto \n");
  fprintf(ofp,"225 10 lineto 225 65 lineto 15 65 lineto \n");
  fprintf(ofp,"closepath 2 setlinewidth stroke } def\n");


/************************************************************
   in function one_tag, the following line was modified to
   include the fillbox and whitebox procedures.
 ************************************************************/

     fprintf(ofp,"fillbox whitebox outline maintitle\n");
```

In the **labelsetup** function, the driver program prompts you for a background string and creates a PostScript procedure to fill a clipped area on the label with that background string. Because background text on the entire name tag may make it difficult to read the main information, a PostScript procedure is written to draw a white box where you want the name. The **whitebox** procedure must be called after the **fillbox** procedure to place the white area on top of the background text.

b. Font Metrics Files

Font metrics or font widths files were introduced in Chapter 15, and can be used to determine the width of a string in a given font. In this program, font widths files are used to determine the maximum point size that can be used to display a given string on a name tag. This enhancement is made only in the interactive version of the program, as it requires you to select the desired point size for each line. The C code added for this enhancement is in Listing 19.5.

Listing 19.5: Listing of Code for Using Font Information

```
/*******************************************************
 Version 3 of the Nametag program contains several
 enhancements.  The major sections of code which changed
 between versions 2 and 3 are included here.
 *******************************************************/

/* global definitions */

#define PTS_W 230L
FILE *ofp,*ifp,*fwfp;      /*fwfp=file ptr for font width file */
long int char_width[200];        /*character widths from file*/
struct line_attrib {char fontname[50];
                    char fontfile[50];
                    long int ptsize;};
struct line_attrib fonts[MAXLINES]=         /*default values*/
           { {"Helvetica-Bold", "helv_b_r.fxw", 24L},
             {"Helvetica-Bold", "helv_b_r.fxw", 18L},
             {"Helvetica-Bold", "helv_b_r.fxw", 18L}};
struct line_attrib print_att[MAXLINES];

/*******************************************************
 In function labelsetup, the user can choose the point
 size for the main title for the nametags.  The titls
 is checked to be sure it will fit according to the width.

 Initialize char_width array to null.  Then open the
 appropriate font width file, and load the char_width
 array.  Use the char_width array to determine the width
 of the string entered, and the maximum point size that
 can be used according to the width.
 *******************************************************/
  char s1[100];
```

```
  int k=0, j =0;
  char ch;
  long int maxpt, sum;
 ....

    for (k=0;k<200;k++) char_width[k]=0;

    if ((fwfp=fopen(main_title.fontfile,"r"))==NULL)
      {cprintf("\r\nFile %s is not present or cannot be opened.",
       main_title.fontfile); exit(0);}

    k=32;    /* character for a space */
    while (fscanf(fwfp, "%c %ld %c", &ch, &char_width[k++],&ch)
           != EOF) {}          /*load char_width from widths file*/
    fclose(fwfp);

    sum=0;
    for (j=0; j<strlen(s1);j++)
      {
      sum = sum + char_width[s1[j]];
      }
    if (sum>0)
      {
      maxpt = (((PTS_W*1000L)*100L)/110L)/sum;
      if (maxpt>main_title.ptsize) maxpt=main_title.ptsize;
      }

    do
      {
      cprintf("\r\nEnter point size for main title (max %ld): ",
         maxpt);
      scanf("%ld",&main_title.ptsize);
      }
    while (main_title.ptsize > maxpt);


/*=================================================================
  Function one_tag: reads in text from input file and writes the
                     postscript to print the tags to output file;
  Returns: 0 if end of file, non zero if not eof.

  Uses the values in the structure print_att to print the text.
  Determines the position to move down in the y direction
  according to the number of strings which will be printed on
  the particular nametag.  This helps to center the text in the
  whitespace printed on the nametag.
  ===============================================================*/

one_tag()
  {
  int lines=0;
  int m=0;
  long int y=60L;
  long int y_incr=0L;

  if (!interactive) lines=get_file_text();
  else lines=get_user_text();
```

```
  if (lines>0)
    {
     fprintf(ofp,"/yval ytitle def\n");
     fprintf(ofp,"fillbox whitebox outline maintitle\n");
     y_incr = 50L/(lines+1);
     y=y-y_incr;
     while (m<lines)
       {
       if (m==0)
         {
         y=y+(y_incr/2L);
         if (y_incr*2L < print_att[m].ptsize)
           print_att[m].ptsize = y_incr*2L;
         }
       else
         {
         if (y_incr < print_att[m].ptsize)
           print_att[m].ptsize = y_incr;
         }
       fprintf(ofp,"/%s findfont %ld scalefont setfont\n",
                    print_att[m].fontname, print_att[m].ptsize);
       fprintf(ofp,"/yval %ld def\n", y=y-y_incr);
       fprintf(ofp,"(%s) centershow\n", names[m++]);
       }
    }
  if (lines == -1) return(0);
  else return(1);
  }


/*=================================================================
  Function get_user_text: get text for one nametag from user
  Returns: number of lines on nametag, or -1 if no more tags

  The font width values are read into the char_width array, and
  are used to calculate the width of the string which was
  entered.  The structure print_att is initialized to the
  default values which are stored in the structure "fonts".
  If the string is too long to fit using the default point
  size, the user is prompted to enter a new font size less than
  or equal to the maximum which is shown, or to re-enter the
  text string.  This process is embedded in a loop so that
  if they enter a new string, it is also checked to make sure
  it fits using the default point size.
  ==============================================================*/
int get_user_text()
  {
  char c;
  char ch;
  int finished=FALSE;
  int i=0;
  int j=0;
  int k=0;
  long int sum;
  long int maxpt;
  int name_long=TRUE;
```

```
while (!finished)
  {
  if (i==0)
    {
    cprintf("\r\nEnter line %d, or CR if done: ",i+1);
    }
  else
    cprintf("\r\nEnter line %d, CR for no text on this line: ",
             i+1);
  if ((getstr(names[i],0)<1) && (i==0)) finished=TRUE;
  else
    {
    for (k=0;k<200;k++) char_width[k] = 0;

    if ( (fwfp=fopen(fonts[i].fontfile,"r")) == NULL)
      {
    cprintf("\r\n%s not present or cannot be opened. Exiting.",
               fonts[i].fontfile); exit(0);
      }
    k=32;
    while (fscanf(fwfp,"%c %ld %c",&ch,&char_width[k++],&ch)
           !=EOF) {}
    fclose(fwfp);

    name_long = TRUE;
    print_att[i].ptsize = fonts[i].ptsize;
    do
      {
      sum=0;
      for (j=0;j<strlen(names[i]);j++)
        {
        sum = sum + char_width[names[i][j]];
        }

      if (sum>0)
        {
        maxpt = (((PTS_W*1000L)*100L)/110L)/sum;
        if (maxpt < print_att[i].ptsize)
          {
          cprintf("\r\nString too long to fit using point size.");
          cprintf("\r\nEnter new point size (max. %ld)" , maxpt);
               cprintf("or 0 to enter string again");
          scanf("%ld",&print_att[i].ptsize);
          if (print_att[i].ptsize > maxpt)
            {
            }

          else
            {
            if (print_att[i].ptsize == 0)
              {
              cprintf("\r\nEnter text %d,  or CR: ",
                           i+1);
              print_att[i].ptsize=fonts[i].ptsize;
              getstr(names[i],0);
              }
            else
```

```
                {
                name_long = FALSE;
                }
              }  /* else line small enough */
            }
          else
            {
            name_long = FALSE;
            }
          }
        else {finished = TRUE; i--;}
        }
      while ((name_long) && (!finished));
      if (++i>=MAXLINES) finished=TRUE;
      }
    }  /* end while(!finished) */

  if (i>0) return(i);
  else return(-1);
  }
```

The appropriate font metrics file is used to calculate the sum of character widths that make up a string. Then, the maximum possible point size is calculated according to the x-width values. You are prompted to enter a point size for each of the name tag lines and given the maximum point size possible for the string has been entered.

c. Results

The PostScript file output from a sample run of Version 3 of the PostScript driver is shown in Listing 19.6. The output produced by that PostScript code is depicted in Figure 19.2.

Listing 19.6: Version 3 Output Listing

```
%!PS-Adobe-2.0
/outline {newpath 5 -5 moveto 235 -5 lineto
235 130 lineto 5 130 lineto closepath
.5 setgray 5 setlinewidth stroke} def
/centershow {0 setgray dup stringwidth pop
240 exch sub 2 div yval moveto show} def
/ytitle 83 def
/maintitle {/Helvetica-Bold findfont 26 scalefont setfont
(Event Name) centershow} def
/newline {currentpoint 8 sub exch pop 5 exch moveto} def
/chknewline {currentpoint pop 230 gt {newline} if } def
/done {currentpoint exch pop -4 lt } def
/strg ( sample ) def
/fillbox { /Helvetica findfont 6
scalefont setfont 0 121 moveto
{ {pop pop chknewline} strg kshow done
```

```
{exit} if } loop } def
/whitebox {newpath 15 10 moveto
225 10 lineto 225 65 lineto 15 65 lineto
closepath 1 setgray fill 0 setgray newpath
15 10 moveto
225 10 lineto 225 65 lineto 15 65 lineto
closepath 2 setlinewidth stroke } def
57 90 translate
/yval ytitle def
fillbox whitebox outline maintitle
/Helvetica-Bold findfont 24 scalefont setfont
/yval 42 def
(Mr. Example) centershow
/Helvetica findfont 12 scalefont setfont
/yval 30 def
(Title Number One) centershow
/Helvetica findfont 12 scalefont setfont
/yval 18 def
(Title Number Two) centershow
0 162 translate
/yval ytitle def
fillbox whitebox outline maintitle
/Helvetica-Bold findfont 24 scalefont setfont
/yval 36 def
(Person's Name) centershow
/Helvetica findfont 16 scalefont setfont
/yval 20 def
(One Title Only) centershow
0 162 translate
/yval ytitle def
fillbox whitebox outline maintitle
/Helvetica-Bold findfont 24 scalefont setfont
/yval 22 def
(Name Only) centershow
0 162 translate
showpage
```

This program could be modified to move more of the required calculations to the C program and further simplify the PostScript program.

You can modify this version of the program to use font width files to enhance the output even when the text is read in from a file. The input text file can be scanned and the longest string length calculated for the given font (for each line). Then the user can be prompted, with the calculated values as the maximum font sizes.

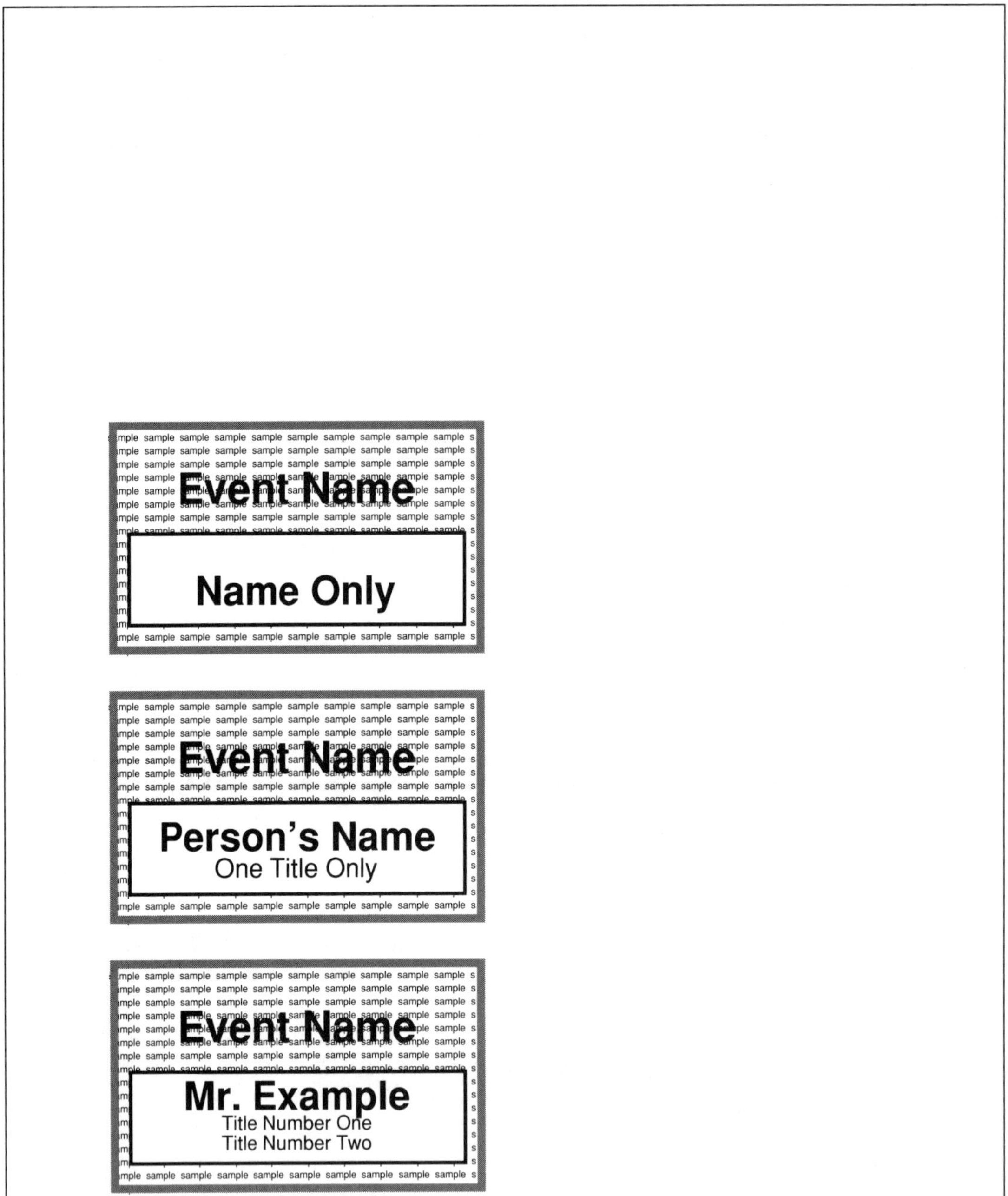

Figure 19.2: Printed Output of Version 3

5. Further Modifications

Several enhancements that might be made to the name tag drivers described in this chapter include:

- Adding a logo or other graphic PostScript procedures in the prologue to print on each name tag. Add additional code lines that write the required graphic procedures to the output file to the text processing procedures.
- Increasing the flexibility and adaptability of the program. The program can be modified to allow the user to define the page size and the size and layout of name tags on a page (two or three across, etc.). Another option is to let the user choose whether to have a title or background printing.
- These programs were not designed to have a particularly user-friendly interface. Verification of the user's entries and loops allowing the user to correct mistakes would be valuable. Procedures can be added to enhance the screen appearance of the program. This includes drawing boxes around prompts or displaying a program name on the top of each page.

Chapter 20
Label Driver in C

1. Introduction

This chapter describes a PostScript driver written in the C programming language which generates labels.[64] The C program allows you to specify labels' format. This provides flexibility, enabling this same program to be used without modification for a variety of label formats.

This program enables you to input the label format, the text to put on the labels, and the font to use for the label text. The label format can be created through a series of interactive questions with the user. The format is stored in a file and can be reused during subsequent executions of the program. The text for the labels can be entered interactively or stored in a file. Each label on the page may be different, as in address labels for each person on your address list, or they may be the same, as in a set of simple return address labels for yourself. In addition, each label can have a different background. This might be helpful printing labels for VCR tapes. You could enter a classification such as "Horror" or "Comedy" to use as the background for each label.

The objectives of this chapter are to show how code can be written That provides a flexible format definition and how to handle multiple input and output files.

[64] The initial concept and code for this chapter, as well as the supporting chapter materials, were developed by Bryan Sorrows.

2. Building the Label Driver

The code for the label driver that is discussed here is provided in Listing 20.3 at the end of this chapter. Sample PostScript code written by this program is included in Listing 20.1, and the output produced by the PostScript code is shown in Figure 20.1. The discussion of the program which follows is divided into three sections: Setup, User Interface, and PostScript Output.

Listing 20.1: Sample PostScript Output

```
%!PS-Adobe-3.0 EPSF-30.
%%BoundingBox: 0 0 612 792
%%Title: (Labels)
%%EndComments

/inch {72 mul} def

/center
  { dup stringwidth pop lw exch sub
    2 div cury ptsize sub moveto } def

/clipbox
  {
  0 0 moveto
  0 lh lineto
  lw lh lineto
  lw 0 lineto closepath clip
  } def

/background
  {/str exch def
   gsave
   120 45 {180 mul cos exch 180 mul cos add 2 div} setscreen
   .9 setgray
   0 ptsize 1.1 mul lh     % set y value every other line
     {
      /y exch def
      0 y sub str stringwidth  pop lw  % set x value
       {y moveto str show} for
     } for
  grestore
} def

/tb .5 inch def
/lb .125 inch def
/tm 1.5 inch def
/lw 2.75 inch def
/lh 2.75 inch def
/la 3 def
/ld 3 def
lb 11 inch tb sub translate
0 lh neg translate
gsave clipbox
/ptsize 10 def
```

```
/Helvetica-Oblique findfont ptsize scalefont setfont
( dbms ) background
/cury lh tm sub def
/ptsize 14 def
/Helvetica-Bold findfont ptsize scalefont setfont
(Database Backup)  center show
/cury cury ptsize 1.1 mul 1 mul sub def
/ptsize 12 def
/Helvetica findfont ptsize scalefont setfont
(Address DBMS)  center show
/cury cury ptsize 1.1 mul 1 mul sub def
/ptsize 12 def
/Helvetica findfont ptsize scalefont setfont
(Date: 11/30/91)  center show
/cury cury ptsize 1.1 mul 1 mul sub def
/ptsize 12 def
/Helvetica findfont ptsize scalefont setfont
(Disk #1)  center show
/cury cury ptsize 1.1 mul 1 mul sub def
grestore
0 lh neg translate
gsave clipbox
/ptsize 10 def
/Helvetica findfont ptsize scalefont setfont
( programming ) background
/cury lh tm sub def
/ptsize 14 def
/Helvetica-Bold findfont ptsize scalefont setfont
(PostScript Programming)  center show
/cury cury ptsize 1.1 mul 1 mul sub def
/ptsize 14 def
/Helvetica findfont ptsize scalefont setfont
(Driver Programs)  center show
/cury cury ptsize 1.1 mul 1 mul sub def
/ptsize 12 def
/Helvetica findfont ptsize scalefont setfont
(C and Pascal)  center show
/cury cury ptsize 1.1 mul 1 mul sub def
/ptsize 12 def
/Helvetica findfont ptsize scalefont setfont
(Fall Term, 1991)  center show
/cury cury ptsize 1.1 mul 1 mul sub def
grestore
0 lh neg translate
gsave clipbox
/ptsize 9 def
/Helvetica-Oblique findfont ptsize scalefont setfont
( word processing ) background
/cury lh tm sub def
/ptsize 16 def
/Helvetica-Bold findfont ptsize scalefont setfont
(Papers) .5 inch cury ptsize sub moveto show
/cury cury ptsize 1.1 mul 1 mul sub def
/ptsize 12 def
/Helvetica findfont ptsize scalefont setfont
(Interactive Systems Class) .5 inch cury ptsize sub moveto show
/cury cury ptsize 1.1 mul 1 mul sub def
```

```
/ptsize 12 def
/Helvetica findfont ptsize scalefont setfont
(Document Processing Class) .5 inch cury ptsize sub moveto show
/cury cury ptsize 1.1 mul 1 mul sub def
/ptsize 12 def
/Helvetica findfont ptsize scalefont setfont
(Interactive Graphics Class) .5 inch cury ptsize sub moveto show
/cury cury ptsize 1.1 mul 1 mul sub def
grestore
lw lh ld mul translate
0 lh neg translate
gsave clipbox
/ptsize 10 def
/Helvetica findfont ptsize scalefont setfont
( programming ) background
/cury lh tm sub def
/ptsize 16 def
/Helvetica-Bold findfont ptsize scalefont setfont
(C Programming Class)  center show
/cury cury ptsize 1.1 mul 1 mul sub def
/ptsize 12 def
/Helvetica findfont ptsize scalefont setfont
(C w/ Imbedded SQL)  center show
/cury cury ptsize 1.1 mul 1 mul sub def
grestore
0 lh neg translate
gsave clipbox
/ptsize 10 def
/Helvetica-Oblique findfont ptsize scalefont setfont
( dbms ) background
/cury lh tm sub def
/ptsize 16 def
/Times-Roman findfont ptsize scalefont setfont
(Database Files)  center show
/cury cury ptsize 1.1 mul 1 mul sub def
/ptsize 14 def
/Times-Roman findfont ptsize scalefont setfont
(Accounting)  center show
/cury cury ptsize 1.1 mul 1 mul sub def
grestore
0 lh neg translate
gsave clipbox
/ptsize 12 def
/Times-Roman findfont ptsize scalefont setfont
( demos ) background
/cury lh tm sub def
/ptsize 16 def
/Times-Roman findfont ptsize scalefont setfont
(Demonstration Files)  center show
/cury cury ptsize 1.1 mul 1 mul sub def
/ptsize 12 def
/Times-Roman findfont ptsize scalefont setfont
(Squares in Motion) .5 inch cury ptsize sub moveto show
/cury cury ptsize 1.1 mul 1 mul sub def
/ptsize 12 def
/Times-Roman findfont ptsize scalefont setfont
(Star Chart) .5 inch cury ptsize sub moveto show
```

```
/cury cury ptsize 1.1 mul 1 mul sub def
/ptsize 12 def
/Times-Roman findfont ptsize scalefont setfont
(Bouncing Ball) .5 inch cury ptsize sub moveto show
/cury cury ptsize 1.1 mul 1 mul sub def
/ptsize 12 def
/Times-Roman findfont ptsize scalefont setfont
(Label Maker) .5 inch cury ptsize sub moveto show
/cury cury ptsize 1.1 mul 1 mul sub def
grestore
lw lh ld mul translate
showpage
%%EOF
```

3. Setup Functions

There are several setup functions for this program. These include using a PostScript prologue file, creating the label formats, and determining whether the label text is entered interactively or from a file.

This program uses a separate file to store the PostScript prologue information, including the PS-Adobe version number and bounding box, and PostScript procedure definitions for procedures used throughout the label program. The prologue file is included in Listing 20.2. Having a prologue hard-coded into the program greatly increases the size of the program code; this is why that option is not used in this example. In addition, having the prologue in a separate text file enables you to modify character encodings and shading without changing and recompiling the program. This program simply copies all the prologue from one file, **LABEL_C1.PSP** into the beginning of any output file it generates. Many PostScript drivers would code the prologue into the driver code. This has many benefits, such as always keeping the program version the same as the prologue version, not needing to keep track of two files, etc. In addition, some of the comments in the prologue, such as **CreationDate** and **Title** could be generated by the program.

Listing 20.2: Prologue File

```
!PS-Adobe-3.0 EPSF-30.
%%BoundingBox: 0 0 612 792
%%Title: (Labels)
%%EndComments

/inch {72 mul} def

/Times-Roman findfont
 dup length dict begin
 {1 index /FID ne {def} {pop pop} ifelse} forall
```

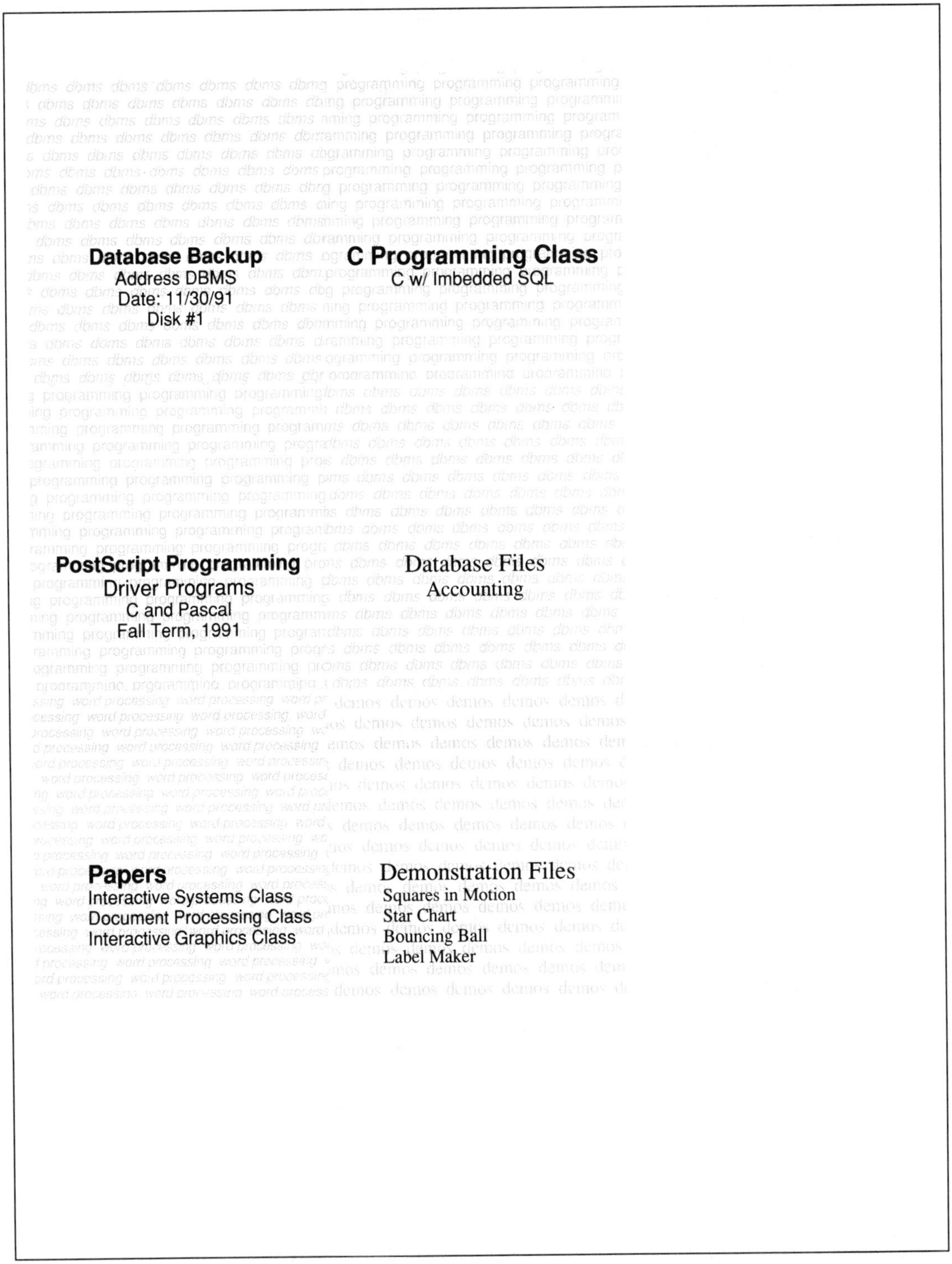
Database Backup
Address DBMS
Date: 11/30/91
Disk #1
C Programming Class
C w/ Imbedded SQL
PostScript Programming
Driver Programs
C and Pascal
Fall Term, 1991
Database Files
Accounting
Papers
Interactive Systems Class
Document Processing Class
Interactive Graphics Class
Demonstration Files
Squares in Motion
Star Chart
Bouncing Ball
Label Maker

Figure 20.1: Sample Diskette Labels

```
  /Encoding ISOLatin1Encoding def
  currentdict end
  /Times-Roman-ISOLatin1 exch definefont pop

/center
  { dup stringwidth pop lw exch sub
    2 div cury ptsize sub moveto } def

/clipbox
  {
  0 0 moveto
  0 lh lineto
  lw lh lineto
  lw 0 lineto closepath clip
  } def

/background
  {gsave
%  0 0 moveto
%  0 lh lineto
%  lw lh lineto
%  lw 0 lineto closepath clip
   120 45 {180 mul cos exch 180 mul cos add 2 div} setscreen
   .9 setgray
   0 ptsize 1.1 mul 2 mul lh      % set y value every other line
     {
     exch dup 3 1 roll            % make a new copy of string
     0 exch stringwidth pop lw    % set x value
       {exch dup 4 1 roll moveto dup show exch } for
     ptsize 1.1 mul add           % set y value for next line
     exch dup 3 1 roll
     dup stringwidth pop 2 div neg exch stringwidth pop lw
        {exch dup 4 1 roll moveto dup show exch } for
     pop
     } for
   grestore} def
```

The **get_format** function determines the format of the label page. You are prompted for the file name for the label format. If the file exists, it is opened, and the structure called "format" is loaded with the format information. If the file does not exist, you are prompted for each necessary parameters. Then the format is then written out to a file so it can be used again. The format information includes the size of the top and left borders, the top margin, the label width and height, and the number of labels across and down on a page. Each size is stored as inches. Once the label format has been read in, a series of **printf** statements are used to write PostScript definitions containing the information to the output file. Because all the math related to the formatting is done in PostScript and not C, it is not necessary to convert the format variable values into floating points; they will just be output as text to the PostScript file.

After the label formats have been defined, the **do_labels** function is called, and it obtains the final setup information for the program. You are is prompted to enter the name of a file containing the text for the labels or to press return to enter text interactively. If the text is be entered from a file, you are prompted to enter the background text and its point size once, to be used for all labels. Then, prompted for whether the labels are all alike.

4. User Interface

The heart of the **do_labels** function is the **while** loop based on the **lines_text** boolean. This variable is set to the value of the **get_user_text** function if the label text is being entered interactively or by the **get_file_text** function if the label text is being read from a file. The loop is performed for each page of labels that is generated. The labels are printed starting at the top left of the page, so this **while** loop starts by writing the translate command to position the axis at the upper left of the page to the output file. The values of the left and top borders are used to determine the appropriate position for the **translate** command.

Within this section are two nested **while** loops which produce the proper number of labels across and down the page. The code to print the label is generated and output by the **print_label** function. If there is text for another label after **print_label**, a **translate** command is written to translate the origin appropriately for the next label, the loop counter is set, and the loops continue.

The text for each label is read using the **get_file_text** or **get_user_text** function, depending on whether you have selected interactive entry. The **get_file_text** function reads in the lines of text for one label. The text is read in character by character. Carriage returns and line feeds are ignored, and each character for the text is added to the **label.text_line.text** array. A comma indicates the end of text string for a line, and a semicolon indicates the end of text for a label. This same function was also used in the C nametag driver program.

The **get_user_text** function is used to get the text for a label if selected interactive entry. This function has two large sections. The first section determines information for the background on the label, and the second section determines information for the main text for the label.

The first section of **get_user_text** asks you for the background text, the font, and the point size to use for the background text. The possible font choices are stored in the **fonts** array; you select them from a simple numeric menu. The text, font, and point size to use are stored in the **label** structure. You are prompted to enter the background information for each label until you indicates the information entered should be used for all remaining labels.

The second section of **get_user_text** is a large **while** loop that gets information for the main text of the label. Inside the loop, you are prompted to enter a line of text for the label. The while loop continues until the **finished** boolean is set to true, which occurs when you enter a null string when prompted for a line of text. Once a line of text is read in, you are asked to enter information about formatting the line. This formatting information includes the font and point size for the text and whether the line should be centered on the label. You are prompted to enter this information for each line of each label until you indicates the formatting information entered should be used for all remaining labels.

5. PostScript Output

When label text has been obtained from either the **get_file_text** or **get_user_text** functions, the **print_label** function writes PostScript code to the output file using the label text, background, and formatting information. A **gsave** is used to save the graphics state stack so it can be recovered after defining a clipping region using **clipbox**. The **clipbox** procedure is defined in the prologue file and define a clipping region so that the label print procedure defines cannot interfere with other labels. The **print_label** function is called for each label, so once a label is printed, the graphics state stack is restored.

The font and point size are set according to the background information, and then the background text is written out. A **for** loop is then used to write out the formatting and text information for each line of text that was entered for the label. The **cury** PostScript variable keeps track of the current Y value to use for positioning the text.

6. Summary

The driver explained in this section could be used for a variety of purposes. A great deal of flexibility is included throughout enabling you to define the labels' format. In addition, the ability to enter label text either interactively or from a file means that this drive can be used for large, repeated jobs just as easily as for small one-time jobs. A prologue file simplifies the driver itself but may introduce problems such as remembering to update it.

7. Program Enhancements

It is easy to imagine giving the user a graphical environment to specify the labels' format. If the user is given the picture of a page on the screen for each parameter of the format, he could drag a line to the dimension that he needs. Programming this kind of interface, although not difficult, is outside the scope of this book and likely would be more device- and compiler-dependent than character-based code.

There are many possible error-checking features that can be added to make this a more user-friendly and robust program. Because that is not the focus of this book, these are left for you to implement. For example, the numeric input allows more than one period and does not check for incorrect negative values.

Allowing the user to modify items from the parameter file also makes the program more useful. Often, the user needs to experiment with format settings to get the output to line up correctly on the label. If the user can make small changes to an existing format file, this process is much easier.

The default values for font and point size are encoded in the program. These values can be stored in a file similar to the format file or with the format file.

8. Possible Errors

There are many things that can go wrong when writing a driver. Of course, there are still the possible PostScript errors; for example, the **bind** operator should not be used for simple lookup definitions, as discovered when writing this program.

In addition, there are errors that may arise due to how the driver program is written and designed. For example when using a prologue file, you need to be sure you do not copy the EOF marker from the prologue file into the PostScript output file.

9. Complete Listing of the Driver

Listing 20.3: Label Driver in C

```
#include <stdio.h>
#include <conio.h>
#include <graph.h>
#define TRUE  1
#define FALSE 0
#define MAXLINE 5      /* number of lines per label */
#define MAXFONT 10     /* number of font choices */


struct format_rec { char format_name[30];
                    char top_bdr[10];
                    char left_bdr[10];
                    char top_margin[10];
                    char lab_width[10];
                    char lab_height[10];
                    int lab_across;
                    int lab_down; } format;

struct text_rec  { char text[80];
                   char font[80];
                   int ptsize;
                   int center; };

struct label_rec { char bkgrnd[80];
                   char bkgrnd_fnt[80];
                   int bkgrnd_ptsize;
                   char spaced[10];
                   struct text_rec text_line[MAXLINE];} label=
                   {"","Times-Roman",18,2};

struct text_rec text_init=
              {"","Times-Roman",10,"1"};


char fonts[MAXFONT][60] =
         {{"Helvetica"},
          {"Helvetica-Bold"},
          {"Helvetica-Oblique"},
          {"Times-Roman"},
          {"Times-Roman-ISOLatin1"},
          {"?"}};


FILE *opfp;  /* PostScipt output file pointer */
FILE *ifpt;  /* pointer to file containing text for labels*/
int done_background=FALSE;
int done_lineinfo=FALSE;


/*============================================================
  Function main();
  ============================================================*/

main()
```

```
  {
  char ch='%';
  FILE *plfp; /* prologue file pointer */
  char opfn[30];   /* postscript output file name */

  printf("This program will produce a postcript output file for\n");
  printf("   printing labels.\n\n");
  do
    {
    printf("\nEnter the output file name: ");
    }
  while (!getstr(opfn,1));
  opfp = fopen(opfn,"w");
  if ((plfp=fopen("labl_c1.psp","r")) != NULL)
    {
    while (!feof(plfp)) {fputc(ch,opfp);
                        ch=fgetc(plfp);}
    fclose(plfp);
    }
  else
    {
    printf("PostScript prologue file LABL_C1.PSP not found\n");
    exit(0);
    }
  get_format();
  do_labels();
  fprintf(opfp,"%%EOF\n");
  fclose(opfp);
  }

/*=============================================================
   function get_format();  Expects nothing; Returns nothing;
   Either retrieves stored setup information from a file, or if none,
      creates a stored setup file.
  =============================================================*/
get_format()
  {
  char fmtfn[30];
  FILE *fmtfp;
  do
    {
    printf("\nEnter file name for format of labels: ");
    }
  while (!getstr(fmtfn,1));
  if ((fmtfp=fopen(fmtfn,"rb")) == NULL)
    {           /* create format file */
    fmtfp=fopen(fmtfn,"wb");
    do
      {printf("\nEnter a description of the format: ");}
    while (!getstr(format.format_name,0));
    do
      {printf("\nEnter number of inches for top border: ");}
    while (!getstr(format.top_bdr,2));
    do
      {printf("\n                           left border: ");}
    while (!getstr(format.left_bdr,2));
    do
```

```
      {printf("\n                              top margin of each label: ");}
    while (!getstr(format.top_margin,2));
    do
      {printf("\n                              label width: ");}
    while (!getstr(format.lab_width,2));
    do
      {printf("\n                              label height: ");}
    while (!getstr(format.lab_height,2));
    printf("\nEnter the number of labels to print across the page: ");
    scanf("%d",&format.lab_across);
    printf("\n                                   down the page: ");
    scanf("%d",&format.lab_down);
    fwrite(&format,sizeof(format),1,fmtfp);
    } /* if there is not a format file */
  else
    {            /* read in rec from format file */
    if (!feof(fmtfp)) fread(&format,sizeof(format),1,fmtfp);
    printf("\nFormat set for %s\n",format.format_name);
    }
  fclose(fmtfp);
  fprintf(opfp,"/tb %s inch def\n",format.top_bdr);
  fprintf(opfp,"/lb %s inch def\n",format.left_bdr);
  fprintf(opfp,"/tm %s inch def\n",format.top_margin);
  fprintf(opfp,"/lw %s inch def\n",format.lab_width);
  fprintf(opfp,"/lh %s inch def\n",format.lab_height);
  fprintf(opfp,"/la %d def\n",format.lab_across);
  fprintf(opfp,"/ld %d def\n",format.lab_down);
  }

/*================================================================
  Function getstr: accepts input from user for a string;
       strtype = 1 if the string is a filename,
       strtype = 2 if getting float number, otherwise, 0.
  Returns: number of characters in string;
  ==============================================================*/
int getstr(instring, strtype)
char instring[];
int strtype;
{
  char c;
  int j=0;
  while((c=getch()) != 13)           /* 13 = Carriage Return */
    {
    if((c==0)&&(kbhit))
      {
      c=getch();
      continue;
      }
    if((c==8)&&(j>0))                /* 8 = backspace */
      {
      j--;
      putch(8);
      putch(' ');
      putch(8);
      }
    switch (strtype)
      {
```

```
      case 1:
        if ((isalnum(c)) ||
              (c==46) ||               /* 46 = period */
              (c==95) ||               /* 95 = underscore */
              (c==92) ||               /* 92 = backslash */
              (c==58))                 /* 58 = colon */
          {
          putch(c);
          instring[j++]=c;
          }
        break;
      case 2:
        if ((isdigit(c)) ||
             (c=='.'))
          {
          putch(c);
          instring[j++]=c;
          }
        break;
      default:
        if (c != 8)
          {
          putch(c);
          instring[j++] = c;
          }
      } /* case */
    }
  instring[j]='\0';
  return(j);
}


/*=============================================================
  Function do_labels(); Expects nothing,  Returns nothing;
  Contains loops for printing all labels.
  ============================================================*/
do_labels()
  {
  char ch;
  int i=0,j=0;
  int lines_text=FALSE;
  int finished=FALSE;
  int all_same=FALSE;
  int interactive=FALSE;
  char ifn[40];

  for (i=0;i<MAXLINE;i++)
    label.text_line[i] = text_init;

  printf("\n\nEnter file name for label text (<CR> for interactive) ");
  getstr(ifn,1);
  if ((ifpt=fopen(ifn,"r")) == NULL)
    interactive = TRUE;
  else
    {
    printf("\nPlease enter background for all labels: ");
    if (getstr(label.bkgrnd,0))
```

```
      {
      printf("\nEnter point size for background: ");
      scanf("%d",&label.bkgrnd_ptsize);
      }
    printf("Enter line spacing for label: ");
    getstr(label.spaced,2);
    }

  printf("\n\nWill all of the labels be the same? (Y/N) ");
  ch = getche();
  if ((ch=='Y') || (ch == 'y')) all_same = TRUE;
  if (interactive) lines_text = get_user_text();
  else lines_text = get_file_text();
  while (lines_text)
    {
    fprintf(opfp,"lb 11 inch tb sub translate \n");
    i=0;j=0;
    while ((lines_text) && (i < format.lab_across))
      {
      while ((lines_text) && (j < format.lab_down))
        {
        print_label(lines_text);
        if (!all_same)
          {
          if (interactive) lines_text = get_user_text();
          else lines_text = get_file_text();
          }
        j++;
        } /* each row  */
      i++;
      j=0;
      fprintf(opfp,"lw lh ld mul translate\n");
      }  /* each column */
    printf("\nOne page of labels will be generated...\n");
    fprintf(opfp,"showpage\n");
    if (all_same) lines_text = FALSE;
    else
      if (lines_text > 0)
      {
      if (interactive) lines_text = get_user_text();
      else lines_text = get_file_text();
      }
    } /*lines_text*/
  fclose(ifpt);
  }

/*==============================================================
  Function print_label;  Prints info in global structure label.  This
  produces one label.
  ==============================================================*/
print_label(int lines_text)
  {
  int i;
  fprintf(opfp,"0 lh neg translate\n");
  fprintf(opfp,"gsave clipbox\n");
  fprintf(opfp,"/ptsize %d def\n",label.bkgrnd_ptsize);
  fprintf(opfp,"/%s findfont ptsize scalefont setfont\n",label.bkgrnd_fnt);
```

```
  fprintf(opfp,"( %s ) background\n",label.bkgrnd);
  fprintf(opfp,"/cury lh tm sub def\n");
  for (i=0;i<lines_text;i++)
    {
    fprintf(opfp,"/ptsize %d def\n",
                 label.text_line[i].ptsize);
    fprintf(opfp,"/%s findfont ptsize scalefont setfont\n",
                 label.text_line[i].font);
    fprintf(opfp,"(%s) ",label.text_line[i].text);
    if (label.text_line[i].center)
       fprintf(opfp," center show\n");
    else
      fprintf(opfp,".5 inch cury ptsize sub moveto show\n");
    fprintf(opfp,"/cury cury ptsize 1.1 mul %s mul sub def\n",
                label.spaced);  /* double space */
    }
  fprintf(opfp,"grestore\n");
  }

/*============================================================
  Function get_user_text()  Returns number of lines user entered.
  ============================================================*/

int get_user_text()
  {
  int i=0;
  int j=0;
  int k=0;
  int finished = FALSE;
  char tmp[80];
  char ch;

  if(!done_background)
    {
    printf("\n\nEnter background (default: %s) ",label.bkgrnd);
    if (getstr(tmp,0)) strcpy(label.bkgrnd,tmp);
    while ((fonts[i][0]!='?') && (i<MAXFONT))
      {printf("\n         %d  %s",i+1,fonts[i]);i++;}
    do
      {
      printf("\nChoose font: ");
      scanf("%d",&k);
      }
    while ((k<1)||(k>i));
    strcpy(label.bkgrnd_fnt,fonts[k-1]);
    printf("\nEnter point size for background: ");
    scanf("%d",&label.bkgrnd_ptsize);
    printf("\nEnter line spacing for label: ");
    getstr(label.spaced,2);
    printf("\nIs this the last time to change the background? (Y/N) ");
    ch = getche();
    if ((ch=='Y')||(ch=='y')) done_background=TRUE;
    }

  j=0;
  while ((!finished) && (j<MAXLINE))
    {
```

```
    printf("\n\nEnter line %d: ",j+1);
    if (!getstr(label.text_line[j].text,0)) finished = TRUE;
    else
      {
      if (!done_lineinfo)
        {
        i=0;
        while ((fonts[i][0]!='?') && (i<MAXFONT))
          {printf("\n        %d  %s",i+1,fonts[i]);i++;}
        do
          {
          printf("\nChoose font: ");
          scanf("%d",&k);
          }
        while ((k<1)||(k>i));
        strcpy(label.text_line[j].font,fonts[k-1]);
        printf("\nEnter point size for text: ");
        scanf("%d",&label.text_line[j].ptsize);
        printf("\nShould this line be centered? (Y/N) ");
        ch = getche();
        if ((ch=='y')||(ch=='Y')) label.text_line[j].center = TRUE;
        else label.text_line[j].center=FALSE;
        }
      j++;
      }
    }
  if (!done_lineinfo)
    {
    printf("\nIs this the last time to change the text font info? (Y/N) ");
    ch = getche();
    if ((ch=='Y')||(ch=='y')) done_lineinfo=TRUE;
    }
  return(j);
  }

/*============================================================
  Function get_file_text:
  Returns: 0 if end of file reached before end of label text;
           otherwise, returns number of text lines read in.
  ============================================================*/
int get_file_text()
  {
  char c;
  int finished=FALSE;
  int j=0;
  int i=0;

  while (! finished)
    {
    if (! feof(ifpt))
      {
      c = fgetc(ifpt);
      switch (c)
        {
        case 13: break;         /* ignore CR when reading file */
        case 10: break;         /* ignore LF when reading file */
        case ';':
```

```
          label.text_line[i++].text[j] = 0;
          finished = TRUE;
          break;
        case ',':
          label.text_line[i++].text[j] = 0;
          j=0;
          if (i>=MAXLINE) finished=TRUE;
          break;
        default:
          label.text_line[i].text[j++] = c;
          break;
        }
      }
    else
      {
      finished = TRUE;
      }
    }
  if (feof(ifpt)) return(0);
  else return(i);
  }
```

Part 4
Command Reference

The programs in the book use a subset of the PostScript operators. This last part of the book takes a look at these operators. The commands are grouped here by their functional type. You are encouraged to look at other commands in the group whenever you come here. To access a particular command, the easiest method is to use the index.

Chapter 21
Operator Reference

It is common to classify PostScript operators based on the types of objects they accept as operands or values they return. This chapter describes the various classes of operators and provides descriptions of the operators that are used frequently in the programs in this book. Some operators fall into more than one category; array operators for example, may also be string or control operators, because procedures and strings are forms of packed arrays. Here is a list the of operators that appear in this chapter:

- add, see page 403.
- and, see page 407.
- arc, see page 391.
- arcto, see page 392.
- array, see page 414.
- begin, see page 411.
- bind, see page 412.
- clip, see page 392.
- closepath, see page 393.
- currentpoint, see page 421.
- curveto, see page 393.
- cvi, see page 424.
- cvr, see page 424.
- cvs, see page 425.
- def, see page 413.
- definefont, see page 396.
- dict, see page 413.
- div, see page 404.
- dup, see page 400.
- end, see page 414.
- eq, see page 407.
- exch, see page 401.
- exit, see page 416.
- fill, see page 400.
- findfont, see page 397.

- floor, see page 404.
- for, see page 417.
- forall, see page 418.
- ge, see page 408.
- get, see page 414.
- grestore, see page 421.
- gsave, see page 421.
- gt, see page 408.
- idiv, see page 404.
- if, see page 416.
- ifelse, see page 417.
- index, see page 401.
- kshow, see page 397.
- le, see page 409.
- length, see page 415.
- lineto, see page 394.
- loop, see page 418.
- lt, see page 409.
- mod, see page 405.
- moveto, see page 394.
- mul, see page 405.
- ne, see page 410.
- neg, see page 406.
- newpath, see page 394.
- not, see page 410.
- or, see page 411.
- pop, see page 402.
- put, see page 415.
- repeat, see page 418.
- rlineto, see page 395.
- rmoveto, see page 395.
- roll, see page 402.
- rotate, see page 419.
- scale, see page 419.
- scalefont, see page 398.
- setdash, see page 422.
- setfont, see page 398.
- setgray, see page 422.
- setlinecap, see page 423.
- setlinewidth, see page 423.
- show, see page 399.
- showpage, see page 425.
- string, see page 399.
- stringwidth, see page 399.
- stroke, see page 400.
- sub, see page 406.
- translate, see page 420.

1. Path Operators

Formally, a path is a mathematical equation which represents the shape of a graphic object. Paths are stored in special data structures to which PostScript programmers have no direct access. However, the name "path" suggests an informal model, an invisible trail which defines the outline of whatever is drawn on the page. The path operators lay down those invisible marks.

arc

Description: This operator expects five arguments on the stack, consisting of two coordinate values, a distance specification, and two angle values. They are removed and the current point and current path are altered according to the following interpretation of the arguments to create a line segment and a circular arc in the user space. Note any scaling transformations alter the shape that is imaged in device space, possibly causing a non-circular shape. The first and second coordinate values are X and Y offsets, respectively, relative to the current origin of the user space that represents the center of the arc. The arc has a radius equal to the distance specification. The arc starts at an angle equal to the first angle value in degrees counterclockwise from the positive X axis and ends at an angle equal to the second angle value, also in degrees counterclockwise from the positive X axis. After the **arc** operator command, the current point is equal to the arc's endpoint. The current path is the aforementioned arc if the current point is undefined or is equal to the arc's starting point. If the current point is defined and is different from the arcs starting point, a straight line segment is appended to the current path before the aforementioned arc is appended to the current path. The line segment starts at the value of the current point at the start of the **arc** operator command and terminates at the start arc's point.

Arguments: $\mathbf{real_1}$ $\mathbf{real_2}$ $\mathbf{real_3}$ $\mathbf{real_4}$ $\mathbf{real_5}$

$\mathbf{real_1}$ and $\mathbf{real_2}$ are the X and Y coordinates relative to the origin of the user space that specify the center of the arc. $\mathbf{real_3}$ represents the distance in user space units from the X and Y coordinate values represented by $\mathbf{real_1}$ and $\mathbf{real_2}$. $\mathbf{real_4}$ and $\mathbf{real_5}$ are the angles relative to the positive X axis of the user space that specify the arc's start and end points.

Results: `none`

<u>**Examples**</u>

Ex. 1. `0 0 100 0 90 arc =>`

If you assume the current point is undefined, this creates the top right quadrant of a quarter circle with a radius of 100 units, leaving the current path equal to the arc and the current point as (0, 100).

arcto

Description: This operator expects five arguments on the stack: four coordinate values representing two X,Y points and a distance specification representing the radius of a circle. The two points (together with the **current point**) represent a pair of intersecting line segments, each of which is tangential to a circle of the specified radius. The five arguments are removed and four coordinate values representing beginning and ending points of the the arc are placed on the stack. Also, an arc and, optionally, a straight line segment are appended to the current path. The arc starts at **(**$\mathbf{num_1}$**,** $\mathbf{num_2}$**)** and follows the circle's circumference between the two points of tangent, ending at **(**$\mathbf{num_3}$**,** $\mathbf{num_4}$**)**. If the current point is different from the first tangent point, a straight line is added to the current path from the current point to the first tangent point **(**$\mathbf{num_1}$**,** $\mathbf{num_2}$**)** before the arc segment is added. After the arc segment is added, the **currentpoint** is always **(**$\mathbf{num_3}$**,** $\mathbf{num_4}$**)**.

Arguments: $\mathbf{num_1}$ $\mathbf{num_2}$ $\mathbf{num_3}$ $\mathbf{num_4}$ $\mathbf{num_5}$

The **currentpoint** *must be defined.* The arguments must be of type integer or real. The **currentpoint** represents the start of the first tangent line and **(**$\mathbf{num_1}$**,** $\mathbf{num_2}$**)** specify the end of the first tangent line. If **currentpoint** is undefined, a "nocurrentpoint" error is generated. Likewise, **(**$\mathbf{num_1}$**,** $\mathbf{num_2}$**)** specifies the second tangent line's start point, and **(**$\mathbf{num_3}$**,** $\mathbf{num_4}$**)** specifies the end point of the second tangent line. Finally, $\mathbf{num_5}$ specifies the radius of the circle in user space units. As with the **arc** operator, if scaling is specified, the shape represented in device space may not be circular.

Results: $\mathbf{real_1}$ $\mathbf{real_2}$ $\mathbf{real_3}$ $\mathbf{real_4}$

The **arcto** operator alters the **currentpath** and **currentpoint** as indicated in the description section and leaves the X and Y coordinates of the two tangent points on the stack.

Examples

Ex. 1. `20 10 20 20 5 arcto =>`

If you assume the current point is (10,10), this operation creates a line segment and an arc with a 5-unit radius. The start of the arc is at (20,10) and the end is at (20, 20). The arc appends to the line segment from (10,10) to (20,10). The example leaves the current point as (20, 20). Also, it leaves the tangent line points as (15,10) and (20,15) on the stack.

clip

Description: This operator does not take any arguments or push any results onto the stack. However, it does alter the current path: **clip** operator takes the area of the user space considered to be inside the current path (as determined by the nonzero winding rule) and the area considered to be inside the current clipping path (as determined by the winding rule in use at the time of the clipping path's creation). It then returns a new path that, generally, is the intersection of both of these areas. It is not possible to enlarge the clipping path unless the **initclip** or **initgraphics** operators are called, both of which reset the clipping region to its initial value.

Arguments: `none`

Results: `none`

closepath Description: This operator does not use any arguments or push any results onto the stack. It is intended to provide an easy way to append a straight line segment to the current path from the current point to the point that represents the start of the current subpath. (This is especially helpful when drawing Bézier curves and arcs, where the required line segment can be tedious to calculate.)

Arguments: `none`

Results: `none`

Note that **closepath** operator terminates the current subpath. Any operator that appends to the current path begins a new subpath. If the current subpath is already closed or the current path is empty, **closepath** operator does nothing.

curveto Description: This operator expects six numbers on the stack and uses them to create a Bézier curve. The arguments are removed from the stack and no objects are pushed onto the stack. If **currentpoint** is undefined when this operator is executed, a "nocurrentpoint" error results.

Arguments: num_1 num_2 num_3 num_4 num_5 num_6

num_1 through num_6 may be either integer or real number objects and represent three pairs of (X,Y) points. **currentpoint** fulfills the requirement for the fourth pair of points. The entire curve is contained within the user space box defined by the four pairs of points. The start of the Bézier curve is the **currentpoint** and the end of the curve is the point indicated by the third pair of arguments, (num_5, num_6). Points (num_1, num_2) and (num_3, num_4) provide input for geometric modifications to the curve, as defined by the following pair of parametric cubic equations: $\mathbf{x(t) = a_x t^3 + b_x t^2 + c_x t + x_0}$ and $\mathbf{y(t) = a_y t^3 + b_y t^2 + c_y t + y_0}$.

Results: `none`

<u>**Examples**</u>

Ex. 1. `23 34 89 76 231 123` **curveto** `=>`

Assuming a current point of (10, 10), this example draws a Bézier curve with a starting point of (10, 10) and an ending point of (231, 123). The curve resembles a shifted parabola.

lineto

Description: This operator appends a straight line segment to the current path from the current point to the point indicated by the two numbers popped off the stack.

Arguments: **num$_1$, num$_2$**

num$_1$ and **num$_2$** may be either integers or real number objects, where **num$_1$** represents the X coordinate and **num$_2$** represents the Y coordinate. Lack of a current point generates "nocurrentpoint" error.

Results: **none**

Examples

Ex. 1. **4 123 lineto =>**

A line segment is appended to the current path from the current point to (4, 123).

moveto

Description: This operator starts a new subpath of the current path. **Moveto** operator sets the current point in the graphics state to the user space coordinate (X,Y) without altering the current path. The (X,Y) coordinate is acquired by popping two number objects from the stack.

Arguments: **num$_1$, num$_2$**

num$_1$ and **num$_2$** may be either integers or real number objects, where **num$_1$** represents the X coordinate and **num$_2$** represents the Y coordinate. If the previous path operation was also a **moveto** operator or an **rmoveto** operator, then the previous point is deleted from the path and the point **num$_1$, num$_2$** replaces it.

Results: **none**

Examples

Ex. 1. **4 123 moveto =>**

The current point becomes (4, 123).

newpath

Description: This operator initializes the current path to be empty, causing the current point to be undefined.

Arguments: **none**

Results: **none**

Examples

Ex. 1. **newpath =>**

After the command is executed there is no path and the current point is undefined.

rlineto

Description: This operator appends a straight line segment to the current path from the current point to the point indicated by the two numbers popped off the stack. Unlike **lineto**, however, the two coordinates are interpreted in a relative manner from the (X,Y) of the current point as opposed to the absolute coordinates, with respect to the origin. Therefore, the line is constructed from the current point (X,Y) to a point relative to the current point by the amount specified in the arguments (X + $\mathbf{num_1}$, Y + $\mathbf{num_2}$). The new currentpoint is (X + $\mathbf{num_1}$, Y + $\mathbf{num_2}$).

Arguments: $\mathbf{num_1}$, $\mathbf{num_2}$

$\mathbf{num_1}$ and $\mathbf{num_2}$ may be either integers or real number objects, where $\mathbf{num_1}$ represents the X coordinate, and $\mathbf{num_2}$ represents the Y coordinate, with the aforementioned special interpretation. Lack of a current point generates "nocurrentpoint" error.

Results: **none**

Examples

Ex. 1. **4 123 rlineto =>**

A line segment appends to the current path from the current point to a new point which is four units to the right of the current point and 123 units up.

rmoveto

Description: This operator starts a new subpath of the current path. **rmoveto** sets the current point in the graphics state to the user space coordinate (X,Y) without altering the current path. The (X,Y) coordinate is acquired by popping two number objects from the stack. Unlike **moveto**, however, the two coordinates are interpreted in a relative manner from the (X,Y) of the current point as opposed to the absolute coordinates, with respect to the origin. Therefore, the new subpath is constructed at a point relative to the current point by the amount specified in the arguments (X + $\mathbf{num_1}$, Y + $\mathbf{num_2}$). The new current point is (X + $\mathbf{num_1}$, Y + $\mathbf{num_2}$). The original current point must be defined or a "nocurrentpoint" error results.

Arguments: $\mathbf{num_1}$, $\mathbf{num_2}$

$\mathbf{num_1}$ and $\mathbf{num_2}$ may be either integers or real number objects, where $\mathbf{num_1}$ represents the X coordinate and $\mathbf{num_2}$ represents the Y coordinate. If the previous path operation was also a **moveto** or an **rmoveto**, then the previous point is deleted from the path and the point $\mathbf{num_1}$, $\mathbf{num_2}$ replaces it.

Results: **none**

Examples

Ex. 1. **4 123 rmoveto =>**

The current point changes to a new point which is four units to the right and 123 units up from the previous current point.

2. Font and String Operators

This book considers font operators and string operators in the same class. Even though they are very different kinds of operators, they are used together to display text. The font operators can be considered a subclass of dictionary operators because they are mainly concerned with locating and manipulating a particular font dictionary and associating it with the current graphics state. The string operators are a specialized form of painting operator.

definefont Description: This operator registers a font dictionary **dict** as the object **key**, usually a name literal. **definefont** operator first checks to see if the dictionary is syntactically correct and can be properly loaded. If so, **definefont** creates an entry with a key **FID** and value of object **fontID**. An error is generated if the dictionary does not have the capacity to hold this value. The **key** value is then associated with **font** in the global **FontDirectory** font dictionary. The **findfont** operator is used to retrieve the font for use.

Arguments: **key font**

The name literal **key** is associated with the dictionary object **font** as specified, allowing **findfont** access to the specified dictionary. The **font** parameter must not have an existing FID associated with it.

Results: **font**

The **font** dictionary object is pushed back onto the stack.

Examples

Ex. 1.
```
/Helvetica findfont dup
length dict
begin
{1 index /FID ne
{def} {pop pop} ifelse} forall
currentdict
end
/hop exch definefont pop
```

This associates a name literal **hop** with the Helvetica font so in all later references, the font may use the name **/hop**. It works by taking a font on the operand stack, normally put there with a **findfont** operator. The font is duplicated, and the top copy is used to determine the length of the dictionary. The **dict** operator uses this number to create a new empty dictionary, which is moved to top of the dictionary stack by begin. This leaves the original copy of the font dictionary on the top of the operand stack. The procedure is pushed onto the stack, and the **forall** operator takes the procedure and the font dictionary off, executing the procedure for each key value pair in the dictionary. The **forall** procedure copies all entries for the font except the one whose key is /FID. When **forall** is done, currentdict takes the dictionary off the dictionary stack and puts it back on the operand stack. The operator **definefont** takes the font and the name literal **`/hop`** off the stack and associates /hop with the font.

findfont

Description: The **findfont** operator consumes a literal key from the top of the stack and returns the font dictionary **`font`** associated with **`key`** in the **`FontDirectory`**. If the font is not found, the action is implementation-dependent. The system may substitute a default font, attempt to search any disk files for the specified font, or it may generate an "invalidfont" error and refuse to continue. You may redefine **findfont** operator to implement different font-finding strategies.

Arguments: **`key`**

`key` is an object defining a font dictionary and can be obtained via a call to **definefont** operator. Fonts built into the output device are usually automatically enrolled into the **`FontDictionary`** and do not need to be registered via **definefont** operator.

Results: **`font`**

The **findfont** operator function returns a font dictionary **`font`** that is associated with the argument **`key`** in the **`FontDirectory`**.

Examples

Ex. 1. **`/Helvetica`** **findfont** => `FONT(HELVETICA,1)`

The given **`key`** /Helvetica is used to obtain the **`font`**. **findfont** operator uses **`key`** to consult the **`FontDictionary`** and returns the associated value, a font dictionary object.

kshow

Description: The term kshow is derived from kern-show and is designed to allow for easy kerning, or adjusting the inter-letter space. The **kshow** operator takes a procedure and a string off the stack and begins by reading the character codes in the string. It shows the first character code at the current point, updating the current point by the first character code width. It then pushes the character codes for the first and second characters onto the operand stack as integers and executes **`proc`**, which may perform any action but typically modifies the current point to affect the subsequent placement of the next character in the string. Basically, **kshow** operator checks for certain pairs of characters. For example, if a *T* were followed by an *o*, the *o* is kerned, or moved closer, to the *T* to give an authentic appearance.

Arguments: **proc string**

Results: **none**

Examples

Ex. 1. `{pop pop showpage 72 72 moveto} (Waste) kshow =>`

The procedure removes the character codes pushed on by **kshow** operator from the stack. It then ejects the current page and moves to a point near the lower left corner of the new current page. Each character in the string "Waste of Paper" is printed on a separate page.

scalefont

Description: This operator expects a number and a font on the stack. They are popped and the **font** is scaled according to **num**.

Arguments: **font, num**

The **font** is scaled from the original 1-unit character coordinate space by the amount **num** specifies in both the X and Y dimensions.

Results: **font**

The **scalefont** function returns a font properly scaled in the X and Y dimensions according to the **num** argument.

Examples

Ex. 1. `/Helvetica findfont`
`12 scalefont => FONT(HELVETICA,12)`

This example obtains the standard Helvetica font, which is defined with a 1-unit line height, and scales it by a factor of 12 in both the X and Y dimensions. This produces a 12-unit high font (i.e. a 12-point font in the default user space).

setfont

Description: This operator expects a font on the stack. It pops **font** off the stack and sets the font dictionary parameter in the graphics state to **font**.

Arguments: **font**

The **font** is used to inform the graphics state of the font to use.

Results: **none**

Examples

Ex. 1. `/Helvetica findfont 12 scalefont setfont =>`

This example obtains the standard Helvetica font, which is defined with a 1-unit line height, and scales it by a factor of 12 in both the X and Y dimensions. This produces a 12-unit high font (i.e. a 12-point font in the default user space).

show Description: This operator pops a string off the stack and displays it at the current point using the current typeface, font size, and orientation as set in the current graphics world.

Arguments: `string`

Character spacing is determined by the character's width, which is part of the font definition. The current point is adjusted by the sum all the imaged characters widths. The current point must be defined, otherwise a "nocurrentpoint" error is generated.

Results: `none`

Examples

Ex. 1. **`(Alistair Cooke)` show =>**

Assuming the font is set to Courier scaled to 24 points, a monospaced font, this example produces a line of text that is added to the current path, and offsets the current point by 201.597 points in the X axis and 0 points in the Y axis.

string Description: This operator removes an integer from the stack, creates a string of nulls equal in length to the integer, and returns that string on the operand stack.

Arguments: `int`

Results: `string`

Examples

Ex. 1. **6 string** => `STRING[6]`

Ex. 2. After execution of the **string** operator, the object on the top of the stack is a string of the length of the integer.

stringwidth Description: The **stringwidth** operator removes a string from the top of the operand stack and replaces it with the X and Y values of the current point that would occur if the string were given as the operand to the **show** operator under the current font settings. See **show** for more information on how the return values are calculated.

Arguments: `string`

`string` is the string of text that **show** uses to calculate the proper width of the string if it were to be displayed on output with the current graphics state. Note the width of the string is strictly defined as the movement of the current point and, as such, the method that **show** uses to calculate the entire string width is irrelevant.

Results: $\mathbf{num_1}$, $\mathbf{num_2}$
$\mathbf{num_1}$ represents the X coordinate and $\mathbf{num_2}$ represents the Y coordinate of the calculated current point.

<u>Examples</u>

Ex. 1. `(Alistair Cooke)` **stringwidth** => `201.597 0`

Assuming the font is set to Courier scaled to 24 points, a monospaced font, this example produces a line of text that, if added to current path, offsets it by 201.597 points in the X axis and 0 points in the Y axis.

3. Painting Operators

The painting operators are responsible for laying "marks" down on the page on top of, around, or within the area defined by the current path and/or the clipping path.

fill

Description: The **fill** operator command paints the area enclosed by the current path with the current shade of gray. If the path is not closed, the **fill** command closes any portions of the current path that are open.

Arguments: **`none`**

Results: **`none`**

stroke

Description: This operator paints a line centered on the path, with sides parallel to the path segments, and in compliance with the settings of the current graphics state. **stroke** operator implicitly performs a **newpath** after it finishes painting the current path. If this concerns, bracket your call to **stroke** operator with **gsave** and **grestore** calls.

Arguments: **`none`**

Results: **`none`**

4. Stack Operators

The PostScript language has four stacks associated with it. The execution stack is under the control of the PostScript interpreter, not the programmer. "The stack" refers to the operand stack and the operators that manipulate it are described in this section. The dictionary and graphics state stack are manipulated with the dictionary and graphics operators, respectively.

dup

Description: This operator duplicates the top element on the operand stack. Only the object is copied, so duplicated composite objects share their values with the original object.

Arguments: **`any`**

The object to be copied may be of any type. The original is popped off the stack.

Results: **any**$_1$ **any**$_2$

Two objects of the same type and value of the argument **any** are pushed onto the stack. Again, for composite objects, the operator **dup** operator only duplicates the reference object. The values of the composite object are shared by both references.

Examples

Ex. 1. **4 dup => 4 4**

This is the simplest example of the **dup** operator. A number object is given as an argument on the stack and two copies of the integer are left on the stack.

Ex. 2. FONT(HELVETICA,1) **dup** => FONT(HELVETICA,1) FONT(HELVETICA,1)

This instance of **dup** places two references to the font on the stack. Because a font dictionary is a composite object, both references point to a shared object; changes to one of the objects will be reflected in the other object, also.

exch

Description: This operator expects two objects on the stack. They are removed and their sum is pushed onto the stack.

Arguments: **any**$_1$ **any**$_2$

num$_1$ and **num**$_2$ may be any object.

Results: **any**$_1$ **any**$_2$

The **exch** function exchanges the top two elements on the stack.

Examples

Ex. 1. **4 123 exch => 123 4**

index

Description: The **index** operator command pops an integer object off the stack and uses that integer as an index to access the **int** entry from the top of the stack. A copy of the **int** entry is pushed onto the stack.

Arguments: **any**$_n$**...any**$_1$**, any**$_0$**, int**

int must be a non-negative integer, and **n** = **int** above. Element counting begins at zero, not one.

Results: **any**$_n$**...any**$_1$**, any**$_0$**, any**$_n$

n = **int** above. The very last instance of **any**$_n$ shown here is the copy of the element that gets pushed onto the stack.

Examples

Ex. 1. **`/a /b /c /d /e 3 index => /a /b /c /d /e /b`**

The **index** operator accesses the 3 position on the stack, with the first position being 0 and moves a copy to the top of the stack, in this case 6.

pop

Description: This operator pops the top object from the stack and discards it.

Arguments: **`any`**

Results: **`none`**

Examples

Ex. 1. **`1 2 3 pop => 1 2`**

The **pop** operator causes the item on the top of the stack, in this case 3, to be removed.

roll

Description: This operator performs a circular shift of the $\mathbf{any}_{n-1}$ through $\mathbf{any}_0$ objects on the operand stack by the amount $\mathbf{int}_2$ specifies. Positive values for $\mathbf{int}_2$ indicate upward motion on the stack, whereas negative $\mathbf{int}_2$ indicates downward motion.

$\mathbf{int}_1$ must be a non-negative integer and $\mathbf{int}_1$ must be an integer. **roll** first removes these operands from the stack; there must be at least $\mathbf{int}_1$ additional elements. **roll** then performs a circular shift of these $\mathbf{int}_1$ elements by $\mathbf{int}_1$ positions.

Arguments: $\mathbf{any}_{n-1}\ldots\mathbf{any}_0$ $\mathbf{int}_1$ $\mathbf{int}_2$

$\mathbf{num}_1$ and $\mathbf{num}_2$ may be either integers or real number objects.

Results: $\mathbf{any}_{(int_2-1)\ mod\ int_1}$ ... $\mathbf{any}_0$ $\mathbf{any}_{n-1}\ldots\mathbf{any}_{int_1}$

If $\mathbf{int}_1$ is positive, each shift removes an element from the top of the stack and inserts it between element $\mathbf{int}_1\mathbf{-1}$ and element $\mathbf{int}_1$ of the stack, moving all intervening elements one level higher on the stack. If $\mathbf{int}_1$ is negative, each shift consists of removing $\mathbf{int}_1\mathbf{-1}$ off the stack and pushing it on top of the stack, moving all intervening elements one level lower on the stack.

The **roll** function returns a number of type real or integer that represents the mathematical sum of the two arguments. The type is determined to be integer only if both arguments are type integer and the result is within the range of representable integers for the PostScript interpreter. A type of real is assigned to the result if both conditions are not met, and some loss in the result's precision may occur.

Examples

Ex. 1. `1 2 3 4 5 3 1 roll => 1 2 5 3 4`

The three items 3, 4, and 5 are rolled once in the counterclockwise direction.

5. Mathematical Operators

PostScript includes a number of operands for mathematical functions, including trigonometric functions and a pseudorandom number generator. The more commonly used operators are:

add

Description: This operator expects two numbers on the stack. They are removed and their sum is pushed onto the stack.

Arguments: $\mathbf{num_1}$ $\mathbf{num_2}$

$\mathbf{num_1}$ and $\mathbf{num_2}$ may be either integers or real number objects.

Results: **num**

The **add** operator function returns a number of type real or integer which represents the mathematical sum of the two arguments. The type is determined to be integer only if both arguments are of type integer and the result is within the range of representable integers for the PostScript interpreter. A type of real is assigned to the result if both conditions are not met, and some loss in the result's precision may occur.

Examples

Ex. 1. `4 123 add => 127`

This is the simplest example of the **add** operator. Two integers are given as arguments and the sum is an integer left on the stack.

Ex. 2. `3490 -34.8 add => 3455.2`

Here the first argument is an integer and the second is a negative real. The result is a real because one of the arguments is type real; also, because the second argument is negative, the operation is equivalent to subtracting 34.8 from 3490.

Ex. 3. `2147483640 10 add => 2147483650`

In this example, the arguments are two integers and the result most likely will be a real number because it is out of the range of most interpreters.

div

Description: This operator expects two numbers onto the stack. They are removed and the result of dividing the bottom number, num_1, by the top number, num_2, is pushed onto the stack.

Arguments: num_1 num_2

num_1 and num_2 may be either integers or real number objects. Argument num_2 must not be zero.

Results: `real`

The **div** operator function returns a number of type real that represents the mathematical division of the two arguments. See the **idiv** function if you desire an integer result.

Examples

Ex. 1. `20 2 div => 10.0`

This is the simplest example of the **div** operator. Two integers are given as arguments and the quotient is real left on the stack. Note the result, 10, is a real number object even though both arguments are integer number objects.

Ex. 2. `-34.8 128.4 div => -0.2710280374`

And, a little more complex example of division.

floor

Description: This operator removes a numeric object from the stack, rounds the value down to the nearest integer value, and then returns the result onto the operand stack.

Arguments: `num`

`num` is the number to be floored.

Results: `num`

The **floor** operator function returns a number as described above.

Examples

Ex. 1. `9.231 floor => 9.0`

Ex. 2. `3490 floor => 3490`

Ex. 3. `-3.2 floor => -4.0`

Note that –3.2 is rounded down to –4.0.

idiv

Description: This operator removes two integers from the stack and divides the first argument by the second argument. The quotient is returned onto the operand stack.

Arguments: int_1 int_2

Results: `int`

The **idiv** operator function returns a number of type integer that represents the result of the division of the first argument by the second argument, with any fraction discarded.

Examples

Ex. 1. `10 5 idiv => 2`

The first argument, 10, is divided by 5 to produce 2.

Ex. 2. `11 2 idiv => 5`

The first argument, 11, is divided by 2 to produce 5.5, which is truncated to 5.

mod

Description: This operator expects two numbers on the stack. They are removed and the remainder from dividing the first argument, $\texttt{int}_1$, by the second argument, $\texttt{int}_2$, is pushed onto the stack. The operation is remainder divisions and not a true modulo operation.

Arguments: $\texttt{int}_1$ $\texttt{int}_2$

$\texttt{int}_1$ and $\texttt{int}_2$ may be either integers or real number objects.

Results: **int**

The **mod** operator function returns a number of type integer that represents the remainder from dividing of $\texttt{int}_1$ by the $\texttt{int}_2$ of the two arguments.

Examples

Ex. 1. `7 2 mod => 1`

Ex. 2. `5 2 mod => 1`

Ex. 3. `-5 3 mod => -2`

These examples illustrates that **mod** is a remainder and not a true modulo operation.

mul

Description: This operator expects two numbers onto the stack. They are removed and the result of multiplying the two is pushed onto the stack.

Arguments: $\texttt{num}_1$ $\texttt{num}_2$

$\texttt{num}_1$ and $\texttt{num}_2$ may be either integers or real number objects.

Results: **real**

The **mul** operator function returns a number of type integer only if both operands are integers and the result is within the representable bounds of an integer for the current PostScript interpreter.

Examples

Ex. 1. `4 2 mul => 8`

neg

Description: This operator expects two numbers on the stack. They are removed and their sum is pushed onto the stack.

Arguments: **num**

num may be either an integer or a real number object.

Results: **num**

The **neg** operator function returns a number of the same type as the **num** argument.[65]

Examples

Ex. 1. `123 neg => -123`

sub

Description: This operator expects two numbers on the stack. They are removed and their difference is pushed onto the stack.

Arguments: $\mathbf{num_1}$ $\mathbf{num_2}$

$\mathbf{num_1}$ and $\mathbf{num_2}$ may be either integers or real number objects.

Results: **num**

The **sub** operator function returns a number of type real or integer that represents the mathematical difference of $\mathbf{num_2}$ substracted from $\mathbf{num_1}$ arguments. The type is determined to be integer only if both arguments are of type integer and the result is within the range of representable integers for the PostScript interpreter. Type real is assigned to the result if both conditions are not met and some loss in the result's precision may occur.

Examples

Ex. 1. `4 123 sub => -119`

This is the simplest example of the **sub** operator. Two integers, $\mathbf{num_1}$ and $\mathbf{num_2}$, are given as arguments and the difference is an integer object placed onto the stack.

Ex. 2. `3490 -34.8 sub => 3524.8`

Here, the first argument is an integer and the second is a negative real. The result is a real because one of the arguments is of type real; also, because the second argument is negative, the operation is equivalent to adding 34.8 to 3490.

Ex. 3. `10 2147483640 sub => -2147483630`

In this example, the arguments are two integers and the result most likely will be a real number because it is out of the range of most interpreters.

---

[65]If the number is the most negative number, the result is a real (otherwise the result is out of bounds of the maximum representable integer for that interpreter.)

6. Logical Operators

PostScript's collection of object types includes the boolean object, which takes values of true and false. Some of the control operators described here expect boolean objects as operands. These operators return boolean values on the stack:

and Description: This operator acts has slightly different actions depending whether the objects are integer or boolean. Both objects must be of the same type. The arguments are removed and a result of the same type is pushed onto the stack.

Arguments (Form 1): **`boolean`**$_1$ **`boolean`**$_2$

Results (Form 1): **`boolean`**

The **and** operator returns an object of type boolean that represents the logical conjunction of the arguments.

Arguments (Form 2): **`int`**$_1$ **`int`**$_2$

Results (Form 2): **`int`**

The **and** operator returns an object of type integer. This integer is the bitwise *and* of the two integer arguments' binary values.

Examples

Ex. 1. `true  true  and => true`

Ex. 2. `true  false and => false`

Ex. 3. `false true and => false`

Ex. 4. `false false and => false`

These are all possible examples of Form 1. The result is true only if both arguments are true, and false otherwise.

eq Description: This operator expects two objects onto the stack. They are removed and a boolean is pushed onto the stack. The boolean object is true if the objects are equal, and false otherwise. Certain objects are considered equal even though they have different types. Integers and reals may be considered equal if they represent the same mathematical value. Strings and names are equal if they have the same sequence of characters.

Arguments: **`any`**$_1$ **`any`**$_2$

`num`$_1$ and **`num`**$_2$ may be any type of object.

Results: **`boolean`**

The **eq** operator function returns a variable of type boolean as described.

Examples

Ex. 1. **4 123 eq => false**

Obviously, 4 is not equal to 123.

Ex. 2. **123.0 123 eq => true**

However, 123.0 and 123 are equal, even though one is a real and one an integer.

ge

Description: This operator expects either two numbers or two strings on the stack. Both arguments are popped and **ge** operator pushes a boolean value on the stack. The boolean value is true if the first argument is greater than or equal to the second, and false otherwise.

Arguments (Form 1): $\mathbf{num_1}$ $\mathbf{num_2}$

$\mathbf{num_1}$ and $\mathbf{num_2}$ are compared by their mathematical values.

Arguments (Form 2): $\mathbf{string_1}$ $\mathbf{string_2}$

$\mathbf{string_1}$ and $\mathbf{string_2}$ are compared element by element for lexical equivalence.

Results: **num**

The **ge** operator function returns a number of type real or integer that represents the mathematical sum of the two arguments. The type is determined to be integer only if both arguments are of type integer and the result is within the range of representable integers for the PostScript interpreter. Type real is assigned to the result if both conditions are not met, and some loss in the result's precision may occur.

Examples

Ex. 1. **4 123 ge => false**

The boolean object false is returned on the stack since 4 is not greater than or equal to 123.

gt

Description: This operator expects either two numbers or two strings onto the stack. Both arguments are popped and **gt** pushes a boolean value on the stack. The boolean value is true if the first argument is greater than the second, and false otherwise.

Arguments (Form 1): $\mathbf{num_1}$ $\mathbf{num_2}$

$\mathbf{num_1}$ and $\mathbf{num_2}$ are compared by their mathematical values.

Arguments (Form 2): $\mathbf{string_1}$ $\mathbf{string_2}$

$\mathbf{string_1}$ and $\mathbf{string_2}$ are compared element by element for lexical equivalence.

Results: **boolean**

The **gt** operator function returns a boolean as described.

Examples

Ex. 1. **`4 123 gt => false`**

Since 4 is not greater than 123, the boolean object false is returned on the stack.

le

Description: This operator expects either two numbers or two strings onto the stack. Both arguments are popped and **le** pushes a boolean value onto the stack. The boolean value is true if the first argument is less than or equal to the second, and false otherwise.

Arguments (Form 1): $\mathbf{num_1}$ $\mathbf{num_2}$

$\mathbf{num_1}$ and $\mathbf{num_2}$ are compared by their mathematical values.

Arguments (Form 2): $\mathbf{string_1}$ $\mathbf{string_2}$

$\mathbf{string_1}$ and $\mathbf{string_2}$ are compared element by element for lexical equivalence.

Results: **`boolean`**

The **le** operator function returns a number of type real or integer that represents the mathematical sum of the two arguments. The type is determined to be integer only if both arguments are type integer and the result is within the range of representable integers for the PostScript interpreter. Type real is assigned to the result if both conditions are not met, and some loss in the result's precision of the result may occur.

Examples

Ex. 1. **`4 123 le => true`**

Since 4 is less than 123, a boolean object **`boolean`** with a value of true is returned onto the operand stack.

lt

Description: This operator expects either two numbers or two strings onto the stack. Both arguments are popped and **lt** pushes a boolean value onto the stack. The boolean value is true if the first argument is less than the second, and false otherwise.

Arguments (Form 1): $\mathbf{num_1}$ $\mathbf{num_2}$

$\mathbf{num_1}$ and $\mathbf{num_2}$ are compared by their mathematical values.

Arguments (Form 2): $\mathbf{string_1}$ $\mathbf{string_2}$

$\mathbf{string_1}$ and $\mathbf{string_2}$ are compared element by element for lexical equivalence.

Results: **`boolean`**

The **lt** operator function returns a boolean as described.

Examples

Ex. 1. **4 123 lt => true**

Since 4 is less than 123, a boolean object, **boolean**, with a value of true is returned onto the stack.

ne

Description: This operator expects two objects on the stack. They are removed and a boolean is pushed onto the stack. The boolean object is true if the objects are not equal, and false otherwise. Certain objects are considered equal even though they have different types. Integers and reals may be considered equal if they represent the same mathematical value. Strings and names are equal if they have the same sequence of characters.

Arguments: $\mathbf{any_1}$ $\mathbf{any_2}$

$\mathbf{num_1}$ and $\mathbf{num_2}$ may be any type of object.

Results: **boolean**

The **ne** function returns a number of boolean as described.

Examples

Ex. 1. **4 123 ne => true**

Obviously, 4 is not equal to 123, so

Ex. 2. **123.0 123 ne => false**

However, 123.0 and 123 are equal, even though one is a real and the other an int.

not

Description: This operator expects an integer or boolean object on the stack. The argument is removed and a result of the same type is pushed onto the stack.

Arguments (Form 1): **boolean**

Results (Form 1): **boolean**

The **not** operator function returns an object of type boolean that represents the logical negation of the argument.

Arguments (Form 2): **int**

Results (Form 2): **int**

The **not** operator function returns an object of type integer. This integer is the bitwise *not* of the integer argument's binary values.

Examples

Ex. 1. ex[true **not** => false]

or

Description: This operator expects two arguments of the same type on the stack. They must either be integer or boolean objects. Both arguments are removed and a result of the same type as the arguments is pushed onto the stack.

Arguments (Form 1): `boolean`$_1$ `boolean`$_2$

Results (Form 1): `boolean`

The **or** operator function returns an object of type boolean that represents the logical conjunction of the arguments.

Arguments (Form 2): `int`$_1$ `int`$_2$

Results (Form 2): `int`

The **or** operator function returns an object of type integer. This integer is the bitwise *or* of the two integer argument's binary values.

Examples

Ex. 1.
```
true  true  or => true
true  false or => true
false true or => true
false false or => false
```

These are all possible examples of Form 1. The result is false only if both arguments are false, and is true otherwise.

7. Dictionary Operators

PostScript uses a number of dictionaries, each of which is stored in the dictionary stack. A dictionary is a data structure organized like a table with each entry having a key identifier and a value. The most important dictionary operator is **def** which expects a value and a literal on top of the stack. Those operands are removed when **def** is executed, and they become a new entry into the current dictionary.

begin

Description: The **begin** operator causes the named dictionary, **dict**, to be pushed onto the dictionary stack so it is the current dictionary (i.e. the first dictionary looked at by later commands).

Arguments: `dict`

Results: `none`

The **begin** operator function makes **dict** the current dictionary. It becomes the first dictionary consulted during implicit name lookups and by the **def, load, store,** and **where** operators.

Examples

Ex. 1. `dictionary[0/25]` **begin** =>

Assume the dictionary stack contained the minimal number of dictionaries—userdict and systemdict. If this example is executed, the dictionary on the operand stack is removed from the operand stack and pushed onto the dictionary stack on top of userdict.

bind

Description: The **bind** operator causes the interpreter to replace all executable operator names in a procedure with the actual operators themselves. This has two effects. First, the procedure executes faster, as operator names do not have to be searched for in the current dictionary stack. Second, if definitions of any of the operators are changed after the procedure has been bound, the procedure operation is not affected. For each procedure object in **proc** whose access is unrestricted, **bind** applies itself recursively to **proc**, makes the process read-only, and returns **proc** on the stack.

Arguments: `proc`

The executable names that refer to operator object values which make up the array **proc** are replaced by the actual operators they refer to.

Results: `proc`

The **bind** function returns the same procedure it was given, except that all references to executable names are replaced by the actual operators they referred to.

Examples

Ex. 1.
```
/ORIGINAL {showpage} bind def =>
/NEWDEF    {showpage} def =>
/showpage {} def =>
/ORIGINAL load =>
/NEWDEF    load =>
```

The first line binds *ORIGINAL* to the meaning of the **showpage** operator; it, images the current page to device space and outputs it. The second line defines *NEWDEF* to mean the same as **showpage**. If *NEWDEF* were executed at this point, it would perform the same action as the original **showpage** (i.e. image and output a page). The third line redefines **showpage** to do nothing. The fourth line executes the bound procedure, *ORIGINAL*. Since this procedure was bound, it images and outputs the current page. *NEWDEF*, on the other hand, executes the current definition of **showpage**, which does nothing. Note both *ORIGINAL* and *NEWDEF* are both defined as **showpage** before the redefinition of **showpage**. Each, however, acts differently after the **showpage** redefinition.

def

Description: This operator consumes two objects of the form **`key`** and **`value`** from the stack and adds them to the current dictionary.

Arguments: **`key value`**

`key` is associated with **`value`** in the current dictionary. If **`key`** exists, the new **`value`** replaces the associated **`value`**. If **`key`** does not exist already in the current dictionary, the dictionary must have room for one more entry. If it does not, a "dictfull" error is generated. **`key`** may consist of any object. If **`key`** is a name literal, it is converted to a name literal prior to storing the entry.

Results: **`none`**

The current dictionary is modified so it contains a **`key`** with an associated **`value`**.

Examples

Ex. 1. **`/PRICE 36.23 def =>`**

This defines the name literal "PRICE" to represent the value of 36.23 in the current dictionary.

`/TAX 0.06 PRICE mul def =>`

This is a more complex example, illustrating the use of the procedure to associate the **`value`** to be associated with **`key`** in the current dictionary. Here, the name literal "TAX" is defined as the result of PRICE multiplied by 0.6. Assuming the previous example has been executed, TAX is defined as 2.1738. Note the **`value`** is stored as an entry in the current dictionary and not returned onto the stack.

dict

Description: The **dict** operator consumes the top value on the stack and creates an empty dictionary with room for that number of key-value pairs.

Arguments: **`int`**

`int` must be non-negative.

Results: **`dict`**

The **dict** operator returns a dictionary object with a maximum capacity of **`int`** key-value pair entries. If an attempt is made to add more than **`int`** key-value pairs to the **`dict`**, a "dictfull" error is generated.

Examples

Ex. 1. **`500 dict =>`** `DICTIONARY[0/500]`

This is an example of the **dict** operator. An integer provides the specification for a dictionary object to be created with a maximum capacity of 500 items. The dictionary object is then placed onto the stack.

end Description: The **end** operator takes the current dictionary off the dictionary stack. The dictionary immediately below the popped dictionary becomes the new, current dictionary. An error is generated if a user-defined dictionary is not on the stack, as the two system dictionaries cannot be popped. This operator does the opposite of the **begin** operator.

Arguments: `None`

Results: `None`

8. Array Operators

PostScript arrays are similar to arrays in other programming languages. However, PostScript arrays are always one-dimensional, and the elements need not be of the same type. For example, you might have an array with some string and some numeric elements.

array Description: This operator expects one argument on the stack. The number is removed and an array of a length equal to the argument is pushed onto the stack. Each item in the array is a null object.

Arguments: `integer`

The **array** operator expects an integer indicating the number of null elements to place in the array before pushing it on the stack. The integer must be non-negative and not greater than the maximum allowable array length.

Results: array

The array object consists completely of null elements.

Examples

Ex. 1. `6 array => ARRAY[6]`

An ARRAY consisting of six null elements is pushed onto the stack.

get Description: This operator gets a single element from the value of an array, packed array, dictionary, or string.

Arguments (Form 1): `array index`

Arguments (Form 2): `packedarray index`

Arguments (Form 3): `dict key`

Results: `any`

Forms 1–3 of the **get** operator command return any data type. For forms where the first operand is an array or a packed array, the data type is accessed by using the second operand as an index. The element the index indicates is then returned. In Form 3, the string is simply used as a key into the dictionary and the associated value is returned.

Arguments (Form 4): **`string index`**

Results: **`int`**

Form 4 of the **get** operator command returns the **`int`** data type. The data type is accessed in exactly the same way as Forms 1 and 2.

Examples

Ex. 1. `[0 1 2 3 4] 3 get => 3`

The values of the numbers in the array happen to correspond to their indices, so getting element 3 from the array returns the number 3 on the stack.

length

Description: This operator behaves differently based the arguments it is given on the stack.

Arguments (Form 1): **`array`**
Arguments (Form 2): **`packedarray`**
Arguments (Form 3): **`dict`**
Arguments (Form 4): **`string`**
Arguments (Form 5): **`name`**

Results: **`length`**

If the argument type is an **`array`**, **`packedarray`**, or **`string`**, **length** returns the number of elements in its value. If the operand is a dictionary, only the current number of key-value pairs in the dictionary is returned. See **maxlength** for information about determining the maximum capacity of a dictionary. Finally, if the argument is a **`name`** object, the number of characters in the text string that defines it is returned.

Examples

Ex. 1. `(Michael B. Spring) length => 17`

The number 17 is returned on the stack because there are 17 characters in the string "Michael B. Spring."

put

Description: This operator has three forms:

Arguments (Form 1): **`array, index, any`**
Arguments (Form 2): **`dict, key, any`**
Arguments (Form 3): **`string, index, int`**

If the first operand is an **`array`** or **`string`**, **put** treats the second operand as an **`index`** and stores the third operand at the position the **`index`** identifies, counting from zero. The **`index`** operator must be in the range of 0 to one less than the length of the array or string. If the first operand is a dictionary, **put** uses the second operand as a key and the third operand as a value, then stores this key-value pair the **dict**. If the key exists for a key-value pair, it is overwritten. Note if the value of **array** or **dict** is in global VM and **any** is a composite object whose value is in local VM, an error occurs.

Results: **none**

Examples

Ex. 1. `ARRAY[6] 2 (hello) put =>`

No value is returned on the stack, but the string "hello" is stored as position 2 in the array, increasing its length from six to seven objects.

9. Control Operators

These operators provide the looping and branching capabilities found in other programming languages.

exit

Description: This operator terminates execution of innermost loop for the procedure which contains it. Valid operator procedures for this command to be executed in are: **cshow, filnameforall, for, forall, kshow, loop, pathforall, repeat, resourceforall.**

Arguments: **none**

Results: **none**

if

Description: The **if** operator command pops two objects from the stack, evaluates the first argument and, if it is true, executes the second argument, the **proc** procedure.

Arguments: **boolean proc**

proc is a set of zero or more PostScript commands.

Results: **none**

While **if** operator is not directly leave results on the stack, the procedure that is executed may alter the stack.

Examples

Ex. 1. `3 4 lt {(3 > 4) show} if =>`

In this, **3 4 lt** is true. The stack has a boolean and a procedure shows a string. The **if** operator takes the procedure **proc** and the **boolean**, and, if the **boolean** is true, executes **proc**.

ifelse

Description: The **ifelse** command pops three objects from the stack, evaluates the first argument and, if it is true, executes the second argument, the $\texttt{proc}_1$ procedure. Otherwise, it executes the third argument, the $\texttt{proc}_2$ procedure.

Arguments: **`boolean`** $\texttt{proc}_1$ $\texttt{proc}_2$

`proc` is a set of zero or more PostScript commands.

Results: **`none`**

Although **ifelse** operator does not directly leave results on the stack, the procedure that is executed may alter stack after the invocation of the **ifelse** procedure has completed.

Examples

Ex. 1. `3 4 lt {(3>=4) show} {(3<4) show} ifelse =>`

In this, `3 4 lt` is true. The stack has a **`boolean`** and two procedures, $\texttt{proc}_1$, $\texttt{proc}_2$, that show strings. The operator **`ifelse`** takes the two procedures and the boolean from the stack and executes the first procedure if **`boolean`** is true or the second procedure if the argument is false. In this case, the expression is true, so the first string is shown.

for

Description: This operator expects a start value, an increment value, a final value, and a procedure on the operand stack. The procedure is executed a number of times, and each execution increments a counter variable by the value of the increment operand. The counter begins at the start value, and when it reaches the final value, the loop ends.

Arguments: $\texttt{num}_1$ $\texttt{num}_2$ $\texttt{num}_3$ **`{operator(s)}`**

The first $\texttt{num}_1$ is the loop counter's starting value. The second $\texttt{num}_2$ is the loop counter's increment value, and the third operator, $\texttt{num}_3$, is the loop counter's destination value. An operator or group of operators enclosed in the curly brackets indicates the number of times the loop executes.

Results: **`none`**

Examples

Ex. 1. `0 1 1 4 {add} for => 10`

In this example, a `0` is placed on the stack followed by `1,1,4` and the procedure **add**. The **for** operator takes the `1 1 4` and uses them as the start, increment, and terminate values of the for loop. The current value of the counter is placed on the stack before each iteration of the procedure—in this case **add**. Thus the `0` on the stack is added to `1` and `1` is returned. `2` is then put on the stack. On the second iteration, **add** takes the `1` and the `2` and returns a `3`. The next two iterations yield sums of `6` and `10` respectively.

forall

Description: The **forall** operator executes a procedure for each element of a string or array. A procedure object is expected on top of the stack (the procedure to be executed) with the string or array underneath it. The **forall** operator pushes each string or array element onto the stack and executes a procedure. The procedure may or may not act the stack element. With strings, the stack objects are codes, or numeric values, of the characters.

Arguments (Form 1): `array proc`

Arguments (Form 2): `packedarray proc`

Arguments (Form 3): `dict proc`

Arguments (Form 4): `proc proc`

Note if the first operand in any of the forms is empty (i.e. has length zero), **forall** operator does not execute at all.

Results: `None`

Examples

Ex. 1. `[(Ho) (Ho) (Ho)] {show 35 0 rmoveto} forall =>`

An array of strings and a procedure are pushed onto the stack. When **forall** is encountered, both arguments are deleted and the procedure `proc` is executed for each string in the array. The **forall** operator itself leaves nothing on the stack, unless the procedure fails to remove each of the array or string elements.

loop

Description: The **loop** operator repeatedly executes `proc` until the **exit** or **stop** operators are called.

Arguments: `proc`

`proc` must execute an **exit** or **stop**, or an infinite loop results.

Results: `none`

Examples

Ex. 1. `{showpage} loop =>`

Since no **exit** or **stop** is included in the `proc` procedure, the loop continues to eject blank pages from the printer indefinitely.

repeat

Description: The **repeat** operator executes `proc int` times, where `int` is a non-negative number, or until the **exit** or **stop** operators are called. If the **exit** or **stop** operators are called, the **repeat** operator terminates prematurely.

Arguments: `int proc`

`proc` is a set of zero or more PostScript commands.

Results: `none`

Although **repeat** operator does not directly leave results on the stack, the procedure that is executed may alter the stack after the invocation of the **repeat** procedure has completed.

Examples

Ex. 1. `1 4{1 add}` **repeat** `=> 5`

In this example, the number 1 is placed on the stack. The number 4 and procedure **1 add** are placed on next. The repeat operator is now encountered. 4 and **1 add** are removed from the stack and **1 add** is executed four times. The first time, it takes the 1 that was initially placed on the stack and adds 1 to it, pushing the result, 2, onto the stack. The second iteration takes the 2, adds 1, and pushes the resulting 3 back onto the stack. After four iterations, there is a 5 on the stack.

Ex. 2. `1 2 3 4 3 {pop}` **repeat** `=> 1`

10. Coordinate Operators

These operators modify the current user space coordinate system:

rotate

Description: This operator expects one or two arguments on the stack. The first argument is always an angle value, either in integer or real form, and the second argument, if present, is a matrix. The horizontal and vertical axes for the current user space are rotated counterclockwise a number of degrees equal to the `num` argument.

Arguments (Form 1): `num`

Results: `none`

Arguments (Form 2): `num, matrix`

Results: `matrix`

The **rotate** function occurs in two varieties: in one, the user supplies a matrix; the other operates on the current transformation matrix (CTM). If a matrix is supplied, the CTM is not altered in any way.

Examples

Ex. 1. `45` **rotate** `=>`

The axes are rotated 45 degrees in a counterclockwise direction.

scale

Description: This operator has two versions, one that operates the current transformation matrix (CTM) and affects the user space, and the other that operates a matrix that is provided.

Arguments (Form 1): num_1 num_2

num_1 and num_2 may be either integers or real number objects and represent the X axis and the Y axis scaling factors, respectively.

Results: **none**

Arguments (Form 2): **num_1 num_2 matrix**

num_1 and **num_2** may be either integers or real number objects, and represent the X axis and the Y axis scaling factors, respectively. In the matrix case, scaling is also done along the X and Y axes. Scaling does not affect the graphics state or, more importantly, alter the CTM.

Results: **matrix**

Examples

Ex. 1. **2 2 scale =>**

The X and Y axes are each scaled by a factor of two.

translate

Description: This operator has two versions:

Arguments (Form 1): **num_1 num_2**

This version of **translate** operator shifts the user coordinate system **num_1** units in the X direction and **num_2** units in the Y direction. The current transformation matrix is updated and the operation relocates the origin point. **num_1** and **num_2** may be either integers or real number objects.

Results (Form 1): **none**

Arguments (Form 2): **num_1 num_2 matrix**

This version of **translate** operator alters **matrix** by providing the transforms for shifting a user coordinate system **num_1** units in the X direction and **num_2** units in the Y direction. The current transformation matrix (CTM) is not altered and the operation has no effect on the current graphics state. **num_1** and **num_2** may be either integers or real number objects.

Results (Form 2): **matrix**

Examples

Ex. 1. **4 123 translate =>**

This is an example of Form 1's **translate** operator. The old point (4,123) in the user space is now the point (0,0) in the user space and all points shift accordingly. For example, the point (–343.3, 23428) would be (–339.3, 23553) after the example **translate** command. The orientation and scale of the CTM are unchanged.

11. Graphics Operators

These operators act on graphics states, which are data structures that store values representing the current user space.

currentpoint Description: This operator pushes two numeric objects representing the current point's the X and Y values. The values are retrieved from the active graphics state.

Arguments: **`none`**

Results: **`num`**$_1$ **`num`**$_2$

The **currentpoint** operator function returns two numbers of type real which represent the X and Y coordinates of the current point in the graphics state. The current point is the trailing end point of the current path. A "nocurrentpoint" error is generated if **currentpoint** is undefined.

Examples

Ex. 1. **currentpoint `operator` => `342 82374892.34`**

currentpoint returns the X coordinate of 342 units and a Y coordinate of 82,374,892.34 units. Remember, these are user-coordinate space values and may be transformed upon conversion to the device and physical spaces.

Ex. 2. **currentpoint** => *ERROR*

In this example, assume **currentpoint** is undefined resulting in a "nocurrentpoint" error.

grestore Description: This operator pops a graphics state from the top of the graphics state stack and makes it active. It undoes any changes that were made to the graphics state since the last **gsave**.

Arguments: **`none`**

Results: **`none`**

gsave Description: The **gsave** operator pushes the current graphics state onto the graphics state stack. This operator is often used before changes that are difficult to recover from are made to the graphics state. It is also used to isolate changes to the graphics state made for a small subsection of the program so those changes do not have unintended effects on commands executed later.

Arguments: **`none`**

Results: **`none`**

setdash

Description: This operator expects an array and a number on the stack. They are removed and their sum is pushed onto the stack.

Arguments: **`array, offset`**

The top value on the stack is the offset into the dash pattern used for each line.[66] The second value is given as an array (placed between [ ]), and it sets the dash pattern as simply the length, in points, of the dash and the gap between the dashes.[67] Once setdash is executed, all lines drawn are in the same dashed pattern until **setdash** operator is explicitly reset.

Results: **`none`**

<u>**Examples**</u>

Ex. 1. **`[ 2 1 ] 0 setdash`**

This sets the dashing to 2 units on, followed by 1 off, 2 on, 1 off, etc.

setgray

Description: This operator expects a number on the stack. It pops **`num`** off the stack, sets color space to DeviceGray, and finally sets the gray shade parameter in the graphics state to a value corresponding to **`num`**. **`num`** may be in the range from 0 to 1, with 0 corresponding to black and 1 representing white.

Arguments: **`num`**

The **`num`** is used to inform the graphics state which gray level to use—if it is above 1 or below 0, the nearest legal value is substituted.

Results: **`none`**

<u>**Examples**</u>

Ex. 1. **`0.95` setgray**

This example obtains sets the grayshade to a very light, almost white shade of gray.

[66] For example, if the pattern is followed by a space of 10 and an offset of three, it starts with a dash of seven.

[67] The array you use may be longer than two. For example, the array [2 2 10 2 5 15] sets the dash pattern to a dash of 2, followed by a space of 2, followed by a dash of 10, followed by a space of 2, followed by a dash of 5, followed by a space of 15. The entire procedure then repeats.

setlinecap Description: This operator expects an integer on the stack. It pops `int` off the stack and evaluates it to determine the shape to put at the ends of open subpaths painted by the **stroke** operator.

Arguments: `int`

`int` must be in the set {0, 1, 2}. If it is not, an error occurs. If `int` is 0, the line has a butt cap: the stroke is squared off at the path's end point. There is no projection beyond the end of the path. If `int` is 1, the line has a round cap: a semicircular arc with diameter equal to the line width is drawn around the end point and filled in. If `int` is 2, the line has a projecting square cap: the stroke continues beyond the path's end point for a distance equal to half the line width and is squared off.

Results: `none`

__Examples__

Ex. 1. `1` **setlinecap** =>

Lines have rounded caps.

setlinewidth Description: This operator expects an integer on the stack. It pops `int` off the stack and sets the line width parameter in the graphics state to the argument value. That number is stored in the active graphics state as the width (in points) for any lines drawn until either the value is changed or another graphics state becomes active.

Arguments: `int`

Specifically, `int` controls the thickness of lines rendered by subsequent execution of the **stroke** operator: **stroke** paints all points whose perpendicular distance from the current path in user space is less than or equal to half the absolute value of `int`. This means stroked lines can vary by as much as 2 device pixels, depending on their positions. Also, an argument of 0 for the `int` causes **stroke** to image the lines at the device's finest resolution.

Results: `none`

__Examples__

Ex. 1. `12` **setlinewidth**

This example sets the linewidth to a line to 12 points in the user space.

12. Conversion Operators

There are a number of type conversion operators. These are three of the frequently used conversion operators:

cvi

Description: The **cvi** operator removes a numeric or string object from the operand stack, converts it into an integer object, and returns an object of type integer on the stack. If the argument is an integer, **cvi** returns that value. If the argument is a real, fractional parts of the number are truncated, unless the real is too large to convert to an integer, in which case an error is generated. If the argument is a string, the characters are interpreted as a number according to PostScript syntax rules. The number obtained is evaluated as described.

Arguments: **`num`** or **`string`**

cvi operator takes either a number or a string as an argument.

Results: **`int`**

If the result of the conversion of the **`num`** or **`string`** argument is too large to convert to an integer, an error is generated.

Examples

Ex. 1. **`89 cvi => 89`**

This is the simplest example of the **cvi** operator. An integer is given as an argument and an integer is returned.

Ex. 2. **`-34.8 cvi => -34`**

Here the first argument is real. The result is an integer.

Ex. 3. **`213634E100000 cvi => ERROR`**

In this example, the argument is a valid string and produces a valid real, but the resultant conversion produces an integer that is out of the range of most interpreters, thereby generating an error.

cvr

Description: The **cvr** operator removes a numeric or string object from the operand stack, converts it into a real object, and returns that object on the stack. If the argument is a real, **cvr** returns that value. If the argument is a string, the characters are interpreted as a number according to PostScript syntax rules.

Arguments: **`num`** or **`string`**

cvr operator takes either a number or a string as an argument.

Results: **`real`**

If the result of the conversion of the **`num`** or **`string`** argument is too large to convert to a real, an error is generated.

Examples

Ex. 1. `89 cvr => 89.0`

This is the simplest example of the **cvi** operator. An integer is given as an argument and a real is returned.

cvs

Description: The **cvs** operator removes any object from the operand stack, along with a string object. It converts the object supplied to a string object and stores it in the supplied string. It then returns the object to the stack.

Arguments: `any string`

cvs operator takes any object and a string as arguments.

Results: `string`

If the `string` argument is too small to hold the resultant string, an error is generated.

Examples

Ex. 1.
```
/tempstr 10 string def
89 tempstr cvs => (89)
```

This is the simplest example of the **cvs** operator. An integer followed by a string is given as an argument and a string is returned.

13. Device Operators

These operators manipulate output device parameters:

showpage

Description: **showpage** transmits the current page to the raster output device, causing any marks painted on the current page to appear. Quite simply, **showpage** converts the information in the user space into the device space, making whatever transformations and modifications are necessary.

Arguments: `none`

Although **showpage** operator does not take any arguments on the stack, certain entries in the device dictionary affect operation, such as the **#copies** userdict variable that defines the numbers of copies that will be produced of each page.

Results: `none`

Index

% percent sign in PostScript programs 16

() parentheses in PostScript programs 16

/ slash in PostScript programs 16

<> angle brackets in PostScript programs 16

Accented characters 238
Add 156, 403
Adobe Font Metric File, excerpts from 233
  character information 234
  composite character 236
  kerning pairs 235
And 407
Angle brackets <> in PostScript programs 16
Angled text 132, 137
Arc 76, 119, 170, 391
Arcto 147, 392
Array 16, 17, 414
Array operators 414

Banner/trailer pages 27
Begin 99, 411
BeginPageSetup comment 32
BeginProlog comment 32
BeginSetup comment 32
Bind 21, 76, 88, 98, 99, 412
Bitmap 18
Borders 153, 242
BoundingBox comment 33
Braces in PostScript programs 16
Braces { } in PostScript programs 16
Brackets [] in PostScript programs 16

Cartesian Coordinate System 37
Centering text 68, 71, 88, 147, 151, 197, 219, 242, 278, 353
  on page 60, 66
  with a device driver 219
Certificate 75
Characters
  accented 238
  clipping path 231
  manipulating 229
  outlining 229
Circular text 190, 195, 346
Clip 77, 189, 392
Clipping 209, 229, 326, 377
Clipping path 51
Closepath 77, 156, 393
Color 51
Comments 16, 148
  DSC 31
  in PostScript programs 16, 25, 29, 64
  required 31
Complexity 214
Composite objects 18
Control operators 416
Conversion operators 117, 424
Coordinate operators 419
Coordinate space 18, 36, 135
  manipulating with PostScript 36, 53
CreationDate comment 31

Creator comment 31
Currentpoint 98, 186, 421
Curveto 77, 393
Cvi 117, 186, 424
Cvr 117, 424
Cvs 425

Dash pattern 51
Def 78, 114, 170, 413
Default imaging area 38
Default unit of measure 41
Definefont 100, 396
Device driver 6, 213
calculation 220
simple 216
Device independence 36, 111, 214
Device interchange language 15
Device operators 425
Device space 39
Dict 100, 413
Dictionary operators 411
Dictionary stack 20
Disk 8
Display PostScript 19
Div 60, 78, 171, 404
Document managers 26
Document Structuring Conventions (DSC) 25
comments/key words 29
compliance 31
Prologue and Script Model 28
Drivers 211
device 6, 213
programs 11, 213
DSC 25
See also Document Structuring Convention
Dup 60, 61, 78, 171, 400

Early binding 21
Encapsulated PostScript 11, 25, 33
End 100, 414
EndComments comment 32
EndPageSetup comment 32
EndProlog comment 32
EndSetup comment 32
EOF comment 32
EPS 11, 25, 33
See also Encapsulated PostScript
Eq 407
Errors 73, 111, 128, 183, 293, 378
Escape character 16
Exch 61, 79, 171, 401
Executable array 17
Execution stack 20
Exit 134, 416

Files
Disk, listing 8
EPS 33
Font Metric 222, 233, 273, 329, 360
PostScript, structuring of 25
Fill 119, 170, 400
Filled characters 231
Findfont 58, 79, 397
Floor 117, 188, 404
Fold marks 122
Font 37, 51
Font families 227
Font metric files 222, 233, 273, 329, 360
Font operators 396
For 79, 120, 417
Forall 100, 186, 418

Ge 408
Geschke, Chuck 4
Get 414
Graphics operators 421
Graphics state stack 20, 49
Grestore 29, 80, 99, 170, 421
Gsave 29, 80, 99, 170, 421
Gt 408

Header 10
Hexadecimal strings 16, 17
High-resolution devices 35
HPGL 5

Idiv 187, 404
If 187, 416
Ifelse 101, 117, 417
Imaging 18, 47
Imaging area 38

Changing the Default 39
default 38
Inch definition 160
Index 101, 401
Interpress 4
Interpretation 18
ISO Latin Encoding 107, 238

JaM 4
Justified text 278

Kerning 135, 236
Keyboard Templates 155
Keyword 29
Kshow 134, 187, 397

Landscape printing 44, 86, 90, 115, 120, 167
Laser printers 4, 35
Late binding 21
Le 409
Leading 135
Length 101, 415
Letterhead 57
Level 2 19
LIFO stacks 19
Line breaks 65
Line join 51
Linecap 51
Lineto 62, 394
Linewidth 51
Logical operators 407
Loop 132, 188, 418
Low-resolution devices 35
Lt 409

Mathematical operators 403
Medallion effect 95, 296
Miter limit 51
Mod 405
Monospaced fonts 229
Moveto 59, 80, 170, 394
Mul 156, 405
Multi-page printing 204, 326

N-Up printing 27
Name literal 17
Ne 102, 410
Neg 80, 118, 406
Nested circles 128, 183
Newell, Martin 4
Newpath 81, 120, 394
Non-decimal representations 16
Not 410
Number objects 16

Object 16
Object based language 14
Octal representation 17
Operator
add 156, 403
and 407
arc 76, 119, 391
arcto 147, 392
array 414
begin 99, 411
bind 76, 98, 412
clip 77, 189, 392
closepath 77, 156, 393
currentpoint 98, 186, 421
curveto 77, 393
cvi 117, 186, 424
cvr 117, 424
cvs 425
def 78, 114, 413
definefont 100, 396
dict 100, 413
div 60, 78, 404
dup 60, 78, 400
end 100, 414
eq 407
exch 61, 79, 401
exit 134, 416
fill 119, 170, 400
findfont 58, 79, 397
floor 117, 188, 404
for 79, 120, 417
forall 100, 186, 418
ge 408
get 414
grestore 80, 99, 421
gsave 80, 99, 421
gt 408
idiv 187, 404

if 187, 416
ifelse 101, 117, 417
index 101, 401
kshow 134, 187, 397
le 409
length 101, 415
lineto 62, 394
loop 132, 188, 418
lt 409
mod 405
moveto 59, 80, 394
mul 156, 405
ne 102, 410
neg 80, 118, 406
newpath 81, 120, 394
not 410
or 411
pop 61, 81, 402
put 188, 415
repeat 81, 148, 418
rlineto 81, 114, 395
rmoveto 62, 81, 395
roll 402
rotate 82, 115, 419
scale 82, 118, 419
scalefont 59, 83, 398
setdash 115, 171, 422
setfont 59, 83, 398
setgray 63, 83, 422
setlinecap 64, 423
setlinewidth 63, 83, 423
show 59, 84, 399
showpage 60, 84, 425
string 116, 399
stringwidth 61, 84, 399
stroke 64, 84, 400
sub 62, 406
translate 85, 116, 420

Operators
- Array 414
- Control 416
- Conversion 424
- Coordinate 419
- Device 425
- Dictionary 411
- Font 396
- Graphics 421
- Logical 407
- Mathematical 403
- Painting 400
- Path 391
- Stack 400
- String 396

Or 411
Orientation of page 90, 99
  See also Landscape printing
Ornament 169
Outlining characters 229, 353
Overdefinition 189

Packed array 16
Page comment 32
Page description language 4, 13
Page independence 27, 215
Pages comment 32
PageTrailer comment 32
Painting operators 400
Parallel printing 28
Parentheses () in PostScript programs 16
Parser 15
Path 51
Path operators 391
PDL 13
Percent sign % in PostScript programs 16
Phototypesetter 36
Place cards 113
Point size 37
Point, definition of 36
Pop 61, 81, 171, 402
Position 51
Poster 185
Postfix notation 14
PostScript
- comments 64
- objects 49
- operators 6
- origins 4

Print server 26
Printer rerouting 28
Printer operation 18
Procedures 16, 146, 169, 189
Processing resources 215

Prologue and Script Model 10, 27, 148, 216
Proportional fonts 229
Put 188, 415

Repeat 81, 148, 418
Repeating text 141, 190, 195, 359
Reserved characters 16
Rlineto 81, 114, 170, 395
Rmoveto 62, 63, 81, 395
Roll 402
Rotate 82, 115, 170, 419
Rotating 41
Ruling lines 37

Scale 44, 82, 118, 171, 419
Scalefont 59, 83, 398
Scaling 39
Scaling text 116, 121, 124, 171, 177, 202
Scan conversion 39
Scanner 15
Scanning phase 18
Scribe iv, 26
Scrollwork 90, 296
Setdash 115, 171, 422
Setfont 59, 83, 398
Setgray 63, 83, 422
Setgrey 170
Setlinecap 64, 423
Setlinewidth 63, 64, 83, 423
Shadowed text 147, 152, 278
Show 59, 60, 84, 172, 399
Showpage 60, 84, 425
Simple objects 18
Slash / in PostScript programs 16
Software templates 155
Stack operators 400
Stacks 7, 13, 19
- dictionary 20
- execution 20
- graphics state 20
- LIFO 19
- operand 13

String 16, 116, 399
String operators 396
Stringwidth 61, 62, 84, 171, 399
Stroke 64, 84, 170, 400
Structured PostScript 10
Sub 62, 406
Systemdict 20

Templates 155
Title comment 31
Token 15
Trailer 10
Trailer comment 32
Transform matrix 51
Transformations of coordinates 39
Translate 85, 116, 170, 420
Translating 41
Type aesthetics 196, 200

Upside down text 151, 242
User interface 11, 214, 376
User space 36
Userdict 20

Version comment 32, 33
Virtual image 18

Warnock, John 4
White space 15
WYSIWYG 211

X width 229

[] brackets in PostScript programs 16